INDIGENOUS CRITICAL REFLECTIONS ON
TRADITIONAL ECOLOGICAL KNOWLEDGE

Indigenous Critical Reflections on Traditional Ecological Knowledge

Edited by

LARA A. JACOBS

Oregon State University Press   Corvallis

Oregon State University Press in Corvallis, Oregon, is located within the traditional homelands of the Marys River or Ampinefu Band of Kalapuya. Following the Willamette Valley Treaty of 1855, Kalapuya people were forcibly removed to reservations in Western Oregon. Today, living descendants of these people are a part of the Confederated Tribes of Grand Ronde Community of Oregon (grandronde.org) and the Confederated Tribes of the Siletz Indians (ctsi.nsn.us).

Library of Congress Cataloging-in-Publication Data
Names: Jacobs, Lara A., editor.
Title: Indigenous critical reflections on traditional ecological knowledge / edited by Lara A. Jacobs.
Description: Corvallis : Oregon State University Press, 2025. | Collection of essays by David G. Lewis and others. | Includes bibliographical references.
Identifiers: LCCN 2025007907 | ISBN 9781962645324 (paper) | ISBN 9781962645331 (ebook)
Subjects: LCSH: Traditional ecological knowledge.
Classification: LCC GN476.7 .I64 2025 | DDC 577—dc23/eng/20250325
LC record available at https://lccn.loc.gov/2025007907

♾ This paper meets the requirements of ANSI/NISO Z39.48-1992 (Permanence of Paper).

Cover art created by Rhode Grayson (Citizen of Muscogee [Creek] Nation with Choctaw heritage). The title of the piece, "PUNAYV EM LVMHE HVTKE," translates to "Story of the White Eagle." Artwork on pages 35, 143, and 241 by Rhode Grayson

"Praise the Rain," from *Conflict Resolution for Holy Beings: Poems* by Joy Harjo. Copyright © 2015 by Joy Harjo. Used by permission of W. W. Norton & Company, Inc.

Oregon State University
OSU Press

Oregon State University Press
121 The Valley Library
Corvallis OR 97331-4501
541-737-3166 • fax 541-737-3170
www.osupress.oregonstate.edu

For our ancestors, Knowledge Keepers,
future generations, and all of our relations.

CONTENTS

Part II Reciprocity

Part III Responsibility

ACKNOWLEDGMENTS

I acknowledge the resistance, strengths, and resilience of all Indigenous Peoples, especially my ancestors and members of my Tribe, who have fought to maintain our cultures, sacred Knowledges, value systems, and the futures of their Peoples throughout history, and those who will continue doing this good work into the future. MVTO (Thank you)!

I also acknowledge and send my deepest gratitude to the many Indigenous Peoples who contributed to this book through their labors, writing, mentorship, consultation, and continued support. This book is built on a historic foundation that was created by Indigenous activists and scholars who, for many generations, have contributed to social, governmental, and academic understandings about the importance of Traditional Ecological Knowledge and Indigenous value systems. I am grateful for their work and the advancements that newer generations of Indigenous Peoples are contributing to these important areas. MVTO!

I also extend my appreciation to my family (my husband Greg, my son Rhode, and my mother Kathryn) for all of your help and assistance while I worked on this collection; to my dearest friends, Cherry Yamane, Serina Payan Hazelwood, and Laney Smith, for all of the time and efforts you contributed in supporting, assisting, and encouraging me through this process; and to my adviser, Ashley D'Antonio, for your mentorship and encouragement throughout my PhD program, especially with all of my many "side projects," such as this book. I acknowledge Samantha Chisholm Hatfield for her assistance in helping me with the earliest stages of this book (e.g., suggesting a publisher, emails, etc.). I acknowledge the incredible amount of assistance I received from Kim Hogeland (Oregon State University Press acquisitions editor), who demonstrated so much patience and support as I navigated the book publishing process for the first time. I also remain grateful to Oregon State University Press for seeing the need for this publication and helping me to make it happen! Finally, I acknowledge the Indigenous peer reviewers of this book who took the time, heart work, and care to help strengthen this book before publication. MVTO

INTRODUCTION
Traditional Ecological Knowledge and Indigenous Value Systems

LARA A. JACOBS AND JOE ANDERSON
POETRY WRITTEN BY KATHRYN CHAMPAGNE
AND TRANSLATED BY BRITT POSTOAK
FIGURES BY RHODE GRAYSON

Positionality Statements

Jacobs: Muscogee (Creek) Nation Citizen with Choctaw and mixed heritage; KVWĒTV Tribal Town; VHVLVKVLKE; raised on Gáuigú (Kiowa), Numunuu Sookobitu (Comanche), Ndé Kónitsąąíí, Gokíyaa (Lipan Apache), Kiikaapoi (Kickapoo), and Jumanos lands; now living on Alsé lands; Oregon State University, College of Forestry, Forest Ecosystems and Society Department.

Anderson: Maternal Muscogee descendant with Paternal CHAHTA heritage; raised and living on the Muscogee (Creek) Reservation; independent scholar focused on Muscogee history and language.

Champagne: Muscogee (Creek) Nation Elder and Citizen with Choctaw heritage; KVWĒTV Tribal Town; VHVLVKVLKE; raised on Popeloutchom (Amah Mutsun), Ohlone, and Awaswas lands; now living on Očhéthi Šakówiŋ and Menominee lands.

Postoak: Muscogee (Creek) Nation Citizen with Chickasaw and Cherokee heritage; TALLAHASSEE WAKOKIYE Tribal Town; FVSWVLKE; born and living on MVSKOKE Nation, College of Muscogee Nation, Native American studies scholar.

Grayson: Muscogee (Creek) Nation Citizen with Choctaw heritage; KVWĒTV Tribal Town; VHVLVKVLKE; raised on Popeloutchom (Amah Mutsun), Ohlone, Awaswas, Tolowa Dee-ni', Siletz, Nüwüwü (Chemehuevi), and Nuwuvi (Southern Paiute) lands; now living on Alsé lands; Oregon State University, School of Language, Culture, and Society.

Introduction

Lara Jacobs: CVHOCEFKV TOS. MVSKOKE MVTOYIS. VHVLVKVLKE TOYIS. KVWĒTV VCULVKE CVNHUMKE FULLVTE. My name is Lara Jacobs. I am a Citizen of Muscogee (Creek) Nation. I am potato clan. My ancestors came from KVWĒTV (Koweta) Tribal Town.

Joe Anderson: AKMORKE CVMECKVTES. NOKOSVLKE HVTHAKV TEPAKEN CENTOWES. KERRETVN VCEYULLET OWIS. I was born in Okmulgee. I am Bear clan and of a peace clan. I am striving to learn.

We begin this book with MVSKOKE EM PUNVKV[1] (the language of the MVSKOKVLKE—Muscogee (Creek) Peoples), so you can understand a piece of our history and the root structures from which our lineages are established. MVSKOKE EM PUNVKV is one of the oldest languages ever spoken in our MVSKOKE homelands, which we refer to as HVSSOSV LECV (below the East) and KVNFVSKE (pointed Earth, referring to the shape of what many people refer to as Florida today). It is also one of the longest-living Indigenous languages spoken on the lands of what many Indigenous Peoples refer to as Turtle Island (so-called North America). We intentionally embed words from the MVSKOKE language into this chapter as a tool of resistance against more than five hundred years of assimilation policies directed at extinguishing our Peoples, languages, and cultures. By privileging our languages and cultures, we reinforce the importance and existence of Indigenous languages that continue to be maintained and revitalized despite colonial attempts to destroy them. In the following chapters, many authors use their Indigenous languages as acts of resistance and cultural sovereignty across Indigenous Nations, communities, and Peoples. We do not italicize

---

1 Some of the MVSKOKE EM PUNVKV that we use in this chapter includes spoken words that are not in the MVSKOKE dictionary. Many of our spoken words were never added to the two published dictionaries, including words for our Tribal Town names, ceremonial ground information, plants, animals, and other such words. The first MVSKOKE dictionary (Loughridge and Hodge 1890) was written by a colonial Christian missionary and does not capture our language in ways that accurately depict the full meaning of our words. The second dictionary (Martin and Mauldin 2000) was not written as a full collaboration with MVSKOKE speakers and provides an inadequate grasp on our language that does not allow for full fluency and understanding by the reader. We also acknowledge there is no correct or incorrect way to spell our words because our language was always passed down orally and not through written methods. Therefore, some of our spellings may not be written similar to what is depicted in the two dictionaries. However, we provide rough translations throughout this chapter to describe the words that we use.

Indigenous language words in this volume; we follow Indigenous writing standards (Younging 2018) that challenge the *othering* of First Languages in order to standardize their use in Indigenous publications. As per these standards, we also capitalize words such as Indigenous Peoples, Native, Tribe, Tribal Nation, Knowledges (when speaking specifically about Indigenous Knowledges), Elders, and similar terms. We think this emphasis is critically important and so have chosen to edit direct quotations from other writers, indicated in brackets. As an act of decolonial defiance, this book also rejects the notion that words like "western" must be capitalized.

This book centers Indigenous voices as an act of resistance and creates space for Indigenous Peoples to lead discussions and contribute critical discourse to the literature on Indigenous Knowledges and value systems. This book uses an all-Indigenous approach to authorship, volume editing, and anonymous peer reviews. Many Indigenous authors in this book have ancestral territories located on Turtle Island, including Native Alaskans, First Nations Peoples from lands now referred to as Canada, Native Americans, Pacific Islanders, and Indigenous Peoples from Central America. Additional Indigenous authors have ancestral homelands located in other parts of the globe, including Aotearoa (New Zealand), Japan, and Siberia. A total of fifty-one Indigenous voices from fifty-nine distinct Indigenous cultures have contributed directly to this edited volume.

This all-Indigenous approach is necessary and was purposefully chosen to resist (1) the colonial and non-Indigenous influences and perspectives that are filtering into academic and governmental management (such as federal land management) conversations about how our Knowledges are understood, explained, and used; and (2) to honor and center the voices of those from our diverse communities who are developing and pushing forward many critical insights into how our Knowledges are used, extracted, maintained, and preserved. Year after year, Indigenous communities face increased pressures to share our Knowledges and braid them with western science in colonial government and academic contexts. Indigenous voices on these topics are often missing in the current landscape of academic and governmental objectives that are directed at researching, using, and collecting Indigenous Knowledges.

This book decolonizes who is considered an expert and can be an author of academic texts by publishing the writings of Tribal governmental workers, nonacademic Indigenous community members, Indigenous poets, and storytellers, alongside the voices of Indigenous academics, including both established and early career researchers. It also provides an opportunity for Indigenous Knowledge holders to share and collaborate rather than looking to outsiders to define Indigenous Peoples' roles. This volume does not cater to a non-Indigenous gaze, but we hope for a wide audience. We invite non-Indigenous allies, governmental managers, academics, students, and other interested parties to read this book, engage with the Knowledges presented here, and embrace this opportunity to learn from multiple, varied Indigenous voices instead of relying on the large body of academic and government work that elevates non-Indigenous peoples to speak on our behalf or ignores our voices altogether. Following in the footsteps of other Indigenous-led publications, this book should be seen as "a sovereign act that is part of a larger movement that supports the disengagement of Indigenous [K]nowledges from the confines and violences associated with western knowledge ordering" (Hokowhitu et al. 2020, 5).

This book employs decolonial methods in many ways, including by deconstructing and unsettling power systems relating to colonialism via the creation and publication of Indigenous critical thought pieces and by centering Indigenous Peoples' voices, concerns, leadership, Knowledges, and value systems. Many chapters within this edited volume also operationalize decolonial methods by creating frameworks that unsettle power systems and center the realities and futures of Indigenous Peoples.

This edited volume focuses on two important aspects of Indigenous Peoples' realities: (1) Traditional Ecological Knowledge (TEK), a term used to describe Indigenous Knowledge-belief-practice systems that Indigenous Peoples have cultivated for tens of thousands of years (or since the beginning of creation) to understand our local environments; and (2) three significant Indigenous value systems (relationships, responsibility, and reciprocity) that are shared across Indigenous communities, yet may be defined in distinct ways among and within cultures. These topics embolden our resilience as Indigenous Peoples and allow us to maintain the permanency of our cultures. This book is organized into three thematic sections, each focusing on one of the specific Indigenous value systems. Within each section, Indigenous authors provide independent critical reflection chapters about TEK and the associated value system in the context of their own cultures.

The book's topics parallel the theme of the inaugural 2022 Traditional Ecological Knowledge Summit held in May 2022 at Oregon State University and facilitated by the Traditional Ecological Knowledge Club. Three Indigenous writing groups were created at the summit, one for each value system, and each group provided one chapter for the book, reflecting on topics discussed at the conference. Each thematic section of the book begins with a poem, followed by a summit essay, and then storytelling and academic chapters. At the beginning of each chapter, the authors provide positionality statements so readers can understand each writer's cultural and geographical background. Similar to the summit, this book creates much-needed space for Indigenous Peoples to privilege their Knowledges and critical perspectives about how TEK is being used and harvested by those outside of our communities.

INDIGENOUS VOICES: CRITICAL INDIGENOUS STUDIES

Indigenous ways of Knowing are "authentic sources of Knowledge" (Turner 2020, 184), and Indigenous voices should be leading all discussions about our distinct Knowledges and Knowledge systems. Despite the long history of Indigenous voices being minimized and undervalued in western scientific contexts, Indigenous Knowledge systems have gradually been given more attention in many academic fields over the past several decades. The emerging field of critical Indigenous studies (CIS) is "a knowledge/power domain whereby scholars operationalize Indigenous [K]nowledges to develop theories, build academic infrastructure, and inform our cultural and ethical practices" (Moreton-Robinson 2016, 5). All of the contributors to this book stand on the shoulders and labors of many Indigenous scholars and activists who have been building the field of CIS for decades, including Vine Deloria Jr. (Standing Rock Sioux); Daniel Wildcat (Yuchi Member of Muscogee (Creek) Nation); Winona LaDuke (Anishinaabe); Ron Trosper (Confederated Salish and Kootenai Tribes of the Flathead Indian Reservation); Leanne Betasamosake Simpson (Michi Saagiig Nishnaabeg); Linda Tuhiwai Smith (Ngāti Awa and Ngāti Porou); Kyle Powys Whyte (Member of Citizen Potawatomi Nation); Gregory Cajete (Tewa from Santa Clara Pueblo); Enrique Salmon (Rarámuri/Tarahumara); Melissa K. Nelson (Turtle Mountain Band of Chippewa Indians); Dennis Martinez (O'odham); Charles Menzies (Gitxaała Nation); Clint Carroll (Citizen of Cherokee Nation); and Nicholas Reo (Citizen of the Sault Ste. Marie Tribe of Chippewa Indians). There are many other Indigenous scholars who also deserve credit for building CIS and furthering the understandings of Indigenous Knowledges and theories. While we do not have room to add everyone, we extend our deepest gratitude to the generations of Indigenous

Peoples who have spent their professional careers dedicated to CIS while remaining accountable to Indigenous Peoples' rights.

Many CIS scholars focus their work on building theories about Indigenous cultures, Knowledge systems, values, experiences, education, and histories, and remain accountable to their communities in their publications by explaining the multitude of colonial issues that Indigenous Peoples have faced through time (including genocide, assimilation, and appropriation). Other areas of focus within CIS include Indigenous sovereignty, self-determination, decolonization, and Indigenization in ways that disrupt dominant western narratives that have for generations preferred colonial versions of history that either ignore Indigenous Peoples' lived experiences, realities, and Knowledges or twist them to suit colonial purposes. CIS is, therefore, a disruptive discipline that replaces westernized and colonial understandings and theories with Indigenous perspectives and philosophies. The authors of this book follow the long legacy of previous Indigenous scholars by staying accountable to Indigenous Peoples' histories, current realities, and futures.

As part of that accountability, in this introduction we honor our ancestors and Knowledges by reviewing MVSKOKE history, written from MVSKOKE perspectives, to give readers an example of how colonial systems have interfered and continue to interfere with almost every facet of Indigenous Peoples' lived realities (including our Knowledges) since colonizers first invaded our lands. We cannot discuss the state of our Knowledges today without understanding the obstacles our communities faced historically and continue to face because of colonial pressures. We discuss some of the many systems of oppression that MVSKOKVLKE have faced and how other Indigenous communities have encountered similar obstacles. Despite what we have lost since the beginning of colonial contact, we reinforce that our Knowledges and cultures remain resilient due to the tools of resistance that our communities have developed and used for generations. Additionally, we also provide an overview of the term TEK and how it differs from and overlaps with other terms such as Indigenous Knowledges, Indigenous/Native Sciences, and western science. Then, we define the three thematic Indigenous value systems that guide the sections of the book and conclude this chapter with a quick summary of the book's contents.

MVSKOKE History:
More Than Five Hundred Years of Colonial Interference

Like many authors in this book, our family roots stretch back to EKVNV ENHVTECESKV MVNETOFVN (in the beginning, when the Earth was young; the beginning of creation) and to the lands that colonial governments now occupy. MVSKOKVLKE are descendants of the Mississippian mound-building societies. Our ancestral territories are located in areas now referred to as the settler states of Alabama, Georgia, Florida, and South Carolina (Muskogee Creek Nation nd a). Our ancestors lived in a good way, using epistemologies (ways of knowing), ontologies (ways of being), and axiologies (value systems) to guide our practices, relations, cultural and spiritual Traditions, and every other part of our lived realities, allowing us to be sustainable stewards of all ecosystem elements since time immemorial.

Similar to many other Indigenous Peoples, our ancestors were scientists who used observations about local ecosystems to understand and inform subsistence-based practices, our relationships with the more-than-human world, and our general lifeways. Our ancestors' incredible understandings of the environment can still be seen today via the surviving complex, earthen mounds, townsites, and fishing weirs that they built using Indigenous-based geotechnical and soil and water engineering practices. Remnants of our mound societies can still be found throughout the southeastern United States, including at Ocmulgee Mounds National Historic Park, in so-called Macon, Georgia. As time evolved, so did our communities, who began constructing TVLWV (Tribal Towns). The center of a TVLWV was organized in a harmonious structure, reflecting many points of MVSKOKE value systems and ways of being, which emphasize the needs to live in a good way and be in good relations. Some MVSKOKVLKE built ceremonial town squares that were flanked on the perimeter by four buildings and located near waterways, thus incorporating an understanding of our worldviews in artistic, architectural, and Traditional ways (Hahn 2004).

Interruptions of MVSKOKVLKE and other Indigenous Peoples' Traditional ways of life on Turtle Island began in the mid-1400s and built into the largest genocide in global history. An estimated sixty million Indigenous Peoples existed on Turtle Island before 1492, and only one century later, our collective populations had dramatically diminished by 90 percent, to only around six million Peoples (Koch et al. 2019). This era began a long history of genocide that Indigenous Peoples have faced and reckoned with since our lands were first invaded. The first invasion of MVSKOKE lands occurred in 1540, when Hernando de Soto stepped foot on our lands; he was later followed by numerous explorers and settlers who brought diseases (including smallpox, measles, and plagues) and other issues into our communities that killed many of our Peoples. Invaders also brought over domesticated animals like pigs that transformed our ancestral landscapes and later became invasive, thus colonizing our animal and plant kin and other relations. From the 1670s through the early 1700s, MVSKOKVLKE traded with settlers from England, France, and Spain and developed diplomatic relations with each government, which led to the establishment of a commerce-based economy (Muskogee Creek Nation nd b). By the 1730s, continued European settlement had increased pressures for settler land rights and led to the era of Treaties and land dispossessions.

TREATIES AND LAND DISPOSSESSION

Some of the first Treaties between European countries and MVSKOKVLKE promised friendship, protection, recognition of MVSKOKVLKE inherent rights to the lands, and acknowledgments of MVSKOKE sovereign powers. The only peaceful and willing land cessation by MVSKOKVLKE occurred in the Treaty with the Lower Creeks (Treaty of Savannah) in 1733, in which the Tribal towns of KVWĒTV and KVSSĒTV TVLWV signed Articles of Friendship and Commerce with the Colony of Georgia under English Law. In 1790, the government of the new United States signed its first Treaty with the MVSKOKVLKE, which guaranteed MVSKOKE claims to land, promised protection from further encroachment by the settler state of Georgia, and approved multiple land cessions (Muskogee Creek Nation nd b). The MVSKOKVLKE and the federal government ratified a total of eighteen Treaties over an eighty-one-year period. Each Treaty brought different ramifications for MVSKOKVLKE, including military occupation, outposts, increased traffic into our territories via major federal roads, land boundaries, and land dispossessions. Each subsequent Treaty further diminished our rights to our homelands and affected our Peoples' abilities to thrive.

Under these Treaties and, later, President Andrew Jackson's Indian Removal Act of 1830, MVSKOKVLKE rights took increasingly hard blows. From 1827 to 1828, an estimated 23,000 MVSKOKVLKE were forced to walk 1,200 miles on the many Trails of Tears from our ancestral homelands to Indian Territory (also known as Oklahoma). It is estimated that

3,500 MVSKOKVLKE died during their journeys. Removals did not just happen on land though; an estimated 2,500 MVSKOKE prisoners were forcibly relocated in shackles on steamboats. Some estimates show that three hundred of them died on the *Monmouth* steamboat in the Mississippi River. An additional removal in the winter of 1838 forced another estimated five hundred MVSKOKVLKE to leave our homelands (Muskogee Creek Nation nd b). Twenty years afterward, census data estimates that 13,537 MVSKOKVLKE were left in Oklahoma; some records claim that more than eight thousand MVSKOKVLKE died during the removal era (NPS nd). However, colonial census and other records are unreliable, and MVSKOKVLKE deaths were likely undercounted. If we sum the estimated numbers of MVSKOKVLKE who were removed during all relocations, then this number totals around 26,000 people. If only 13,537 MVSKOKVLKE remained thereafter, then a more likely number of individuals who died is approximately 12,463, or about 48 percent of MVSKOKVLKE.

Similar to the MVSKOKVLKE, other Indigenous Peoples on Turtle Island share histories of forced removals and were often relocated from their homelands into new and/or smaller territories (Dunbar-Ortiz 2014). Indigenous Peoples in the United States are estimated to have lost almost 99 percent of our ancestral lands because of colonization, or about 94 percent of the total geographic areas we sustainably stewarded since time immemorial (Farrell et al. 2021). Today, 42 percent of Tribes have no recognized lands, and the ones that do have only about 2.6 percent of their original territories. The removals of Indigenous Peoples from our ancestral lands and waters were a coordinated and systematic tool of colonialism that forced our ancestors to move into areas deemed by colonizers as less valuable—lands less able to support European-style agriculture and colonial extraction practices—while at the same time, Indigenous Peoples were explicitly prevented from practicing our Traditional food customs. Many of these areas are today at increased risk from the complex hazards of climate change (Farrell et al. 2021). Additionally, on lands that settlers found to contain valuable minerals such as uranium, Indigenous Peoples today are subject to the health and community effects of environmental degradation and pollution. Therefore, these removals should be understood as not just historic incidents that affected our ancestors generations ago, but as a long, ongoing, systematic tool of dispossession that continues to impact our communities today and threatens the futures of our Peoples.

ASSIMILATION AND GENOCIDAL POLICIES

Beyond the near decimation of Indigenous Peoples' populations and removals from our ancestral territories, settler colonial relations affected Indigenous cultures, lands, waters, and additional aspects of our ancestral ecosystems in many other ways (Jacobs et al. 2022b). The history and current reality of most Indigenous Peoples is fraught with assimilationist and genocidal colonial policies that intend to erase us, our Knowledges, and our cultures. Colonialism is situated at the root of these issues because of its inherent requirements for domination, control, and exploitation (Horvath 1972). Colonialism is an ongoing culture-change process and is about genocide and access (Horvath 1972; Liboiron 2021b). Colonialism requires settler dominance and access to every part of our cultures and identities, including our Knowledge systems, values, practices, cosmologies, ontologies, lands, and even our Indigenous bodies and lives.

As the United States and Canada became more powerful colonial occupying entities, Indigenous children were forcibly taken from their families and required to attend genocidal federal boarding schools that were created to address the "Indian problem" and to "kill the Indian, and save the man" (Pratt 2013). Governmental policies, via school administrators and the curricula and regulations they imposed, literally and figuratively focused on "Killing the Indian." For 150 years, boarding schools intended to kill Indigenous cultures, Indigenous Knowledges, value systems, Traditions, and religious practices, and subsequently replace them with western ways of knowing, ways of being, values, worldviews, and religions.

Indigenous children as young as three years old were forcibly taken away from our families and sent hundreds of miles away to be brainwashed by colonial educational agents (Galindo 2022). Part of this brainwashing included forcibly assimilating Indigenous children to European Judeo-Christian norms by forbidding them to practice our cultural Traditions, wear Traditional clothing and braided hair, and speak our languages (Lomawaima 1993; Dunbar-Ortiz 2014; Stevens 2014; Fisk et al. 2021; Jacobs et al. 2022a,b). To further destroy connections to Indigeneity, boarding school officials would strip Indigenous children of all of their belongings, including their clothing, medicine bags, and other sacred items that protected them from harm, and then set the items on fire (Galindo 2022). Federal policies were geared at a westernized domestication of Native girls in the practices of regimenting, training, and clothing their bodies (Lomawaima 1993). This process included "a rigid and detailed military discipline that scheduled every waking moment, organized classrooms and work details, and even mandated a 'correct' physical posture, 'correct' ways of moving and exercising, and 'correct' details of dress'" (Lomawaima 1993, 228). In place of their Traditional practices, Indigenous children were subject to "systematic militarized and identity-alteration," including new English names, woolen military-like uniforms (worn even in summer), short hair, military-style regimentation and drills, manual labor (brick-making, lumbering, railroad work, domestic labor), corporal punishment (solitary confinement, beatings, withholding food), and numerous other forms of trauma (Galindo 2022; Newland 2022). These calculated harms were aimed at achieving social objectives to civilize and Christianize, and thus assimilate young Indigenous Peoples so that they would withdraw from our Indigenous identities and ways of living and being (Lomawaima 1993).

However, our belongings and practices were not the only things destroyed or restricted: "Children died, killed themselves, ran away, and were beaten badly. . . . The newborns of young girls raped and impregnated by the clergy were thrown into fiery furnaces or killed in other ways and buried on school grounds" (Galindo 2022, 26). Countless Indigenous children died at federal boarding schools. The death of an Indigenous child results in the literal deaths of possibilities and futures: it is the genocide of future generations of Indigenous Peoples that were not allowed to come into existence. It is the killing off of future family members, Knowledge transmission systems, and the cultural root structures that are so deeply integrated into Indigenous family systems and Knowledge processes. The actual number of Indigenous children's deaths have remained unreported for generations; however, progress is slowly being made in the United States and Canada to uncover the truth of how many children died and were buried at boarding schools.

Boarding schools were not enough, though, and before 1978, 25–35 percent of Indigenous children in the United States were forcibly removed from our families; 85 percent of these children were subsequently placed into white and non-Indigenous households, where assimilation was again the goal (NICWA nd). Though the Indian Child Welfare Act of 1978 tried to halt these harmful practices, the rights of Indigenous children to live within our communities are contested in US courts on a regular basis. As of the date of this writing (spring 2023), the Supreme Court of the United States is determining the constitutionality of ICWA in the case *Haaland v. Brackeen*.

Indigenous Peoples have navigated and continue to navigate other issues, especially around our rights to practice our religions and Traditions—which were not cemented into law until the passing of the American Indian Religious Freedom Act of 1978 and even now are often misunderstood and threatened by colonial governments—and our rights to birth children, as generations of Indigenous women suffered from forced, nonconsensual, and non-informed sterilization practices via the Indian Health Service (Lawrence 2000). For hundreds of years, colonial governments and policies have intended to destroy every part of our Indigeneity: our lives, our future generations, and our connections to land, languages, families, cultural and spiritual practices, and, importantly, our Knowledges and values. Many Indigenous communities have remained resilient and steadfast in our resolve to maintain all these factors: we continue practicing our cultures, languages, values, and maintaining our sacred Indigenous Knowledges, no matter the cost. Despite more than five hundred years of targeted oppression, we still persist today because we have long roots of resistance.

A METAPHOR FOR GROWING ROOTS OF RESISTANCE

As VHVLVKVLKE (Potato People), Lara's clan came from the Earth, and to these People, potato plants carry significant and sacred meanings, which we will not describe in this book. However, potato plants provide a strong metaphor for how Indigenous Peoples may grow roots of persistence and resistance to maintain their identities, cultures, values, and Knowledges from one generation to the next. Figure I.1 contains an illustration of a potato plant and many of its structural elements. Potato plants consist of a mother tuber, underground stems, roots, stolon (underground connections to other plants), and daughter tubers, among other parts. The mother tuber is planted into the soil and subsequently develops stolon and tuber-root systems. The underground stem grows upward, from the mother, and breaks through the soil surface to form the aboveground greens of the plant (Zhao et al. 2020). The mother also grows downward roots, which absorb and provide nutrients to the plant and create the ability for the plant to repair itself. The roots help to stabilize the plant and allow it to absorb life-sustaining water. The underground stem generates a creeping root structure that grows laterally and later produces new tubers called daughters (Zhao et al. 2020). It is through this entire structure, from the underground stem

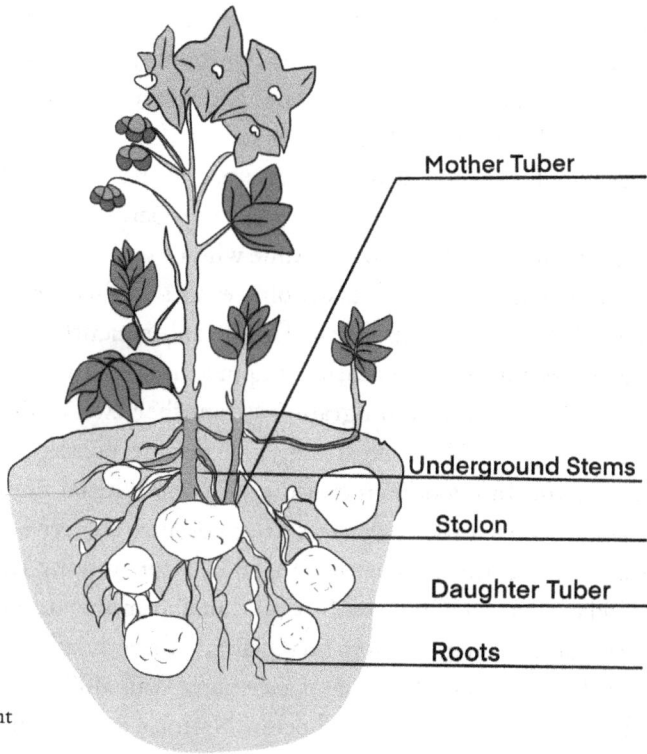

Figure I.1. Potato plant by Rhode Grayson.

to the tuber-root systems, that the mother is able to pass its characteristics and strengths to her daughter tubers (Merk 2019).

To put it simply, the potato plant begins with a mother that grows roots and connections to land, and then passes all of her strengths and abilities to her offspring, which remain connected to the mother through roots and other structures. The potato plant provides a strong metaphor for how Indigenous Peoples connect to the land, water, family and community, and the continuity of strength and resilience we hold and maintain from one generation to the next. Similar to the Mother tuber, our Elders carry our connections to land, water, culture, Knowledge, values, and the strengths of our ancestors and pass all of these characteristics down to others within our communities, who later pass the same traits onward to future generations.

Similar to humans, potato plants are subject to diseases, especially potato late blight, which is caused by the fungus *Phytophthora infestans* (Yuen 2021). Symptoms of potato late blight typically appear in the fall as lesions on the leaves, which grow into darker-colored dead material and white sporulation on the stems, the underside of the leaves, and other plant parts. As the fungus colonizes the potato plant, the sporangia (where fungal spores are formed) can be transported by wind and water to other parts of the plant, including the mother and daughter tubers, that, when infected, succumb to tuber blight and die (Yuen 2021; Arora, Sharma, and Singh 2014).

Potato late blight was a contributing factor to the devastating Irish potato famine of 1845–1849, a time when English imperial rule both created and exploited such catastrophic events to further colonial objectives (Nally 2008). The Irish potato famine subsequently created food shortages across Europe, the deaths of approximately two million people, and the displacement and emigration of another two million people (Large 1940; Yuen 2021). Interestingly, the famine overlapped with the later years of the Indigenous removal era in the United States (1820–1850), which was also a tool to meet settler colonial objectives, and Indigenous Peoples noted the similarities. In 1847, after walking the Trails of Tears to Oklahoma, the Choctaw Nation donated money to help prevent mass starvation in Ireland. Their financial gift directly affected the survival of many Irish people (Towes and Germany-Wall 2022). Today, a statue in Ireland commemorates the Choctaw Nation's investment in Irish people's well-being.

Even at the plant level, colonization (in this case, fungal colonization) proves problematic when left to grow unchecked. However, tools of resistance such as early planting, increased circulation, targeted watering—tools derived from knowledge, observation, human-plant relations, and experience—exist for potato growers just as assimilation resistance tools exist for Indigenous Peoples.

MVSKOKVLKE are matriarchal Peoples; our social and community organizations originate from our mothers. Similar to the potato plant, our family roots stretch down deep into the ground and are fertilized by the subsequent connections to our mothers, ancestors, Elders, lands, and waters. Late potato blight destroys many of these important connections in potato plants, just as US colonization and assimilation policies disrupted and attempted to destroy many Indigenous Peoples' root systems. Where the potato plant has roots and stolon, we have roots of resistance that carry the stories, value systems, Knowledges, cultural practices, memories, and the seeds of our ancestor's hopes and dreams from generations of the past to our Peoples today who transmit these characteristics to our future generations. Just as MVSKOKVLKE have maintained our Indigeneity,

Knowledges, and values over time, many Indigenous communities have cultivated and preserved theirs too, despite hundreds of years of colonial contact, reform, mass genocide, displacement, assimilation, and other disruptions to our root structures. Our Indigenous resilience is rooted in resistance to these oppressions, and these forms of resistance are passed down through generations of our families and communities. Such root-based generational transmissions have allowed our cultures, identities, Knowledges, and values to persist since time immemorial and are what will continue the perseverance of our ways of living into the future. One of our most sacred forms of Knowledge, which has been maintained and carried through generation after generation of Indigenous Peoples, is Traditional Ecological Knowledge (TEK), a western science term that describes the sacred environmental Knowledge-belief-practice systems of Indigenous Peoples that are rooted in our histories and current realities and carried to the futures of our Peoples.

KERRETV VCAKE TOWES (To Know Is Sacred): Traditional Ecological Knowledge

KERRETV VCAKE TOWES
UEWV VCAKE TOWES
EKVNV VCAKE TOWES
PONVTTV VCAKE TOWES
AHOCKV VCAKE TOWES
TECATE VCAKE TOWES
KERRETV VCAKE TOWES
MOMES TOWES

Knowledge is Sacred
Water is sacred
Land is sacred
Animals are sacred
Plants are sacred
Native Peoples are sacred
To know is sacred
It is so

Since the beginning of our species, basic human survival has depended on understanding and forming scientific Knowledges about the environment: data relating to harvesting and hunting techniques and seasonal abundance of food, water availability, animal and plant characteristics, and agricultural functions. Western scientists suggest that early humans developed such Knowledges as a survival mechanism that allowed them to understand which foods could be eaten and which ones would result in an early death or illness, among other reasons (Lindberg 2010). However, many Indigenous Peoples across the globe have sacred Creation/origin stories that detail how our Knowledges were given to us as gifts, sacred laws or moral codes, and instructions from Creator: they are not just Knowledges we learned along the way as a matter of survival.

Indigenous Knowledges (IK) are sacred and contain some of the oldest forms of environmental sciences known to humans. They are often the products of tens of thousands of years of scientific inquiries and observations by Indigenous Peoples, who have studied, observed, developed, and passed down Knowledges through generations of our communities since time immemorial. Indigenous Peoples' understandings of our local environments are increasingly seen as viable forms of science and are slowly being integrated into practice by the same western academic and colonial officials that once derided and dismissed them. Today, Indigenous Knowledges about the environment increasingly play a critical role in western sciences, including in ecology and other subjects pertaining to land, water, more-than-human animals and plants, natural resources and land and water management, climate change, cultural resources, and similar topics.

TERMINOLOGIES

Many terminologies are used to describe Indigenous ways of Knowing: terms such as Indigenous Knowledges (IK) or Indigenous Knowledge Systems (IKS), Traditional Knowledges (TK), Traditional Ecological Knowledges (TEK), Indigenous Sciences (IS), Native American Sciences (NAS), and many others are often used interchangeably, especially in academic literature. Anishinaabe and Métis scholar Melissa K. Nelson (2014) acknowledges the multidimensionality and interconnectedness of IK terminologies that are connected and nested at different scales: "TEK arises out of Indigenous Science, which arises out of larger-scale Knowledge systems" such as IK (Nelson 2014 189). Because of the nested nature of such

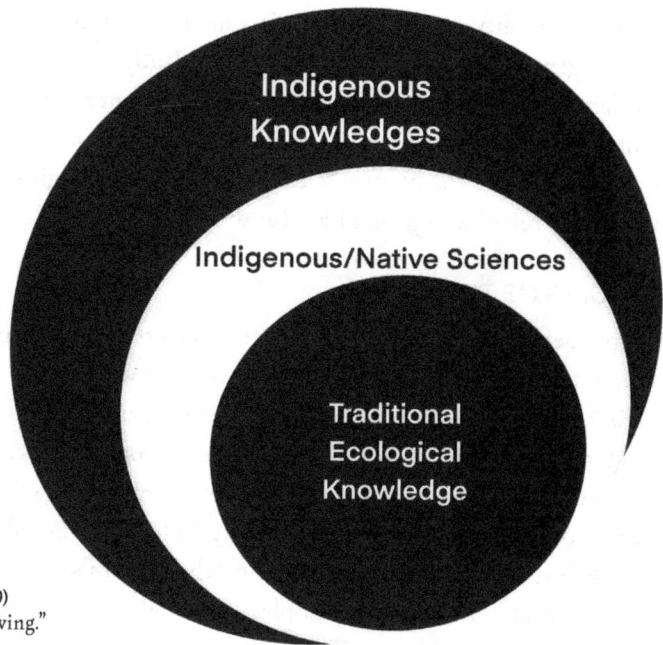

Figure I.2. Adaptation
of Nelson's (2014, 189)
"Nested Ways of Knowing."

Knowledge systems, Indigenous Peoples may simultaneously hold IK, NAS/ IS, and TEK (figure I.2).

We acknowledge that many distinctions exist between definitions of IK, NAS/IS, and TEK, depending on who is writing about them. For the purpose of this book, IK refers to all of the Knowledges held by Indigenous Peoples that originate from Traditional and non-Traditional avenues such as Indigenous cultural and spiritual practices, IS, TEK, cosmologies, modern technology, media, Indigenous forms of education, and formal and/or western-based education. IK describes the interactions between Traditional and non-Traditional ways of Knowing. In other words, IK encompasses all of the types of Knowledges that Indigenous Peoples carry. Gregory Cajete (2004, xxi), Tewa Indian from Santa Clara Pueblo, describes Native Science as including "philosophy, art, agriculture, ritual, ceremony, technology, astronomy, farming, plant domestication, plant medicine, hunting, fishing, metallurgy, and geology." However, he explains that it also goes beyond these categories to include other factors, such as spirituality, community, creativities, sustainability-based technologies, and "the exploration of basic questions such as the nature of language, thought, and perception; the movement of time-space; the nature of human knowing and feeling; the nature of proper human relationship to the cosmos; and other such questions related to natural reality" (Cajete 2018, 17). Cajete also states that Native Science is an Indigenous paradigm that incorporates Indigenous Peoples' relationships "to land, plants, animals, community, self, cosmos, spirit, and the creative animating processes of life" (Cajete 2018, 15). As Cajete's descriptions illustrate, a large part of Native Science focuses on ecological topics, which fall under the terminology of TEK. But what exactly is TEK?

ORIGINS OF TEK

Before defining TEK, it is important to understand its origins. The term TEK was not created by Indigenous Peoples but by western scientists (McGregor 2005). Many settler scientists (e.g., Fikret Berkes) helped form and define the western understandings of TEK in academic contexts. As an act of resistance against colonial interpretations of our epistemologies, practices, and beliefs, in this chapter we intentionally employ Indigenous Peoples' interpretations and definitions instead of highlighting those from settlers.

For many Indigenous Peoples, cultural and Ecological Knowledges relating to the environment are inherent parts of our understandings and cultural Knowledge systems. Many Indigenous communities did not need a word or term to define these aspects separately from the ways we understand other parts of our realities because our Knowledges are seeded in the lands and all of our relations (plants, animals, and other more-than-human kin). For example, MVSKOKVLKE have no phrases or words to describe our specific Knowledges about local environments. We do not have a word for "ecology" or any words to describe Indigenous Science. We refer to these as simply KERRETV (Knowledge or to know), and HÓPOREN'KV (wisdom). TEK is not often a term recognized by our Elders and other members of our Indigenous communities, beyond those with academic and governmental involvements. It is not a term many Indigenous Peoples use at all: it is mainly used by academic, governmental, and nonprofit entities.

The roots of the term TEK stretch back to the 1950s, when academics first began systematically considering non-western forms of Knowledge (Inglis 1993). In the 1980s, non-Indigenous scientists who were interested in Indigenous ways of Knowing began using the term more frequently in their research (McGregor 2005; Ramos 2018). During this same time, Indigenous scholars such as Ron Trosper, Dennis Martinez, and others challenged standard definitions of TEK by incorporating Indigenous value systems into TEK discourse and literature. Through the years, many academics, both non-Indigenous and Indigenous, have tried to define TEK as a means of generalization. However, defining TEK can prove difficult because, as Anishinaabe scientist Deborah McGregor (2006) emphasizes, the defining characteristics of TEK are dependent on who is providing the definition. McGregor states, "Whoever 'studies' TEK gets to define it, and has control over what types of things are studied, and which are ignored" (Luckey 1995, 55 [Metis], as cited by Simpson 1999, 18). Distinctions in definitions also exist in the literature, especially between academic and policy publications, according to Potawatomi scientist Kyle Whyte (2013). Such differences can create controversial situations and disagreements because of the implied differences "about 'whose' definition of TEK gets privileged, who is counted as having expert authority over environmental governance issues, and how TEK should be factored into policy processes" (Whyte 2013, 1). Also problematic is the issue of using TEK as an all-encompassing term that homogenizes global Indigenous Knowledges (McGregor 2008). Indigenous Peoples are not monolithic; therefore, it is imperative to recognize that TEK and similar terminologies have many differences and definitions among and even within Indigenous communities and differ drastically based on cultures, languages, Traditions, ontologies, axiologies, cosmologies, geographies, ecosystem elements and functions, kinship relations, and much more.

DEFINING TEK IN COMPARISON TO WESTERN SCIENCE

Despite these difficulties, many Indigenous scientists use generalized definitions that describe the term's basic characteristics. Many of these define TEK as a form of Native Science that is in many ways similar yet remains distinct from western science. For example, Kimmerer (2002, 433) explains that both forms of science "yield detailed empirical information of natural phenomena and relationships among ecosystem components"; they both "have predictive power, and in both intellectual traditions, observations are interpreted within a particular cultural context." TEK often contains empirical data related to biology and ecology; resource assessments and monitoring; climate and seasonality; species relations and interactions; naming systems for plants and animals; sustainable uses of foods, plants, animals, waters; adaptive management histories and strategies; and disturbance ecology (Kimmerer 2002). Such subjects are found within many western scientific disciplines. However, TEK is not just limited to these factors and can and does overlap into other fields, such as engineering (for example, MVSKOKE geotechnical and soil engineering Knowledges that helped build our long-lasting mounds), and other scientific disciplines within the western academy. TEK includes abstract and philosophical modes of thinking and practical and applied Knowledges (Nelson 2014). The similarities and overlaps between TEK and western science are abundant and may be why Deloria (1997) refers to TEK as the "intellectual twin" to western science.

However, TEK and other Native Sciences originate from "lived and storied participation with natural landscapes and reality" (Cajete 2004, 46). This is where some of the distinctions between TEK and western sciences can be seen. In a 2012 article, Nicholas Reo (citizen of the Sault Ste. Marie Tribe of Chippewa Indians) and Kyle Whyte describe TEK as a multifaceted, interconnected, and inseparable structure that consists of three main systems: Indigenous Knowledges, practices, and beliefs. Belief systems are not typically associated with western science. However, as Cajete states, "Our stories, ceremonies, and prayers at once speak and create a moral universe, or practical, lived [K]nowledge" (Cajete 2004, xviii). This lived Knowledge is specific to each community and can vary among clans and other groups within the community; it is based on distinct geographies (place-based); and it accumulates through generational experiential Knowledge sharing (Reo and Whyte 2012; Menzies and Butler 2006). Western scientific paradigms do not have such community and geographic boundaries, nor do they pass down specific data through familial and community generational processes.

Another contrast between TEK and western science can be seen in data ownership. Western science and colonial copyright standards typically situate ownership with scientists, institutions, and authors of scientific papers and reports. However, TEK data are collectively owned by Indigenous communities and inextricably linked to the community's identities, experiences with local environments, and land and cultural rights (Trosper 2012). Ron Trosper (member of the Confederated Salish and Kootenai Tribes of the Flathead Indian Reservation) describes this generational aspect of Knowledge distribution as crucial to sustaining Indigenous Knowledges, cultures, and identities. Much of this is tied directly to an inherent reliance on relationships. For example, Charles Menzies (member of the Gitxaala Nation) leans more into the relational aspects of the term, defining it as "the local understandings of plant, animal, and habitat relations held by Indigenous [P]eoples" (Menzies 2006, 87). Reo and Whyte (2012) echo this sentiment when considering the epistemological underpinnings of TEK that integrate ecological relations, ecosystems and associated components, and places. TEK is not static: Indigenous communities evolve our TEKs by accumulating experiences and responding to factors inside and outside of our communities, just as western scientists do (Grenz 2020; Reo and Whyte 2012; Menzies and Butler 2006).

As a system of practice, TEK refers to "the application of accumulated, intergenerational Knowledge[s], using best practices, economic relationships, expertise, skill, and formal or informal rules" (Reo and Whyte 2012, 15; Berkes 1999). Applied TEK exists in Traditional activities such as community-based hunting, fishing, gathering of plants, and understandings of kinship systems, and the associated movements or trading of goods. As a belief system, TEK incorporates Indigenous values and moral codes that constitute Indigenous communities' worldviews (Reo and Whyte 2012). Drawing from previous work from other Indigenous authors, particularly Standing Rock Sioux author Vine Deloria Jr. (1990), Dan Wildcat (Yuchi member of Muscogee (Creek) Nation) and Indigenous ally coauthor Ray Pierotti (2000) explain that an underlying assumption embedded within TEK is that humans have historically and will forever be connected to all life and that "nature" does not exist in a metaphoric vacuum, independent of humans and their associated activities. Instead, TEK emphasizes and incorporates relations.

TEK is acquired through an intergenerational process of direct and indirect observations representing historical and current understandings about the environment. TEK includes oral stories, experiences, and observations made by Indigenous Peoples and Indigenous communities, much like western social sciences that rely on qualitative forms of data (Grenz 2020; Menzies and Butler 2006). Unlike western science, sacred Indigenous oral histories, stories, and observations were historically (and sometimes even today, for cultural reasons) never written down. As a sacred form of science, these types of data necessitate safeguarding and a recognition of Indigenous data sovereignty (the rights of Indigenous Peoples to fully control all aspects of the data, including data collection and transmission processes). However, as Rarámuri (Tarahumara) scholar Enrique Salmón (2017) writes, such oral Traditions should still be considered historical texts.

Our Knowledge storage practices also differ from western scientific practices, which typically house knowledge in scientific journals, textbooks, and libraries. Comanche scholar Jared Wahkinney (2019, 3) explains that IK are "not stored in physical libraries. Elders are our libraries." Our Elders, especially our ceremonial leaders, medicine Peoples, and storytellers store large bodies of our cultural and ecological data and are therefore living bodily libraries of Indigenous Science. As living libraries, Elders play a crucial role in the ways Indigenous data are acquired and shared within our Indigenous communities. As Nlaka'pamux scholar Jennifer Grenz describes,

> Traditional [E]cological [K]nowledge is [K]nowledge shared by Indigenous [K]nowledge keepers. It is important. Knowledge acquired from our deep relationship with the places we are from. Intergenerational [K]nowledge, passed through our lineages about plants, animals, places, and things we did. Ancestral [K]nowledge that is also simply "in" us. (2020, 1)

In comparison, western scientists collect and analyze data according to the scientific method and publish data in scientific journals and technical reports. The collected data are not often from lived and embodied knowledge because of western scientific paradigms that necessitate "objectivity" and prioritize outsider collections, storage, and data analyses. The focus on objectivity is a dramatic distinction between western science and TEK (Pierotti and Wildcat 2000; Kimmerer 2002).

> TEK is much more than the empirical information concerning ecological relationships. Unlike [scientific ecological knowledge], [T]raditional [K]nowledge is woven into and is inseparable from the social and spiritual context of the culture. Traditional [K]nowledge can rival [w]estern science as a body of empirical information, but [T]raditional [K]nowledge may also extend its explanatory power beyond the strictly empirical, where science cannot go. TEK is laden with associated values, while the scientific community prides itself on data that are "value free." TEK includes an ethic of reciprocal respect and obligations between humans and the nonhuman world. In [I]ndigenous [S]cience, nature is subject, not object. . . . TEK offers not only important biological insights but a cultural framework for environmental problem solving that incorporates human values. (Kimmerer 2002, 434)

Kimmerer provides additional information about the distinctions between western science and TEK, including how TEK tends to be qualitative while western science incorporates quantitative and qualitative data;

TEK is diachronic (originating from very long time intervals and associated with local ecosystems) while western science relies more on synchronic data that originates from multiple locales and is collected over shorter time intervals. Kimmerer also notes that such differences also relate to who is collecting the data: TEK is collected by Indigenous Peoples and Indigenous communities who are observing environmental phenomena, often while participating in activities, such as subsistence food gathering and hunting practices, while western scientific observations originate from small groups of professionals who are highly trained and educated and are conducting the work according to the scientific method.

Despite these many distinctions, for a few decades now, TEK has been integrated into western scientific frameworks to inform scientific research endeavors and colonial governmental management processes. TEK is applied far and wide, including in ecology, biology, engineering, marine science, fisheries and wildlife management, food science and agriculture, land and water management, and plenty more disciplines. Colonial governments and international bodies (such as the United Nations) have called on recognizing the importance of incorporating TEK into scientific understandings of local environments and into governing frameworks. However, a crucial part of TEK is typically missing when western scientific research and governmental processes implement the TEK they harvest from Indigenous communities: the application of Indigenous value systems.

Indigenous Value Systems

Similar to TEK and other Indigenous Knowledge Systems, Indigenous value systems cannot be seen as monolithic. Several Indigenous value systems have been recognized in academic literature as generalized values that many, if not most, Indigenous communities share across cultures, including relationships, responsibility, reciprocity, redistribution, rights, respect, relevance, reconciliation, and redistribution (Jacobs et al. 2022a,b; Donner et al. 2021). But such value systems are not defined or "expressed" in similar ways within and among Indigenous communities.

This book (and the 2022 Traditional Ecological Knowledge Summit that preceded it) is structured around three Indigenous value systems: relationships, reciprocity, and responsibility. Each value is intimately linked to the Knowledge-practice-belief systems inherent to TEK (figure I.3). We outline some general definitions of these systems below, but other chapter authors explain their interpretations of these values in ways that

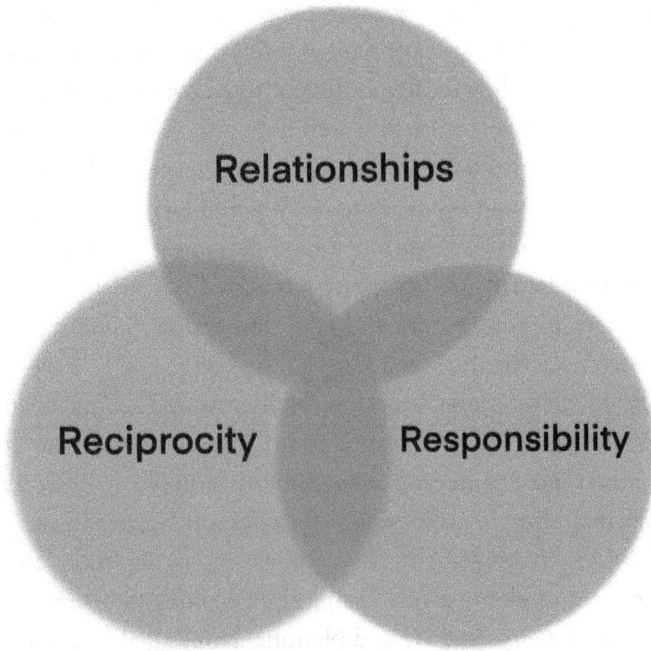

Figure I.3. The intersections of relationships, reciprocity, and responsibility.

are grounded in and remain accountable to their distinct cultures and communities. As an example of this, we begin by defining these terms in MVSKOKE and use storytelling to illustrate how each of these value systems relates to each other and to TEK generally. We encourage readers to carefully consider how each value system is written about and operationalized in later chapters and how or whether such uses differ from our generalized definitions.

CVNAHVMKE is the MVSKOKE word for relationships. We do not have a specific word that translates to reciprocity in MVSKOKE EM PUNVKV. After some careful consideration, we decided that our word ARAKKUECKV (which translates to respect) is appropriate to use here because we cannot have systems of reciprocity without respecting the entire system in which reciprocal interactions can occur. We also do not have a specific word for responsibility in MVSKOKE EM PUNVKV. The closest word that we have is the word VNOKECKV, which means love. Our concept of VNOKECKV includes all the associated responsibilities we must maintain to all our relations. To be responsible means that we must practice love and we must maintain our responsibilities to all our relations.

CVNAHVMKE: Relationships

Comanche scholar LaDonna Harris and Cherokee scholar Jacqueline Wasilewski (2004) describe the Indigenous value of relationships as a kinship obligation that contains the notion that humans are related to other humans and to everything else (more-than-human animals, plants, rocks, land, water, and even to the chemical components of stars: to all of creation) just as they are to blood relatives. Such kinship relations are valued as a sort of extended family in which all beings have specific roles and tasks and make specific contributions. However, as Métis scholar Max Liboiron (2021b) explains, a "cosmic sameness" of relations does not exist among Indigenous communities, which is why specificity is necessary when we discuss relations.

A good example of this is demonstrated in the distinctions between relations in MVSKOKE clanship systems. A MVSKOKE clan (e.g., VHVLVKVLKE (potato); NOKOSVLKE (bear); HOTVLKVLKE (wind); etc.) can be passed down directly only by a MVSKOKE mother to her children (via matrilineal descent). Although we do not carry forward our father's clan, we still honor and respect those relations as distant yet connected kin. Each MVSKOKE clan is either HVTHAKV (White/Peace clans) or CELOKE (Red/War clans). All clans are directly related to our ETVWLV (ceremonial grounds), which strictly follow our creation story: OFULVNKV EMVLIKVTV VHAKVN EMONYAKVTES (the Creator gave the laws for the clans).

Our creation story is a sacred MVSKOKE law, and the details of this story and our laws cannot be shared outside of our communities. However, we provide our readers with an example of relational distinctions within a Tribal community: Lara's clan, VHVLVKVLKE, has distinct relations, laws, and Knowledges compared to MVSKOKVLKE from other clans. Joe's clan, NOKOSVLKE, has an entirely distinct form of relations, rules, and Knowledges to bear species and in ceremonial processes. As these examples illustrate, other Tribal cultural laws, rules, or moral codes about relationships may differ between clans within an Indigenous community and definitely differ among Indigenous communities that may have other clanship or relational systems. However, this does not mean that all relations are distinct within Indigenous communities. For example, MVSKOKVLKE honor the concepts of HER'KV (peace), VNOKÉCEV (love), and MERRTV (compassion) with all of our relations. So, there are overlapping and distinct relations within our specific community, and distinctions and overlapping similarities (like the need to live in a good way) between MVSKOKVLKE and other Indigenous communities.

Additional relationship elements include time and other factors of Indigenous Peoples' practices, belief systems, and ways of being. Time is embedded into Indigenous relationships in a way that embodies a form of intergenerational accountability connecting the pasts, the present, and futures of all things together (Clarkson, Morrissette, and Régallet 1992; Jacobs et al. 2022a,b). In terms of the potato, time can be seen by the ancestral connections of the Mother tuber and her connections to generations of past Mother tubers and her future progeny. The stolons that connect them together operate similar to the way Knowledges, stories, and spiritual connections relationally bind Indigenous Peoples at the same time to their ancestors and to future generations. Relations are also embedded into spirituality, ceremonies, languages, subsistence practices, medicines, songs, and the physical, social, emotional, and mental health of our Peoples and communities (Salmón 2000).

This relational binding to the past, present, and future, can be seen through MVSKOKE ceremonial and healing relations, which use only plants. They are, for a lack of a better MVSKOKE-to-English translation, a culturally and ceremonially defined, balanced chemical equation that has never and cannot ever be changed. MVSKOKE medicinal and ceremonial ways are set in stone and to change them would be to challenge OFULVNKV EMVLIKVTV VHAKVN EMONYAKVTES. A good example of this is illustrated by how we heal certain human ailments: specific plants are gathered through strict and relational methods that adhere to MVSKOKE laws. None of the relational formulas (songs, ceremonies, and other rituals) in MVSKOKE methods can change because of the laws that hold and bind together our entire MVSKOKE medicinal ways. These examples show how relations to plants, songs, ceremony, human health, multiple elements of time, and the relational connections between each factor play a role in MVSKOKE TEK and medicinal practices.

Raramuri scholar Enrique Salmón states that "the use of plants for healing and for food offers a fundamental relationship from which Raramuri view themselves as participants in their natural community. The Raramuri understand that they were placed here as caretakers of their land, but also to aid in the health of the Creator, who works hard each day to provide for the land and its inhabitants" (Salmón 2000, 1329). Relations are central to how Raramuri Peoples use plants for healing and food and see their inherent positions among their ecosystems and their relational roles with Creator. Relationships are tied intimately to other Indigenous value systems of reciprocity and responsibility.

ARAKKUECKV: Reciprocity

Indigenous value systems are often interconnected and woven together in a way that makes them difficult to define separately because they often work together and inform one element to the next (figure I.3). In the Raramuri example, Indigenous Peoples are involved in a cycle of reciprocity that provides for the land and Creator, which, in turn, maintain fruitful realities for the Raramuri. In the MVSKOKE plant medicine example, a similar system of reciprocity is demonstrated by the relational and respectful care that is formulated into each step of the process that ultimately benefits human health. These examples show how reciprocity is often an exchange practice that offers cyclical benefits from one life being to another (Jacobs et al. 2022a,b; Harris and Wasilewski 2004). "Reciprocity principles integrate Indigenous understandings of socioecological, ceremonial, cosmological, and spiritual connections within Indigenous communities, kinship systems, lands, and waters" (Jacobs et al. 2022a, 285). Reciprocity is also something that is often promised to Indigenous Peoples in our origin stories. In situations where Indigenous Peoples' origins stories offer rules and laws for how they should take care of specific other lifeways, a subsequent promise of abundance and sustainable lifeways for humans is often part of the reciprocal cycle embedded within the story.

To illustrate this, we return to the potato, which demonstrates an embedded system of reciprocity between humans and plants. Caring for a potato plant requires a grower to understand the plant's needs and how to respond to those needs in specific ways. To prevent potato blight, the grower needs to develop an intimate relationship with the plant and spend time with it to understand its health and needs. Growers have to understand how their actions (e.g., planting intervals, watering practices, etc.) can ensure the success of the plant and respond accordingly in times when the plant may be stressed or starts to show signs of blight. When growers develop good relations with plants in ways that make them capable of responding to the plant's needs—by *listening* to the plant's needs—then they are investing in a cycle that will subsequently provide them with potatoes for food and other purposes. Therefore, the potato plant gifts the fruits of its labor to the grower, who develops the relations needed to be responsible and maintain good relations with the plant. This is one form of reciprocity in action. On a cultural level, such processes can occur through other methods, and often engage with other elements (spirituality, ceremony, and other cultural practices).

Reciprocity exists in most cycle-based systems, including the living and dying processes of all beings. For humans, Coyote Marie Hunter-Ripper (Cherokee/Choctaw; 2022, 45) states, "we live so we know how to die and we die to live again." The cyclical aspects of reciprocity transcend time, lives, and species, and guide all beings on a cyclical trail into other realms of existence where one life passes through death into a new reality. Reciprocity then becomes a connection to the cosmos, the spirit world, and a process in which all living beings participate wittingly or unwittingly. It is the gifting of life, the gifting of death, and the gifting of connections. Each gift in this reciprocal system, much like the relationships discussed above, holds different types of responsibilities that Indigenous Peoples honor in various ways.

VNOKECKV: Responsibility

Embedded factors of the Indigenous value system of responsibility can be found in the examples above. Responsibility is shown in the roles that Raramuri Peoples honor as caretakers of the land and in their responsibilities for the health of Creator. The potato grower has a responsibility and therefore practices VNOKECKV within the relationship to the potato—to understand, see, care for, and listen to the plant, and act upon the plant's needs in a way that contributes to its well-being. In many ways, this type of responsibility to relations, the practice of VNOKECKV, ties back to the sense of kinship and relations that are demonstrated by mothers who look after their children: potato mother tubers ensure that their daughter tubers have strength and other necessary characteristics to grow, similar to how Indigenous Peoples ensure that all things to which they are related are loved and cared for over time through a critical system of reciprocity. The intersections between responsibility, relationships, and reciprocity are hard to ignore.

However, as an Indigenous value system, we see responsibility as "the obligations that Indigenous Peoples hold to lands, waters, plants, and animals" and to other members of our human communities, including the responsibilities we hold to past and future generations of our Peoples (Jacobs et al. 2022a, 285). Max Liboiron extends this understanding by defining responsibility as "the obligation to enact good relations . . . and to account for our relations when they are not good. And you can't have obligation without specificity" (2021b, 24). Indigenous lifeways often follow the mantra of living and being in a good way with all things and all relations. But as Liboiron points out, not all relations are good. So, an inherent responsibility exists within many Indigenous communities to right the wrongs of bad relations to avoid interrupting the reciprocal systems embedded within good relational ways of being.

In terms of bad relations, many Indigenous communities honor our responsibilities to maintain our cultures and relations with all beings by rejecting forms of assimilation and western dominance through more than five hundred years of colonial contact. Honoring our responsibilities to our languages, ceremonial practices, values, Traditions, Knowledges, and sacred ways is what maintains our cultures and ensures that the future generations of our Peoples have opportunities to connect to the long roots our communities have grown with lands, plants, animals, and all of our more-than-human kin. Honoring our responsibilities is the practice of VNOKECKV.

Similar to reciprocity and relationships, responsibilities may differ between and within Indigenous communities and also may originate from sacred origin stories and other forms of oral histories. Therefore, specificity matters and not all responsibilities are the same, nor accountable to the same relations and systems of reciprocity. This is why it is essential for Indigenous Peoples to explain such value systems from our distinct perspectives and a reason why we shouldn't homogenize Indigenous values into one understanding. Responsibilities guide us on our reciprocal lifeways with all beings to which we are related to ensure that the health of everything around us, including our own communities, remains sustainable and resilient.

Storytelling: Connections between TEK and Indigenous Value Systems

We offer our readers a non-Traditional fictional story that illustrates the integration of TEK and the specific Indigenous value systems we highlight in this volume:

> PUCA (Grandfather) and I walked slowly to the banks of the river. The water flowing in this river has sustained our family and other relations since the beginning. I carried the SVMPV (basket) that my PUSE (Grandmother) had woven years ago when she was just a young girl. Her ECKE (mother) taught her to weave the basket

from reeds that they harvested and dried: reeds that came from the wetlands near the river. Reeds that were fed by the river and our People. Reeds that our family has sat by, listened to, and taken care of for generations.

Our family has long-rooted relations to the reeds, to the waters they grow by, and to the VHV (potatoes) that we will be harvesting today. We also have relations to the basket that I hold, which has been used by our family to collect VHV and other AHOCETV (plants) for a long, long time. VHV are our kin—they are like family to our community. We, too, came from the soils in which they grow. Before this basket, there were other baskets that our family used, and each one holds the memories of our families, the Knowledges of how they should be created, and the relations we have to the foods we harvest for our community—foods like the VHV. We cannot eat the VHV but harvest them as gifts meant for other community members.

PUCA brings gifts for the water, the land, and VHV. We sing a song as we give our relations these gifts. Our relations with VHV, the river, and the reeds include a system of giving and receiving. The gifts we lay down contain Knowledge—Knowledge about what each of our relations need and what responsibilities we hold: what will help them grow, what will purify them and bring needed nutrients that will be absorbed by the waters, the VHV, and the reeds that will be later distributed back to our Peoples. Knowledges that were passed down through generations of our Peoples. Before we harvest the gifts from our relations, PUCA reminds me of our responsibilities.

Embedded within our Knowledges is an understanding about our roles and responsibilities in maintaining our relationships to the river, the reeds, and VHV: What do they need from us? What can we do for them? How can we make sure they thrive? When should we bring them our gifts? When can we harvest the gifts that they provide to us? What medicines do they need? What songs do they need to hear to grow strong? What songs do we sing when we harvest, when we weave, and when we give gifts to our relations? How do we care for them as they transition to different seasons of their lives and as we transition in ours? What instructions were given to us by Creator for all of these tasks? What instructions have our families passed down to us? How do we make sure our relations have enough gifts to provide to their other relations? How do we honor them and help them continue in the future? What new Knowledges are they teaching us? How are we listening to them and telling their stories to our children? Are we in good relations?

This story shows some of the central components of TEK as a Knowledge-belief-practice system that incorporates relationships, reciprocity, and responsibility as integrated value systems that guide the entire system. We ask our readers to challenge themselves here and look for the science and methodologies embedded within the story. Look for how Knowledges, practices, and beliefs are distributed and enacted within the family. As you consider these factors, also reflect on how some of the questions posed at the end of the story create an Indigenous scientific form of inquiry that is ongoing and embodied. How does such inquiry overlap with western forms of science? How and why does it differ? Keep these questions in mind as you navigate other stories and poems in this book, and as you learn from the gifts that Indigenous authors offer you in their chapters in the coming sections.

Indigenous Values as Themes

The first section of this book, part I, focuses on the Indigenous value system of relationships. Authors in this section incorporate their understandings of relationships with TEK to cover multiple subject areas, including relations among humans, plants, and foods; with water, fire, air, and Earth; with Tribal regalia; with Indigenous Knowledges in western colonial institutions and curricula; to protect, honor, and provide gratitude to Mother Earth through Tribal governmental management practices; with the co-production of Knowledges between Indigenous Knowledge systems and western science; and with standpoint and Native Hawaiian identities and concepts in the context of the geosciences.

The second section, part II, engages with the Indigenous value system of reciprocity in the context of TEK by focusing on the gifts of rain; restoration work and science education; reciprocity as a process that holds Indigenous communities together; the survival practices, culture, and relations to place; reciprocal sovereignty and the dignity of the natural world; pyroepistemology (a merging of cultural fire burning with Knowledge systems) and university education systems; abolition as a pathway to building reciprocal futures; building a critical declaration of decolonization and Indigenization for scientific research and the academy; storytelling.

The third section, part III, is guided by the Indigenous value system of responsibility as it pertains to TEK. Authors in this section focus on the gifting processes of teachers, memories, offerings, and returning; intergenerational responsibilities that are owed to the past, present, and future; the history of manifest destiny and the current reality of land conservation; honoring Indigenous responsibilities while doing science; storytelling; the responsibility of relational consideration in the context of invasive and nonnative species; growing an authentic voice and connecting to community; responsibilities to Indigenous data; and responsibilities of Indigenous Peoples to manage their ancestral homelands.

The chapters in this book are far-reaching and at times provide contrasting perspectives on situations and resolutions to specific issues. These distinctions reinforce the need to listen to the plurality of Indigenous voices and opinions, while understanding that there is no one-size-fits-all model or approach that will meet the needs, values, and interests of every Indigenous community. We encourage readers to lean into the differences and recognize that the critical thought pieces shared in the following chapters do not present the only existing critiques or the only paths forward, but examples of how Indigenous Peoples feel about different topics and the futures that they hope to see in resolving the issues they are navigating. We ask our readers to keep these thoughts in mind as you navigate the book and to reflect on ways that you can enact good relations, reciprocity, and responsibility as you engage with the material in each chapter.

We end this introduction with poetic words of wisdom from MVSKOKE Citizen Kathryn Champagne, who thoughtfully provides stanzas that were translated into MVSKOKE by Britt Postoak about the Indigenous value systems of relationships, reciprocity, and responsibility.

CVNAHVMKE

OFULVNKV APVK'ETV EPHOPEYET

EM-PVL-SV'LKE OKETV: HOFUNVNKE, MUCV-NETTV,
    NETTV-OCEN

EM-PVL-SV'LKE VPVLTAKE: AHOCKV, PONVTTV, UEWV,
    EKVNV

ESTE MVSKOKVLKE: ARAKKUECETV, YVHIKETV, MVLIKETV,
    CUCO-HVMECVLKE, KERRETV

CVFEKNETV-HOMPETV, HELESWV, SE-EM-MVHAYETV
HESAKETVMESE APVK'ETV PUME
MOME TOWES

Relationships

Creator connects us
To our time relations: past, present, and future
To other relations: plants, animals, water, and land
To our Peoples: ceremony, song, clans, family, and Knowledge
To our health: foods, medicine, and practices
Creator connects us
It is so

ARAKKUECKV

MVTO OFULVNKV
MVTO PONVTTV MOMEN AHOCKV
MVTO EKVNV MOMEN UEWV
MVTO PURKE-TATE MOMEN NET'TV-OCEN EM-PVLSV'LKE
MVTO PUN HELES HEYVLKE
NAK EMKV VRAKKUECES
MOMES TOWES

To respect (reciprocity)

Thank you Creator
Thank you animals and plants
Thank you land and water
Thank you to our medicine people
We honor your gifts
It is so

VNOKECKV

EKVN UEWV TEPAKEN VCAYECET
AHOCKVLKE PONVTTVLKE VCAYECET

PUM ESTVLKE VCAYECET
ESTECATE OPUNVKV VCAYECET
MOMES TOWES

To love (responsibility)
Take care of the land and water
Take care of our plant and animal family
Take care of our people
Take care of the language of your ancestors
It is so

PART I

Relationships

1
HO'N A:WAN HI:DOSHNA

KOBE NATACHU

Positionality Statement

Enrolled in the Pueblo of Zuni (Shiwi) with Navajo (Diné) and San Felipe Pueblo (Katishtya) ancestry.

Ho'n A:wan Hi:doshna:we
FOR BRICE, LOVE KU'KYA

K'yałami, I want to share this gift with you

Open your hand and receive these kernels
Hold them close . . . listen for their stories spanning generations
Collected from harvests long before your time
By those who dreamed of your arrival one day
Feel each galaxy held within kernels waiting to expand

Ho'n a:wan hi:doshna:we, our responsibility tending to the world they
    left for us to continue
A daunting task we know but remember . . .

Our Knowledge is everywhere

Draw from collective memories to maintain what is sacred
Listen for instructions whispered between each flutter of humming-
    bird's wings
View cartographies embedded in red sandstone, orient yourself to the
    horizon
Recognize the familiar scent of burning cedar heavy in the air

Welcome each new day with serenity and become the stewards to of all
    our kin
Dom i:yaniki:na:we

This is lovework
To love is to uphold ho'n a:wan hi:doshna:we
Given to us all upon entering this world
Sow these kernels and continue our memory

Remember summers where your stretch bridged land and sky
Where I cradle you in my arms
Feel my cornsilk hair drape across your face
Laughter calling upon clouds heavy with bounty
Grow alongside these lands and breathe life into them once more
Watch shumak'olo:wa rest on leaf blades of mi:we
Curious tsyuyya:we visiting udenna:we of squash, emerald bellies
    dusted with pollen
Your harvest much later than theirs yet you still bear gifts
May you love this life more deeply than those before you
Find your place of belonging sooner than we did
Share this message with your kin as we watch from the garden, leaving
    our blessing
We lock eyes as the wind carries us to the west alerting you of our
    departure
Delapba you say as your prayers carry us Knowing we will return
This lovework never ends . . .

2

SACRED RELATIONSHIPS IN TRADITIONAL ECOLOGICAL KNOWLEDGE

MONIQUE WYNECOOP, TOMÁS A. MADRIGAL, JONI TOBACCO, AND DON MOTANIC

Positionality Statements

Wynecoop: Maternal Pit River (Atsugewi)/Mountain Maidu with paternal Italian American Heritage; raised in Mountain Maidu ancestral homelands for my younger years and then near helitack bases where my father's fire career took us to Idaho in Nimiipuu ancestral homelands; my children are enrolled Spokane, and we are now living in the ancestral homelands of the Spokane, Colville, and Kalispel Tribes; Tri-Regional Fire Ecologist, Bureau of Indian Affairs, NW, AK, & Rocky Mountain Regional Fire & Fuels Programs.

Madrigal: P'urhépecha (P'urhécheri) now living on Duwamish lands; community to community development (www.foodjustice.org); PhD.

Joni Tobacco: My name is Joni Tobacco, "Woksape le ca Teca Yuha Mani Win" (Oglala Lakota); Oglala Lakota Tribal Member, South Dakota; raised in a traditional Lakota family on the Pine Ridge Indian Reservation; I am the mother of Leroy, Nettie, and Emmett; I worked in natural resources management for the Oglala Sioux Tribe before returning to school; currently attending school full time in the field of forestry and hydrology within the ancestral homelands of the Salish Kootenai Tribes.

Motanic: Paternal Umatilla Tribal Member and maternal Coeur d'Alene; raised in Seattle and then was able to live and work on the reservations where my parents grew up before attending the Chemawa Indian School and to pass on some of the stories and language to our three daughters and numerous Native students through my forty-one years with the American Indian Science and Engineering Society; retired forester of forty-four

Figure 2.1. "This place is healing and so are we. We are here, healing together." Artwork by Monique Wynecoop, Atsugewi/Mountain Maidu, showing the four elements involved in the Spokane Tribe's Cultural Burn at their Food Sovereignty Garden, x̣x̣súl̓eʔxw ("a nice little place of good ground").

years, having worked and lived within Yakama, Umatilla, and Spokane ancestral homelands.

Sacred Relationships in Traditional Ecological Knowledge

Tata Juan Chavez Alonso, a P'urhépecha Elder from Nurio, Mexico, once asserted that Indigenous Peoples "have been stewards of both [water and the Earth] for generations" (Madrigal 2015, 1). He explained, "without our territory, without air, without water, and without warmth, all we have is death" (1). Across the western hemisphere, Indigenous Peoples' voices resonate with this worldview that incorporates their Traditional Ecological Knowledges (TEK): our collective responsibility to steward our relationships with fire, water, air, and Earth while keeping at least seven generations in mind. Healing these sacred relationships is necessary for cultural recovery and provides the basis on which Indigenous Peoples preserve and perpetuate life projects for generations yet to come through the four elements in a Traditional medicine wheel that include fire, water, wind, and Earth. In this chapter, we use case studies to briefly illustrate the power of Indigenous Peoples' relations with fire, water, air, and Earth and connect these factors to the need for healing such relations.

FIRE

The relationship between fire and the wellness of our communities and ecosystems is inseparable (see figure 2.1). Indigenous women and youth are taking back roles as leaders and stewards of the land, water, air, and fire, which are crucial positions needed for healing our communities. In 2021, in eastern Washington, the Spokane Tribal Network held its first community cultural burn on the Spokane Tribal Food Sovereignty Garden, x̣x̣súleʔxw (Melodi Wynne, a Spokane Tribal member, translated the Spokane Salish word as "a nice little place of good ground"; Sherwood 2021, 1). This burn was led by mostly women from different generations and was extremely powerful, as the Spokane Tribal women have held specific fire súméŝ (a Spokane Salish word for spiritual power regarding the Tribe's relationship with fire) since time immemorial (Boyd 2021; Wynecoop et al. 2019). As Frank Kanawha Lake, a Karuk Tribal Descendant with Yurok family, writes, "Fire is a gift from the Creator, and we humans have a responsibility to reciprocate and replenish what we use from the lands and waters we live among" (Boyd 2021, vi–xvii). For the Spokane Tribe specifically, cultural burning has been inhibited since the first Catholic Mission was established

on the upper Columbia (NPS 2019), the subsequent US military and settler occupation of Spokane Ancestral Territories in 1858 (Spokane Tribe of
Indians nd), and more recent federal policies (e.g., the 1935 10 A.M. Policy)
prevented, controlled, and criminalized cultural burning and wildfire (Pyne
2015, 13). In reconnecting with our cultural relationship with fire and our
ecosystems, we heal, as Melodi Wynne, Spokane Tribal member explains:
"When our land heals, we heal" (Sherwood 2021, 1).

WATER

In the ancestral homelands of the Lakota, water is scarce. Unpredictable
winter, spring, and summer precipitation events bring their own energy
and spirit, shaping the land and water bodies. The Lakota believe water has
a spirit and is a living being (Marshall 2002). Similarly, the Lakota relationship to their main food source, the Buffalo Nation, as told by Pete Catches
Sr. (Lakota Tribal member; personal communication with Joni Tobacco, nd),
was one of brotherhood. Tim Mentz Sr. (Lakota Tribal member; personal
communication with Joni Tobacco, July 13, 2022) discussed how the Lakota
knew where to find the purest spring water on the vast plains and often
depended on this Knowledge for survival (Marshall 2002).

Water is our First Medicine, given to us by our mothers at the beginning of our existence. Its presence in all of creation connects us, a belief
embodied in the Lakota principle Mitakuye Oyasin, "we are all related."
This belief defines the Lakota worldview and is integral to all their ceremonies. The nature and quality of water bodies are often described in their
Traditional names. As John Goes In Center (Lakota cartographer, personal
communication with Joni Tobacco, nd) explains, "Water quality, and many
other ecological factors, once determined the location of camps at different
times of the year."

WIND

The wind created "displaced relatives" when Yakama Nation root gatherers faced a barrier to their Traditional root areas among the new wind
turbines (Hernandez 2022, 24). The PacifiCorp Company leased land for
the turbines and closed off the property to the root gatherers who had a
previous agreement with the rancher. The Department of Energy failed
to mitigate the cultural impacts on Tribal members, and subsequently, the
roots and the Indigenous Peoples became displaced relatives until the issue
was resolved after several agency and community-based meetings. However,

implementing the recommendations of the Climate and Traditional Knowledges Workgroup, *Guidelines for Considering Traditional Knowledge with Climate Change Initiatives*, would have provided a process to calm the wind of dissension between the federal agency, the Yakama Nation, and the energy company before these relatives were displaced (CTKW 2014). Additionally, this example underlines the need for the wind to also be viewed as a living subject, part of the community, and, as described by Potawatomi scholar Robin Wall Kimmerer, a relative (Kimmerer 2015, 123–124). Our Tribal languages and TEK can help reconnect displaced relatives with their verb-oriented existence.

EARTH

The shared struggle waged by Indigenous Peoples to defend life on Earth, as asserted by the late Tata Juan Chavez Alonso, have been described in this hemisphere as "eco-wars" (Hernandez 2022, 125). Like many hemispheric Indigenous Peoples' beliefs, the P'urhépecha worldview holds that all creation is complementary and creates the unique conditions necessary for life to exist on Earth. It is for this reason that the obligation for Indigenous Peoples to take care of the Earth is sacred (Kuákari 2021, 13). Securing Indigenous stewardship of the Earth in our hemisphere, thus, has continued to be the terrain on which struggles by Indigenous Peoples have been waged to protect the future of all life and to ensure the ability of future generations to have a sacred relationship with the Earth.

One of the diasporic practices that Indigenous Peoples bring with them through place-based TEK is soil remediation, healing the soil so that it can thrive. In Washington State, Mixteco, Triqui, Maya, and P'urhepecha farmworkers who are displaced Indigenous Peoples often cultivate small patches of Earth for subsistence farming needs. Often the soil is not healthy to begin with, so they make soil via composting based on TEK, taking the best of their harvest and burying it beneath the soil in a ceremony where they speak to the Earth and honor the Earth for giving life. Each of these diasporic Indigenous Peoples has their own specific way of doing so. The ceremonial aspect during harvest Traditionally requires the participation of the Indigenous Nation who hosts the displaced relatives, and they are also honored.

As Felimon Pineda, a Ñuu Savi (People of the Rain; Mixteco-speaking) vice president of the independent farmworker union Familias Unidas por la Justicia (Families United for Justice) in Washington, says, "The work we do is life, because we plant the plants that bear fruit so that people can eat in order to be strong, to be healthy, in order to have energy, in order to survive. With our own hands, we plant, we sort, and we harvest the fruit. And so, the work we do is life—the life of the entire country" (McKinley 2014, 0:19). For Indigenous Peoples in diaspora, the relational way we cultivate the Earth is fundamental to perpetuating life upon it.

HEALING RELATIONSHIPS

The four elemental stories provide place-based, contextual examples of what is essential for sustainable stewardship. TEK provides the balance to sustain the environment with protections that connect instead of separating the system. These elements and their relationships are interconnected in more ways than we will ever know. Federal, state, and local agencies, national organizations, and university programs dedicated to natural resource management are just beginning to realize the critical need to incorporate different ways of knowing into their decision-making and operating capacities (Hoagland 2017).

The relationships between and protection of the elements described in this chapter are common themes found in different Indigenous communities. The environment has been sustained for millennia because these elements have been connected. Today, a need exists for each of these elements to be reconnected through TEK to heal lands and our Peoples.

3

MY DRESS HAS WINGS

MICHELLE M. JACOB

Positionality Statement

Enrolled Member, Yakama Nation; professor of Indigenous studies; co-director, Sapsik'ʷałá Program, University of Oregon.

Introduction

In this poem, I reflect on teachings learned from my Yakama Elders which affirm the rich relationships that surround the Tradition of wearing one's Tribal regalia. In this way, clothing and jewelry become more than simply fashion or entertainment. Rather, regalia connects one meaningfully and powerfully to place and a deep sense of love and respect for relationships past, present, and future. When one internalizes these lessons, central components of Traditional Ecological Knowledge, the importance of place-based Knowledges and relationships, are honored. My poem honors and affirms Indigenous joy and is primarily a space to dream powerful Indigenous futures. I center my Yakama ways of Knowing and being, focusing on tł'píip (wingdress), a Tradition in clothing we share with many Indigenous Nations. I juxtapose western views of animal/creature/beast with an Indigenous perspective of honoring our More-than-Human Relations. I destabilize the rigid and destructive human/nature dichotomies and hierarchies that feed ongoing settler colonial violence on Indigenous lands. I draw from a feminist critique of dichotomies by naming the analytical tool of both/and, while also playing off Indigenous Traditions of refusing to explain everything in terms that settlers may find easy or comfortable (magic!). The conclusion of my poem names and reclaims the power of Indigenous communities as a process of becoming, moving (from feeling, hearing, seeing, sensing) to an embodiment of the many strengths within our communities (Ancestors, Elders, Lands, Waters, More-than-Human

45

Relations). The poem expresses possibilities for what self-determined and
decolonized relationships can be for Indigenous Peoples—as we engage in
Traditional Ecological Knowledge research within our own communities to
feel, hear, see, sense, and create scholarship with transformative possibilities. Such approaches help us understand that we indeed have wings to fly
into beautiful Indigenous futures.

My Dress Has Wings

When I wear my Tribal regalia
I feel the power of my Ancestors
I hear my Elders' loving voices
I see the kindness in our Lands and Waters
I sense the generosity of our More than Human Relations.

When I wear my Tribal regalia
Strangers often ask if they can take a photo with me
What will happen to that image, I wonder
When they go home or to their next academic conference
How will my image be consumed by people with whom I have no
    relation?

When I wear my Tribal regalia
Strangers often ask to touch my clothing and hair
They ogle my jewelry and beadwork
Under their gaze, I am here to entertain
Am I exotic beauty, noble creature/beast, or simply an object?

When I wear my Tribal regalia
I see, feel, and sense how comfortable people are
In their own skin, hair, clothes, jewelry, and footwear
I move toward people who are gentle and welcoming
I seek distance from those with a greedy desire to consume.

When I wear my Tribal regalia
I feel my Ancestors urging me on
To move powerfully and humbly through the world
To assert my beautiful vision grown under the care of our teachings

To use my tɬ'píip (wingdress) to rise above settlers' problems, both
    petty and catastrophic.

When I wear my Tribal regalia
I'm both grounded and lifted
How can that be, small western minds might ask
Maybe someday they'll grasp the both/and
Until then, I'll simply explain: my tɬ'píip is stitched with magic!

When I wear my Tribal regalia
I am connected to Peoples and Places
Rich with Traditions, linguistic and spiritual
Just like our Lands, Waters, and Ancestors, I am strong, flexible,
    gorgeous
It is good to be a Yakama woman wearing a tɬ'píip.

When I wear my Tribal regalia
I am the power of my Ancestors
I am my Elders' loving voices
I am the kindness in our Lands and Waters
I am the generosity of our More than Human Relations.

4

BUILDING PILINA
Reconnecting to ʻIke Kūpuna

ULULANI KEKAHILIOKALANI BRIGITTE RUSSO OANA

Positionality Statement

I am a Native Hawaiian born and living on Oʻahu, Hawaiʻi. I am a science and Hawaiian studies teacher at Waiʻanae Intermediate and a University of Hawaiʻi at Mānoa PhD graduate in curriculum studies and instruction.

Introduction

Kānaka[1] have passed down ʻike kūpuna (Ancestral Knowledge—including Traditional Ecological Knowledge, TEK) through many generations of family and community. In Hawaiʻi, our ʻike kūpuna was often based on oral histories of our moʻokūʻauhau (genealogy) (ʻĪʻī 1959).

However, our moʻokūʻauhau expands beyond the typical family tree and includes the whole universe. Since time immemorial, Kānaka Maoli have recited moʻokūʻauhau for the cosmos, land, ocean, gods, and our Peoples through chants and stories (Malo 1951). Our pilina (close relationship) with the universe is deeply embedded in our everyday lives, and our oral histories have been recited from one generation to the next for thousands of years (Kamakau 1992).

---

1 Kānaka ʻŌiwi, ʻŌiwi, Kanaka, Kānaka (plural), Kānaka Maoli, Hawaiian, and Native Hawaiian are terms used in this manuscript to address the Indigenous Peoples who have genealogical ties to humans that lived in Hawaiʻi before western contact. These terms are capitalized as a sign of respect and solidarity for the movement toward sovereignty and to follow guidelines for writing about Indigenous Peoples as outlined by Younging (2018). This discussion shifts between terms to remind the reader that the term Hawaiian does not work as a residency marker but as reference to descendants of the Native Peoples of Hawaiʻi. This book purposefully does not italicize Hawaiian words in an effort to normalize Hawaiian language and not perceive it as a foreign or *other*.

Unfortunately, for some families, their moʻokūʻauhau and ʻike kūpuna were disrupted after western[2] contact. We still see this disruption today, perpetuated through the desecration of land to a western-centric education system. The disruption of ʻike kūpuna began when our population was decimated by the introduction of diseases that killed a majority of the Indigenous populations. This sudden disruption of ʻike left a lot of our People in crisis and a lot of our land empty. The desecration of our land is another major form of disruption. Military bombing, poisoning of our waters, machine gun testing, Rim of the Pacific exercises (RIMPAC), and overdevelopment of homes and hotels are just a few examples of the ongoing desecration of our land. This disrupted connection to land has led many families to be displaced and disconnected from their ancestral homes.

Furthermore, grounding our Native Hawaiian families in western-centric education systems is another form of disruption between moʻokūʻauhau and ʻike kūpuna. Western-centric education is rooted in imperialist ideologies, the polar opposite of our ʻike kūpuna, where the foundation of our Knowledge is based on our land, skies, seas, and other natural phenomena. Western-centric educational systems have successfully been used as a tool to oppress countless numbers of our ancestors and living Peoples via US-based assimilation policies that support the erasure of Indigenous ways of Knowing. Nonetheless, many ʻŌiwi are fighting to bridge this recently created disruption to our histories in many ways, such as implementing decolonization-based practices to dismantle and unsettle educational institutions and their foci and praxes.

One of the numerous examples includes Waiʻanae Intermediate School, which is located in Oʻahu, Hawaiʻi, and encompasses a student body consisting of predominantly Native Hawaiians. Within this educational institution, a few Kānaka teachers intentionally reshape the science curriculum to be ʻike kūpuna and community-centered. This work is extremely important to me, my students, and their parents. Our work is a tool of resistance for Indigenous communities to use against the tools of oppression that we face as students and teachers at western-centered institutions. Therefore, it is critical that we all continue the decolonizing and Indigenizing work that we are doing. Although we discuss the illegal occupation and not colonization, it is crucial to recognize the impacts that literature focusing on

2 The terms western, and west, are used interchangeably to represent the dominant culture of the Judeo-Christian western European region that colonized and dominated two-thirds of the world.

decolonization has had in the world. Therefore, I use the words decolonization and colonization with the focus on dismantling the western oppressive forces that have oppressed our People. I understand that we are not a colonized nation, but I recognize the body of literature that Indigenous Peoples have created to decolonize western institutions. With similar goals in mind, I use the word decolonization knowing that Hawaiʻi seeks de-occupation.

This chapter recounts my experiences as a Kanaka ʻŌiwi teacher who is advocating for her students and their needs. Through the process of reflexive methods rooted in decolonizing methods, I critically analyze my experiences and lived reality working within this educational system and share them through storytelling. Themes of pilina emerge among students and land, ancestral stories, me, and community.

ʻIKE KŪPUNA: ANCESTRAL KNOWLEDGES

Indigenous[3] Peoples around the world understand that Ancestral Knowledge systems (e.g., TEK) are at the core of our identities. It is crucial for Indigenous Peoples to work toward restoring and reconnecting to these Knowledge systems, while also maintaining opportunities to practice such systems in their everyday lives. In Hawaiʻi, much of our ʻike kūpuna is grounded in our ʻāina (land). Oliveira (2014) spoke of the pilina Kānaka Maoli have with ʻāina, oceans, and even celestial lines. Many of our moʻolelo (ancestral stories), chants, hula, and culture revolve around mountains, valleys, beaches, rivers, and other aspects of ʻāina (Oliveira 2014). For many Native Hawaiians, connections to ʻāina and specific places are the foundation of our identity. Anderson-Fung and Maly (2002) explain this concept by describing how Native Hawaiians hold emotional connections with our surrounding ecosystems and that these connections are manifested in every facet of our lives. These connections are woven into our moʻolelo (stories), ʻoli (chants), mele (songs), lei, and also form the foundation for the ethics and practices we have historically and currently employed in managing our surroundings.

Formations of ʻāina often have an exhilarating moʻolelo. Hawaiians spent multiple generations cultivating and working the same land, deeply rooting it as part of family moʻokūʻauhau, and embedding ʻāina deep into our senses of self, identities, and genealogies. For example, the famous ʻōlelo noʻeau (Hawaiian language proverb) states, "he aliʻi ka ʻāina; he kauwā ke

---

3 The terms Indigenous and Native are used with the understanding that these are both groups that have been oppressed and experienced loss of land and culture by the west.

kanaka," which translates to "the land is the chief; man is its servant," meaning, "land has no need for man, but man needs the land and works it for
a livelihood" (Pukui 1983, #531). 'Āina was seen as a Chief, and Kānaka
as the servants who depended on our 'āina. Therefore, the disruption of
these ontologies via the historic and current structures of colonization have
resulted in a turbulent time for our Peoples. Although some families are
still lucky enough to have these lands, most have been displaced. Today,
'Ōiwi leaders continuously work to create programs and 'ike kūpuna-based
nonprofits to restore 'āina and our connections to it (Maunakea 2019). The
erasure of our culture has oppressed our Peoples for too long, making it
extremely important for Kānaka to continue to reconnect to 'ike kūpuna
and build pilina to all things through a Hawaiian lens.

Post western contact, Kānaka experienced mass deaths of our families, pressure to change religious beliefs, losses of land, and much more
(Kameʻeleihiwa 1992). Numbers of Hawaiians dropped from an estimated
1,000,000 to 400,000, and then to 40,000 by 1890: a massive genocide
that was rooted in colonization and occupation (Stannard 1989; Trask
1999). Ultimately, the Hawaiian People lost sovereignty after the illegal
overthrow of the Hawaiian monarchy by twelve businessmen and the US
government in 1893 (Liliʻuokalani 1898). Subsequent occupation and other
forms of injustice have historically and, in many instances, still, disparately
affected Hawaiian Peoples through racial oppression, homelessness, high
incarceration rates, high numbers of special education placements, drug and
alcohol abuse, and the ban of the Hawaiian language and cultural practices
(Aken 2018). However, 'Ōiwi continued to persevere and work tirelessly to
reconnect to 'ike kūpuna (Kanahele 1986).

The Hawaiian Renaissance began in the 1970s and went beyond the
spread of Hawaiian culture and practices by involving an extensive list of
Hawaiian activists who protested multiple oppressive acts on 'āina, the evic-
tion of Hawaiians, and the abolishment of Hawaiian language in schools
(Chait 1999). The ban on Hawaiian language was lifted in 1978, and the
first Hawaiian-language immersion schools, referred to as Ka Papahana
Kaiapuni Hawaiʻi (the Hawaiian immersion project), were founded in 1987
(Fox et al. 2012). In these educational facilities, Hawaiians created opportunities for Kānaka to learn about Hawaiian culture—an education that many
previous generations were deprived of. "Over the course of the next three
decades the [I]ndigenous [P]eople of Hawaiʻi continued to peacefully protest
and doggedly lobby state, federal, and international entities, like the United

Nations, for Native Hawaiian rights to sovereignty and self-determination" (Wright 2003, 30). This strenuous fight to rebuild pilina to 'ike kūpuna is seen throughout the pae 'āina (archipelago) today.

WAI'ANAE INTERMEDIATE SCHOOL

One of the many ways Kānaka 'Ōiwi are rebuilding pilina to 'ike kūpuna is through educating our next generations. Wai'anae Intermediate School, located on the rural side of O'ahu, Hawai'i, provides education for seventh and eighth graders, and encompasses a student body of about a thousand students, with a high percentage of Native Hawaiians (66.2 percent) (SSIR 2018). The science department has worked to rebuild pilina to connect students to 'ike kūpuna. As a Kanaka 'Ōiwi kumu (teacher) who teaches predominantly Native Hawaiian students, it is my kuleana (responsibility) to provide my students with opportunities my parents and myself did not have (e.g., sharing ancestral mo'olelo about place, education on the illegal overthrow of the Hawaiian monarchy, the impacts of oppression Kānaka had to withstand, and the negative impacts of blood quantum ideologies). These are important topics of our history that need to be discussed; however, the "controversial"[4] nature of these topics means they continue to be frowned upon. After years of protesting, teachers have begun to implement these lessons within curriculums, although doing so often feels like a never-ending protest. Nevertheless, I was fortunate to cocreate a curriculum with Science Coach Kekaha Spencer and the former Science Department Head Kanani Blue. Many 'Ōiwi teachers make it their kuleana to bridge western standards with Hawaiian culture to create opportunities for our students in the public school system (e.g., connecting to 'āina through field trips, sharing ancestral mo'olelo about place, teaching hands-on cultural practices, and providing education on the "controversial" topics mentioned above). Many of these teachers are often criticized and not supported by their administrators when veering away from a western-centric curriculum. However, at our institution, we are lucky to have a Native Hawaiian principal, John Wataoka, who supports our endeavors.

My first year teaching, in 2015, was precarious, to say the least. Our department had no curriculum, and I was told to google state science standards. Inspired by my mother, Natalie Kekahiliokalani Oana, who taught

---

4 The word "controversial" is placed in quotes because our history is not controversial, but it makes non-Hawaiians uncomfortable and is deemed controversial by the Department of Education.

Hawaiian science at Hālau Kū Māna (a small public charter school), I followed in her footsteps by integrating ʻike kūpuna into my lessons. I facilitated monthly lessons that I referred to as "moʻolelo days," in which I shared the moʻolelo I learned from ʻŌiwi leader Eric Enos about the Waiʻanae area. Immediately, I noticed a shift in my students; they were attentive, perfectly behaved, and kept requesting for more moʻolelo-based lessons. I quickly learned that my students needed much more from me than just monthly moʻolelo days.

After struggling through my first year and having half of our department members quit their jobs, Kekaha, Kanani, and I built a curriculum together based on ʻike kūpuna. When we first started to implement this curriculum, we saw an immediate change in students. Students were suddenly more engaged, more invested in the lessons, and began to build a sense of responsibility for our ʻāina. The curriculum was grounded on moʻolelo from our kūpuna (ancestors) and focused on our community, mountains, streams, and valleys. Today, we begin our curriculum with the stories our kūpuna had about each mountain that surrounds our campus. Through these stories we begin to discuss their implications, deeper meanings, and the associated scientific phenomena.

As of 2024, Hawaiʻi public schools provide standardized Hawaiian culture curricula for only one semester in fourth, seventh, and eleventh grades, and an optional Hawaiian Studies elective for twelfth graders. Even these small offerings provide opportunities that do not really exist in the United States in standardized curricula. In many parts of this country, there is an active war on teaching anything from Indigenous perspectives: continued forms of assimilation and Indigenous erasure. Although Hawaiian public schools offer more Indigenous-centered educational opportunities than what may exist in other states, it still feels like it is not enough. Hawaiʻi seems to be leading the way in incorporating Indigenous-cultural teachings into our public school system, but we are still working toward enriching this as a more sustainable and decolonial education model. While these are important and necessary additions to public school standards, the lack of constant immersion into our Knowledge systems creates a situation wherein students often know little to no Hawaiian language and ʻike kūpuna by the time they get to eighth grade. This is insufficient. Private, Hawaiian-immersion, and Hawaiian-focused charter schools are doing an amazing job of providing students with opportunities to build pilina with ʻike kūpuna, but the standard public school system has yet to catch up. My students are very proud to be Native Hawaiian, but they often lack the opportunities to reconnect to ʻike kūpuna. Although the Department of Education (DOE) has initiated efforts to do so, there is much work to be done to create curricula that center Hawaiian culture and teacher training.

The importance of our curriculum became evident when my students shared the moʻolelo with their families. Parents called me in tears, thanking me, expressing how their children came home and shared moʻolelo they had never previously heard. They expressed how they wished they had this type of education when they were going through school and how they were happy their child had such opportunities. It still brings tears to my eyes because I also did not have those opportunities in school, but I was privileged enough to have a mom who taught me ʻike kūpuna. The school is helping to mend some of the disturbances from colonization by bringing students into closer communications with their Ancestral Knowledges so they can share that with others within their communities, including their parents. This is a form of resistance and resilience to settler colonialism. The children are becoming teachers to reclaim their histories and teach their older family members. It is really quite meaningful and beautiful.

Through the several years of developing, redesigning, applying, and rethinking this curriculum, some best practices became evident. I quickly learned that if I do not build pilina with my students, the curriculum will not be as meaningful. I teach in a low-income community that includes a large population of houseless individuals and people who live in multigenerational homes. School often provides a safe place for students, with free food and many friends, but it can also be a place where my students feel inadequate. Working at a public school usually entails the administration of western-centric curriculum that is driven by state testing requirements. Because of this, school is often an intimidating space for many of my students who are riddled with trauma from past academic experiences. Many students talk about feeling dumb, incompetent, being told they would never make it, that they will never go to college and so on. My teenage students are often dealing with not just academic trauma but a lot of intergenerational trauma. Like those in many Indigenous communities, they come from families suffering from alcoholism, houselessness, drug abuse, domestic violence, and other such situations. They have shared many stories with me and expressed how they need someone who believes in them, listens to them, and cares about them. However, my students are not the only ones learning in the classrooms: I am continuously learning from my students and their experiences. They often crave safe spaces to build trust and share their own stories, so I have integrated that as part of my teaching practices through one-on-one check-ins, truth circles, and *talk story* sessions (as described below). Unfortunately, this is not a normalized practice in western-centered institutions, and it is extremely important for Indigenous students to have these safe spaces. Creating such spaces is rooted in social justice and decolonizing practices, where we break down barriers to learning, centering the student's lived realities and cultural norms.

Building pilina with my students often begins during the first week of school with simple group check-ins where students can share anything they might be going through. Although some do not share at first and choose instead to listen to their brave classmates' heartbreaking hardships, eventually this storytelling practice inspires all students in the classroom to share with others. I listen to their stories, provide them with resources to help when needed, and, most importantly, this process helps me to build pilina with all members of the classroom. Creating a safe space for students to share, be vulnerable, and, most importantly, be accepted and cared for is the most critical work I do as a teacher. Building pilina is a foundational practice that embodies such care work for younger generations. Once that pilina is established, students become more invested in coming to class and school. Furthermore, when students ask me to share about myself, I often include why I became a kumu and why I teach what I do. I explain how I am trying to provide them with the education that I wished I had while growing up. I discuss the utter disconnect and oppressions our kūpuna went through after the illegal overthrow of the Hawaiian Kingdom. I share my intentions for the school year, the overview of the curriculum, and why I believe it is so important to rebuild pilina to 'ike kūpuna. These moments of vulnerability lay a foundation of our pilina for the rest of the school year.

Once a base layer of pilina is established, our curriculum begins with the mo'olelo of the mountains surrounding our campus. The mo'olelo guides our dive into the geosphere, hydrosphere, biosphere, and atmosphere. Science is all around us, and our kūpuna were the best scientists. They observed their local ecosystems and used those observations to make sense of the relations among species and information regarding environmental systems. They knew about the relationships that connect the land to the ocean, the sky, and the stars. Once students see that scientists do not just wear a lab coat, but are people who navigate with the stars, farm kalo (cultivated taro, *Colocasia esculenta*), and much more, they believe our kūpuna are scientists and that they can be, too. Once they see that their own People, who look like them, speak like them, and embody their cultures, are scientists too, it is very powerful.

A very important way we physically build pilina with 'ike kūpuna is by creating opportunities for our students to take care of our 'āina. I connect with multiple organizations that restore 'āina to find opportunities for students to mālama 'āina (take care of the land). We average about eight field trips every school year through which students remove invasive plants and plant native species. These opportunities create spaces for students to build that pilina with 'āina and heal our 'āina. Building pilina with 'āina is foundational for Kanaka 'Ōiwi; however, it is now rare for our children to have such a connection to land because of urbanization and loss of ancestral lands.

The experiences students have during mālama 'āina field trips are often my favorite memories. Students share that healing our 'āina makes them feel a sense of pilina to 'āina that I could not have taught them within the four walls of our classroom. Instead, our 'āina is our classroom, just like it was for our kūpuna. Field trip days are usually the days I see all my students shine, especially my rascal ones: students with less confidence in the classrooms are repeatedly the ones who thrive more outdoors. These opportunities give those students their time to shine and create a sense of pride and confidence that all students subsequently carry back to our classroom.

This work is also very healing for me. I often find myself reconnecting to my kūpuna when I am working the land, trying to revive it from the invasive species that suck our soil dry (e.g., California grass, haole koa, and guinea grass). This is similar to western-centered educational systems that act like these invasive entities by draining our cultures and languages away from our everyday practices, especially when they do not focus on Ancestral Knowledges and teachings. We have a kuleana to help heal our 'āina and protect our 'āina from the harm we have done to it. Students recurrently relay similar feelings after seeing a large space we cleared, or how big a native plant has grown since previous visits.

Throughout the curriculum and mālama 'āina field trips, students develop a sense of kuleana to restore and protect our 'āina. A large part of our curriculum revolves around resource management and environmental justice issues within our community (e.g., overdevelopment of land, military desecration of land, illegal dumping, and so on). We give the students the opportunity to research one of the many environmental justice issues within the Wai'anae moku (district) and present possible solutions for them.

Students create a deeper connection to the kuleana they feel for 'āina by picking a specific place they want to protect. The places they choose usually involve their favorite fishing and hunting places, and places that are significant to their families. Depending on the 'āina they choose, they design a solution that will provide protections for that specific 'āina. This project gives students autonomy and creates opportunities for them to engage in community stewardship. Students learn about different environmental justice issues about which they may have previously been unaware, and the educational process results in student activism as they demand justice to overcome the issues. Some examples are the cleanup of military unexploded ordinances, creating fire breaks to protect endangered native plants, de-channelizing rivers, restoring overdeveloped land, and much more. We also organize a Science Showcase, where students present their environmental justice solutions to their families, community members, and judicial leaders. The showcase creates opportunities for community discussion around a variety of environmental justice issues within our Wai'anae moku. The showcase has given partners a view into our classroom work. Creating partnerships with state entities and community leaders provided opportunities for our students' voices to be heard.

KEAWA'ULA

The largest program our curriculum has created is our adoption of 'āina at Keawa'ula. In partnership with state and federal entities, we adopted an acre of land at Keawa'ula, Ka'ena, located at the end of our Wai'anae moku. We visit this 'āina four times a year. During these trips, students form a sense of kuleana to reclaim and restore this 'āina. On our Keawa'ula field trips we create different stations integrating 'ike kūpuna, western science, and Indigenous Science (depending on the current unit). However, the station that stays constant is mālama 'āina. Students spend about 45 minutes per station and rotate through all of them. Seeing this 'āina change over the years has incredibly shaped our students. They know exactly which plants they planted and which areas they cleared. Many students mālama 'āina over the weekends. For example, they bring water bottles filled with water to the site to water the plants. They even bring their families to the location and teach them the names of the different native plants, what our kūpuna used them for, and the associated mo'olelo.

I will never forget Ke'ala, who said to me, "This is the place you come to the beach and party, but now it's the place I have to take care of" (Ke'ala

2020). Keawaʻula is notorious for local beach parties, which we witness long
after the parties have ended by seeing the green bottles scattered around
our ʻāina. However, because of our program, this ʻāina is slowly becoming
more than just a good party spot. As my students get older and the program
grows, fewer amounts of trash have been found around our plants, thanks to
the students spreading the word of our project throughout our community.
It is evident that Keawaʻula is becoming a place our community cares for
and stewards.

The sense of kuleana students maintain with this ʻāina is demonstrated
in their desire to come back and lead our Keawaʻula field trips for new generations of students. I created a partnership with the local high school, so
my former students are able to come back and maintain relations with ʻāina
and be able to continue their responsibilities and leadership skills. I initially
intended this partnership to provide me with more support for the different
stations, but I was shocked to realize what it actually meant to my former
students and to learn of their passions to lead the mālama ʻāina station. The
pilina they had built with Keawaʻula was something they missed incredibly.
Another surprise came from the amount of admiration my current students
had for my previous students. I expected my eighth graders to be in awe of
the high schoolers, but I did not expect them to look up to their older peers
because of their passions. When I see my former students, I meet them
with a jog and a hug, followed by both of us saying how much we miss each
other, and then the conversation always turns to how much they miss my
class and the mālama ʻāina field trips. They quickly share with my current
students how they should be grateful for being in this class and how much
they will miss this once they get to high school. It always humbles me when
they share this, and often brings tears to my eyes. I remember one time, a
current student looked at me and said, "I hope you are that happy to see me
when I come back."

I had not realized that the pilina that I built with my former students
would have such an impact on them, to the point where current students
were already planning to come back to the program once they were in
high school. However, the biggest shock for me came out on the field. My
students began to work a lot harder clearing ʻāina than in previous years.
Thinking it was just a "good year," I moved on and continued with our work.
At the end of the field trip, I shared with the students how amazing their
work was and they responded by telling me that they worked really hard so
they could come back and be leaders next year too. My heart melted. The

pilina my former students built with my current students inspired them to work harder and to become leaders that continue to reinvest in pilina with 'āina, younger generations, and me.

Unbeknownst to me, the high school leaders were asked by my current students how they were picked to come back. They responded and told the students that they were the hardest workers, which inspired my current students to give it their all. Stories of these high school leaders continuing to take care of Keawa'ula on weekends filled my ears and overflowed my heart. They all shared a sense of responsibility they felt to keep working this 'āina. Moreover, reciprocity is also an important aspect of my work. The pilina that is being built with 'āina also creates a sense of responsibility to 'āina that continues to funnel through different generations of students, one year after another, while we work with 'āina as land protectors.

These lessons showed me that the curriculum cannot stand on its own but must be accompanied by a kumu who builds pilina with their students. It is important for kumu relations to engage in a way that decolonizes systems of power in the classroom and to empower relational dynamics between students and teachers by relying on these cultural responsibilities as a kumu. Students from other classes who come to Keawa'ula often share that watching the pilina that my students and I have has inspired their mālama 'āina efforts. Without the pilina, our 'ike kūpuna might just live within the classroom, something that is not a Traditional practice. It is the pilina created with our 'āina, kumu, and community members that reinforce this sense of responsibility for our People. The implementation of this curriculum has helped me to teach in a more Traditional format. This program will continue to evolve and grow. Keawa'ula continues to be healed while healing us in the process. What this 'āina was once known for is now being shared by our students.

Now What?

Former students are very vocal in sharing their needs for an 'ike kūpuna-centered curriculum. They often express their disappointment in the lack of field trips and Hawaiian culture within high school classrooms that do not engage in such curricula. Some students enter Wai'anae High School's amazing agricultural, marine biology, and Hawaiian Studies programs that integrate 'ike kūpuna-centered curriculums, but most do not. So, the question follows: Now what? Although DOE teachers like me are creating 'ike kūpuna curriculum, it still feels like we are swimming against the current. I have been challenged before by questions and comments from people who ask, "What is the point of this curriculum? What happens after they leave you? What if they never use any of this information for their future jobs?" Comments like these continue to invalidate teachers and students who are desperately seeking to create an education journey where they can learn about their own ancestors.

Thinking that this type of curriculum is not important if it does not serve students in their future jobs is fundamentally centered around western ideologies. Such thinking does not take into consideration that an adult could have interests, hobbies, practices, or family and cultural value systems that exist within and outside of their jobs. Additionally, questioning whether an 'ike kūpuna-based curriculum is even Hawaiian creates an idea that anything existing within a western-centric system cannot be considered Hawaiian. In the early days of western contact, our kūpuna adapted quickly. They used western resources, such as metal, to adapt their tools (e.g., placing metal at the end of fishhooks). They did not abandon their Hawaiian practices, but rather adapted them to be more efficient with the materials to which they were introduced. Education is merely the same. Indigenous Peoples are creating Indigenous Knowledge–based programs around the world. Leading many of these programs are Indigenous Elders and Indigenous academics who have written extensive books and articles that validate Indigenous Knowledges[5] and recognize their capacity to evolve over time. Receiving a western degree is what often gives us the voice and credentials that will be heard and listened to by others. Until our community members' voices become loud enough, many of us continue to pursue higher education degrees in western systems so we can share the validity of our Knowledge systems with the masses and in the scientific literature. This is a tool of resistance that Indigenous scholars are using to insert our Knowledges as (1) scientific understandings; (2) to decolonize the types of Knowledge that are accepted by western science; (3) as a responsibility to our past, current, and previous generations; and (4) as a responsibility to 'āina.

Perplexed by these questions, I decided to ask them to my students. Without sharing much of my opinion, I asked them what they think the answers might be. The reactions they had were priceless. Many students articulated how they wished all their classes were like the one that I facilitate.

---

5 Mary Kawena Pukui, Samuel M. Kamakau, Haunani K. Trask, Jonathan Osorio, Kū Kahakalau, and Lilikalā Kameʻeleihiwa, to name a few.

One student began to cry in her response and shared that if this was the only time in her whole life she would ever learn 'ike kūpuna, then she is glad that she did. She said that even if she never used it at her job, she would pass it down to her kids and grandkids. She broke down as she continued to share that, yes, this curriculum made her feel good, it made her feel like she belonged, like she finally knew more about her Hawaiian heritage, and how she felt like she had a bigger purpose in life. Others continued to share similar feelings, and that even if they were working in western-centric systems, the importance of Knowing their culture took precedence. They also wished this was a standard way and model of teaching.

Therefore, the question continues, Now what? Although the western-centric education system is strongly in place, do we wait to create a Hawaiian-centric education system? What do we do with our students until then? Should we just focus on private Hawaiian immersion and Hawaiian charter schools? Should we just give up on public school students? Or do we continue to fight and resist? Do we give our students whatever we possibly can until Hawaiian-centered educational systems are created? These are questions I consider very often. However, no matter what, I will continue to try my hardest and work to include 'ike kūpuna in all avenues of life. As a kumu, I find it my kuleana to do so within the realm of education. I am guided by my kūpuna to provide such opportunities to my students. Our kūpuna were beaten when they spoke Hawaiian, and they were oppressed throughout their educational journeys. If they could see my students now, they would rejoice. It is not perfect, and I am always trying to evolve my methods and praxis, but as my students shared, it is better than doing nothing. If our kūpuna saw them restoring and advocating for our 'āina, they would be so proud. They truly are living our ancestors' wildest dreams.

FUTURE HOPES AND DREAMS

As our ancestors dreamed, I also dream of a Hawaiian-centric education system. My hope lies in those of my kūpuna: the hope to help students and future generations rebuild pilina to 'ike kūpuna, to rebuild pilina with our 'āina, and most importantly to one another. It is crucial that we create spaces where we, as Kānaka Maoli, can connect to 'ike kūpuna. Our children are the future. Through the next generations, I hope the pilina and kuleana my students feel will be passed down to their children and grandchildren.

With these thoughts in mind, I believe that curriculum based on 'ike kūpuna should be normalized in public schools. Western-centric curriculum and standardized testing should not be the only metrics to gauge student successes and inform their futures. Thankfully, there are many teachers who are working tirelessly to unsettle western-centric standards in a way that creates room for the practices and Traditions from our kūpuna. Most of us understand that curriculum should not only be ʻike kūpuna-centered, but it should also be grounded in the ʻāina surrounding the school itself. So, it is time we prioritize our own Peoples on our own lands.

I hope all teachers will make strides to include many of the afore-mentioned elements into their praxes and that they are met by principals and administrators with full support. However, they may encounter some obstacles, such as knowing ʻike kūpuna and being able to see the connections of our ʻike kūpuna in all of the things around us. Connecting to community members, Elders, reading primary source books, and doing research will be necessary to overcome such obstacles. Nevertheless, I hope programs such as these continue to validate the importance of integrating ʻike kūpuna within our education system.

Conclusion

Over the past decade, the Science Department at Waiʻanae Intermediate School has advocated and created opportunities for students to rebuild pilina with ʻike kūpuna. Reflecting on the experiences my students and I have had helps me to clarify the importance of the work that I am doing and the best practices that work with my specific students. This type of education is imperative for our People. My students, their parents, and myself included, have all benefited from a curriculum grounded in ʻike kūpuna. Through time, I have learned the importance of building pilina with my students, continuing the opportunities beyond my classroom, and giving students autonomy in their learning. However, unexpected outcomes, such as increases in attendance, classroom engagement, grades, and Hawaiian identity, also occurred and therefore should be considered as additional successes in this praxis.

To all the Indigenous educators reading this: I hope you feel inspired and validated by this chapter. This program invests in Indigenous value systems of relationships as a foundation to the curriculum. I hope this chapter inspires you to include land work within your curriculum, too. To all admin reading this: I hope you see the value of such work and allow your teachers and staff to implement similar transformative educational practices within your schools. In doing so, we can all play an important role in decolonizing and Indigenizing the oppressive forces that are deeply rooted in western-centric education systems.

Acknowledgments

Mahalo nui to my mother Natalie Kekahiliokalani Oana for inspiring me to be a teacher and all my kūpuna before her for guiding me. I would also like to thank my Wai'anae Intermediate 'ohana for supporting my wildest dreams. Finally, mahalo nui to all contributing partnerships who make our curriculum come to life.

5

DECOLONIZING KALAPUYAN ANTI'P (CAMAS)
Histories and Studies

DAVID G. LEWIS

Positionality Statement

Descended from the Santiam Kalapuya, Chinook, Takelma, Molalla Tribes, and Citizen of the Confederated Tribes of Grand Ronde; assistant professor of anthropology and Indigenous studies, Oregon State University. David lives at Chemeketa, in the Traditional Homelands of the Santiam Kalapuya People.

Introduction

Camas, Anti'p,[1] is a beautiful blue to purple flower that erupts in spring each year in the Willamette Valley, the original illahee,[2] or land, of the Kalapuya Tribes and Bands. This illahee is now a large area of the state of Oregon. Between April and May, where there had previously been early season unplowed fields, there will suddenly erupt a purple sea of camas flowers. Early explorers reported this sight appearing as if it was a large inland sea of flowers.

Anti'p was one of the primary staples of the Kalapuya Peoples, and yet the environments to host this flower are relatively rare today. Much of the valley has been turned into a vast number of agricultural fields, with few areas left traditional and undisturbed enough to host a field of camas. As such, large fields of camas are rare, and most communities host only a handful of parcels unmanaged enough to grow Anti'p. Tribal communities who associate with the valley, such as members of the Grand Ronde and Siletz

---

1 The Kalapuya word for "the camas" with camas being "ti'p" or "di'p."
2 Illahee is a Chinook wawa word for land that was commonly used in the region and common enough in usage today.

communities, have struggled to find fields of the plant to practice their cultural Traditions of digging the roots with Traditional digging sticks.

Every Tribal member will have their own story of rediscovering this amazing plant and the culture around it. This is my story, but it is also about my family, of which I am from a branch of the Mercier and Hudson families of the Grand Ronde Reservation. My Tribal ancestry is with the Chinook, Takelma, Santiam Kalapuya, and Molalla Peoples of western Oregon. At least one of my ancestors, Duniwi, was a Yoncalla and Upper Umpqua woman from the Umpqua Valley. The Hudson family are Santiam, and I grew up in the Santiam homelands near the village of Chemeketa, which was a band of the Santiam Tribe. Family members are leaders at the reservation, many relatives and direct ancestors serving on Tribal Councils and in the government for decades. I am the result of modern generations of my family already integrated with American culture, growing up going to high schools, getting jobs as laborers, farmers, and timbermen, and living alongside other peoples in the area. Yet, growing up, I never encountered the history and culture around this plant that sustained our Peoples since time immemorial. This context was shrouded in a settler overlay that veiled the true nature of this place before colonization so completely that few have questioned how and why we got here and what was here before. This work of rediscovery and restoration is important to recovering who we are as Native Peoples.

DECOLONIZING ANTI'P

In Salem, Oregon, there are three large Anti'p fields, including areas at the State Fairgrounds where Anti'p inhabit the overflow parking areas and the large fields of Bush Pasture Park. Neither area has ever been developed, and the Anti'p patches grow thick with overlapping camas plants. Both Bush Pasture Park and a small grove of heritage oaks bordering the Fairgrounds on Seventeenth Street have Anti'p growing under a protective oak overstory. The small heritage grove, an official state-recognized heritage site, has very old and tall varieties of Anti'p, which grow to nearly five feet tall. The third camas area includes several prairies at Minto-Brown Island Park.[3] The park is a restored "natural landscape" carved from several early settler farms.

---

3 John Minto, an early settler to this land, was a great proponent of agriculture in the valley. He established orchards and brought Merino sheep to Oregon. He served on the first Oregon State Fair board and helped develop the institution in early Oregon. Minto also knew and worked with many Native Americans in and around Salem. He learned the Chinuk wawa language and could easily communicate with Kalapuya People.

Much of the park contains fields, groves of trees, heavy underbrush of invasive plants, and walkways. The fields are reclaimed from European hazelnut groves and the City of Salem water supply settling ponds. Many of the hazelnut groves are still extant (or existing), if unproductive. At least three fields at Minto-Brown Park have Anti'p. The central Farm Field has a mixed variety of common camas (*Camassia quamash*) and giant camas (*Camassia leichtlinii*), while the two other areas, a field on the north side and the edge of a tree grove on the west side, contain common camas. More than twenty years ago, much of the park was replanted with trees and bushes and then groomed to create a parklike landscape. The Anti'p in the park were subsequently planted by park visitors who broadcast Anti'p seeds along trails.[4]

I have visited these locations continuously for the past ten years, every year taking numerous photos documenting the Anti'p cycles, and every year noticing more about the plant than ever before. One year, I noticed the many colors of Anti'p at the fairgrounds parking site on Sunnyview Road. Where I had previously assumed that Anti'p were simply variations of purple and blue, I noticed white, blue streaks with white, washed-out reds of many tones. Dark-blue-colored Anti'p predominates the area, but there is quite a lot of variation. There are several white true Anti'p at Bush Park as well, and they are rare enough that I counted the individual plants, one year getting to seventeen plants. These were not the much-heralded death camas (which is *Toxicoscordion venenosum*, not an Anti'p at all but a white flower that grows in a cone-shaped formation), but simply a white variation of the blue Anti'p. Looking closely at the base of most of the white flowers, I noticed blue veins. There are a few white Ant'ip at the Farm Field too, and park visitors have been tearing them from the ground, assumedly misidentifying them as death camas.

Death camas has a small bulb, a white flower, and grows in the same field as camas. Eating the bulb of death camas is deadly, and Native Peoples would normally pull the plant from camas fields. As such many People will not eat any white flower plant, just in case.

The flowers are not the most important part of Anti'p for Indigenous Peoples. Anti'p bulbs have been eaten for thousands of years by Tribal Peoples as a major food staple in the valley and throughout the Northwest. The Willamette Valley was famous for having large prairies full of Anti'p, and the

---

4 Initially I thought they may be surviving or volunteer fields of camas, but a comment on my blog, the *Quartux Journal*, stated that they had been broadcasting camas seed in the park to stimulate its growth.

Salem area (with the original name of Chemeketa (Tcimikiti)), was noted in oral histories as the "Camas place" (Jacobs 1945). Anti'p were so common and well harvested in the Willamette Valley that the plant became synonymous with the Kalapuya civilization. So numerous were the Kalapuyans that they were described to Lewis and Clark in 1806 by a Clowwewalla guide: "Multnomah (Willamette) above the falls was crouded [sic] with rapids and thickly inhabited by Indians of the Cal-leh-po-e-wah Nation" (Thwaites 2001 [1905], 241–242). Anthropologists estimate that there were approximately 16,000 Kalapuyans before settler-period epidemics. Smallpox first decimated Native populations in the 1770s, then malaria in 1830 destroyed Kalapuya populations by an estimated 85–97 percent (Boyd 1999).

DECOLONIZING KALAPUYA HISTORY

Before Treaties, settler land appropriations had fully claimed the Willamette Valley by 1851, leaving no large areas available for Tribal settlements. By the 1840s, Kalapuyans were forced to adapt to settler foods because their Traditional prairies were plowed under or fenced in for livestock. Hogs are noted as eating well on the Anti'p and getting fat off the Native foods (Palmer 1854; Lewis 2021). Kalapuyans and other Native Peoples were forced from their normal foods and pressured into poorly paid servant roles with settlers and subsequently began stealing food from the settlers to survive. They were labeled as thieves and vagrants when unable to find food or places to live in their own lands—lands that had been illegally taken by settler encroachment. The Kalapuya Peoples knew they had mistakenly allowed the settlers to take their lands and were being sandpapered away to nothing. When Indian Superintendent Joel Palmer made an offer to buy their lands and move them to a secure reservation that was safe from further encroachment and violence, and where they could live among their own People, they accepted the Treaty.[5] It was not until March 3, 1855, that the Willamette Valley Treaty was ratified by the US Congress and signed by the president. The processes of encroachment, disease, settlement, colonization, genocide, and removal of the remaining Kalapuyan Peoples to reservations parallels similar histories that occurred to all Native Tribal Nations across the continent.

Treaties did not give Native Peoples citizenship in the United States, and most Native Peoples were forcibly removed from their lands to federal

---

5 See the Willamette Valley Treaty Commission journal of proceedings for the transcribed comments by Kalapuya chiefs.

reservations. By April 1856, an estimated six hundred Kalapuyans remained; most were removed by the United States Indian Agents to the Grand Ronde Indian Reservation.[6] At the Reservation, the Kalapuyans (there were at least thirteen Kalapuya Tribes and Bands)[7] joined about nineteen other Tribes, represented in seven ratified Treaties,[8] removed there in the same period. The thirty-two Tribes had to learn to live together for the first time and subsequently intermarried and integrated cultures; now, most people from the reservation have numerous Tribal ancestries. The Tribes remained on the reservation for about one hundred years, for much of that time unable to leave without a pass from the Indian agents.[9] Descendants of the Kalapuyans still live in the valley and nearby. However, settler towns sublimated and replaced the Native towns, consequently modifying the lands of the Kalapuyans into arid agricultural lands with few Native spaces remaining.

I did not begin to discover these facts until I attended the University of Oregon some thirty-five years ago. I took classes and attended events and went on outings with Native Peoples from several local Oregon Tribes. Members of the Coquille Indian Tribe and the Confederated Tribes of Coos, Lower Umpqua, and Siuslaw invited a group of Native students to a private field on Crow Road outside of Eugene, Oregon, and there we dug Anti'p together for hours. At the time, the field was muddy and the Anti'p were not thick. Through this experience, I discovered much about Anti'p and was told that it was a major staple of all the Tribes in this region.[10] This experience led me to years of rediscovering our culture, history, ethnobotany, Traditions, and the Traditional environments of the Native Peoples

---

6 By April 16, 1856, the majority of Kalapuyans were at the Grand Ronde Indian reservation.

7 Those Kalapuya Tribes and Bands listed on the Willamette Valley Treaty are eleven; on the Umpqua and Kalapuya Treaty, one; and there is an additional Santiam Band, the Chiwean Band, found in 2021 on a previously undiscovered signature page for the WVT. Some five Tribes signed the Treaty late and the signatures were one year late arriving in Washington, DC (see Lewis 2021).

8 Ratified Treaties for western Oregon include Cow Creek 1854; Rogue River 1853, 1854; Chasta 1854; Umpqua and Calapooia 1854; Willamette Valley 1855; Molalla 1855.

9 Native Americans were not made citizens of the United States until June 2, 1924, with passage of the Indian Citizenship Act (https://www.loc.gov/item/today-in-history/june-02/), but until at least 1900, "Indians" had to have a pass to leave the reservation or be subject to imprisonment and forced return. The passbook was only used for about twenty years; after the Dawes Act of 1887, the controls over Natives leaving the reservation appear to have loosened.

10 Camas is a commonly accessed staple of Tribes from California to British Columbia and east to the Rockies. Some areas, valleys like the Willamette Valley, have preferential soils, water, and climate and appear to produce greater amounts of camas.

of Western Oregon. Over the years, I was joined by many other Native Peoples, students, and teachers on this journey of rediscovery, and today many of us are now professionals working to understand deeper levels of Native histories, TEK, and ethnobotany, leading others to take our research further.

We are in this situation today because our lands and Peoples were colonized by American settlers in the nineteenth century. Those settlers took our land and forced our ancestors to accept Treaties and sell their lands to the United States. My ancestors had to move to the Grand Ronde and Coast Reservations, and over generations, they completely adapted to living in American society through assimilation programs of the Indian department. Their children were forced into boarding schools, and the adults became farmers to prove they were civilized members of American society. Tribal children were literally rounded up by boarding school officials and taken to boarding schools to live, where they were forced to learn the culture of the settlers and see their parents for a few months in the summer. Western-style farming practices were pressed onto many Tribes. The Kalapuya People, like many other Tribes who did not have western-based agriculture previously in their cultures, were made to become farmers to prove they could become civilized and deserved American citizenship and therefore more freedom in American society. At the Grand Ronde Tribe, farming became a way to survive the abuses of the Indian office, which did not adequately support Native Peoples or administer resources and aid to better their situations. Once resources and lands were finally made available, through community efforts in agriculture, the Grand Ronde Peoples found ways to survive the many abuses of reservation life. By 1880, our Peoples were called "self-sufficient" by Indian agents (Lewis 2018).

Many of the promises made to the Tribes in their Treaties were not honored, and many of these Peoples died waiting for support from the federal government. Promises made in Treaties included housing, food, services like education and health care, and land. However, from 1856 into the 1870s, the People on the reservation lived in poverty. They had not been given land or enough food, they lived in poorly constructed shacks and were poorly supplied with services like health care and education.[11] Verbal promises by Joel Palmer were made in 1856, offering more food, housing,

---

11 Informal land allotments were not given at Grand Ronde until 1872, at the earliest, and formal Dawes Allotment Act land not until 1889. The Dawes Act was passed in 1887 but took a few years to implement.

and money to get the Tribes to remove to the reservation, yet these promises were not honored at all.[12] The Native Peoples never experienced the
benefits of a "better life on the reservation," as promised by Palmer. Palmer
made promises to convince the Tribes to move because he knew that he
had to protect the Tribes from genocide and allow white settlers to claim
additional lands, and if the Tribes remained on their lands, they would soon
be reduced to nothing.

Once on the reservation, Native Peoples were also forced to give up
their Traditional spirituality and accept Christianity as part of becoming
civilized. European Christian missionaries were placed on reservations to
save the souls of the heathens and help them become civilized by becoming
Christians (Prucha 2014). US assimilation policies sought to teach Tribal
Peoples to be civilized and suppress their Tribal cultures. With assimilation
would come the freedom to move around in American society and not be
discriminated against. Through the teachings of Christianity, farming, and
the forced assimilation of Native children who attended boarding schools,
many families lost connections with their Traditional cultures. Yet, even
as Native Peoples were being converted to farmers, the resources needed
to make this cultural change were not provided to Tribes by the Indian
Department. In 1858, after more than a year of near starvation, extreme
poverty, and the death of nearly a quarter of the Peoples from illness (Lewis
2016b), the Tribes at Grand Ronde were allowed to go back to gathering and
eating their Traditional foods (e.g., Anti'p, huckleberries (An'iwam), native
blackberries (Antkwililek), and salmon (Amhuya)) to supplement their diets.
At the Grand Ronde Reservation, a salmon fishery began on the Nechesne
River (Salmon River) to allow the Native Peoples to sustain themselves off a
local fishery only twenty miles away (Lewis 2016a).

Federal records show that federal officials lacked the training and
resources to effectively manage Indian reservations.[13] Despite promises
made in Treaties for land, the Tribal Peoples had to wait nearly twenty
years, until the early 1870s, to receive up to a hundred acres of allotment

---

12 The Molalla have a story of their final negotiation with Palmer, which included these
promises, but Palmer resigned, and they never saw any of the promises honored.
13 See numerous letters addressing difficulties on the reservations in microfilmed correspondence from the Indian office, National Archives Records Administration RG 75, M2
& M234 microfilm series, Records of Letter sent to the Commissioner of Indian Affairs,
Washington DC.

land.[14] However, the land allotted contained the poorest soils because most Indian reservations were placed on the poorest quality lands, lands that were not desired by settlers. Much of the Grand Ronde valley floor is full of clay, and there are poorly available water sources. The mere 240 acres received in allotment were not enough to make a living, but many Native Peoples decided to become farmers in hopes of becoming American citizens. Colonization, removal, and assimilation were largely successful in taking away Tribal rights to land, resources, and cultural identities. By the twentieth century, many Native Peoples on the reservation lost their connections to their Traditional cultures, including Knowledge of Traditional plants and systems of stewarding the land. Even so, many Peoples at Grand Ronde continued harvesting wild foods, materials for weaving baskets, fishing, and hunting, and maintaining some contact with their Traditional cultures. Even Natives from the boarding schools did not always lose their cultures and would return to the reservations and participate in the cultures by fishing and hunting.

The gathering of some Traditional foods continued for some time, but over decades and generations, many began losing connections with their Traditions. For example, using Anti'p and other roots for food was no longer being practiced by the Kalapuya Peoples and the other thirty-one Tribes at the Grand Ronde Reservation. Instead, they worked hard on their farms, attempting to make a living as American farmers. When Native Peoples dug and ate Anti'p, they were considered backward and poor, and the Traditional practice was admonished.[15] Each subsequent generation would learn less, and many children would be forced to attend boarding schools far away from their homes (e.g., Carlisle Indian Boarding School in Kansas and Sherman Indian Boarding School in Riverside, California). The boarding school system forced Native children to assimilate and learn American culture, and because of this, many students forcibly lost contact with their Tribal cultures (Collins 2000).

Despite assimilation pressures, some individuals maintained their cultural practices. Because the Grand Ronde Reservation was a confederated Tribe, it comprised some thirty-two different Tribes and many different cultures, represented by Tribes as far south as the Rogue River Valley and as far north as the Columbia River. By 1900, Native Peoples at Grand Ronde

---

14 For nearly twenty years, the Tribes at Grand Ronde had no land, even though it was promised to them in six ratified treaties.

15 Henry Zenk, personal comment 2022.

were related to at least three or four Tribes through intermarriage at the reservation and between regional reservations. A few spoke Traditional languages and knew oral histories of how to practice the cultures of their ancestors. These oral accounts were collected by anthropologists who published them in a series of language texts, many of which are being accessed today to help our Peoples relearn the Traditional philosophies and methods of collecting foods and processing them. For many Kalapuya Peoples, there are the Kalapuya Texts by Melville Jacobs (1945), a collection of tribal oral histories.[16]

During settlement, Americans saw Tribal Peoples as being of a lesser culture than the "civilized" Euro-American culture. Natives were termed as "savages" and "barbarous," and their cultures and lifeways were looked down on as primitive, with no meaning (without value) in a "civilized" society (Whaley 2006). Tribal Knowledges of land, oral histories, and the like were ignored and disregarded as useless and primitive. Tribal cultures and languages were studied because they were curious, quaint, primitive cultures (Deloria 1997). Scientists, anthropologists, folklorists, and linguists were interested in the mechanics of Tribal languages but had no interest in the meanings of Tribal oral histories (Mihesuah 1998). American society at large was fascinated by the primitive character of "Indians" and Tribal cultures. Native languages were widely collected and published in the Native language texts, and field manuscripts were placed in archives and museums, alongside collections of "natural history."[17] These collections were joined by vast collections of human remains and funerary objects, because collecting Native curios was a common amateur activity (Cole 1995). Native human remains are now subject to repatriation under federal laws, like NAGPRA (1990), but no such law addresses the recovery of Native cultures collected in manuscripts. Instead, Tribes and Native scholars are recovering relevant manuscripts as they work to recover, restore, and revitalize Native cultures and Traditions (Lewis 2015).

By the 1940s, only a few Native People at the Grand Ronde Indian Reservation—mostly Elders in the Tribe—knew or practiced their Traditional cultures. Their relationships with the land of their ancestors were severely

---

16 Because of the nature of the confederation of Tribes at the reservation, there are oral histories for most of the Tribes (e.g., Takelma Texts by Sapir, and Clackamas Texts by Melville Jacobs).

17 See the National Anthropological Archives and the American Philosophical Society for thousands of manuscripts of collected Native languages.

affected by forced removal to the reservation. Native languages were barely surviving during this time. In the 1950s, the federal Indian Termination Policy (1953) terminated the Tribes of Western Oregon (1954–1956) causing the remaining Peoples on the reservation to disperse to American cities to find work (Lewis 2009). From 1954 to the 1980s, many Tribal members found ways to survive with parts of their culture intact despite having no Tribal reservation on which to practice their cultures. During this period, because of the lack of education about Native Peoples, the American public forgot the people of the Grand Ronde Indian Reservation ever existed. Many assumed that the Kalapuyans and other Tribes had gone extinct, or were not Native enough, because of low blood quantum, to be a legitimate Tribe.[18]

In the 1980s, even though Tribal Nations were being federally restored, impacts on their cultures resulted in a need for some Peoples (e.g., some members of the Grand Ronde Tribe) to relearn their ancestors' cultures and restore relationships with the land of the original Tribes. The Peoples of Grand Ronde had been removed from their lands for 147 years (1856–1983) and terminated as a Tribe for twenty-seven of those years (1956–1983).[19] Yet, many believed that the reservation was where they belonged. Many recently enrolled Tribal members knew nothing of what their original Tribes were, nor where they had originally lived (i.e., on all the lands of western Oregon), much less anything substantial about the environments and cultures of their ancestors. It is not surprising that the Grand Ronde Tribe had to begin sponsoring community education classes to teach current generations who their ancestors were, the locations of their lands, and information relating to their cultures and languages.

It was confusing for me, when first working at the Tribe as the Culture Department manager in 2006, to hear from Tribal members that the reservation was the homeland of the Tribe. My research and family histories underlined how my Tribal ancestors had lived in the Willamette Valley, on

18 Letters to Oregon politicians during this restoration period stated that the Grand Ronde people were too diluted in blood quantum to be legitimately Indians. See the collections of Les AuCoin at Oregon Historical Society library. In addition, personal experiences at the University of Oregon, with students who stated that the Kalapuya were extinct, suggest that people had forgotten we ever existed and had no good reasons to be a tribe again. The blood quantum measurement, initially imposed by federal authorities, is not a legitimate measure of "nativeness."

19 The Western Oregon Termination Act PL 588 was passed in 1954 but was not implemented until 1956.

the Columbia River, and in the Umpqua and Rogue River valleys before their removal to the reservation. The reservation was the place to which we were forcibly removed and allowed to live at, enforced by federal Indian agents. However, I also knew how poorly our history was written and passed down by scholars, as well as the history of assimilation, the effects of which are still being felt today via the extreme lack of community Knowledge about our Tribal contexts. I count myself among many of our Peoples who were affected by removal and assimilation, as a secondary population of Tribal members who did not ever live on the reservation or attend boarding schools. In part, this is because I was born within the Termination period, a time when there were no services that I had the rights to access. I, therefore, learned little about Tribal history and culture until I concentrated my efforts on uncovering the histories and restoring the relationship with the lands and cultures of my ancestors.

Even today, the histories about our Tribes, the reservation, and our cultures are still being discovered and written by Tribal scholars who are engaged in rediscovering the silences of our past: silences created by generations of poorly written histories of the settlement of Oregon and the forced removal of the Tribes to the Grand Ronde Reservation. Most of these histories never captured the perspectives of Native Peoples and sought to tell only the story of the settlers. For example, histories of the Rogue River Indian War placed the full blame for the war on the Tribes involved and did not ask Tribal Peoples about their experiences, or provide the context of why the Tribes went to war. Ignored was the fact that the Tribes were being encroached upon and felt there was no justice because no white men were held accountable for murder and genocide (Lewis and Connolly 2019).[20] We now understand these histories to be part of the settler culture. These are colonized histories that negate the continued presence of our Peoples and cultures and foreground settler experiences as the only significant and valid accounts. The colonization of Native histories was effective in perpetuating the assimilation of Native Peoples by attempting to erase the Indigenous past so completely that it is now difficult for some to find their way back to it.

---

20 There are many early histories of the Rogue River War: a sampling includes Alice Applegate Sargent, "A Sketch of the Rogue River Valley and Southern Oregon History," *Quarterly of the Oregon Historical Society* 22, no. 1 (1921): 1–11; Harvey Robbins, "Journal of Rogue River War, 1855," *Oregon Historical Quarterly* 34, no. 4 (1933): 345–358; Hubert Howe Bancroft, *History of Oregon: 1886–88*, vol. 30, AL Bancroft, 1888; Charles Henry. Carey, *History of Oregon*, vol. 3, Pioneer Historical Publishing Company, 1922.

Amid our work to recover our Tribal history is our struggle to relearn how our Native Peoples related to the lands on which we lived: our Traditional territories and Traditional Knowledges of the Tribes. For decades, because of the lack of deep scholarship on our Tribal cultures, our Peoples were considered to be primarily hunter-gatherers.[21] The Kalapuyans were thought to have spent most of their time hunting. Other Tribes in the area, like the Chinookan Peoples, were considered "complex hunter-gatherers" and spent much of their time fishing for salmon and doing some trading.[22] But these cultural descriptions are poor representations, even stereotypical characterizations, of Tribal cultures in western Oregon. Yes, the Tribes hunted and fished, but the major economic activity was trading. The Kalapuyans participated in the Columbia River Trade Network (Stern 1998) by trading Anti'p and wapato (m'amptu) to the Clowwewalla, Clackamas, and Multnomah Chinookans (Henry and Thompson 2015).[23] Their contribution then joins the efforts of thousands of Tribes to make unique products and trade their goods within the network, making products from extreme regions easy to find at trading villages. Regarding Kalapuya trading practices, the term "camas wheel" is born, which describes our understanding of a packet of soft-cooked Anti'p cooked and dried, that has been mashed together in an ovoid shape and covered with large leaves for easy storage, transport, and trade. In exchange for this packet of cooked Anti'p, the trading partner would obtain dried and smoked salmon, or other cultural products (e.g., baskets, woven mats, dentalium, and buffalo robes) that were made and gathered by other Tribes and traded down the Columbia from faraway locations. Therefore, the anthropological categorizations of the Tribes do not do justice to the complexity of their intertribal trade, or their social and political activities.

In times when Kalapuyans had excess processed foods, they would dry them and store them for winter food and trade. An oral account from *Kalapuya Texts* helps contemporary descendants of the Kalapuya Peoples to

---

21 Hunter-gatherer is a common anthropological term, used to describe Northwest Coast peoples including the Kalapuyans (Kenneth M. Ames and D. G. Maschner Herbert, *Peoples of the Northwest Coast: Their Archaeology and Prehistory*, London: Thames and Hudson, 1999).

22 These are commonly used terms in anthropology today; local sources are Kenneth M. Ames, "The Northwest Coast: Complex Hunter-Gatherers, Ecology, and Social Evolution," *Annual Review of Anthropology* (1994): 209–229; Kenneth M. Ames, and D. G. Maschner Herbert, *Peoples of the Northwest Coast: Their Archaeology and Prehistory* (London: Thames and Hudson, 1999).

23 Henry (Henry and Thompson 2015) does provide one of the rare journal accounts of the Kalapuyans bringing foods to Willamette Falls to trade.

properly prepare their Anti'p and other foods. The account also gives us hints as to how much planning and care went into preparing foods for winter storage.

> Now then it had become cooked camas, they dried some of it in the sun. And they took care of it (turned it over) all the time (it lay drying). And when it was dried, they then put it away. They ate it in the wintertime, when there was a lot of snow on the ground. . . . That is the way they did everything. They always put it away. They dried Chinook salmon for the wintertime, and then they ate it. They dried meat, and in the wintertime they also ate hazelnuts, and acorns, and tarweed seeds, and dried berries. They dried all sorts of things, and in the wintertime they ate them at the time when there was a lot of snow, they dried eels which they ate in wintertime, in the summertime they picked tarweed seeds, and they dried them on the fire, and when they were done, then they put them away. (Jacobs et al. 1945, vol 1, 19–20)

Kalapuyan lifeways are vastly different from Tribes such as their Chinookan neighbors. The Chinookan Tribes had lots of salmon, steelhead (Anya'i), lamprey (Antau), and sturgeon to capture from preferential and highly productive capture sites, like Celilo, Cascades Rapids, and Willamette Falls. The Kalapuyan Tribes also had fish, but not highly productive areas, and so they spent most of their time harvesting food plants like Anti'p, wapato, acorns (An'ulik), huckleberries, and many species of root plants. These food plants grew so well in the valley and the foothills that the Kalapuya Peoples learned to depend on them and make detailed plans about how and when to harvest them each season.

The Tualatin calendar (figure 5.1) provides many clues about annual harvesting activities. This twelve-month calendar focuses on the northern Kalapuya Tribe, the Tualatin (Atfalati), and their activities during each monthly period, including harvesting and processing Anti'p and wapato, another nutritious bulb, harvested from wetlands. The focus of the calendar on root plants suggests that the Kalapuya Peoples followed root plant cycles for their annual harvesting (Gatschet 1877). They would travel to known fields of root plants (especially Anti'p and wapato) and remain for a month or more harvesting foods for winter storage. The Tualatin Calendar might not fully represent all Kalapuyan Tribes and bands in the Willamette

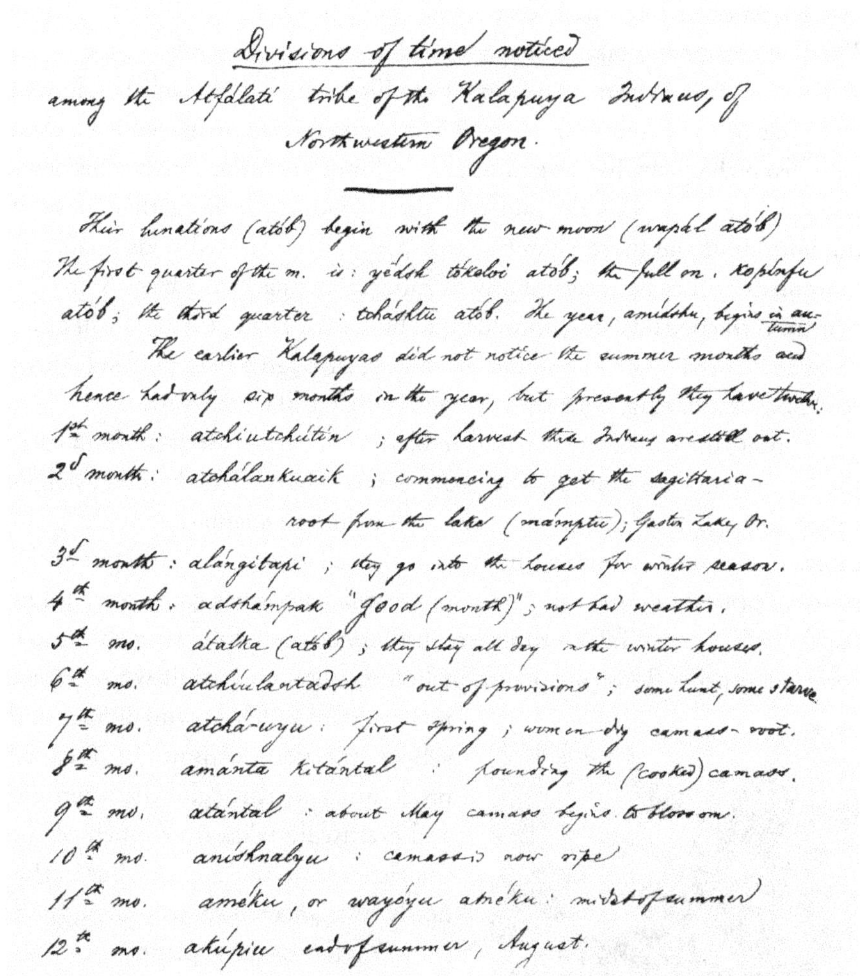

Divisions of time noticed
among the Atfalati tribe of the Kalapuya Indians, of
Northwestern Oregon.

———

Their lunations (atób) begin with the new moon (waphl atób)
The first quarter of the m. is: yédsh tókeloi atób; the full on. Koplofu
atób; the third quarter : tchashtú atób. The year, amidshu, begins in au-
tumn
         The earlier Kalapuyas did not notice the summer months and
hence had only six months in the year, but presently they have twelve.
1st month : atchiutchitín ; after harvest these Indians are still out.
2d month : atchalankuaik ; commencing to get the sagittaria-
                         root from the lake (mámptú); Gaston Lake, Or.
3d month : alángitapi ; they go into the houses for winter season.
4th month : adshámpak "good (month)"; not bad weather.
5th mo. átalka (atób) ; they stay all day at the winter houses.
6th mo. atchíulantádsh "out of provisions"; some hunt, some starve.
7th mo. atchá-uyu : first spring ; women dig camass-root.
8th mo. amánta Kitántal : pounding the (cooked) camass.
9th mo. atántal : about May camass begins to bloom.
10th mo. aníshnalyu : camass is now ripe
11th mo. améku, or wayóyu améku : midst of summer
12th mo. akúpiu end of summer, August.

Figure 5.1. Calendar of the Atfalati by Albert Gatschet 1877, a twelve-month calendar with monthly names in Kalapuya and their translated meanings.

and Umpqua Valleys, because not all these Peoples had vast shallow lakes full of wapato, like Wapato Lake. The wapato-rich environments in highly productive ponds and swales appear to have existed as far south as Lake Labish north of Chemeketa (Salem) and Minto-Brown Island Park west of Salem. There are not yet confirmed highly productive resources for Tribes in the southern Willamette Valley, or in the Umpqua Valley. Contemporary studies of the Anti'p fields in the Salem area have revealed forgotten lessons about the plant. For example, Anti'p plants begin to erupt in March, and by April and May, all the plants are up and flowering. The plant's flowers occur in a sequence of four to at least six layers of flowers from bottom to top. The flowering cycle takes about a month, and there is rarely a time when all the flowers are open at the same time (figure 5.2). This cycle is followed by a cycle of the plant going to seed. Large green triangular seed pods then hang from the plant for several weeks. In June, when the weather becomes warmer, the seed pods dry out and the remaining seeds gather loose at the bottom of the three-chamber seed pod. Once the seed pods open, any movement will cause a cacophony of rattling as small hard black seeds are cast from the pods. Winds, animals, and humans stirring the field will cause seeds to be broadcast. The sound of walking through a field of dried Anti'p seed pods is amazing, with the seed pods ringing like little rattles.

In June, the last of the Anti'p is in bloom. At Minto-Brown Island Park, the last blooms are typically the giant camas. They reach the exact height to top the prairie of tall grasses. This seems like an adaptation of the giant camas to remain visible to pollinators in the tall grasses at the height of the summer prairies. By July, all Anti'p on the valley floor has gone to seed. The Anti'p cycle is early fall to summer, and immediately following the Anti'p come many other flowering plants, including yellow cinquefoil, white prairie

Figure 5.2. Anti'p (Camas) with its second layer of flowers open. Photo by David Lewis, summer 2022.

mallow, purple thistle, wild onions, and yellow tarweed (Ansawal). Tarweed predominates through the summer and eventually takes over much of the prairie. Yarrow, too, appears, but in this newly reengineered environment, there are just a few of these plants.

The flower and plant cycles lead me to think about the summer as being not one season but a series of micro-plant seasons within the two growing seasons. The Anti'p are the first to appear in large quantities, and they dominate the early summer period and are ready to dig by mid-summer. Then, because the Anti'p fields are well-known locations to the Tribes, Anti'p will be dug again whenever there is an occasion to revisit, usually in late summer when other roots, fruits, nuts, and seeds are being gathered. The Tualatin have oral histories of digging Anti'p in late summer and cooking them in the same pits used to process acorns. Evidently, the Tualatin Kalapuyans co-harvested both foods at the same time.

> Long ago the people after they had dug a hole (for acorns), then they would build a fire right there (in the hole). Now they would put a lot of stone (on top of the fire) Then when the rocks got hot, then they would say to a shamen,[24] "Look at the rocks now! Is it right for us to put camas on them?" Now then the shamen would step (barefooted) on the hot rocks, he would cross over on them, he would look at his feet, and he would say, "Oh pretty soon the camas will be good (well cooked)." That is how they used to do once in a while. So then they placed all their camas there. (Jacobs et al. 1945, vol. 1, 18)

Kalapuyan oral histories collectively suggest there are at least three times to harvest Anti'p, and that it may be dug nearly any time of the year as a food source, except perhaps when it is flowering. The Tualatin Calendar notes that our People would harvest Anti'p just before the plant flowered in the spring. This suggests that Anti'p may have been a starvation food because the Anti'p fields were dug in the later winter when People had run out of winter stores and may have been struggling for food. As Anti'p would erupt for the season, they would still be preserved underground. The Tualatin Calendar notes some four months later when the Anti'p were ready to be harvested in mid-summer. This is part of the Traditional Ecological Knowledge (TEK) of the Kalapuyans, preserved in oral histories that we are now accessing and analyzing to recover the cultural Knowledge of our ancestors.

For the other fields in the area (i.e., at the Fairgrounds and Bush Park), the City of Salem will mow after the Anti'p go to seed. We rarely get to see the Anti'p there in the mid-summer, as fears of fire danger cause landscape managers to mow all the fields. This is a very real fear today because, in recent years, fires have threatened and burned down many towns in the west. In 2020, nearly every river valley in the western Oregon Cascades had a major fire, including the Santiam Canyon fires (Beachie Creek and Lionshead), which burned down the town of Gates and parts of Mill City and threatened Salem, the state's capital. Just days before this chapter was

---

24 Normally spelled Shaman, in the Northwest those spiritually gifted would be called Doctors as well.

submitted, on July 30–31, 2022, the town of Klamath River in Northern California was burned down.

Unfortunately, the City of Salem has yet to embrace Indigenous Traditional Knowledge about setting fires in its parks in the fall as a deterrent for catastrophic fire. If the city adopted this practice, especially in parks where fire could be easily controlled, there may not be a buildup of fuels, which continues to happen when they mow down the fields. Many areas of Minto-Brown Park present the overcrowded understory of vegetation that is typical of so-called fire-suppression practices. The understory is full of invasive species such as English ivy and Himalayan blackberry, which would be somewhat controlled if a regular fire cycle were imposed. The Kalapuya Peoples knew fire well and would set fires on the whole Willamette Valley prairies in late September when the rains began. Their food plants of underground bulbs, like Anti'p, biscuit root (Antbuitsuk), and wapato, would be preserved underground and ready to be harvested, while tarweed seeds would be roasted on the plant, with the sticky tar burned away, and then harvested with bats and baskets from the burned prairies.

In 1843, Jesse Applegate, a settler in the Willamette Valley, lived among two Kalapuya Tribes—Luckiamute and Yoncalla—and wrote extensively about his experiences with them. Applegate learned the Kalapuya and Chinuk Wawa languages to communicate well with the Tribal Peoples. He wrote about the fires he experienced on his homestead at Salt Creek, west of Dallas, Oregon. The Tribe who set these fires was likely the Yamel (Yamhill) Kalapuyans, who had a major village in the vicinity of Amity, Oregon.

> It was a custom of these Indians, late in the autumn, after the wild
> wheat was fairly ripe, to burn off the whole country. The grass
> would burn away and leave the pods well dried and bursting. Then
> the [women], both young and old, would go with their baskets
> and bats and gather the grain. It is probably we did not yet know
> that the Indians were wont to baptize the entire country with fire
> at the close of every summer; but very soon the fire was started
> somewhere on the south Yamhill, and came sweeping up through
> the Salt Creek gap. The sea breeze being quite strong that evening
> caused the flames to leap over the creek and come down upon us
> like an army with banners. All our skill and perseverance were
> required to save our camp. The flames swept by on either side of
> the grove; then quickly closing ranks, made a clean sweep of all the

country south and east of us. As the shades of night deepened, long lines of flame and smoke could be seen retreating before the breeze across the hills and valleys. The Indians continued to burn the grass every season until the country was somewhat settled up and the whites prevented them; but every fall for a number of years, we were treated to the same grand display of fireworks. On dark nights sheets of flame, tongues of fire, and lurid clouds of smoke made the picture both awful and sublime. (Applegate 1914, 134–135)

Changes made to the valley by farmers have affected all the plants, animals, and human cultures of the Willamette Valley. In their attempts to create better more arid soils and a longer growing period, farmers dug ditches to help drain the valley of excess water (Lewis 2021a,b, 2023). The valley normally would collect seasonal rains in flat wetlands that grew into ponds and shallow lakes when rains came. These wetlands threatened the new farmers' fields when rains came during the growing season by drowning crops before they were ripe. Digging ditches to drain the seasonal rains into the Willamette River became standard practice for farmers in the valley. Because of this practice, Lake Labish (in North Salem) and Wapato Lake (near Gaston, Oregon) were drained in 1918 and 1936 using a ditch digger to dig a combination of extensive ditches (Lewis 2021a,b). These projects were undertaken by land speculators Jay and Abraham Hayes, who purchased large areas of the lakebed for cheap prices because they were worthless lands; after ditching was concluded, they sold the land at a premium and made large profits. Their investments were supported by all the farmers owning land near the lakes because they stood to make money as well, by increased crop yields. But their projects destroyed large resource areas full of wapato and other marsh and lake plants, as well as environments to many thousands of animals, fishes, and waterfowl.

If Anti'p and other native plants are to be restored, then we will need to recreate the environment in which they thrived for thousands of years in the valley. This means filling in many of the ditches and allowing water to collect in shallow ponds again in the valley. This is the proper environment for the native plants to reestablish themselves in large enough quantities that Native Peoples can harvest them for food again. Tribal projects to restore Native cultures may be dependent on the restoration of the Traditional foods that Native Peoples used and based a large portion of their cultural lifeways around. Therefore, restoring the environment of the Traditional lands and resources of the Kalapuya Peoples is a necessary step to aid in the restoration of our Tribal cultures.

Traditional Ecological Knowledge developed over thousands of years in response to the environmental resources of each territory. The Kalapuya Peoples developed a culture that subsisted on Anti'p as one of their staple foods, and today, Anti'p exists only regionally in a few fields in significant quantities. However, not many of these fields are in public or Tribally accessible areas for the food to become a staple for local Tribal Peoples again. The amount of land that contains Traditional resources needs to increase along with the rights for Native Peoples to harvest these foods when they need them.

Research continues today on the Traditional environments of the Willamette Valley and the Kalapuya Peoples and their cultures. We are just beginning to reconstruct what their Traditional environment was like. Today, significant developments attract energy from a variety of peoples, including Natives, non-Natives, allies, and environmentalists working to decolonize and restore land in large parcels back to their original states. Native experiences and Knowledges must be centered in such efforts. Projects that do not engage with Native Peoples run the risk of advancing futile efforts that will never fully restore landscapes. Restoration projects that do not include Traditional Ecological Knowledge can never address the culture of the original Tribes who stewarded the lands to produce food. Tribal cultures and stewardship created the supposed "pristine" landscapes of the valley much lauded in settler histories. Examples of oak savanna restoration projects are everywhere in the valley; however, most, if not all these efforts, never address the need to harvest acorns semiannually, which is what the Kalapuya Peoples did. Similarly, the Anti'p restoration project at Bush Pasture Park, one of the three large camas fields in Salem, does not have a plan for harvesting the Anti'p, nor are there gather plans for any large Anti'p sites in Salem. Sections of the Anti'p beds are wildly overgrown near the Willamette University stadium in Bush Park, with stalks of the plants closely packed and falling all over each other. The Anti'p beds would benefit greatly from measured annual harvesting of the bulbs by Native Peoples. It must be noted that Salem City parks has been receptive to restoration efforts and even occasional test projects by Native People.

During a study in the summer of 2022, I visited the Farm Field at Minto-Brown Island Park each week in May through July to observe the growth cycle of the Anti'p. The area happened to have rains well into May, which delayed the summer by at least a month in the valley. In May, seasonal flooding was observed in the Anti'p field, which seemed to approximate a natural cycle. During the first weeks of May, the common Anti'p was midway through its flowering cycle, the giant Anti'p just beginning to erupt. Week three there was a rainstorm. I visited the field again the next day, May 17, and there was a shallow swale that covered a large section of the field. Many Anti'p were completely submerged as well as much of the juncus (*Juncus* spp.). The next week, the water had receded, and the Anti'p showed no negative effects after several days of being under water. This cycle happened a few more times before the warm summer weather took hold and dried everything out.

This experience cemented notions of what the character of the valley was like prior to settlement, a valley where it was a common occurrence that shallow swales created by regular rainstorms would creep into and cover the valley for a week at a time. The Anti'p in the valley were then adapted to thriving in a seasonal wetland. During the past twenty years, in the valley, temperatures have gotten progressively higher in the summers, and the regular rainstorms I had experienced growing up in the valley were not occurring as frequently as before. My impressions of the character of the valley mirror that witnessed by Lieutenant George Foster Emmons when travelling through the valley in the summer of 1841. Emmons recorded his impressions when traveling with the US Exploring Expedition, down the west side of the valley, near the Long Tom River, when the expedition came upon this sight:

> September 10, 1841—"Skirted the margin of a small lake of fresh water, the surface but about a foot below the surface of the prairie, ... the banks being steep and mirey. Soon after came upon the banks of a small river called Lum tun-buff [Long Tom] which in many places assumed the appearance of small lakes with high abrupt banks.[25] (Emmons 1841)

The restoration of fire to the valley is happening in scattered sections, some owned by METRO (e.g., Quamash Prairie in 2019), and others in

---

25 This same scene was recorded by Henry Eld as well. Charles Wilkes was not with this southern survey expedition, but instead took the Columbia River route, and so much of the original first-person impressions of the valley south of Chemeketa are not detailed in the published journals and are available only in the unpublished journals.

Figure 5.3. May 10, flooded area of Farm Field. Photo by David Lewis 2022.

Figure 5.4. May 19, flooding abated at Farm Field. Photo by David Lewis 2022.

the southern valley (e.g., Mount Pisgah in 2021 and the Andrew Reasoner Wildlife Reserve in 2021). Fire will make a huge difference and aid in restoration projects, but a parallel analysis of the changes to water systems and benefits of restoring water systems needs to occur to have maximum benefits. The study of the fire and water relationships in the valley will help restoration efforts to fully understand the conditions under which Kalapuyans stewarded their lands. Changes made in the valley to water systems during the last hundred years, as noted in this essay, are continually draining prairies, swales, marshes, and lakes to make more arid lands. As such, the seasonal rains in all parts of the valley drain out to the ocean too fast to help the valley maintain Traditional landscapes. As climate change makes the valley drier and hotter, it will be necessary to reverse many of the settler changes to water systems to keep water in the valley for restoration purposes and to support Native Peoples' futures.

In all these efforts, Native Knowledges and experiences need to be a central part of the conversation if these projects are to be successful. It is not acceptable simply to take the Knowledge and use it without Native Peoples' involvement. That is just tokenism and intellectual theft. Too often throughout history, theft of Indigenous Knowledges has occurred and subsequently leaves Indigenous communities with less power and access and no benefits. Tribal Nations, if invited to participate in any projects, will ask the question, "How will we benefit from the project?" before they will collaborate. Decolonization theories suggest that Native Peoples need to be a part of the solutions, as equal partners, from the very beginning stages of project planning to the very end, with long-term benefits to the environment and Native Peoples, like harvest rights. These types of practices ensure that everyone shares the benefits. A holistic reveal of the histories and contexts of the Tribes and their cultures needs to be a central part of all such efforts. If we have a true recognition of our histories and cultures and a restoration of our rights and lands, this will go far in helping all Tribal Peoples restore a personal relationship with the lands of their ancestors, lands we were removed from in 1856, lands where more than five hundred generations of our Peoples are buried, and lands that have adapted with our Peoples since time immemorial.

6

SWINOMISH PLACE-BASED SCIENCE, CULTURE, AND ENVIRONMENTAL EDUCATION
An Indigenous Approach to Environmental and Resource Issues

TODD A. MITCHELL swəlítub

Positionality Statement

Swinomish Tribal citizen; raised on sdukʷalbixʷ (Snoqualmie), sduhubš (Snohomish), dxʷsəq̓ʷəbš (Suquamish), and Coast Salish Lands; now living on Swinomish Lands; Swinomish Indian Tribal Community, Department of Environmental Protection.

Introduction

The Swinomish Indian Tribal Community (Swinomish, SITC, or Tribe) is among those descended from the Indigenous Tribes and Bands that have lived in the Skagit River Valley and islands of the central Salish Sea since time immemorial. These Coast Salish Peoples maintain a culture centered on abundant saltwater resources that include salmon, shellfish, and marine mammals, as well as upland resources like cedar, camas, berries, and wild game. Natural resources remain vital to present-day Tribal members for subsistence harvesting activities and other Traditional life practices and remain inextricably tied to Swinomish cultural beliefs and values. The environment cannot be adequately protected without being attentive to our cultural values, and Tribal cultural values cannot be maintained without protecting the environment.

> Close your eyes, you can feel the sense of spirituality of all the living things. They are all living: trees, earth, air, sky, wind. It means something to us. And we have to respect it, take care of it. —Joseph

86

McCoy, Swinomish Spiritual Leader. (Mitchell, Lekanoff, and Schultz 2011)

The Swinomish Indian Tribal Community is a federally recognized Indian Tribe and political successor in interest to certain Tribes and Bands that signed the 1855 Treaty of Point Elliott. The 1855 Treaty of Point Elliot, among other things, reserved fishing, hunting, and gathering rights in vast areas of land and water in northern Puget Sound and beyond and established the Swinomish Reservation on Fidalgo Island in Skagit County, Washington. As a federally recognized Tribe, Swinomish operates under a constitution originally approved in 1936 that created the Swinomish Senate as an elected body to self-govern and manage the affairs of the Tribe, including natural resources protection, policy development, and regulatory authority.

This chapter briefly describes who we are as Swinomish and why our place is important and then discusses our Indigenous environmental management approach, which includes feedback loops of regulatory and community engagement activities that overlap with environmental monitoring activities. Several case studies of special projects will show how our work comes together and incorporates Traditional Ecological Knowledges (TEK). It is important to provide an example of the work of incorporating Native Traditional Knowledges with "western" science and of how an Indigenous-led approach can provide long-term relationship building or rebuilding for Indigenous resilience into the future.

Place and Swinomish Culture

While the Tribes and Bands included in SITC certainly used the area now defined as the Reservation, their cultural practices, Traditional Ecological Knowledge (TEK), and lifeways were not historically limited geographically to the modern Reservation footprint. I have wondered whether our ancestors who signed the Treaty could fully understand the Treaty language translated first from English to Chinook Jargon and then into Lushootseed, our Native language. However, our ancestors understood the proposed Treaty well enough to reject relocation from the Skagit Valley or from the Puget Sound and Salish Sea to reservations elsewhere. Instead, they chose to cede their lands and accept the limitations of the Reservation and use of their ceded lands (referred to as Usual and Accustomed Areas in the Treaty) because their relationships to our place, homelands, and natural resources were important.

Today, Swinomish Peoples maintain strong relationships with our Usual and Accustomed Areas as well as strong family and cultural relationships with other Tribes in the region. Our regional Tribal relationships were built on familial and cultural similarities, and language familiarity, as many of the Treaty of Point Elliott Tribes speak variations of the same language, Lushootseed. Chief Seattle said in his 1854 Oration that many of our ancestors' relationships to the land are so strong that they continue into the spirit world:

> Our dead never forget this beautiful world that gave them being.
> They still love its verdant valleys, its murmuring rivers, its
> magnificent mountains, sequestered vales and verdant lined lakes
> and bays, and ever yearn in tender fond affection over the lonely
> hearted living, and often return from the happy hunting ground to
> visit, guide, console, and comfort them. (Suquamish Tribe 2015)

Our ancestors' relationships with their lands, culture, TEK, and even families changed greatly in the new world as federal and state governance began over lands deemed as parks and protected areas and settlers occupied our Usual and Accustomed Areas, including on parts of the Reservation. These altered relationships may have been part of the assimilation to a more "western" or modern lifestyle but were also a product of United States Indian policies of the late 1800s to early 1900s. For example, Indian boarding schools were established to assimilate, educate, or "civilize" native youth while prohibiting and denying the use of our languages, culture, and cultural practices (Marr and Fernando 2013). Many who attended boarding schools would not teach their children the culture or the Native Lushootseed language because of their school experiences (King 2008). Those experiences led to long-term historical trauma for many Native families.

My grandparents, Dewey and Winifred Mitchell, attended the Tulalip boarding school in the early 1900s. I can only assume their experiences there led to lost generations of Indigenous Knowledge and relationships with our culture. My late father, Raymond Mitchell, would say his parents and other Elder Tribal Native speakers would never talk about their experiences in the boarding schools, and "When they didn't want us kids to know what they were talking about, they would speak in Indian (Lushootseed)." A decade ago, this story would raise a chuckle with audiences, but now with more information coming out about boarding schools, it does not—a very

Figure 6.1. Swinomish Tribal Members beach seining for salmon at Lone Tree Point, September 2009. Photo courtesy Todd Mitchell, SITC.

recent and modern change in our relationship with this past. "It's a miracle that [N]ative [P]eoples have survived at all," said Sousan Abadian, a Harvard doctoral graduate and cultural trauma expert. "It reflects their unbelievable resilience" (King 2008).

> Cultures, to be able to survive, have to adapt. They go through cycles of change. Nothing ever stays the same. And if our culture is to be important, we need to adapt to our current conditions. That's the strength of who we are as Indian [P]eople.—Larry Campbell, Swinomish Tribal Elder. (Mitchell, Lekanoff, and Schultz 2011)

Our resilience is in our adaptation to the changing world, where modern Swinomish, People of the Salmon, still maintain our values and lifeways of a fishing and natural resource economy. Though we are a small Tribe with an enrollment of about one thousand Tribal citizens/members, our People still participate in subsistence fishing, shellfishing, hunting, and gathering in the lands our ancestors used since time immemorial (figure 6.1).

Indigenous Environmental Management Approach

The Swinomish Department of Environmental Protection's (DEP) work on the Reservation's environmental and natural resource issues is strongly place-based and centered on protecting our natural resources while maintaining access to the cultural practices they support. This centering is reflected in our vision and mission statements that rely and build on our relationships to our TEK:

- **Vision**: Preserving our culture by connecting our Tribal citizens to their natural resources.
- **Mission**: To protect and restore the natural environment, and the health and welfare of the Swinomish Indian Tribal Community for present and future generations.

The DEP management approach to fulfilling this vision and mission can be visualized as two cyclical processes or feedback loops of environmental regulatory activities and community engagement activities that stem from and overlap our environmental monitoring and research activities (figure 6.2). Our regulatory approach functions as a feedback loop through which environmental monitoring and research across various media (land, air, water) feed environmental data and analytical products to Tribal law or code development. Code implementation activities performed by the Planning Department (permitting/environmental reviews, code enforcement/violations, restoration of violations, etc.) that DEP supports

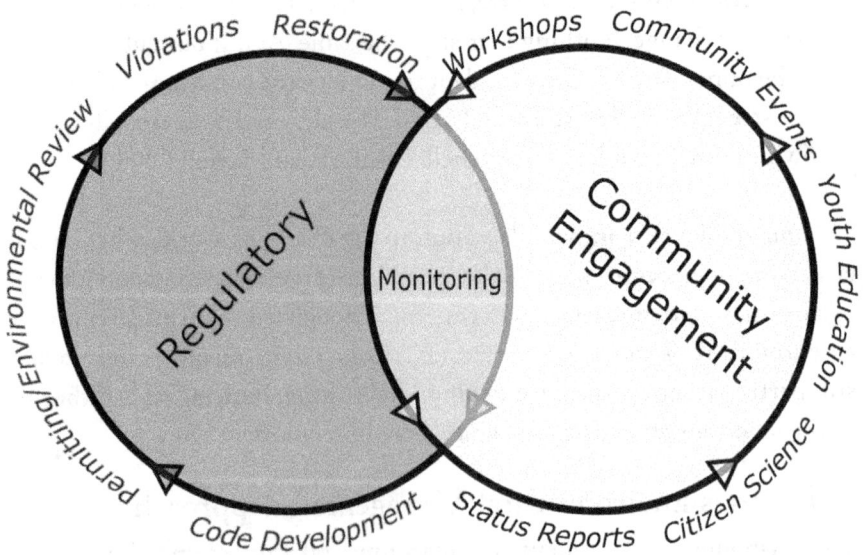

Figure 6.2. Visualization of an Indigenous approach to environmental/resource protection. Environmental monitoring and research are at the center and service regulatory functions and the community's connection to resources.

may in turn feed back into research performed by Fisheries, Skagit River System Cooperative (SRSC, a science and research consortium supporting the Swinomish and Sauk-Suiattle Tribes), DEP, or others to apply lessons learned in the cycle. Our community engagement approach uses our monitoring and research outputs to (1) inform the community about the condition of their resources; (2) aid in the teaching of Traditional Knowledge and activities; (3) provide opportunities to engage in stewardship and Traditional management; and (4) solicit community input about environmental concerns and priorities. Both the regulatory and community engagement loops are somewhat flexible; the steps need not be sequential or comprehensive. The loop analogy merely reflects the iterative relationship between data collection and application and, importantly, the function of research and monitoring in connecting community values with the regulatory framework. The following sections provide more details about these sectors and their relationships.

ENVIRONMENTAL MONITORING

Our monitoring and research work contribute to the preservation of Treaty-Reserved Rights with respect to on-Reservation salmon rearing, shellfish habitat issues, Traditional plants, water quality, physical shoreline habitats, and maintaining harvesting access to each of these resources. DEP primarily works on-Reservation and addresses resource-oriented issues on a site-specific basis to support resource availability and accessibility where they have Traditionally been found. Multiple Tribal departments work in off-Reservation terrestrial, aquatic, and marine habitat types, overseeing various ecosystems and life-stages. These departments include the Fisheries Department, which has a large shellfish team; Community Environmental Health Department; Environmental Policy Department; Hunting and Gathering Department; and SRSC.

The core of our program is ambient (systematic and long-term) or programmatic monitoring of several classes of environmental data. We are able to leverage thousands of years of TEK along with our collected numeric data to develop a deep understanding of our place. Rather than focusing on responses to specific problems, we maintain a proactive strategy of regular, consistent observations and measurements of a broad suite of parameters designed to characterize conditions and alert us to incipient problems or opportunities for improvement.

Monitoring on the Reservation includes:

- Basic water quality in freshwater bodies, marine waters, wetlands, and groundwater seeps (figure 6.3)
- Water quantity monitoring, including groundwater, stream discharge, and wetland stage
- Air quality monitoring, including meteorological measurements, particulates, and pollutants
- Nearshore characteristics, including morphology and substrate texture
- Vegetation monitoring with noxious weeds, timber assessment, and Traditional plants

Data and observations collected as part of these programs support ongoing Tribal regulatory programs and community engagement (table 6.1).

DEP also conducts targeted research projects on the Reservation that build on our programmatic monitoring. These projects arise from various community needs or address concerns (e.g., beach erosion affecting fisheries or refinery emissions impacts to children). Special research projects may be responsive to issues identified via ambient monitoring (e.g., investigating recurrent bacterial contamination at a recreation site that poses a human health risk or low stream flows affecting habitat availability). Targeted monitoring is also incorporated in remedial or restoration activities to evaluate

Figure 6.3. Swinomish DEP technicians collect ambient marine water quality data by boat, Swinomish Channel, June 2019. Photo courtesy Lindsay Thomason Logan, SITC.

Table 6.1. DEP routinely monitors several classes of environmental parameters, collecting data used to support both regulatory and community engagement activities on the Reservation.

Monitoring Target	Regulatory Use	Community Engagement Use
Water Quality	Data inform regulation of discharge, zoning, and allowed uses, identify illicit discharge	Communicate safety of waters for recreation and shellfish consumption
Water Quantity	Identify areas at risk for seawater intrusion, over-appropriation; inform regulation of groundwater withdrawals; evaluate water availability for building permits	Encourage conservation and maintenance of water systems; teach community about relationships among precipitation, surface water, groundwater
Air Quality	Data inform regulation of emissions, burn ban declarations, air quality advisories	Communicate risks and mitigation strategies for adverse air quality events; teach community about air quality impacts
Nearshore Characteristics	Data inform regulation of shoreline structures/armoring, evaluation of shorelines/sensitive areas permits	Teach community about relationships among nearshore character, shoreline structures, and habitat
Vegetation	Inform regulation of forestry activity, wetland areas; noxious weed management	Re-engage community with Traditional plants/foods; involve community in the management and harvesting of resources

the effects of the action and support adaptive management to maximize project success and/or limit any negative impacts. Special research projects typically have limited duration, but we generally extend post-action monitoring at restoration sites to ensure long-term success (figure 6.4).

REGULATORY STRATEGY

Through sovereign authority and delicate management of complex cross-jurisdictional regulatory relationships, the Tribe has developed and maintains the necessary capacity to regulate land use and activities within the Reservation to protect and advance the Tribe's sovereign interests, cultural values, and the interests of both member and nonmember Reservation

Figure 6.4. Targeted habitat status monitoring at Kukutali Preserve, June 2013. Photo courtesy SITC.

residents. This includes the development of culturally relevant natural resources protection ordinances and policies.

Data collected by DEP via our environmental monitoring programs and special projects is used to support and inform development and ongoing revision, in collaboration with the Planning Department and Office of Tribal Attorney, of Tribal ordinances related to monitored parameters, including Shorelines and Sensitive Areas Ordinance, Tidelands (management) Ordinance, Aquifer and GW Protection Code (draft), Water Quality Standards Code, and Swinomish Clean Air Act. The data and their analyses also provide other regulatory tools used in conjunction with the codes to guide code application. Some examples of such tools are the Air Quality Tribal Implementation Plan, wetland ratings and prioritization criteria, delineated wellhead protection zones, and geohazard maps.

DEP also supports the implementation of the codes and regulatory tools. We provide environmental management services to identify and prioritize remediation projects via a brownfields program and conduct forest management activities. DEP provides technical support and review of on-Reservation environmental permit applications, including development of alternatives or mitigation recommendations as appropriate. We also support code enforcement staff with identification of unpermitted actions or permit violations and provide technical assistance with identification and implementation of restorative actions.

This regulatory model relies on formal codes and tools to guide activities that affect the Reservation environment and community. These codes also prescribe penalties and remedies for unauthorized activities that create negative impacts. Cultural values, therefore, need to be incorporated within the codes by selecting culturally appropriate thresholds and effective penalties that deter willful violations and provide for restoration of cultural losses. Our Indigenous management approach helps to ensure that the regulatory framework is informed by our community's priorities and values.

COMMUNITY ENGAGEMENT

Our efforts to protect and restore our natural resources are driven by community needs and values. Part of our approach is to engage the community as informed partners in environmental management, nurturing the relationship between Peoples and the Reservation environment. It is important that our activities are accessible to all members of the Tribal community, regardless of age, education, employment status, or socioeconomic position. All community voices are valued, and we strive to meet our People where they are throughout our engagement work so that we continue to remember our ancestors' teachings:

> Everything has its own life and we respect these lives. We take what we need and no more. If it wasn't for our [E]lders, and the [E]lders before them, we wouldn't know what our resources were. They used them for a reason, they used them out of respect, and they were thankful. Be thankful. —Brian Porter, Swinomish Tribal Leader (Mitchell, Lekanoff, and Schultz 2011).

DEP uses a variety of media and activities to ensure the community is informed about environmental status and the relationships between the human and natural environments. Urgent information that may impact health and safety, like fire risks or toxic shellfish, are disseminated quickly via posted flyers, public reader boards, community text services, social media, and the Tribal website. More general information about resource issues, active studies, and the connections between human activities and the environment are shared via a monthly community newsletter or the Tribal website. DEP also writes and collaborates on books related to Traditional resources and practices that are printed and made available to the community.

We also offer active educational and engagement opportunities that are designed to improve understandings of our environment and resources and promote stewardship. DEP organizes work parties for community members and Tribal staff to participate together in management activities like noxious weed removals, vegetation plantings, or harvest events. We organize cleanup activities as part of our Tribal Earth Day celebrations, focusing on hazardous waste management, derelict fishing gear removal, and other stewardship protective of environmental quality. These engagements are grounded in our Indigenous values that are guided by TEK and "western" science and provide opportunities for Knowledge exchange between staff with "western" scientific backgrounds, community members, and Keepers of TEK.

DEP has developed environmental education curricula used for community workshops, student field trips, and in our Between Two Worlds (BTW) Indigenous Science program at the local high school (figure 6.5). BTW, the first Indigenous Science class taught at the local school district, was developed with several goals, including (1) making science accessible to our Tribal youth by teaching our TEK; (2) centering Tribal citizens as teachers and Tribal scientists as guest speakers; (3) providing opportunities for students

Figure 6.5. Nearshore beach unit for Swinomish Tribal youth attending the Between Two Worlds Indigenous High School science class at Kukutali Preserve, February 2020. Photo courtesy Todd Mitchell, SITC.

to earn science credit; and (4) providing information about Tribal Science, government, sovereignty, Treaty-reserved rights, and their relationships to our culture. The BTW class is guided by the question I asked our first class of students: "What is the simplest definition of science?" The answer to this question is "observing the world to understand it," which relates to how our Tribal Peoples used/use Indigenous Science to survive and thrive (i.e., a fisher needs to know a lot about salmon habits, fishing equipment technology, tides, currents, and weather to be successful) and to western science's more monitoring and numbers-driven data collection and analysis work. We hope that some of the Tribal youth may persist in studying science and return to build our workforce from within. Even if few youths come back to work for the Tribe, we hope that learning about Native ways of Knowing—noted by Dominique David-Chavez (Taíno) et al. (2020) as "centuries of observations of Earth's natural systems, innovation, and application of technology" that can "include unique cultural concepts, such as our relational accountability towards Mother Earth as a living being"—will help our youth relate to our culture, relate to Mother Earth as stewards, and become ambassadors to relate Tribal values to those outside our Tribe.

> The youth are the ones that are going to inherit this land and this community. We need to . . . encourage our children to get as much education as they possibly can . . . and understand that the [E]lders are the keepers of [Tribal] wisdom. Education is the key. That's going to be our safeguard against all those forces out there that are trying to impact us. —Raymond Mitchell, late Swinomish Elder. (Mitchell and Kobel 2024)

We support and participate in community events related to environmental and natural resources. The Community Clambake held each August brings our People to Lone Tree Point to enjoy Traditional foods like clams and salmon and to sustain their relationship with both the resources and our sacred place. The annual blessing of the fleet and the First Salmon Ceremony include offerings brought by fishers to the four water directions, honoring the returning salmon, and asking for the protection of our fishers in the upcoming fishing season (figure 6.6). Our fishers in turn support Tribal seafood harvests for the community and put the harvests away for upcoming events throughout the year because it is important to our culture and spirituality. These practices help maintain community-based

Figure 6.6. Swinomish First Salmon Ceremony in the Swinomish Village, May 2015. Photo courtesy Todd Mitchell, SITC.

TEK through educational and community engagements and are vital to strengthening the relationships with our Elders, our natural resources, and hence our culture.

Honorable community engagement does not mean just giving them information and opportunities for participation, though. While these actions help ensure a common understanding of environmental management and science, our goal is not to indoctrinate the community. Rather, we seek to be taught by them about the Traditional Knowledges of their ancestors, to learn about community priorities and values, and to hear their concerns for the future. By being open, communicative, and inclusive, we hope to create a familiarity that encourages Knowledge sharing throughout our activities while actively seeking out community input to identify issues and prioritize the foci of our work. We conduct direct interviews to gather information from willing Elders, participate in community events, and conduct workshops specifically to gather input on emerging issues. Most importantly, we treat the Knowledge shared (and the Knowledge-holders themselves) with necessary respect, including careful, culturally appropriate use and sharing of Knowledge; accurate attribution and data sovereignty; and gifting to show our appreciation and respect for the gifts they are giving us.

We view the role of DEP in many ways as a facilitator, fostering relationships between the community and the Reservation environment, TEK and western science, and place-based science and environmental regulation. The following case studies section describes several of our special research projects that illustrate ways we have practiced our Indigenous Environmental Management Approach while incorporating a focus on relations.

Case Studies
WETLANDS CULTURAL ASSESSMENT

The Swinomish Wetlands Cultural Assessment Project provides a tiered regulatory strategy for wetland areas based on a ranking analysis using TEK about wetland plant species as a cultural value scoring criterion. An initial wetland ranking assessment that was established via a contracted consultant included an assessment of cultural values using a standard state approach that did not reflect Tribal priorities and cultural uses. In response to this gap, an Indigenous approach was created to assess and incorporate the TEK of Traditionally used native wetland plant species.

Development of the Swinomish cultural value metric comprised two research activities. The first was a botanical survey of Reservation wetlands to determine all plant species present, conducted by a botanist (figure 6.7).

Figure 6.7. Surveying wetlands in Snee-Oosh Creek Wetland, February 2002. Photo courtesy Elissa Kalla, SITC.

The second was the identification of Traditionally used species that was conducted through Elder interviews and research of historical Swinomish accounts. By combining the botanical surveys with the Traditional uses, a ranking tool was developed based on the availability and accessibility of Traditionally used wetland plants. The tool is based on the number of Traditionally used plant species in varying use types, wherein more species present in a wetland leads to a higher ranking (Mitchell et al. 2024a).

The wetland rankings are incorporated into wetlands protection code used for permitting, with higher rankings stipulating stronger protections for the wetland from disturbances. Throughout this project, we have related TEK directly to environmental protection. We are also working on ways to share or return this extensive and detailed TEK of plants to the community to rebuild our relationships with our Traditionally used plants. This TEK has to a large extent been lost as common Knowledge through assimilation and historical trauma; thus we hope our work will provide revitalization and interest in plant Knowledges as well as a written record for future Tribal use, all in the context of proper Knowledge protection.

SMOKEHOUSE FLOODPLAIN RESTORATION

The Smokehouse (Fornsby) project is located on Reservation farmland that was converted from estuarine habitats, retaining the former distributary channels as drainages or ditches. Routine monitoring identified water quality issues in Fornsby Creek and the distributary sloughs on the Smokehouse floodplain behind Traditional flap-style tidegates. Traditional tidegates allow water to drain only from the farm/estuary side to the main channel and prevent tidal prism or fish from passing, effectively isolating the distributary channels from habitat use.

The Swinomish community identified that preserving and enhancing habitat for migrating salmonids is a priority to preserve and/or enhance salmon rearing and escapement leading to increased returns and spawning. Both the water quality impairments and the tidegates limited the accessibility and quality of habitat in the creek and sloughs. We responded to the community's priorities by using our approach to develop a restoration project aimed at increasing the amount and quality of available salmonid-rearing habitat.

Our work replaced the traditional tidegates with self-regulating tidegates and, later, muted tidal regulators to increase connectivity of the sloughs and the Swinomish Channel for water and fish passages (figure

Figure 6.8. Smokehouse double-door Muted Tidal Regulator installation, July 2014. Photo courtesy Todd Mitchell, SITC.

6.8). The distributary channel habitats were restored by increasing channel sizes and riparian buffer plantings. We established a robust monitoring design to document pre-restoration conditions and the effects of restoration. We continued monitoring the site after initial restoration and documented water quality improvements, increased fish usage, and minimal water quantity/groundwater impacts to adjacent farmed fields (Mitchell et al. 2024b). We have further used our monitoring data to adjust tidegate operations for more optimal conditions for fish, during migratory windows, and for farms, when salmonids aren't present. Adaptive management continues by using our continuous data and observations to develop additional restoration and habitat improvement activities at this site to further improve habitat.

TRADITIONAL NAMING OF TRIBAL STREAMS

The losses of our Native language significantly damaged our relationship with our TEK. Youth who weren't taught Lushootseed were not able to fully access the Knowledges held by Lushootseed speakers. The prevailing use of English names deepened the disconnection of our Peoples from their Traditional places. However, we approach the strengthening of our community's connection to and ownership of their lands and resources by recovering and restoring these Traditional names.

The Reservation includes four named creeks and additional unnamed streams. All four creek names are either anglicized or colonial names. One unnamed stream contributes to an area undergoing restoration and needed a new designation for use in identifying it in project monitoring and development. Rather than perpetuating the English naming pattern, we opted to identify a Lushootseed name for this creek and, at the same time, reclaim Lushootseed names for the other named creeks.

Two of the creeks were referred to with names that were anglicized versions of Lushootseed names. The stream known as Snee-Oosh Creek was named using a phonetic spelling of its Lushootseed name: sdiʔus (SNEE-oosh). Lone Tree Creek was named using the English translation of its Traditional place name: in Lushootseed, Lone Tree is dádčulqid (DAHD-chool-keed), meaning one tree standing.

Two other creeks were named for local people: Fornsby Creek was derived from the name of the original Tribal allottee of the land over which it flows; and Munks Creek, which we believe to have been named for a local non-Indigenous person. After speaking with community Elders and researching archival materials, no Lushootseed names could be found for these creeks. It was, therefore, necessary to work with Swinomish Elders and cultural Knowledge holders to find new and culturally consistent Lushootseed names for these creeks and the unnamed stream of interest. The subsequent names acknowledge the original allottees or Tribal landowners who were allotted the land these streams flow through after the 1887 Dawes (or Allotment) Act, which designated that Reservation lands were no longer owned in common but were divided up among individual Tribal members to use or sell as they saw fit, a process designed to colonize and eliminate reservations. The names on the Bureau of Indian Affairs map were

Figure 6.9. dádčulqid Lone Tree Creek stream crossing sign, April 2022. Photo courtesy Todd Mitchell, SITC.

phonetic spellings of the Traditional names, which were then converted into Lushootseed by one of our Tribal language scholars. The unnamed creek became dxʷsdaxʷəb (DOOS-da-whub); Fornsby Creek received the Lushootseed name šuxʷšukʷáal (shoo-shoo-QUA-all); and Munks Creek's Traditional name is šiistal (shees-tal).

We are working to normalize the use of Lushootseed names in our work and the community. To increase awareness and usage, we designed and installed stream crossing signs to be placed on Reservation roads where they pass over the streams. The installation work required cross-jurisdictional coordination with our local county that was facilitated by our Tribal Planning Department, as the roads and right of ways are maintained by the county. Sign specifications including sizing and reflectivity needed to be provided by the county to us for road safety requirements. DEP selected and identified the stream crossing locations (culverts) using global positioning systems (GPS) for the county Public Works installers. Installation was timed to ensure the availability of our Tribal Canoe Family to bless the unveiling of the signs (figure 6.9). Our Teachings say we bless our completed projects to protect them from harm and to tell our ancestors about the projects and honor their presence through this spiritual work.

Conclusion

Many things may have changed since the Treaty was signed, but the spirit remains: place remains central to our Indigenous identity and Swinomish culture. Swinomish Peoples maintain generational ties to our Traditional harvesting areas. Our community events and environmental protection work are centered around nurturing the relationship between the community and its resources. Even when the changing world and environment have depleted or made our resources scarce, our cultural ways must continue.

> This depletion of our natural resources has already changed our
> culture. When salmon is not available for the community to
> have on the table when there is a ceremony, it is detrimental to
> the community. —Lorraine Loomis, Late Swinomish Elder and
> Fisheries Director (Mitchell, Lekanoff, and Schultz 2011)

Our approach to environmental protection and management honors our connections and relationship to our homelands. We prioritize and invest in foundational research that helps us "know" our landscape and its resources and recognize any changes or opportunities for improvement. We use that understanding to develop a regulatory framework and tools that prioritize Swinomish values and emphasize restorative, rather than simply punitive, responses to violations. We honorably engage with the community, sharing our Knowledges and embracing the TEK shared with us and input about concerns and needs to guide our work. We create and support opportunities to affirm and deepen the relationships between the community and their resources.

> We didn't inherit this earth from our grandparents, or our parents, we borrowed it from our children. It's just loaned to us, we are stewards of this earth. —Brian Cladoosby, Swinomish Elder/former Chairman (Mitchell, Lekanoff, and Schultz 2011)

I am so grateful to our ancestors who had the foresight and determination to hold on to this place, preserving the relationship with our lands and resources that define our culture.

I have embraced what I have learned from my father, our Elders, and community throughout my lifetime as a Tribal citizen and my more than twenty-year career as a protector of our environment. Their teachings guide me in taking a long view in my work, looking ahead to seven generations, to ensure that the values of stewardship and relationships to our TEK aren't lost, but strengthened for my children and the generations to come. I am guided by these words I hold close to my heart, thinking of my own children's future:

> The land and the location is what makes Swinomish, the People, who they have become, it's tied to the water, it's tied to the sea, the mountains. —Raymond Mitchell, Late Swinomish Elder (Mitchell and Kobel 2024)

Often as Indigenous scientists or researchers we are challenged with combining "western" scientific norms with our cultural practices. Both require comprehensive knowledge, experience, and practice, and often do not fit perfectly together without significant consultation in both realms. To work in collaboration with or as an ally of Indigenous scientists, one should take the necessary time to build a relationship of mutual understanding and defer to Indigenous needs through Indigenous-developed

Figure 6.10. The author and child, Anneka (they/them), near Kukutali Preserve, June 2015.
Photo courtesy Karen Rittenhouse Mitchell, SITC.

projects or in response to direct requests from Indigenous Communities (as
they often have limited time and resources to respond and/or collaborate
on new projects), respecting that these communities have a depth of understanding that, while it may not conform to western scientific norms, is no
less valid. Work should reflect Tribal values, including usage of Traditional
languages and place-names.

Our relationships to our Knowledges go back countless generations, and
the sensitivity of using those Knowledges as both an Indigenous and "western" scientist must be balanced to maintain protection of our Knowledges.
Knowledges from Indigenous scientists used in any context should be used
only as taught and treated as data, analyses, or reports with appropriate
citation and authorship to any products or deliverables. All information,
data, and products should be returned to the Indigenous communities in
whole so that current and future generations can benefit from and easily
access the work.

The approach and projects described in this chapter provide a snap-
shot of our work to date to honor Traditional Swinomish values in environmental monitoring, regulation, and stewardship. While Indigenous

communities are diverse, I believe this framework is a transferable starting point to values-based management and honorable engagement and hope readers can apply this work to theirs.

Acknowledgments

I would like to thank my Swinomish Tribe, Elders, and leaders for their Knowledge, guidance, and faith in my work by allowing me to use my education and skills for the betterment of the Community. Thank you to my parents, Raymond and Jennifer, in letting me chart my own path in education and the world. With the recent loss of my late father, it really puts into perspective the education, culture, and family history he taught me. To my children, Anneka and Colin, and my wife, Karen, thank you for supporting me in all my Tribal and artistic work. Karen has also been my coworker for more than twenty-two years and has been instrumental in supporting the development and implementation of the above approach, programs, and projects—this work is that much stronger with you.

7

CO-PRODUCTION OF KNOWLEDGE IN ARCTIC RESEARCH
A Paradigm Shift or Another Cycle of Oppression?
ANAMAQ MARGARET H. C. RUDOLF

Positionality Statement

Enrolled Member of the King Island Native Community; born and raised on Dena'ina lands; raised and now living on Lower Tanana Dene lands; University of Alaska Fairbanks, International Arctic Research Center

Positionality—Relationship to the Work

The Indigenous methodology concept of positionality (Kovach 2009) is a process through which a researcher is self-reflective and understands their relationship to the work. My Inupiaq name is Anamaq, after my great aunt. My mother is from the Mayac family, who originally came from King Island, Alaska. My father, a Polish, Irish, and English man from the Seattle area, was a political philosopher, Native education high school counselor, and community college professor. Both sides of my family instilled deep values of humility, respect, empathy, equity, collaboration, sharing, and self-determination in myself and others. The relationship, responsibility, and reciprocity highlighted in this book are also crucial elements within my work. I bring these values as my holistic approach to apply to the fragmented projects, committees, and initiatives inherent within academia. These values and my holistic mindset are often at tension within academic spaces. However, Indigenous methodologies and Indigenization literature allow me to incorporate my values while doing science differently from a place that is inherently transdisciplinary.

At the time of this writing (early 2023), I am an interdisciplinary PhD candidate at the University of Alaska Fairbanks. My background is in permafrost and engineering, but I struggled to find inclusive environments and meaningful mentorship in these areas. I always envisioned researching with communities to overcome challenges, but finding mentors who did that work was hard, even in engineering research. As an early career scientist, I noticed the still pervasive concept that scientists need to be separate from society to be objective (Pielke Jr. 2007). I remember being trained to distrust non-scientists, including myself, as the scientific method brought about "unbiased truth." I remember hyper-focusing on impressing and modeling other scientists seeking promotion and funding. I remember seeing researchers not allowing themselves to become rooted in the community and hearing comments about how odd it was that I did not go out of state for my education. After years of dealing with implicit biases and stereotypic threats, my self-confidence was gone, and I took a break from my PhD program. After returning, I decided not to try to fit into academic culture. I was going to find my path and ways of doing research, which led me to the co-production of knowledge approach (CPK, explained further in the next section of this chapter). This positionality is my relationship to the work. My journey has been to understand why and how I, and other Indigenous Peoples, generally do not fit within typical academic research models and programs. This journey includes studying critical methodologies to understand where there are issues in research and Indigenous methodologies to learn better approaches. It is charting my path to understanding what being an Indigenous scientist means.

Introduction

CPK semantically means doing research with communities instead of on them. Intuitively, this term means sharing decision-making, prioritizing relationships, and creating co-produced outputs. I became interested in CPK as an approach to working with Indigenous communities and doing science that is inclusive of Indigenous Knowledge Systems. CPK is also an approach Indigenous leaders advocate for in the Arctic research community (Ellam Yua et al. 2022).

CPK is a methodological approach that has recently grown in popularity, especially within the Arctic, due to the National Science Foundation's (NSF) Navigating the New Arctic (NNA) program, which started in 2019. NNA emphasizes doing CPK with Arctic Indigenous communities for outcomes that "enable resilient, sustainable Arctic communities" (NSF 2018). While the National Science Foundation's definition of CPK aligned with the broader literature, the progressive concepts were new and confusing to the research community. In response to the first round of NNA proposals, Indigenous leaders from western Alaska sent a letter to NSF regarding the lack of meaningful Indigenous engagement within individual proposals and the NNA program itself (Bahnke et al. 2020). The Indigenous leaders that authored the letter included Kawerak, Inc., representing twenty Tribes in the Bering Strait region; Association of Village Council Presidents (AVCP). representing fifty-six Alaska Native villages in the Yukon-Kuskokwim Delta; Bering Sea Elders Group, with an association of Elders from thirty-eight Tribes in the Bering Strait and Yukon-Kuskokwim areas; and the Aleut Community of St. Paul. The letter describes researchers approaching their organizations and communities at the last minute with fully written proposals, showing a lack of understanding of CPK. It also requests NSF support in building the capacity of Indigenous Peoples, moving away from western approaches and derived topics, having Indigenous representation in the peer-review process, and ensuring the competency and expertise of the researchers to engage Indigenous communities ethically. These issues were never met, which led to a follow-up letter (Bahnke et al. 2021) with more explicit recommendations for changes, including pausing the program.

While I became interested in studying CPK because of its semantic and intuitive meaning, CPK practice and theory are often challenging to achieve because of persistent colonial ideologies and a lack of addressing issues having to do with equity and power. CPK was not initially developed for working with Indigenous communities. Newer literature on CPK with Indigenous communities builds off the methodological approaches of Traditional Ecological Knowledge (TEK) research practices and has some similarities to the Indigenous methodological approach of Two-Eyed Seeing (Bartlett, Marshall, and Marshall 2012).

This chapter offers me space to critically self-reflect on CPK as a methodological approach and how it intersects with Indigenous methodologies and best practices. Significant tensions exist between CPK, the aspirational theory, and the real challenges in its implementation. These challenges are compounded when working with Indigenous communities, where recognizing colonization and systemic inequity is necessary. This chapter first lays out how research can be colonial acts, which includes key concepts from Indigenous critical methodologies. Using these "research as colonial acts" concepts, I self-reflect on CPK literature, which includes the need to address power and politics. These sections lead to me critically self-reflecting on NNA and the implementation of CPK.

RESEARCH AS COLONIAL ACTS

There are distinctions between Indigenous methodologies and critical methodologies, as it is functionally learning versus unlearning. Māori scholar Linda Tuhiwai Smith's (2021, originally published in 1999) foundational work in critical methodologies from an Indigenous perspective shows western research's long history of oppressing and justifying the colonization of Indigenous Peoples. Smith describes how the Scientific Revolution happened in the same period as the end of absolutist monarch rule, so western culture was looking to redefine itself. The development of individualism and rational rules of law supported individual economic self-interest. Black scholars, like psychologist Beverly Daniel Tatum (2017 [1997]), also discuss the oppressive and colonial history of research. The Scientific Revolution occurred at the same time as imperialism, when people sought justifications for colonialism. Tatum describes how research was able to place the "other" in devalued positions, allowing White men to be placed into valued positions in the social construct of society.

Standing Rock Sioux Member Vine Deloria Jr. criticized anthropologists in his 1969 book *Custer Died for your Sins: An Indian Manifesto*, for getting thousands of dollars, even millions over a career, to study Indigenous Peoples, while Indigenous research participants may only get an occasional small honorarium. He described the results of a particular anthropologist as a "compilation of useless knowledge 'for knowledge's sake'" (Deloria Jr. 1988 [1969], 94). He called for Tribes to require researchers to go through Tribal review processes and have budgets for Tribes equal to the amount the researchers are getting.

Colonial ideologies exist today in the dominant culture, education, and research. For example, western knowledge and science are still perceived as superior, while all other knowledge systems, including Indigenous Knowledge Systems, are anecdotal without being validated by scientific ways of thinking (Nadasdy 2003). The situation with NNA is not an isolated occurrence but part of a long history of research upholding and justifying colonial ideologies. There are also decades worth of critical methodologies that lay out what research as colonial acts look like, which are explored in the following sections.

CO-OPTING OF INDIGENOUS KNOWLEDGES AND METHODOLOGIES

Within Smith's foundational work, she wrote that "colonialism was not just about the collection. It was also about re-arrangement, re-presentation and re-distribution" (Smith 2012, 65). The emphasis on the "re-" is because scientists often re-define Indigenous Knowledges and cultures without objectively or accurately representing how Indigenous Peoples understand them. This crucial concept is important as scientists could naively attempt to validate Indigenous Knowledges with science, treating it as anecdotal. Misrepresentation through misunderstanding can also happen within a project, such as how translating Indigenous words that represent Indigenous concepts inherently changes their meaning. Furthermore, while Indigenous scholars have put Indigenous methodologies into CPK, there is the potential to co-opt Indigenous concepts.

I often worry that my research will become a conduit to co-opting and reinterpreting Indigenous methodologies. Indigenous scholar Margaret Kovach (2009) defines Indigenous methodologies as Indigenous Peoples looking at our Tribal epistemologies (ways of knowing) and working with our communities to do research completely within the context of our ontologies (ways of being) and epistemologies. Additionally, using our Tribal Knowledges defines ethics, methods, decision-making, communication, and all aspects of research (Kovach 2009; Sandoval et al. 2016; Neeganagwedgin 2013). Under this lens, CPK, being inherently pluralistic, does not fit within Indigenous methodologies, which is not a value judgment.

An Indigenous scientist, like myself, can study Indigenous methodologies and pull our community-based principles and practices into our research. The Ellam Yua et al. (2022) CPK model uses concepts and conceptual modeling from Indigenous methodologies (Kovach 2009; Topkok and Leonard 2015; Inuit Circumpolar Council—Alaska 2015) to make it more culturally responsive and should be a framework adopted by all researchers. But CPK does not represent Indigenous methodologies; to say it does would be co-opting and reinterpreting it. So, I am cautious with my words to try not to directly associate the two within my writing so that no misunderstanding can occur. I usually describe the integration of community-based principles and values within the process of positionality instead of stating it as "pulling from Indigenous methodologies." While I think this is an important disclaimer in not co-opting, I think all researchers interested in working with Indigenous Peoples should study Indigenous methodologies to make their research more culturally responsive. Science technology and society researcher Pielke Jr. (2007) states that science is used when values are perceived to be aligned and uncertainty is perceived as low. Following Indigenous ethics and concepts can create an alignment of values. Understanding Indigenous ways of Knowing and Indigenous value systems may prevent researchers from rejecting Indigenous Knowledges because of uncertainty. It also creates an understanding of the concept of relationships. which leads to better practices. The best way forward is for scientists to recognize, credit, and learn from Indigenous methodologies before applying them to their work, while being careful not to co-opt them or allow others to do so.

OTHERING

Equitable and ethical CPK is challenging to achieve because of the prevalence of WEIRD (western, educated, industrialized, rich, and democratic) researchers (Brady, Fryberg, and Shoda 2018). As of 2018, full-time faculty in degree-granting postsecondary institutions are 75 percent White, 12 percent Asian/Pacific Islander, 6 percent Black, 6 percent Hispanic, and less than 1 percent for Indigenous and two or more races (Hussar et al. 2020, 151). Consequently, with the lack of diversity, faculty tend to normalize their own experiences and worldviews (Brady, Fryberg, and Shoda 2018). This normalization is also discussed in anti-racism literature wherein the perception of White is the norm, and everyone else is therefore deemed abnormal—a process commonly termed as *othering* (Tatum 2017; Oluo 2019; Saad 2020). For example, when listing identities, People of Color typically name their race, while White people list their occupation, character, and many other types of descriptors besides being White (Tatum 2017, 102). Identity is taken for granted in the dominant White society because "the person's inner experiences and outer circumstances are in harmony with one another, and the image reflected by others is similar to the image within. In the absence of dissonance, this dimension of identity escapes conscious attention" (Tatum 2017, 102). However, culture includes differences in visible behaviors and invisible ideas, assumptions, and values. The visible and invisible parts shape the cultural products of societal institutions and prevailing individual thoughts and behaviors. When you have a majority, dominant group of people within academia that are WEIRD researchers, they develop systems based on their experiences and worldviews, believing such factors will fit everyone (Brady, Fryberg, and Shoda 2018). For example, climate scientists perceive users as just like themselves because they lack past experiences and interactions with non-climate scientists and the broader society (Porter and Dessai 2017). Therefore, even though academics have made progress in diversification, statistics and literature show much work is still needed.

An example of othering in Arctic research is shown in how often scientific and Indigenous Knowledge Systems are pitted against each other in the context of their commonalities and differences (Eicken 2010; Barnhardt and Kawagley 2005). While this can be a necessary step in developing understanding, it requires tokenizing Indigenous Knowledge systems to present them simplistically. Furthermore, othering as a colonial act occurs when non-Indigenous peoples define the roles of Indigenous Knowledges and Indigenous Peoples within research and academia. In comparison, allowing Indigenous Peoples to self-define their roles and the roles of Indigenous Knowledge Systems is a better practice. Othering is a form of power, and power dynamics are central to the success or failure of community-focused projects (Lemos et al. 2018; Daly and Dilling 2019; Turnhout et al. 2020). Instead of thinking of individuals only fulfilling roles and projects only producing outputs, preventing othering requires the prioritizing of relationships and listening to each other to create understanding and trust.

However, with the current popularity of working with Indigenous communities, the researchers seeking funding often have no prior knowledge of Indigenous societal needs, cultures, or Knowledge systems. This naivety is often the root of the problem for colonial acts in research. Arctic Indigenous Peoples have for decades dealt with wildlife management scientists collecting Traditional Ecological Knowledge (TEK), redefining it, or only accepting aspects of it that align with western knowledge and values. Nadasdy (2003) describes such practices as non-Indigenous researchers defining Indigenous Knowledge Systems and retaining the defining power instead of allowing Indigenous Peoples sovereignty over life, land, and waters.

"AT RISK" PEOPLES

Unangax̂ scholar Eve Tuck and K. Wayne Yang (2012) created the concept of "a(s)t(e)risk peoples," wherein Indigenous Peoples are not studied because of their population being low and at the margins (asterisks people) or studied under the framing of being "at risk." The "at risk" concept is shown in early TEK research that was conducted by non-Indigenous scientists because they thought Indigenous Knowledges and Peoples would eventually disappear and such Knowledges would be critical to possess (Berkes 2012). These scientists collected Indigenous Knowledges in hopes that one day they would be used, when the Knowledge-holders were gone. It is also an example of "asterisks peoples" in the assumption that Indigenous Peoples would become assimilated to a point where they became like the dominant western society. These ideologies tokenize Indigenous Knowledge Systems as static and archaic instead of living Knowledges rooted in relationships. They also ignore the resilience and cultural continuity of Indigenous Peoples. Unfortunately, such research got Indigenous Peoples' buy-in so that TEK could be added to wildlife and resource management decision-making. But generally, the research did not affect management policies or the decision-making processes that control resources, which, in turn, limited Indigenous Peoples' relationships to the land, water, animals, and plants (Nadasdy 2003). Instead of having researchers focus on collecting TEK, Nadasdy (2003) advocates for Indigenous leadership in resource management and states that such leadership should be a system that prioritizes the relationships with Indigenous leaders and their relationships with the land, water, animals, and plants.

A similar concept to "a(s)t(e)risk peoples" is the omission and commission framework, by Tulalip psychologist Stephanie Fryberg and Arianne Eason (2017). Omission focuses on what does not exist or what is left out, such as the lack of Indigenous representation in education and the sterilization of history. Commission refers to what exists and whether it upholds biases and inaccurate representations of Indigenous Peoples, such as what occurred in the Barrow alcohol study (Mohatt et al. 2004). Commission is the victimization versus presenting the non-romanticized truth about how Indigenous Peoples' realities can be related to the concept of survivance. Anishinaabe scholar Gerald Vizenor (2008) describes the concept of survivance as Indigenous Peoples telling their stories in their ways. The omission and commission framework challenges dominant research frameworks and authoring protocols by allowing Indigenous Peoples to define themselves. It prioritizes the researcher's relationship with Indigenous partners instead of asking them to fulfill a predefined role. It also honors the self-direction of Indigenous communities, which is an important element within Free, Prior, and Informed Consent (FPIC).

Free, Prior, and Informed Consent (FPIC) is a universal research ethic that has been contextualized for Indigenous Peoples in the United Nation's

Declaration on the Rights of Indigenous Peoples (UNDRIP; Food and Agriculture Organization of the United Nations 2016). Free within this context is a process that is self-directed by the community without expectations or timelines. Prior is defined as before any activities occur, including authorization, thus consent must occur early in the planning process. As projects change, it is recognized that informed consent must be an ongoing process. The fundamental difference between typical research FPIC ethics and UNDRIP's FPIC is the prioritization of having respectful, trusting relationships between researchers and community partners—things that are missing from most western scientific frameworks.

SETTLER MOVES TO INNOCENCE

Unangax̂ scholar Eve Tuck and K. Wayne Yang (2012) created the concept of "settler moves to innocence," while recognizing how decolonization is used too loosely in academia and has subsequently been co-opted and redefined into different meanings. Tuck and Yang state that decolonization means the repatriation of Indigenous lands and lives. It is important to recognize that research can be a colonial act and distract from repatriations of Indigenous lands and lives. The concept of "settler moves to innocence" details strategies people use to avoid guilt and responsibility, which include claiming naivety, deflecting settler identity, adopting Indigenous practices and Knowledges to claim space, emphasizing equality over equity in discussions of colonization, and focusing on the mind and intentions over land and power. Settler moves to innocence is a fitting last concept within this section of "research as colonial acts," because it puts responsibility onto researchers and funders to do better and prioritize relationships with Indigenous Peoples instead of prioritizing western and colonial interests.

Critical Self-Reflection—Co-Production of Knowledge

With the understanding of research as colonial acts, I reflect deeper on CPK, which is an emerging concept through the convergence of many disciplines and worldviews. There is no set definition, but a consensus is forming that it incorporates a high level of engagement with shared decision-making power at every step of the research process (Norström et al. 2020; Ellam Yua et al. 2022; Djenontin and Meadow 2018; Wall, Meadow, and Horganic 2017; Mach et al. 2020; NSF 2018). To differentiate CPK from other community engagement approaches, a large group of practitioners developed the four principles of CPK (Norström et al. 2020). The first principle is interactive and aligns with the above definition. The second is pluralistic, meaning it must blend scientific knowledge with local and/or Indigenous Knowledges (e.g., TEK). The third and fourth are context-based to the community partners and goal-oriented in solving community challenges, instead of creating generalizable knowledge, which is typical in western research. CPK increases the perceived credibility, relevancy, and legitimacy of the research, which leads to usable outcomes (Arnott and Lemos 2021; Sarkki et al. 2015). CPK brings together scientists with the communities and/or policymakers that would benefit from their research (Norström et al. 2020; Dilling and Lemos 2011; Lemos et al. 2018).

Conceptually, CPK calls for a new and aspirational way of doing research, but CPK practitioners find it difficult to create systemic changes. There is a growing body of literature about the difficulty of accomplishing CPK due to lack of funding, institutional reward systems, community capacity and infrastructure, training, cultural competency, willingness to collaborate, power dynamics, and politics (Arnott and Lemos 2021; Lemos et al. 2018; Daly and Dilling 2019; Turnhout et al. 2020; Arnott, Neuenfeldt, and Lemos 2020; Wall, Meadow, and Horganic 2017; Chambers et al. 2021). However, accumulating shifts in the broader scientific community (such as more emphasis on being inclusive, equitable, and actionable) may initiate a paradigm shift within community-based research (Kuhn 1996). I personally find alignment as an Indigenous scientist with CPK because it attempts to prioritize the Indigenous value system of relationships. However, I remain simultaneously frustrated to see projects and academia continue to fail to reach their potential in using CPK.

There has been a shift in CPK literature in recent years, which can be highlighted in two synthesis papers that categorize different CPK approaches. The first paper is Bremer and Meisch (2017) which provides categories based on approaches and purposes. The second paper, published four years later, is Chambers et al. (2021), which developed the six modes of CPK that focus on utilization, power, politics, and impacts: researching solutions to inform; empowering voices within policymaking; brokering power to develop solutions; reframing power to change narratives; navigating differences to develop relationships; and reframing agency to create safe spaces for perspectives. Chambers et al. (2021) highlight the challenges and risks associated with each mode in reinforcing the status quo, worsening inequalities, and creating echo chambers. The shift is characterized by key pieces of literature about power and politics that were published from

2018 to 2020 (Lemos et al. 2018; Daly and Dilling 2019; Turnhout et al. 2020). Both frameworks provide interesting perspectives on CPK, but I prefer the Chambers et al. (2021) framework because it assists in clear communications between researchers and community partners. However, the framework does not address decolonization (Tuck and Yang 2012). Instead, it works within colonial systems to create beneficial changes. Being able to communicate a project's purpose clearly will assist in FPIC for project partners (Food and Agriculture Organization of the United Nations 2016) yet it will not work toward Indigenous Peoples' reparations of land and lives.

Lövbrand (2011) states that CPK faces challenges with two concepts: the logic of accountability and the logic of ontology. The first concept shifts from scientific autonomy to projects focusing on utilization. The second recognizes how incorporating diversity and other ways of knowing changes the role of science. However, projects can fail when researchers shut down discussions about conflicting values, interests, and power dynamics that lead to partners disengaging. In addition, putting accountability power into the hands of the users in situations where users stop engaging or do not engage in the first place can cause the project to fail (Lövbrand 2011; Bremer and Meisch 2017). These issues show the significance of having relational accountability to project partners.

Critical CPK literature shows how researchers consider CPK as an aspirational cure-all rather than exploring the realities of its application (Lemos et al. 2018; Turnhout et al. 2020). The practice of CPK means relationships are given significant time, caretaking, and resources, which community partners may not be able to give, thus leading to research fatigue (Lemos et al. 2018). Turnhout et al. (2020) explicitly underline a need for addressing politics and power within a project and how conflict-avoidant consensus decision-making can leave out marginalized peoples' viewpoints, creating a need to address power and politics directly. While I agree with Turnhout et al. (2020), I acknowledge that feminist methodologies may conflict with Indigenous methodologies in creating a culturally responsive project. Even when dealing with politics and power, projects can still lead to research fatigue because it takes time and energy for research partners to explain how research can be a colonial act.

For CPK in Arctic research, the seminal paper, under the first author Ellam Yua (2022; Ellam Yua is Yup'ik for the spirit of the universe), provides a conceptual framework for working with Arctic Indigenous communities. The other authors include Social Science Program Director Julie Raymond

(Yakoubian with the Inupiaq organization Kawerak, Inc); Yup'ik researcher Raychelle Daniel (Pew Charitable Trust), and Indigenous Knowledge/Science Advisor Carolina Behe with Inuit Circumpolar Council. The Ellam Yua et al. CPK framework differs from the rest of the CPK literature because of the inherent tension of scientific and Indigenous methodologies. The "cornerstone" of this CPK model is equity, not usability, and by incorporating equity in all parts of the research process, there is a higher likelihood for CPK to be achieved with Indigenous communities. The authors developed their model from critical and Indigenous methodologies and the Two-Eyed Seeing approach. They criticize how most of the broader CPK literature has participants with similar ways of knowing to the researchers or forces integration into a western scientific knowledge system. Within Arctic research, the term equity is often used instead of colonial acts. I sometimes think focusing on equity instead of colonial acts reinforces the notion of settler moves to innocence (Tuck and Yang 2012). Using softer terms can support the understanding to create changes, but it does not necessarily address the root cause.

The Ellam Yua et al. (2022) CPK framework layers Indigenous ethics and best practices on top of CPK. These conceptual tools within the CPK framework align with the broader critical methodologies: decolonization, sovereignty, ethics, trust and respect, relationships, empowerment, and being deliberate and intentional. In addition, two of the conceptual tools are prevalent in the CPK literature (Lemos et al. 2018; Wall, Meadow, and Horganic 2017; Djenontin and Meadow 2018), which are the researcher's capacity to engage and Indigenous partners having the means and ability to participate in the project. The shared decision-making power is a fundamental part of CPK, which respects Indigenous sovereignty and self-determination within a project. Using CPK allows the broader research community to understand and accept it because it aligns with their western research approaches. However, I question whether the current practice of CPK in Arctic research co-opts Indigenous methodologies, redefines them, and inappropriately applies them back onto Indigenous Peoples.

CRITICAL SELF-REFLECTION—NAVIGATING THE NEW ARCTIC

There is a difference between the theory of CPK and the implementation, which can have compounding challenges when working with Indigenous communities. This is shown within NSF's Navigating the New Arctic program (NNA). NSF uses a CPK definition that aligns with the literature, but there are failures in its implementation. I named this section "critical self-reflection" in recognition that I am part of the NNA community—not separate from it. I am not an outsider critiquing this system but an insider trying to understand and fix the issues.

While CPK is a progressive and fundamentally different methodological approach than other approaches scientists use, claiming naivety in not correctly implementing, it is a settler move to innocence (Tuck and Yang 2012). Additionally, the peer-review process should critically analyze the claimed expertise of researchers claiming to do CPK, but as the letters to NSF state, researchers without such expertise often get funded (Bahnke et al. 2020, 2021). This validation by NSF disregards CPK and Indigenous critical methodologies as whole fields of study that need to be centered in proposal evaluations.

Ellam Yua et al. (2022) apply the CPK methodological approach within the context of critical and Indigenous methodologies. Layering Indigenous concepts onto CPK does not change the definition of CPK but can create confusion within Arctic research when someone says CPK: do they mean Ellam Yua et al. (2022)'s version of CPK, or science-policy CPK, or the misuse of CPK? The misuse of CPK does not meet the standard of shared decision-making at every step of the research process. Because the definition of CPK is not well understood in Arctic research, people are trying to incorporate its use into projects that are not inherently CPK-based. This is so common that these practices could co-opt and redefine CPK, which includes the Indigenous concepts within the Ellam Yua et al. (2022) CPK model. We are at the precipice for a paradigm shift within Arctic research. If the co-opted misused CPK definition gets adopted, then the status quo remains, but if the Ellam Yua et al. (2022) CPK conceptual model dominates, then genuine power-sharing may occur, with meaningful relationships and positive societal benefits.

However, when researchers fail to commit to power-sharing and develop meaningful relationships, it maintains processes of othering (Tatum 2017), especially when researchers do not reach out to Indigenous leaders before initiating a project. While it was a good step to recognize the omission (Fryberg and Eason 2017) of Arctic Indigenous Peoples within Arctic research, often, the result of such research is commission instead of co-production. For example, funded researchers have power to define gaps, needs, and methods for Indigenous communities instead of co-defining these important elements with the communities. Thus, researchers perform an act of commission and limit the potential usefulness of the project to the community, which tokenizes the role for Indigenous Peoples, by not allowing them to self-define their roles. This is frustrating for Indigenous individuals involved in Arctic research because these continued shortcomings mean the message is not getting across, nor are the concepts of CPK. The broader literature of CPK supports respecting partners as experts in their role of policy and decision-making, but that does not seem to translate into respecting Indigenous leaders as experts in knowing community needs. The reason for the call to co-produce the NNA program (Bahnke et al. 2020, 2021) is that representation matters because WEIRD researchers cannot define Indigenous societal benefits (Brady, Fryberg, and Shoda 2018). When Indigenous Peoples can self-define their roles, there are better chances to create credible, relevant, and legitimate outcomes for communities and research members.

The justification for NNA starts with the risk of an ice-free Arctic Ocean by mid-century and continues with this: "The rapid and wide-scale changes occurring in response to this warming portend new opportunities and unprecedented risks to natural systems; social and cultural systems; economic, political and legal systems; and built environments of the Arctic and across the globe" (NSF 2018). "Unprecedented risks" sets up the perception of Arctic Indigenous Peoples as "at risk" peoples (Tuck and Yang 2012) that need saving by science. It also supports colonial ideologies, with the ice-free Arctic leading to "new opportunities," which will likely be extractive economic opportunities (e.g., shipping and oil production). Even the name "Navigating the New Arctic" provides the image of colonial extraction, as it was also a *new* Arctic for the whalers, fur traders, and gold miners. The follow-up letter to NSF states, "Tens of millions of dollars of federal funding has been invested in research that does not achieve societal benefits for Arctic [P]eoples who are currently experiencing disproportionate and extreme impacts of climate change" (Bahnke et al. 2021). So, the perception of NNA is colonial extraction of the Arctic and Arctic Indigenous Peoples through research and the inequitable funding distribution.

FPIC (Food and Agriculture Organization of the United Nations 2016) provides a critical framework for examining NNA. Indigenous and Tribal leaders within Alaska were not made aware of the program to give prior consent (Bahnke et al. 2020). NSF did not try to educate researchers on FPIC or CPK, so researchers followed typical research processes in creating tokenized roles for Indigenous partners. This lack of awareness led to most

NNA proposals being submitted without Indigenous communities' consent or to situations in which consent was asked after the proposal had been fully written and methods and budgets defined, not following free or prior consent (Bahnke et al. 2020). Additionally, NNA and funded projects establish a situation of coercion due to the limited time frame and competition of proposals. It creates a situation wherein Indigenous leaders would feel pressured to sign on to proposals to gain access to funding or potentially lose it to another project or different community that is more willing to sign on. If NNA had a slower rollout that centered and required Indigenous Peoples' engagement and that planned for projects being granted directly to Indigenous communities, it would follow FPIC ethics and prevent harm and conflict.

Where Do We Go from Here?

NSF's Navigating the New Arctic (NNA) program was planned to run for five years, making the NNA RFP 2023 the last cycle. The projects funded during the first cycle should finish by 2023, and the last cycle of funded projects will finish in 2028. The central question remains, "What is the purpose of NNA?" Is the program to fund scientists (thereby maintaining the status quo) or to fund projects that create societal benefits for Arctic Indigenous Peoples? If NSF wants to fund projects that work toward societal benefits, then the answers to fix the issues exist within the letters from Indigenous leaders of western Alaska (Bahnke et al. 2020, 2021). NSF needs to prioritize relationships with Arctic Indigenous leaders to co-produce programs to create societal benefits for Arctic Indigenous Peoples instead of causing harm with colonial acts. Positive changes for Indigenous Peoples cannot happen without respecting Indigenous sovereignty. Indigenous leaders can self-define what needs to be researched, which methods are practical and necessary, and what success metrics are culturally responsive. This chapter provides context to the issues they have raised. Further research, especially by Indigenous Peoples, is needed to understand how to formally evaluate and critique funding programs like NNA regarding equity and sovereignty (David-Chavez and Gavin 2018).

Positionality and self-reflexivity are important concepts within Indigenous methodologies, so researchers can analyze where they have succeeded and failed. As a scientist, I am not separate from what is happening with NNA, nor can I detach my Indigenous identity from my work. To continue doing research, I must advocate for a research paradigm shift in Arctic research and establish examples of how scientists can work better with Indigenous communities. Some key concepts I ask myself when considering Indigenous community-based research include these: Does this project support Indigenous sovereignty and work toward creating positive changes with community partners? Do Indigenous partners have self-determination within the project? Are we following free, prior, and informed consent? Does the project align with my values? Does the project align with the Indigenous community partner's values? What are my motivations, positionality, and purpose for wanting to do the project? There are nuances to answering these questions, but fundamentally it comes down to prioritizing relationships with Indigenous communities and incorporating a sovereignty-based focus into research practices.

Acknowledgments

I am grateful to the large community of mentors and peer-mentors that support me and discuss CPK and NNA ad nauseam. This chapter is also presented within my doctoral dissertation, completed in 2023. In the direct writing of this chapter, I would like to acknowledge my committee members Sarah Trainor, Alexander Hirsch, Richard Hum, and Asikłuk Topkok. I heavily cited the work of Julie Raymond-Yakoubian, Carolina Behe, and Raychelle Daniel, with their Ellam Yua (2022) CPK model. Also, the Indigenous leaders of western Alaska, Melanie Bahnke, Vivian Korthuis, Amos Philemonoff, and Mellisa Johnson, including the support of Lauren Divine, Ecosystem Conservation Office director at the Aleut Community of St. Paul Island. I want to acknowledge their leadership and continued advocacy in Arctic research. I am funded through Alaska Center for Climate Assessment and Policy (ACCAP) (NOAA - NA16OAR4310162) at the International Arctic Research Center (IARC) at the University of Alaska Fairbanks (UAF) and supported by the USDA National Institute of Food and Agriculture, Hatch project 1018914.

8

GEOSCIENCE OBLIGATIONS TO DECOLONIZATION
An 'Ōiwi Methodology of "Makahanalimukaikeea" in Ainu Mosir

ANDREW KALANI CARLSON

Positionality Statement

Multiracial Kanaka 'Ōiwi (Native Hawaiian); raised in international dias-pora; kulāiwi (ancestral lands) in the ahupua'a (Traditional communities) of Waiākea, Niuli'i, Honu'apo, Wailuku, and Waihe'e; now living on Ainu homelands. Hokkaido University, Graduate School of Environmental Science.

Part One: Kuleana and Kūlana in Geoscience Research

Conventional geoscience research operates within and upholds the ongoing settler-colonial systems of oppression at the root of the climate and plan-etary crises and must be confronted. Therefore, researchers must rigorously investigate their roles in advancing decolonization and sovereign liberation, even through laboratory-based and so-called basic science, or else remain complicit. To do so, geoscientists should articulate and reorient their research methodologies to address their standpoint-derived (positional) obligations to the local Black and Indigenous Peoples, communities, and environments affected by their research. This will allow for critical exami-nation of the worldviews, ways of knowing, ways of being, value systems, background, and motivations researchers have for doing science. This is essential for meaningful and ethical science, especially within the context of settler-colonial governments and institutions. Ultimately, ethical and sustainable science requires a decolonized future, so our scientific objectives must be aligned with Black and Indigenous sovereign liberation.

In this chapter, I share my attempt to develop a decolonial research methodology as a diasporic Kanaka 'Ōiwi (Native Hawaiian, person of the bone) environmental scientist and transient settler/outsider in Ainu Mosir (the Indigenous homeland of Ainu People). To do this, I investigate my kūlana (position, station, situation)–derived kuleana (rights, responsibilities, authorities, obligations) as a case study. Rooted in 'Ōiwi scholarship, this methodology uses an 'upena of pilina (fishing net of social-ecological relationships) worldview, my moʻokūʻauhau (genealogies), and 'ōlelo Hawaiʻi (Hawaiian language) concepts and values. While this methodology remains flawed and is case-specific, it may provide some guidance for other scientists to engage with their own standpoint-derived research obligations to decolonization.

As a starting point, it is imperative that scientists more critically engage with reflective questions, such as, "What is my kuleana here?" (The Mauna Kea Syllabus 2021). Kānaka 'Ōiwi scholars and activists explain that in 'ōlelo Hawaiʻi (Hawaiian language, translations from Pukui and Elbert 1986), kuleana evokes the rights, privileges, and responsibilities one has to people and place as well as the authority and justification to act in different contexts (Goodyear–Kaʻōpua, Hussey, and Wright 2014; Aikau, Goodyear–Kaʻōpua, and Silva 2016). Kuleana is also central to Kanaka 'Ōiwi research methodologies broadly (Oliveira and Wright 2016). In this paper, I critically examine my kuleana and kūlana (station, position, situation) while engaged in noiʻi (Knowledge-seeking, research) by articulating my research methodology and standpoint.

From an 'Ōiwi perspective, understanding kuleana requires understanding kūlana and our relationality to our places of research, especially in the context of outsider identities and local familiarity. For example, one 'ōlelo noʻeau (wise saying) related to kuleana instructs "E mālama i ka 'ōlelo, i kuleana e kipa mai ai" ("remember the invitation, for it gives you the privilege of coming here") (Pukui 1983). Moreover, even with an invitation, one's place-based experience and expertise (and therefore, rights to conduct research) may be limited. This is illustrated by the 'ōlelo noʻeau, "No nehinei aʻe nei nō; he aha ka 'ike?" ("[You] just arrived yesterday; what do [you] know?") (Pukui 1983). With these values in mind, the Kūlana Noiʻi Working Group was formed through broad community input to provide guidance for "how an individual carries themselves as they seek knowledge or information," particularly in the place-based context of community engaged scientific research in Hawaiʻi. These guidelines are fundamentally concerned with building and nurturing strong, mutual pilina (relationships) between researchers and community members, in addition to sharing 'ike (Knowledge, awareness, understanding, vision) and aloha (love, affection, compassion) (Kūlana Noiʻi Working Group 2021). This shows that the Kūlana Noiʻi are focused primarily on kūlana in terms of how individual researchers physically and socially conduct themselves, particularly in relation to the local community and place.

Here, I focus on kūlana in the more abstract sense of standpoint. Taking this step back makes kūlana relevant to research objectives, framing, and applications, even for primarily laboratory-based or so-called basic (i.e., not applied) science. A focus on kūlana as standpoint and how it relates to kuleana as responsibility allows for a more critical assessment of researcher motivations, justifications, and obligations beyond conventional standards for research ethics. This framing also aligns with other Indigenous research methodologies, such as those described by Smith (Ngāti Awa, Ngāti Porou), Wilson (Cree), Walter (Trawlwoolway), and Andersen (Métis) (Smith 2021 [1999]; Wilson 2008; Walter and Andersen 2016). Essentially, if a researcher does not understand their own standpoint (including their ways of knowing, ways of being, value systems, and social position), they cannot assess whether they have the authority to conduct the research or how to ensure their research is relevant. This is why articulating a research methodology and standpoint is critical.

Ultimately, decolonial research methodologies require objectives aligned with material outcomes (Deloria Jr. 1988 [1969]; Tuck and Yang 2012; la paperson 2017). While defining specific visions of decolonization and Indigenous sovereignty is beyond the scope here, it is essential to emphasize a few key points. First, Eve Tuck (Unangax̂) and K. Wayne Yang (settler/trespasser) emphasize that decolonization must mean material land back, with restoration and empowerment of Indigenous self-sufficiency and sovereignty in our homelands (Tuck and Yang 2012). In the geosciences, examples include Indigenous scientists working in the context of restoring Indigenous sovereignty over parks and protected areas (Fisk et al. 2021), biocultural restoration, food sovereignty, and community-based management in Hawaiʻi (Delevaux et al. 2018; Montgomery and Vaughan 2018), as well as conservation management and ecological restoration that centers Indigenous value systems (Grenz 2020; Jacobs et al. 2022a,b). The abundance of Indigenous-led science oriented toward sovereignty makes it clear that the path forward is already being forged.

Next, joint and overlapping solidarity among Black, Indigenous, and Afro-Indigenous Peoples, as well as other oppressed and colonized Peoples, is essential (Fanon 2004 [1961]; Freire 2018 [1968]; Lorde 2012 [1984]; hooks 2014 [1994]; King 2019; Mays 2021b) and must be considered in decolonial geoscience methodologies. From the classic work of Walter Rodney (Guyanese) to contemporary work by Andrews (British African-Caribbean), it is well established how the structures of colonial oppression are intimately dependent on the ongoing oppressive effects of the colonization of the African continent (Rodney 2018 [1972]; Andrews 2021). Black authors in the United States have shown how historical (structural) enslavement is not a relic of the past but lives on in the ongoing systems of caste (Wilkerson 2020), mass incarceration (Alexander 2020 [2010]), and Afropessimism's theory of Black social death (Wilderson III 2020). Since 1979, Robert D. Bullard's scholarship on the racist impacts of pollution on Black communities in the US South and his now classic book, *Dumping in Dixie* (Bullard 2018 [1990]) paved the way for the fields of environmental and climate justice, leaving no room for doubt that environmental science must consider and address anti-Black racism. Meztli Yoalli Rodríguez Aguilera (Mestiza Mexicana) also provides a relevant example of how ecological grief and environmental racism impacts Black and Indigenous Peoples in Oaxaca, Mexico (Rodríguez Aguilera 2022). Therefore, geoscience methodologies that aspire to be decolonial but only consider a narrow conception of Indigenous sovereignty will ultimately fail if they still perpetuate environmental injustice and anti-Black racism.

With this context, the research methodology described here establishes the standpoint-derived obligations for my research project. While Liboiron (Métis) has previously explained the importance of standpoint, obligations, and decolonization within the realm of basic geoscience research (Liboiron 2021a,b), this chapter develops those ideas into a specific and explicit research methodology that is firmly grounded in 'Ōiwi methodologies, values, and language. The additional context of my Indigenous upbringing in diaspora and current displacement in Ainu Mosir also create complications that may offer insights for others navigating and disrupting settler-colonial science. Therefore, I share my methodology and standpoint as a case study and call for all geoscientists, even those conducting basic research, to investigate their standpoint-derived obligations and reframe how they discuss their data and results in terms of those obligations. From the successes and flaws of this case study, as well as the broad decolonial scholarship it stands on, I hope that the path forward for other geoscientists may be made clearer.

CASE STUDY:
RESEARCH KULEANA OF A KANAKA ʻŌIWI IN AINU MOSIR

Even as a Kanaka ʻŌiwi well-versed in the importance of kuleana, I had not fully engaged in questioning my kūlana-derived kuleana as a researcher before embarking on a five-year PhD program at Hokkaido University. Yet, the history of diasporic kuleana is well documented (Chang 2019) and cannot be overlooked since "resistance to settler-colonialism is a responsibility for both Kanaka ʻŌiwi in Hawaiʻi, as well as those in the diaspora" (Vaughn 2019). Therefore, I have had to critically examine the limitations of my positionality as an invited guest of the Japanese government (MEXT Scholar), while also being an uninvited outsider/transient settler from the perspective of the Indigenous Ainu People.

PARALLELS WITH PARACHUTE SCIENCE

Given this context, I discuss how my background informed my initial and evolving motivations for pursuing a PhD in environmental science at Hokkaido University specifically. More personal motivations included a lifelong interest in Japan and Japanese culture, having grown up with both genealogical and place-based Japanese cultural influences, and taking my first Japanese-language class when I was eleven years old. In terms of education and research opportunities, Hokkaido specifically was of interest because of its well-known wild and commercial kelp, combined with the relevant resources and experts at Hokkaido University for researching kelp carbon dynamics.

Yet, despite these ties and interests, I am still of course an outsider, and so it is important to investigate the similarities and differences between my positionality and the extractive practice of "parachute science" (Asase et al. 2021; de Vos 2022). Conducting research as an outsider is often fundamentally flawed (Said 2014 [1979]), and even Indigenous researchers operating from the diaspora face many ethical obstacles (Aikau 2019; Mwampamba et al. 2022). In my case, as an outsider with kuleana outside of my current residence, my research objectives are inherently extractive and center an outsider's perspective. Despite this, my situation is critically distinct from typical parachute science because of my context of working in an all-Japanese lab at a public Japanese university, without exerting power structures to dominate local Japanese People, places, and Knowledges.

PERPETUATING AINU COLONIZATION

However, this narrative is disrupted by the fact that while Japanese People can be considered Indigenous to the main island of Honshu, they are indisputably settler-colonizers in Ainu Mosir (Hokkaido), which is the Indigenous homeland of Ainu People. Uzawa (Ainu), explains that the Japanese government first recognized Ainu People as a minority ethnic group in a 1991 report to the United Nations, then as an Indigenous People by a 2008 resolution, and, most recently, as an Indigenous People by a 2019 law. Yet, Ainu People still do not have legal rights to self-determination or sovereignty (Uzawa 2020). Even though the area where I collect seawater and macroalgal samples (within Oshoro Bay) has been managed through a Hokkaido University marine station since 1908 (Yotsukura 2021), it is still part of the Ainu homeland. In fact, conducting conventional research anywhere in Hokkaido is a form of perpetuating settler-colonialism, as there is no legal requirement to consider the rights of Ainu People or communities to manage the use of their ancestral and modern homelands for research purposes.

Unfortunately, historical and ongoing settler-colonial violence has oppressed open identification as Ainu People, which also complicates issues surrounding ethical accessibility and community engagement. For example, Ishihara describes herself as an "Ainu Liminar"—her term for those of Ainu heritage who have had their Ainu voices stolen from them by Japanese settler-colonialism and do not feel that they can identify as Ainu People (Grunow et al. 2019; Ishihara 2019). Ishihara also uses the term "Silent Ainu" for People who may identify as Ainu but do not feel comfortable publicly identifying their Ainu ethnicity because of issues of discrimination and pressures of assimilation (Ishihara 2018; Ishihara 2020). These issues complicate the validity of government demographic surveys on the Ainu population in Japan (Uzawa 2020). Therefore, while it might be expected that the survey results of zero Ainu respondents in the Shiribeshi region where Oshoro Bay is located (Uzawa 2020) is an underestimate, it is an indication that there isn't a publicly active local Ainu community in the broader region with whom I can engage.

Despite these issues, it would be unethical to dismiss the relevance of Ainu sovereignty in Hokkaido as too complicated a topic for this research project. Indeed, Ainu People elsewhere in Hokkaido may have their own genealogical and personal relationships to Oshoro Bay maintained diasporically throughout and beyond Hokkaido. Therefore, regardless of the apparent absence of Ainu People living near Oshoro Bay, this research must engage with the broader Ainu community and ensure its relevance to them.

My standpoint, therefore, includes both my identity as an invited guest and researcher (MEXT Scholar) of the Japanese government, and as an uninvited transient settler from the perspective of Indigenous Ainu People to whom Hokkaido is their present and ancestral homeland. As an outsider, reconciling these identities with a kuleana to not conduct extractive research is inherently complicated. For example, it would generally not be appropriate for me to attempt to use or discuss Ainu Knowledge without the co-production of that Knowledge (Lock et al. 2022). Also, attempting to re-center my research toward primarily benefiting Ainu People would likely be disingenuous and fundamentally flawed due to my positionality.

However, this positionality should not be used as an excuse to engage in the "moves to innocence" (Mawhinney 1998; Tuck and Yang 2012) that are characteristic of resistance to anti-racist and anti-oppression activities. Instead, I have to look to my standpoint-derived kuleana and investigate how I can have a positive impact while centering my Indigenous positionality in my research. I, therefore, have kuleana to ensure that the insights generated by my scientific research are advancing a restoration of Indigenous sovereign management of these macroalgal ecosystems, most especially for the Ainu People and communities on whose land and waters this research is based.

In other words, based on this kūlana, I have kuleana to advance decolonization and Indigenous sovereignty through my research on macroalgal biogeochemistry and Blue Carbon, with particular attention to 'Ōiwi and Ainu Peoples. As figure 8.1 shows, my kuleana, kūlana, and mo'okū'auhau are all linked and collectively informed by an 'Ōiwi/Indigenous relational worldview. This methodology is therefore born from the complex identities and contexts of my standpoint and represents a flawed starting point for my research; nevertheless, this case study may provide useful insights to others.

SUMMARY AND OBJECTIVES

Explicitly stating a research methodology according to one's own cultural and place-based contexts is critical for engaging in one's positionality relative to the various places one has relationships and responsibilities to (standpoint-derived kuleana). Even geoscientists conducting basic research must investigate how their positionality and their research impact Black

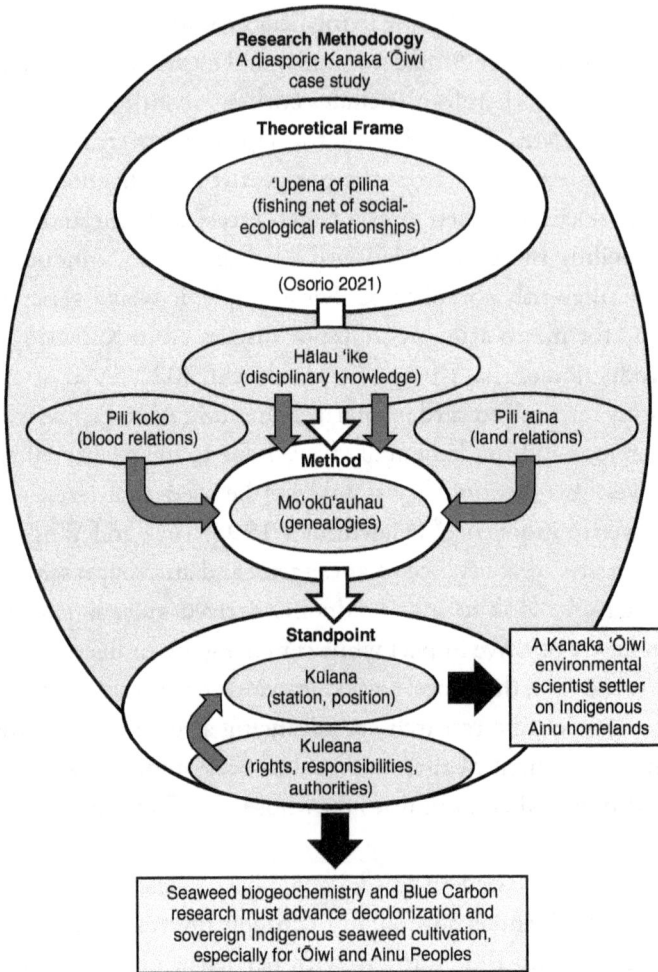

Figure 8.1. Components and outcomes of this diasporic Kanaka ʻŌiwi research methodology. This methodology is guided by an ʻupena of pilina worldview as its theoretical frame and foundation for shaping the other methodological components. Various moʻokūʻauhau (genealogies) inform my kūlana (standpoint) as a Kanaka ʻŌiwi environmental scientist settler on Indigenous Ainu homelands. This positionality informs my kuleana (rights and responsibilities), which are framed through the broader social-ecological worldview. Ultimately, this framing indicates that my macroalgal biogeochemistry research should advance Indigenous sovereignty, especially for ʻŌiwi and Ainu Peoples. Specifically, my macroalgal biogeochemistry research must be oriented toward and made useful for sovereign Indigenous seaweed cultivation, stewardship, and social-ecological health.

and Indigenous Peoples, communities, and environments, and whether oppressive systems are upheld or decolonization objectives are advanced. Therefore, I offer three primary objectives for this chapter, as follows:

1. To situate my research on macroalgal dissolved organic carbon dynamics and implications for Blue Carbon strategies in the context of my responsibilities and limitations

2. To encourage other Kanaka ʻŌiwi as well as other Indigenous scientists to confidently and explicitly incorporate our Indigenous-based methodologies into our research to benefit and center Indigenous Peoples, communities, environments, and sovereignty

3. To encourage geoscientists broadly to engage in their methodologies and standpoints to investigate how their science perpetuates settler-colonial systems or advances decolonization

Part Two: Methodologies of Moʻokūʻauhau

One meaning of "I ka wā ma mua, ka wā ma hope" is that the past informs and secures the future (Kameʻeleihiwa 1992; Wilson-Hokowhitu 2019). Through moʻokūʻauhau (genealogies), we can therefore better understand kūlana and ultimately kuleana, even in the context of research objectives and outcomes (figure 8.1). First, the cultural centrality of moʻokūʻauhau to Kānaka ʻŌiwi can be illustrated by the genealogical nature of the various Kumulipo (cosmogonic creation chants), which are primary kumu (sources, teachers) for understanding where all living entities come from and their context in the world (Kanahele 2011; Nuʻuhiwa 2019).

Looking to modern ʻŌiwi scholarship, moʻokūʻauhau and the Kumulipo are also central to research methodologies and broader ʻŌiwi ways of Knowing and Being (Wilson-Hokowhitu 2019). Notably, they serve as the foundation for Papakū Makawalu (Kanahele 2011), which describes a "methodology and pedagogy for understanding the Hawaiian Universe" from multiple perspectives (Nuʻuhiwa 2019). Papakū Makawalu is particularly relevant to decolonial geoscience because of how it has been combined with grounded theory to construct land stewardship policy (Kanahele-Mossman and Karides 2021) in the context of Kānaka ʻŌiwi opposition to the proposed Thirty Meter Telescope on Mauna Kea (Alegado 2019; Kahanamoku et al. 2020). Personal moʻokūʻauhau have also been critically applied across disciplines (e.g., Kurashima et al. 2018; hoʻomanawanui 2019; Osorio 2021), including in the context of sustainability science (Kealiikanakaoleohaililani et al. 2018).

Ultimately, how much and in what ways personal moʻokūʻauhau are shared methodologically, if at all, will vary based on the nuances of each situation, and should never be coerced or required as a standardized practice. This is especially important to emphasize given the context of colonial violence, trauma, and blood quantum (Kauanui 2008). Therefore, this methodology refers to my moʻokūʻauhau as a starting point to center kuleana and pilina without explicitly reciting my moʻokūʻauhau pili koko (blood relation genealogy).

ʻŌiwi methodologies of moʻokūʻauhau also incorporate moʻokūʻauhau pili ʻāina (genealogy of land connections) and moʻokūʻauhau hālau ʻike (disciplinary genealogy). Considering these moʻokūʻauhau together in a research methodology, therefore, informs kūlana. In addition, clarifying research-relevant social position informs what or how research questions are asked and answered. For Kānaka ʻŌiwi scientists, using moʻokūʻauhau as methodology, including their relationships to ʻŌiwi worldviews of kuleana and pilina, can provide a powerful way to investigate how pono (righteous, good, correct) oneʻs research concept, conduct, and impacts may be.

CASE STUDY: MOʻOKŪʻAUHAU
MOʻOKŪʻAUHAU PILI KOKO

Based on moʻokūʻauhau pili koko and cultural upbringing, I am a Kanaka ʻŌiwi with a multiracial heritage raised in the international diaspora. Before both my birth and my motherʻs birth in the diaspora, the one hānau (sands of birth) of our kūpuna (grandparent generation, Elders, ancestors) were most recently in the ahupuaʻa (community-level land division) of Waiākea in the moku (district) of Hilo on Hawaiʻi Island, while those of previous generations included the ahupuaʻa of Niuliʻi and Makapala (Moku o Kohala) and Honuʻapo (Moku o Kaʻū) on Hawaiʻi Island, as well as the ahupuaʻa of Waiheʻe and Wailuku (Moku o Pūʻali Komohana) and the ahupuaʻa of Kanahena (Moku o Honuaʻula) on the Island of Maui. It is also worth remembering that some of my living kūpuna still have memories of their kūpuna who were born, even became mākua (parents), in the internationally recognized Kingdom of Hawaiʻi. This time of Indigenous sovereignty and period when ʻōlelo Hawaiʻi was the primary language has therefore not been forgotten and may yet be reclaimed.

In terms of our many kulāiwi (ancestral lands, where bones are buried), Niuliʻi in particular is home to additional kuleana and pilina for our ʻohana. This is one place we know our kūpuna signed the 1897 Kūʻē petitions—the democratically and legally successful protest against annexation to the United States of America (Silva 2004; Goodyear-Kaʻōpua, Hussey, and Wright 2014). Today, ʻohana from the Hussey line in Niuliʻi continue to steward kuleana land that was distributed in the Great Māhele (mid-1800s land division policy of the Kingdom of Hawaiʻi). In addition, Niuliʻi is a piko (umbilical cord, navel, focal point) for connecting both the Malakaua and Hussey lines to the Maui kūpuna who can be traced all the way back to Papahānaumoku and Wākea (Earth Mother and Sky Father).

Briefly summarizing my genealogy, by the time of my upbringing, my Hawai'i-based Kanaka 'Ōiwi mo'okū'auhau had largely assimilated and integrated aspects of English (beyond five generations) and Okinawan (within five generations) cultural identities. Additional ancestors within five generations (with English, German, Irish, and West African ethnocultural identities) from separate genealogies were largely assimilated into the white majority culture of the United States. Therefore, my standpoint is primarily influenced by Kanaka 'Ōiwi and white-US cultures, both mediated in the context of an international diaspora, as I describe below.

MO'OKŪ'AUHAU PILI 'ĀINA AND HĀLAU 'IKE

Here, I briefly summarize mo'okū'auhau pili 'āina (genealogy of land connections) and mo'okū'auhau hālau 'ike (disciplinary genealogy). I was born on the homelands of the Patwin and Miwok Peoples (in the area currently referred to as Davis, California, United States) with my upbringing and grade-school education beginning there at César Chávez Spanish Immersion School. My grade-school education then continued at the North American–curriculum international schools where my parents taught: International School Bangkok, which is on land first settled by the Tai People (Nonthaburi, Thailand); Colegio Internacional Puerto la Cruz, which neighbors lands of the Kalina/Kariña, Waikerí, and Taíno Peoples (Barcelona, Venezuela); and American School of Doha, which is on land of the Indigenous Arab Peoples (Doha, Qatar). I then earned a BS in environmental engineering from Northwestern University, which is situated on lands of the Peoria, Bodwéwadmi (Potawatomi), Myaamia, Očhéthi Šakówiŋ, Hoocąk, and Kiikaapoi (Kickapoo) Peoples (Evanston, Illinois, United States). After graduating, I lived and worked as an environmental engineer on lands of the Tséstho'e (Cheyenne), Očhéthi Šakówiŋ, hinono'eino' biito'owu' (Arapaho), Núu-agha-tʉvʉ-pʉ (Ute), and Ndé Kónitsąąíí Gokíyaa (Lipan Apache) Peoples (Denver and Aurora, Colorado, United States). Now, I am currently earning a PhD in environmental science from Hokkaido University (Sapporo, Japan), which is within Ainu Mosir, the homelands of Ainu People. From these mo'okū'auhau I establish my kuleana and kūlana as a diasporic (displaced and transient settler) Kanaka 'Ōiwi environmental scientist.

These moʻokūʻauhau clarify the combination of my experience in conventional science and engineering with sources of Indigenous Knowledges, ways of Knowing, and ways of Being. For me, these sources include kūpuna, ʻōlelo noʻeau, the unique worldview understood through ʻōlelo Hawaiʻi, oral histories and recordings, environmental observations, naʻau (intestines, mind, heart), ʻike ʻohana (family Knowledge), Traditional Ecological Knowledges, and so on. These various moʻokūʻauhau-derived ways of Knowing and Being are therefore integrated into this transdisciplinary academic and cultural methodology.

MOʻOKŪʻAUHAU LIMU: MACROALGAL RESEARCH MOTIVATIONS

Next, I discuss how my moʻokūʻauhau motivated my interest in pursuing a PhD program in which I investigate macroalgal biogeochemistry and Blue Carbon more specifically. Because of my moʻokūʻauhau, I have had a lifelong relationship with coastal environments, with an awareness of and concern for the impacts of climate change since early childhood. It is also relevant that through an ʻŌiwi worldview, the environment and sea are not resources for extraction but rather living ʻāina and akua (elemental gods) that feed and sustain people. According to this worldview, they must be respected and cared for within sustainable, mutual relationships (McGregor et al. 2003). This context provided my broad motivation for initially studying environmental engineering and then narrowing my interests to marine biogeochemistry for a graduate degree.

Regarding macroalgae specifically, limu (seaweed, as well as other submerged plants or algae) are an important part of ʻāina in Hawaiʻi and provide an example of how ʻāina sustains Kānaka both nutritionally and culturally (Abbott 1978). Even in the diaspora, my upbringing has always included seaweed as a food source. Various limu species (e.g., limu kohu, līpoa, paheʻe, and līpalu) are also featured in mele (songs) such as "Ka Uluwehi O Ke Kai" by Aunty Edith Kanakaʻole, popularly performed during kanikapila (impromptu music playing sessions) including in my ʻohana. Other important cultural roles include limu kala in hoʻoponopono (family conferences to set relationships right) and the food kapu (restriction, consecration) on pakaiea (a particular limu) for ʻohana with a manō (shark) ʻaumakua (deified ancestor).

In the Kalākaua version of the Kumulipo ("He Kumulipo"), the importance of limu is also established from a moʻokūʻauhau perspective by appearing in the first era, long before Kānaka, and only after coral polyps, earthworms, sea urchins, and shellfish are born (Keaulumoku 1700; Liliʻuokalani 1898; Kanahele 2011). All told, "He Kumulipo" explicitly names the birth of the following limu in the sea, along with their respective inland forest kiaʻi (protectors): ʻēkaha, ʻakiʻaki, manauea, kōʻeleʻele, puakī, kīkala moa, limu kele, limu kala, līpuʻupuʻu, loloa, nē, and hulu waena. In fact, there are up to 149 documented traditional names for various limu in ʻōlelo Hawaiʻi, with more names likely known historically (Abbott and Williamson 1974).

Taken together, limu have a strong importance to Kānaka ʻŌiwi in general, and also to me personally. This also motivates my deeper connection to and interest in macroalgal cultivation specifically, compared to other climate change mitigation strategies such as geological sequestration. Even other Blue Carbon ecosystems such as mangroves, which are an invasive and harmful species in Hawaiʻi (Möhlenkamp et al. 2018), cannot hold the same cultural meaning to me as macroalgae. This reality that mangroves may have Blue Carbon value yet be ecologically damaging in Hawaiʻi underscores the fact that social-ecological health can be better understood through place-based genealogies and culture rather than a narrow fixation on accounting services such as Blue Carbon.

SUMMARY

This case study reflects on and honors my moʻokūʻauhau as a way to understand my research kūlana and kuleana, so this framing and process is most relevant to other Kānaka ʻŌiwi researchers. Other Indigenous scientists will have their own Traditions and methodologies that similarly incorporate genealogies but should be sure to root their work in the specific values of their own cultures. Likewise, non-Indigenous geoscientists can turn to the social sciences for more general methodologies, such as auto-ethnography. Broadly, these genealogical relationships and histories are critically relevant to geoscientists because they inform the rights a researcher has to conduct research and the responsibilities that a researcher has to the local land.

In my case, based on my cultural worldview and genealogies, combined with formal experience (academic and professional) as an environmental engineer, I developed a motivation for pursuing research on macroalgal dissolved organic carbon in relation to its Blue Carbon potential (i.e., its potential to meaningfully contribute to climate change mitigation through carbon sequestration). Despite the many potential research areas with as great or greater potential to contribute to climate change mitigation or other positive contributions to society, my moʻokūʻauhau were essential to motivating (through cultural values) my engagement in this specific field and will continue to shape my motivations going forward.

These genealogies give me the rights and obligations to do this research in a way that empowers Indigenous sovereignty. However, they also limit how and where I can responsibly do research—an aspect that conventional geoscience commonly overlooks. Conventional geoscientists too often assume that their academic degrees give them the right to conduct any kind of science anywhere. Instead, we must look back to where we came from to see where we are allowed to go.

Part Three: An ʻUpena of Pilina Worldview

The intrinsic relationship between moʻokūʻauhau and key ʻŌiwi ethics means moʻokūʻauhau are of primary importance in understanding one's kuleana within an ʻupena of pilina (fishing net of social-ecological relationships; Osorio 2021). In Osorio's conceptualization, each intimate cord that connects Kānaka to each other and to ʻāina needs nurturing to keep our social-ecological systems healthy. This relational worldview is also reflected in modern ʻŌiwi science by integrating written and oral histories of Traditional Ecological Knowledge in marine (Puniwai 2020) and terrestrial (Kamelamela et al. 2022) ecosystem restoration toward the goal of ʻāina momona—"thriving and productive communities of people, place, and natural resources" (Andrade et al. 2022). New Indigenous Knowledge is also generated through rigorous and intimate observation (Puniwai et al. 2016; Morishige et al. 2018; Andrade and Morishige 2022). More broadly, the worldview of lōkāhi refers to the balance between humans, ʻāina, and spirits, but again, this balance is dependent on the agency of the kuaʻāina (backbone of the land) who cultivate land and culture in the countryside (McGregor 2007). Unfortunately, modern imbalances have resulted in a period of hulihua (upheaval, turning), manifestly visible through the hōʻailona (signs) of climate change and other global crises (McGregor et al. 2020).

This ʻŌiwi relational view of social-ecological balance is wholly distinct from the worldview of modern "western" environmentalism that separates humans and the natural environment (McGregor 2007) and so the distinction deserves explicit emphasis. The European concept of nature espoused by conventional conservationists is genealogically linked to the ideas of Alexander von Humboldt (1769–1859). While von Humboldt critiqued Spanish colonization in South America and expressed some sympathy and respect toward Indigenous Peoples, he and those who were inspired by him (including Charles Darwin, Henry David Thoreau, George Perkins Marsh, and John Muir) championed ideas of conserving or preserving a "wilderness" that was isolated from inherently negative human impacts (Wulf 2015). Ultimately, this idea of nature as an isolated recreational space was far from benign and was weaponized in the violent displacement of Indigenous Peoples from their homelands—all in the names of conservation and preservation (Dunbar-Ortiz 2014; Bennett et al. 2021; Xego and Obioha 2021).

However, from many Indigenous perspectives, one cannot visit nature because nature is not and cannot be separate from society, and this is reflected in our languages. Actually, in ʻōlelo Hawaiʻi there is no word for nature in the sense of an outdoor environment (Pukui and Elbert 1986). The closest word to nature or the environment is ʻāina, which again literally means those who sustain or feed, a definition that requires mutual relationships among Indigenous Peoples, nonhuman beings, and the lands, air, and waters. These relationships are not trivial given that Indigenous Peoples steward vast and ecologically intact landscapes (Garnett et al. 2018) and that environmental stewardship by Indigenous Peoples is quantifiably more effective than other conservation strategies (Dawson et al. 2021)..

In fact, in ʻŌiwi Indigenous statecraft, social-ecological systems were defined by a deep and complex pilina between humans and ʻāina that sustainably supported intense populations (up to one million people, comparable to modern numbers) for at least hundreds of years (Beamer 2014; Osorio 2021). For example, within an ahupuaʻa (social-ecological community, with boundaries organizing resource access and kuleana) there was productive equilibrium between loko iʻa (multi-trophic fishponds cultivating fish, shellfish, and limu), loʻi kalo (taro fields), and areas kapu (forbidden, sacred, protected) to resource use (Keala, Hollyer, and Castro 2007; Beamer 2014; Winter et al. 2018). Moreover, the complexities of the biocultural resource management systems extended to the scale of moku (social-ecological region or district) within an island (Winter et al. 2018). This shows why it is useful to look to our histories of Indigenous sovereignty to envision future decolonization.

When considering these social-ecological relationships and systems, it is also important to be clear that the Kingdom of Hawaiʻi was a multi-ethnic sovereign Indigenous Nation. Therefore, a future Indigenous government of Hawaiʻi can and should be multi-ethnic while still centering

Kānaka ʻŌiwi sovereignty and social-ecological relationships, value systems, and worldviews. More specifically, Nitasha Tamar Sharma (Hawaiʻi-born Indian-Jewish settler) discusses the ways Hawaiʻi has been a haven for Black People (including Black Kānaka ʻŌiwi) as well as the ways anti-Black racism still needs to be confronted (Sharma 2021). Such havens are not only compatible with, but also necessary for, the joint struggle toward Black and Indigenous sovereign liberation and are critical threads in this vision of an ʻupena of pilina. The expansive concept of an ʻupena of pilina forces us to understand how the biocultural and social-ecological elements of an ahupuaʻa or moku system conceptually and meta-physically form a decolonial future that is co-created.

CASE STUDY: MACROALGAL BLUE CARBON IN AN ʻUPENA OF PILINA

In this research methodology, I focus on ʻŌiwi ethics as articulated through an ʻupena of pilina because it focuses on the importance of deep relationships between and among Indigenous Peoples and the land within a complex fishing net whose cords need constant tending. This interconnected and multifaceted framing helps bring together many ʻŌiwi Values into a more integrated and holistic worldview. This conceptualization also helps serve as a reminder of the various cords that must be tended. This framing emphasizes that all projects, no matter how well or ethically executed, are simply one piece in a greater collaborative effort. Understanding and articulating one's positionality within an ʻupena of pilina is therefore important for being an effective and ethical part of greater efforts and communities.

Indeed, this positionality of centering ʻŌiwi ethics has specific implications for macroalgal Blue Carbon research. For example, much discussion surrounding macroalgal Blue Carbon includes large-scale projects either for biofuels, offshore kelp forests, or even deep-sea biomass sinking, all of which have a substantially weaker or nonexistent social-ecological relationship between people and macroalgae. Such projects are generally antithetical to a Kanaka ʻŌiwi worldview, at least as they are currently articulated by non-Indigenous people. Some of their specific limitations and negative consequences, as well as broader questions surrounding carbon dioxide removal projects, have also been highlighted in the scientific literature (e.g., Morrow et al. 2020; Boyd et al. 2022; Ricart et al. 2022).

Despite the need for greater funding and empowerment for sovereign Indigenous cultivation of macroalgae, monetization of Blue Carbon credits could result in perverse outcomes. I critique the coloniality of the broader Blue Carbon credit market in greater depth elsewhere (Carlson 2024) but highlight a few key points here. Cautionary examples can be seen in the history of terrestrial carbon offset projects, with tensions between the government and Indigenous control (Asiyanbi 2016), as well as uneven benefits (Poudyal et al. 2016). More fundamentally, there is increasing recognition of the need to move beyond the transactional context of ecosystem services accounting (Pascua et al. 2017). By looking to the successful social-ecological systems of Hawai'i, it becomes clear that macroalgal Blue Carbon must exist within a sustainable and productive context of an 'upena of pilina and not simply a narrow fixation on sequestering carbon at the expense of all else.

This conceptualization is also helpful for conveying that if the pilina connecting macroalgal cultivation to the rest of the 'upena are frayed or broken, or if macroalgal cultivation is attempted outside the 'upena—outside the boundaries of the ahupua'a—then such activities are not contributing to the long-term, sustainable health of the social-ecological system. Therefore, 'Ōiwi sustainable aquaculture and agriculture systems serve as important examples of ecomimicry (Winter et al. 2020) and a circular economy (Beamer et al. 2021) for not only reestablishing a social-ecological equilibrium but also for achieving far greater productivity and independence than the present-day colonial system has been able to provide.

Indigenous cultivation of macroalgae is also important beyond Hawai'i, as demonstrated by modern and historical accounts. However, I do not have the positionality or relationality to discuss the specifics of other Indigenous social-ecological systems. While I am engaging in discussions with local and Ainu People, it is not within my authority to be specific regarding historical or current efforts by or prioritized interest of Ainu People to engage in macroalgal cultivation. However, my efforts to bridge knowledge gaps regarding macroalgal dissolved organic carbon dynamics and its potential Blue Carbon role may offer some value to macroalgal cultivation by Ainu People. For example, macroalgal dissolved organic carbon could be considered a culturally relevant proxy for coastal social-ecological health, and quantitative data insights could help guide Indigenous coastal management and monitoring (Carlson, Yoshimura, and Kudo 2024). Therefore, it will be important to communicate relevant results to Ainu communities and maintain an active role to ensure that any Blue Carbon funding is redirected to Ainu People in Hokkaido over larger-scale industrial and commercial interests. This also represents an opportunity to grow relationships between 'Ōiwi and Ainu Peoples that will persist far beyond the scope of my research project. Building solidarity among sovereign Indigenous Peoples by sharing Traditional Ecological Knowledges of seaweed cultivation can be an important component of the global Land Back movement.

SUMMARY

I have kuleana to these places and environments because my research is based in, related to, and has benefited from them. Therefore, I must be active in providing relevant Knowledge and advocacy for sovereign Indigenous cultivation of social-ecological systems and their contributions to Blue Carbon. However, this relational framing also confronts the value of transactional carbon offsets and ecosystem services accounting. Instead, the central objective should be Indigenous social-ecological health, with Blue Carbon acting only as a supporting tool, if at all.

The result of articulating my standpoint through 'Ōiwi methodologies and re-centering macroalgal biogeochemistry toward decolonization can also be expressed in a new 'ōlelo no'eau that will guide my research: "Makahanalimukaikeea." Consistent with other 'ōlelo no'eau, there are various kaona (hidden meanings) embedded in the phrase, but one translation offered here is this: "There is life and sovereignty in the work of seaweed." This kuleana must not only benefit Kānaka 'Ōiwi in Hawai'i but also other Indigenous Peoples worldwide in their efforts for sovereign coastal management and cultivation.

Conclusions and Recommendations

My methodology is informed by both various personal mo'okū'auhau (pili koko, pili 'āina, and hālau 'ike) and "He Kumulipo" more broadly. My ways of Knowing are guided by extensive 'Ōiwi scholarship on research methodology, culture, values, Traditional Ecological Knowledges, and environmental science, combined with 'ike na'au and 'ōlelo no'eau. My hālau 'ike also includes academic and professional experience in conventional environmental science and engineering. These various sources of Knowledges, values, and ways of Being provide me with the motivation to research macroalgal biogeochemistry and Blue Carbon sequestration potential, within a framework that centers research objectives and outcomes around Indigenous Peoples and sovereignty. In particular, greater consideration of social-ecological ethics (as expressed here through an 'upena of pilina worldview) and systems (as evidenced by the moku and ahupua'a systems of

Hawaiʻi) can lead to a deeper awareness of whether and how one's research advances a sustainable and just future or maintains conventional settler-colonial systems of extraction, oppression, and the separation of humans from "nature." From an ʻŌiwi perspective, just as research is ceremony (Wilson 2008), research is—and must be—aloha ʻāina.

To guide other geoscientists, I offer three reflective questions. For one, geoscientists should continuously address the question, "What are my obligations, rights, and responsibilities here?" Understanding one's research standpoint clarifies responsibilities to and authority within scientific, social, and environmental communities. We must also ask, "How does my research perpetuate settler-colonialism?" and "How can my research advance Black and Indigenous sovereign liberation?"

In fact, the answers to these questions can and should be embedded in published research manuscripts, as they are particularly relevant to the introduction (objectives and motivations) as well as the discussion (applications, implications, and conclusions). Just as it is now conventional to frame the relevance of geoscientific results within the context of climate change, sustainability, or other global environmental crises, so too should basic research be framed within the transdisciplinary context of ongoing colonialism.

For geoscientists broadly, we not only can, but also must, ensure our research is advancing decolonization. Colonialism is inseparable from the climate crisis (Táíwò and Cibralic 2020; Ghosh 2021; Sultana 2022a, b) as well as issues of environmental justice and racism (Bullard 2018 [1990]; Whyte 2018; Gilio-Whitaker 2019). Research attempting to solve or mitigate these issues as strictly geophysical or environmental is deeply incomplete without a concurrent effort toward decolonization. Colonialism is not sustainable.

To conclude, this process of articulating a research methodology facilitated deeper investigations of my moʻokūʻauhau, kūlana, kuleana, and pilina, thereby reorienting my research toward deliberately advancing decolonization and sovereign Indigenous cultivation of seaweed through aloha ʻāina. In doing so, this paper hopes to help more Indigenous scientists conduct science in a way that is true to themselves and their communities. If all geoscientists apply these concepts according to their unique contexts and their own standpoint-derived obligations, we can make truer progress toward the inseparable objectives of decolonization, Black and Indigenous sovereign liberation, and a thriving planet.

Acknowledgments

Mahalo piha to the following amazing ʻŌiwi scientists who were gener-
ous with comments, discussions, and encouragement that helped shape
this work: Anela Akiona, Rosie ʻAnolani Alegado, Steven Manaʻoakamai
Johnson, Aurora Kagawa-Viviani, Sara Tenamoeata Kahanamoku, Katie
Kamelamela, Kelly Luis, and Cherry Yamane. Much appreciation to Lara
Jacobs for both broad and detailed feedback across many versions. Me ke
aloha pumehana e kuʻu ʻohana for being the first reviewers and supporting
me the whole way. Me ke aloha nō e kō mākou kūpuna a me nā ʻaumākua,
e mālama pono e kuʻu aloha. I am supported by a Ministry of Education,
Culture, Sports, Science and Technology (MEXT) scholarship (No. 190358)
from the Japanese government.

PART II

Reciprocity

9
PRAISE THE RAIN

JOY HARJO

Positionality Statement
Citizen of Muscogee (Creek) Nation

> Praise the rain; the seagull dive
> The curl of plant, the raven talk—
> Praise the hurt, the house slack
> The stand of trees, the dignity—
> Praise the dark, the moon cradle
> The sky fall, the bear sleep—
> Praise the mist, the warrior name
> The earth eclipse, the fired leap—
> Praise the backwards, upward sky
> The baby cry, the spirit food—
> Praise canoe, the fish rush
> The hole for frog, the upside-down—
> Praise the day, the cloud cup
> The mind flat, forget it all—
>
> Praise crazy. Praise sad.
> Praise the path on which we're led.
> Praise the roads on earth and water.
> Praise the eater and the eaten.
> Praise beginnings; praise the end.
> Praise the song and praise the singer.
>
> Praise the rain; it brings more rain.
> Praise the rain; it brings more rain.

10

RECIPROCAL RESTORATION WITH TRIBAL NATIONS
Natural Resources Management and STEM Education

JOSEPH GAZING WOLF, CELINA GRAY, ORAL SAULTERS,
AND STEPHANIE KELLEY

Positionality Statements

Gazing Wolf: See chapter 13 for positionality statement.
Gray: Little Shell Chippewa, Blackfeet; University of Montana
Saulters: Apache; Kansas State University
Kelley: Te-Moak Band Shoshone; Portland Public Schools

Indigenous communities across space and time have often refrained from documenting their histories, stories, languages, and philosophies through the written word. Though historically this has been viewed as evidence of the Native's lack of intelligence and sophistication, in reality, those engaged in relationships of reciprocity with the Earth and with one another understand that both individual and collective Knowledge of specific realities undergoes near constant evolution. Hence, the written word, along with current ideas about certain events or realities within the scope of human experience, are like an image in time, a static projection of a particular thing that is constantly undergoing growth and change. The written word, like the dogmatic thought, may act to prohibit this evolution in a system, a phenomenon, an institution, or a person.

When reciprocity is discussed as a collective action that is under constant flux, the opportunity to view the action as an adaptive and enduring part of a collective experience, known as Traditional Ecological Knowledge (TEK), presents itself. Herein, we provide brief reflections on both the practice and reverberating impacts of reciprocal restoration in natural resources management and STEM education. We encourage our readers to reflect on their practice of reciprocity, or lack thereof, in their personal, professional, research, and educational endeavors.

As we explore the roles of reciprocity and TEK in restoration, it is helpful to examine the meaning of our work and center our discussion. In this regard, before we view TEK as another resource or set of methods for potential mining, appropriation, and/or personal exploit, a reflection on our embodied paradigms and worldviews is essential. Kimmerer, for example, states that "reciprocal restoration is grounded in a positive feedback relationship between cultural revitalization and land restoration. Revitalizing language and culture protects and disseminates TEK, and builds relationships of reciprocity and respect, all of which are good for the land. What's good for the land is good for the people" (2011, 258). Valuing reciprocity, therefore, reaches far deeper than merely supporting environmental restoration in any narrow sense that is exclusive of human community and human relationships.

Reciprocity may begin with self-restoration, which requires the understanding of oneself in the context of one's community and the broader political and global contexts. This begins by situating ourselves in the greater context of giving honor to that which our communities, families, and parents afforded us through their sacrifices, so we could succeed both personally and professionally. The realization that our very self is an impossibility without our kin, centers what we do and how we think. As much as possible, nothing is done for the sole sake of the self without genuine effort to increase the collective good for our communities and beyond.

Reciprocity continues with the reconciliation or, at the very least, the civil interfacing of diverse worldviews and value systems. Reconciling Traditional upbringings in a Tribal context with colonial STEM training and its value systems is often a great struggle. The struggle begins in leaving our communities behind to fulfill the call by our Elders to complete a formal education as an act of reciprocity to our communities. The struggle continues as we encounter colonial institutions that understand our values and worldviews as simplistic and unsophisticated. Upon returning home, having for years clashed with a western value system antithetical to our own, we find that the struggle continues as our Tribes continue to restore our ways of life on the land. In particular, the struggle to restore native species and access to homelands on and off the reservation while negotiating with white settler landowners in a racialized landscape can be soul-sucking and even dangerous. Furthermore, as professionals and mentors within our

communities, we often encourage our youth to enter natural resources pro-
fessions and seek STEM education, knowing well that the institution will
only frustrate and fail them.

Indigenous students of the ecological and environmental sciences often
find themselves in contexts that were not designed with them in mind.
These foreign Euro-centric systems of knowledge (e.g., western-based
disciplines of biology and ecology) are fundamentally exclusive of alternative worldviews and epistemologies (ways of knowing). Settler institutions
(e.g., university systems) have historically understood Indigenous Peoples
as uncivilized *savages*,[1] ignorant of the white man's god and his perfect
and eternal design of nature. The place-based, relational approach of the
Native has no place in the positivism that is embedded within western
understandings of reality. Despite a vast literature highlighting the importance of cross-cultural exchanges of knowledges and value systems (Russell
1948; Van Doren 1992; Hall and Tandon 2017), the academy continues
to lack any deeper sense of reciprocity and, therefore, maintains its colonial footing. However, the complexity of modern environmental problems
and their many social repercussions demand adaptive reciprocity between
knowledge systems. Such reciprocity requires interfacing with diverse value
systems and culturally embedded, place-based Knowledge systems such as
TEK (Keane 2008; Deloria et al. 2018). Efforts must therefore be made to
unsettle western academia to the extent that diverse knowledge systems are
braided together to find solutions to complex local to global issues.

One way to begin this process is in the classroom. Academic institutions may design programs and persistent funding mechanisms to provide
STEM instructors with the necessary training to create curriculum and
instruction informed by Indigenous Ways of Knowing (IWOK), including TEK. When IWOK is missing, Indigenous scientists and instructors
must make up the difference by relying on their Indigenous Knowledges
and cultural training or through IWOK-based education within and from
their communities. Culturally relevant curriculum developed by or taught
by Indigenous faculty is the optimum method to interface western science
with IWOK and potentially weave the two knowledge systems for the benefit of Tribal youth, Indigenous communities, and our allies. We must tread

---

1 The term *savage* is derived from the French *sauvage*, "wild"; from the Latin *silvaticus*, "of
the woods." It was historically utilized by imperialistic nations to degrade Indigenous communities as people who were vicious, violent, and brutal, and thus needed to be controlled
or eradicated, as did the wilderness that was home to them.

lightly, though, on a pathway of reciprocity with constant awareness and considerations of Tribal sovereignty, education, and science to reconnect intergenerational gaps caused by colonization. This is the call from our ancestors, Elders, and communities.

Another way to begin the restoration process through reciprocity is in the field. In our work with Tribal communities, an enduring quality of reciprocity is that, collectively, we continue to center the Tribe's current priorities as well as long-term vision for land and community restoration. Though some government agencies have attempted to consider TEK in their restoration work for example (see US EPA 2017, "Considering Traditional Ecological Knowledge (TEK) during the Cleanup Process"), these attempts are often limited in terms of their ambition and specificity. We propose a more robust and adaptive, whole-community framework that includes practical principles and opportunities for TEK to become central in fieldwork/restoration. This framework includes the following principles, which, when practiced, are mutually restorative:

- **Understanding Vision, Assets, and Vulnerabilities.** In order to understand the current needs and long-term vision of the community, put in the work and time required for genuine relationship development.
- **Promoting Health and Well-Being.** From an Indigenous perspective, there is no such thing as ecosystem restoration without human restoration. Prioritize the community's physical and mental safety and health in your work.
- **Protecting Environmental Quality.** Understanding the history of colonization will help you understand why Tribes tend to live in degraded environments and how your work can help mitigate that. This will often require some policy work and, sometimes, legal proceedings.
- **Strengthening Economy, Infrastructure, and Technology.** Tribal communities stand out historically in terms of their adaptability. In the modern age, everyone needs functional economies that serve their populations, safe and efficient infrastructure, and technology that addresses needs and problems. Shape your work in such a way that it has positive impacts on these long-term needs.
- **Enhancing Self-Determination, Leadership, and Partnerships.** Never approach a Tribal community with your priorities in mind. Tribal Nations have been fighting for self-determination for centuries, and

basic human dignity affords everyone the right to self-determination. Moreover, the fact that Indigenous Nations across the world are doing incredible restoration work, with virtually no resources, is evidence that we should all be following their lead.

- **Preserving Cultural Heritage.** While protecting the environment on multiple fronts, Tribes are also fighting to protect their culturally significant spaces. Combining ecological restoration with the protection of cultural sites is a strategy many researchers and natural resources managers are implementing in their work with Tribes. Look into it.

- **Emphasizing Community Engagement.** Make sure the community is always invited to participate in your work with them. If you need people in the field collecting data, invite our youth. If you need to hire people to enter data or run samples, try to hire within the community.

In this brief reflection, we have attempted to (re)seed, nurture, and regenerate TEK consciousness through community resilience and reciprocal restoration in collaborations with Tribes, with a focus on natural resources management and STEM education. The current state of ecosystems, economies, education, health, and the like, in North America and throughout the world, require solidarity toward the common good among disparate communities and their different worldviews and value systems. The complex problem of climate change, and its many economic, health, and ecological repercussions, was caused by man's isolation and dehumanization of man. TEK teaches us that solidarity may be most deeply experienced in our shared humanity, our shared home (Mother Earth), our shared need for basic necessities, our shared love of beauty, and our shared struggle for a dignified existence. In a good way we encourage all to move forward, knowing reciprocity is a shared responsibility, in some cases a burden, that conditions us for a more resilient future.

11
WHAT WAS TAUGHT TO ME

SAM SCHIMMEL (TRANSCRIBED BY LILY PAINTER)

Positionality Statements

Schimmel: Kenaitze Indian Tribal member and Siberian Yupik; raised in Kenai, Alaska, and the Native Village of Gambell, St. Lawrence Island, Alaska (my own a Tribal lands); now attending school on Piscataway and Pamunkey Lands; subsistence hunter and fisherman; Georgetown University, Law Center, JD (Juris Doctor) candidate.

Painter: Kiowa Tribe of Oklahoma and Citizen of the Winnebago Tribe of Nebraska. Raised on Kiowa, Comanche, and Apache Land Reservation in Anadarko, Oklahoma.

Reciprocity is a promise, the promise that holds our communities together.

The promise is that my Elders will teach me what was taught to them by their Elders. The promise is that I will use that Knowledge to take care of them. The promise that we will one day, through living by the rules of that Knowledge, become like them in that we too will pass on to our children and grandchildren the Knowledge that our Elders passed on to us.

This cycle of intergenerational strength and reliance is the reciprocity that our communities are built upon. This is how our people have existed since time immemorial. It's the steady hum of culture and Tradition passed on and improved from each generation to the next but never so inexorably changed as to be unrecognizable. The changes that our young people bring into our communities are tempered by the wisdom of those who have been around far longer than us. My great grandmother, Estelle, was born in the 1920s and raised by her grandparents who were born in the 1860s: a time before missionaries or cargo ships, a time when the only white people who came to our island were Yankee whalers hunting the same animals we always relied on for food. The Traditional Knowledge (e.g., Traditional Ecological

Knowledge) that she passed down to me is something that stretches back to a time before contact. I remember her talking about growing up and being a little girl. About the expectations that were placed on our young people and about the rules that had to be followed. Rigid, unbending structures passed down from generation to generation and only edited at the corners. She talked about how the role of men in our community was to ensure that everybody had enough to eat, the role of women was to let men think that they were in control, and the role of those in between was just that: to be in between.

She talked about how not everybody in the community needed to know how to do everything. Not every person needed to know every single Tradition. But how everyone needed to know something and to do something. She talked about the importance of good leadership. Leadership that listened and leadership that ensured everyone not only had what they needed to survive but what they needed to thrive. Leadership that knew the importance of Tradition and had a steady hand. In those times spent sitting on the floor around a cardboard box, flattened and piled high with muktuk, she taught me these things. Now today when it comes to Indigenous pathways into the future, we must remember these teachings, the idea that youth are to work, that Elders are to teach, and that one should not be cast aside because they do not know everything.

That leadership means the insurance of mutual prosperity and that our continued thriving—our continued ability to thrive—is rooted in the reciprocity that we have with our Elders.

This is what has been taught to me.

12

RELATED TO ʻĀINA
The Reciprocity of Living with Place
ʻALOHI NAKACHI AND KAIKEA NAKACHI

Positionality Statements

ʻAlohi Nakachi: Kanaka Maoli with mixed heritage; raised on the Kona coast of Hawaiʻi Island; currently residing on the island of Oʻahu; University of Hawaiʻi at Mānoa Department of Natural Resources and Environmental Management.

Kaikea Nakachi: Kanaka Maoli with mixed heritage; born and raised on the Kona coast of Hawaiʻi Island; independent scholar focused on Native Hawaiian and biocultural research management.

A Hawaiian Worldview—He ʻĀina Hōʻihi

Hawaiian survival and prosperity on remote islands, as well as the development of our Knowledge systems, religion, attitude, and morality, stem from our worldview. In this Hawaiian worldview our kānaka (human) life cycle is intimately woven into the seen and unseen components of the island environment. This complex weaving of the visible and invisible connections between kānaka and ʻāina (land) has continued to develop for generations. Throughout time, this process has reflected a system of reciprocity in which our understandings and deepening connections to natural phenomena shape our Traditional Ecological Knowledge (TEK) and practices, which in turn, strengthen our ties to ʻāina; thus, further weaving kānaka together with place. The root of this complex weave is aloha, which can be defined in many ways. One of our ancestors, Pilahi Paki, said, "Aloha is the word my kupunas (Ancestor/Elder) attributed to the universe. Aloha is the universe." In what would later be codified as the Aloha Spirit Law (HI Rev Stat §5-7.5a), she also defined aloha as an acronym with the following meanings:

A: Akahai – kindness to be expressed with a feeling of tenderness
L: Lōkahi – unity to be expressed with a feeling of harmony
O: ʻOluʻolu – agreeable to be expressed with a feeling of pleasantness
H: Haʻahaʻa – humility to be expressed with a feeling of modesty
A: Ahonui – patience to be applied with perseverance

Pilahi Paki also said, "Aloha is something that is there. We can feel it but we cannot touch it. Aloha is a way of life because it takes your heart. The five ways to bring aloha out are: your eyes, your spoken words, your hands, your hearing, and your breath" (Hawaiian Civic Club of Wahiawā Meeting Minutes, November 9, 1962). Individuals who live in Hawaiʻi are unwittingly doing some of these things on a daily basis and are thereby participating in the sacredness of reciprocity (kapu aloha) (Kanakaʻole Kanahele et al. 2017). Knowing our place in Hawaiʻi and our connections or our genealogy to these places helps to reveal and understand our aloha to place (Kealiikanakaoleohaililani et al. 2018).

As the complex definition of aloha above shows, Hawaiian language is important in articulating a Hawaiian worldview. Many layers of meanings within words and within our belief system often do not translate well to other languages and can be lost within conveyance (Kaʻanehe 2020). The word "reciprocity" does not exist in the Hawaiian dictionary. However, like aloha, reciprocity is rooted in our language, as it is foundational to our relationships with place and others. The closest literal translation we may have to reciprocity is a phrase, "kekahi i kekahi," which means "from one to another." An additional Hawaiian word that could be used for reciprocity is hōʻihi, which can be defined as "to treat as sacred" (Hoihi—Wehe[2]wiki[2] Hawaiian Language Dictionaries). Pilahi Paki described that "the language of my ancestors has three very distinct characteristics. They define the poetic, literal, and esoteric aspects in language—each characteristic connotating and defining mind and heart in spirit." (Speech to the International Society of Ministers at Mauna Kea, January 23, 1984). The literal, poetic, and esoteric uses of hōʻihi, aloha, and reciprocity may help illuminate the sacredness of ʻāina and how our belief systems, our TEK, our actions in place, and our genealogy to place are rooted in this sacredness.

Hawaiians know that we come from ʻāina, we are related to ʻāina, and we are the youngest members of this interrelated family (Beckwith 1972; Kameʻeleihiwa 1992). In our creation stories, the genesis and interconnectedness of our interrelated family are explained as humans being the last-born members (Beckwith 1972; Kikiloi and Graves 2010). Our akua (elemental deities) and ʻaumakua (family deities) are embodiments of elemental forces, plants, animals, rocks, and places (Kameʻeleihiwa 1992; Kikiloi and Graves 2010; Kikiloi et al. 2017; Kurashima et al. 2018). Knowing this genealogy and understanding the inherent sacredness of ʻāina is foundational to a Hawaiian worldview that sets forth a need for respect and reciprocity in our interactions and practices with ʻāina (Andrade 2013; hoʻomanawanui 2012; Kealiikanakaoleohaililani et al. 2018; Kikiloi and Graves 2010; Kurashima et al. 2018). By viewing the environment as kin, the subsequent reciprocal aspects of practice by Hawaiians and our worldview create a philosophy called aloha ʻāina (Andrade 2013; Beamer et al. 2021). Aloha ʻāina articulates and embraces aloha to place. Our worldview and the philosophy of aloha ʻāina were woven into TEK, food systems, land divisions, management practices, and governance systems before Anglo-European contact in Hawaiʻi (Kameʻeleihiwa 1992; Kikiloi et al. 2017; Kurashima et al. 2018; Winter et al. 2018). In doing so, ʻāina became paramount and central to a Hawaiian way of life that requires the elevation of ʻāina and the understanding of the root of reciprocity in all interactions and practices with ʻāina. Our ways of life also connect our governance, belief systems, TEK, lifestyles, and practices and thereby result in flourishing social, cultural, and ecological systems (Kameʻeleihiwa 1992).

In this chapter we first outline some examples of Traditional practices that highlight reciprocity-based management practices achieved through Hawaiian worldviews, TEK, and relationships to place that enabled ʻāina momona (environmental abundance). We then go into some of the obstacles to Hawaiians today that stem from continued impacts from settler colonialism and affect access and ability to show aloha to place. Finally, we discuss how, despite these obstacles, Hawaiians, including our family, find ways to continue reciprocal practices and show aloha to place.

Aloha ʻĀina Traditional Practices

Hawaiian worldviews, intimate relationships, and Knowledges of ʻāina allow for the development and successful implementation of reciprocity-based management praxes, such as rotating fishing seasons, and the vertical and horizontal land divisions and food production within them, as well as the practice of taking care of patron sharks. These aloha ʻāina practices equally benefited our People and ʻāina. Their continued refinement and use over generations allowed for a potential state of resource abundance referred to as ʻāina momona (Andrade 2013; Beamer et al. 2021; Gon et al. 2018; Kurashima et al. 2019; Winter et al. 2018).

NĀ IʻA KAPU—TRADITIONAL FISHING REGULATIONS

One way that Hawaiians were able to fish and thrive with minimal impacts to fisheries was through rotating fishing seasons of two important species: ʻōpelu (mackerel scad, *Decapterus* spp.) and aku (skipjack tuna, *Katsuwonus pelamis*). In this system, ʻōpelu are actively fed (hānai) in their natural aggregation areas (koʻa) during the restricted (kapu) season, which is associated with their spawning period (Winter et al. 2018; Maly and Maly 2003). When the ʻōpelu are kapu, the aku fishery is unrestricted (noa), which compounds its conservation effect. During this time, ʻōpelu are being fed and not being fished, and subsequently, their predators are being harvested, which simultaneously reduces ʻōpelu natural mortality. Families have assigned koʻa to hānai during the kapu season for ʻōpelu. If they fulfill that responsibility, they are allowed to fish within any of the koʻa during noa season after first harvesting from the one they tended. If, however, a family does not fulfill their responsibility to hānai during their designated koʻa in the kapu season, they lose their privilege of fishing for ʻōpelu in the following noa season. When the kapu is lifted for ʻōpelu fishing, the six-month kapu for aku fishing begins and allows for population recovery of that species (Kamakau 1976; Maly and Maly 2003; Winter et al. 2018). In these practices, reciprocity is maintained through the care and application of hanai and kilo (observation). These practices elevate Hawaiian TEK, which is then applied to ensure proper restrictions are in place and followed so that fish populations thrive and abundant harvests can be sustained.

MEA ʻAI MOKU—LAND DIVISIONS AND FOOD PRODUCTION

Additionally, Hawaiian worldviews, intimate reciprocal connections with ʻāina, and the resulting TEK can be seen in the design and essence of forested landscape (wao) and seascape divisions (kai) listed in tables 12.1 and 12.2, and their integration of moku (social-ecological regions). Wao and kai zones span across the moku to vertically influence the management of ahupuaʻa (individual social-ecological communities) while horizontally connecting ahupuaʻa within a moku (figure 12.1) to enable coordinated management of important biocultural resources (Friedlander, Shackeroff, and Kittinger 2013; Winter et al. 2018). This design allows reciprocal practices to be integrated into resource management in Hawaiʻi to minimize impacts

Vertical divisions
for system-based
management
within social-
ecological
communities
(ahupua'a).

Horizontal
management of
population
dynamics within
social-ecological
zones (wao/kai)
across social-
ecological regions
(moku).

```
                    wao ı akua
                    wao ı kele
                    wao ı nāhele
                    wao ı lā'au
                    wao ı kānaka
    ahupua'a   ahupua'a   ahupua'a   ahupua'a
                    Moku
                ka po'ina nalu
                  kai lūhe'e
                  kai koholā
                   kai 'ele
                   kai uli
                  kai pualena
        kai pōpolohua-a-Kāne-i-kahiki
```

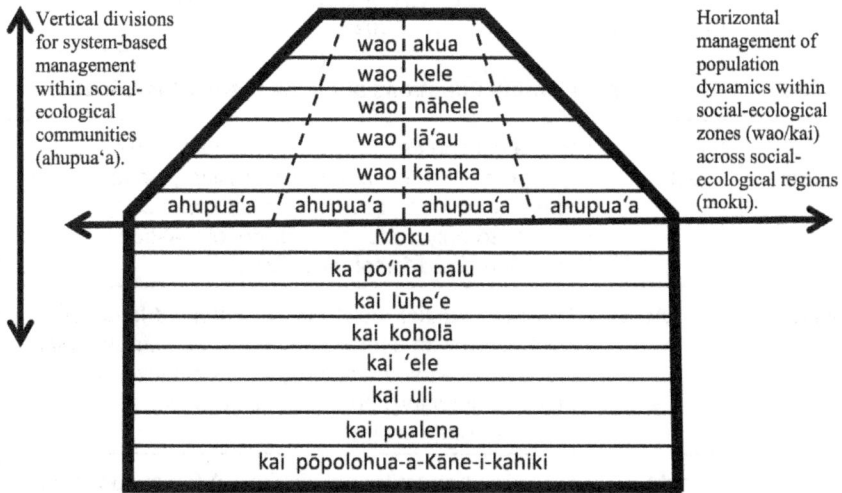

Figure 12.1. A schematic model depicting the layout of a single social-ecological region (moku) including the structure of both social-ecological zones (wao and kai, designated horizontally) and of social-ecological community boundaries (ahupua'a, designated vertically) to convey the framework for the biocultural resource management of the moku system in the Hawaiian archipelago in the precontact period. Figure adapted from Winter et al. (2018).

on 'āina and all that 'āina represents to Hawaiians. The vertical divisions of land established societal boundaries, managerial hierarchies, and duties based on status and occupation. The horizontal zones are generalizations of the resources and ecosystem types that have certain conditions for care, interaction, restriction, and occupation/practice (such as engineering, architecture, botany, medicine, fishing, farming, and sports). Reciprocity was rooted not only in management of 'āina but also in social institutions. The vertical divisions of social management hierarchies ensured that restrictions and practices were properly followed within horizontal zones to ensure ecosystems and food systems flourished. Within the social hierarchies, all beings had a close kinship. Leaders had a duty to care for both 'āina and our People; and with care and respect shown, the People of the land had more motivation to ensure the continuation of 'āina and food systems and care for leaders (Kame'eleihiwa 1992; Kurashima et al. 2018). If reciprocity with 'āina and People were not maintained, then ecosystems declined, food systems suffered, and the People of the land could leave to seek other leadership (vertical divisions) (Kame'eleihiwa 1992; Kurashima et al. 2018).

Land divisions and coordinated reciprocal-based management have historical rooting in Hawaiian Traditions. For example, before contact, less

Table 12.1. List of potential terrestrial social-ecological zones (wao) and their management implications (based on Table 2 from Winter et al. 2020).

Zone	Translation	Primary Functions and Management Implications
wao akua	Sacred forest	Perpetual source population for endemic biodiversity. Designated as "sacred forest," making it a restricted forest zone for a native-only plant community, accessed only under strict protocols. Associated with montane cloud forest, elfin forest.
wao kele	Wet forest	Maximize aquifer recharge. An untended forest zone associated with core watershed areas (remote upland, wet forest below the clouds) left as a native-dominant plant community. Impractical access except for transit-through via trails.
wao nāhele	Remote forest	Maximize habitat for native birds. A forest zone that was minimally tended (generally remote upland, mesic forest) and left as a native-dominant plant community. Impractical for access except by bird catchers and feather gatherers.
wao l ʻau	Agro-forest	Maximize the availability of timber and non-timber forest products. A zone allowing for the management of a highly tended forest via an integrated agroforestry (native and introduced plants) regime: Native and introduced hardwood timber, introduced food trees, native and introduced biofuel sources, maximization of native biodiversity for non-timber forest products, cordage and weaving material, medicine and dyes, and ceremonial and adornment plants.
wao kānaka	Habitation zone	Landscape-scale augmentation to maximize the availability of food, medicine, and housing. A zone allowing for (but not mandating) the conversion of forest to field agriculture, aquaculture, habitation, recreation, and/or temple worship. Native and introduced trees tended, individually or in groves, for regular and specific cultural services.

than 15 percent of Hawaiʻiʻs total land area was utilized to provide 100 percent of human needs to a population estimated to be near 800,000 Peoples (Gon et al. 2018). The use of limited land areas demonstrates successful sustainability and resource management praxes that were made possible via the operationalization of Hawaiian worldviews that regard ʻāina as familial and ancestral (Gon et al. 2018). Additionally, it is estimated that before contact, approximately 100,789 hectares (ha) of land could support Indigenous agriculture, resulting in the estimated potential of more than 1.02 million

Table 12.2. List of potential marine social-ecological zones (kai) and their management implications (adapted from Winter et al. 2018; Maly and Maly 2003).

Zone	Translation	Primary Functions and Management Implications
ka poʻina nalu	Surf-break sea	Fringing reef with breaking waves that often represented the seaward boundary of an ahupuaʻa. Terrestrial nutrient input, sunlight penetrating shallow depths, and oxygen from wave energy allows abundant primary production that supports a rich reef ecosystem. Strategic placement and management of walled fishponds allowed these processes to provide easily harvested fish while still contributing to replenishment of surrounding reefs and reducing need to harvest from them.
kai lūheʻe	Octopus lure sea	Shallow shelf of varying benthic topography utilized for fishing using octopus lures. Continued environment of various shallow marine habitats providing niche space for a wide variety of marine flora and fauna whose harvest for food, medicine, tools, materials, and ceremony was controlled by the konohiki of each ahupuaʻa directly shoreward.
kai koholā	Whale sea	Section of the sea with submerged volcanic shelves that is frequented by humpback whales (Megaptera novaeangliae). This intermediary zone exhibits the limit of photosynthetic benthic species and reef habitat and transitions to deeper more pelagic habitat. The potential for upwelling from these submerged shelves provides nutrients that allow the flourishing of transecting reef and pelagic habitats. Potential fishing grounds, but also a respected area due to seasonal presence of whales (Koholā).
kai ʻele	Black sea	Deep-sea area, possibly between volcanic shelves. Continued pelagic environment with potential for upwelling and a shift in planktonic primary productions supporting a large biomass of pelagic species including planktonic forms of reef species. Important seasonal fisheries are also controlled by Traditional customs and regulations.
kai uli	Dark sea	Deep-sea area, possibly beyond the islands' volcanic foundations. Continued pelagic environment with some potential for upwelling and increased daily vertical migration (dvm) of pelagic species. While fishing is potentially productive, the distance from shore limits use to infrequent excursions.

Zone	Translation	Primary Functions and Management Implications
kai pualena	Dawn light sea	Sea along the horizon that gets the first yellow touch of the sun's morning light. Total pelagic zone dominated by dvm of pelagic species. Similar potential for productive harvest, but distance is even more of a limiting factor on use.
kai pōpolohua-a-Kāne-i-kahiki	Purplish sea of the travels of Kāne	Distant, dark, and deep-sea area beyond the sight of land associated with the travels of the deity Kāne. Division of the vast ocean (moananuiākea) mostly visited and fished only during long distance voyaging trips.

metric tons (mt) of food per year, or 1.34 billion kilocalories annually (Kurashima et al. 2019). These estimates could have supported a theoretical maximum population of more than 1.2 million people each year (Kurashima et al. 2019). However, these estimates do not include animal proteins from fishing, fishpond aquaculture, or livestock, which accounted for about 22 percent of the Traditional Hawaiian diet (Kurashima et al. 2019).

Before contact, the annual yield of fishponds could have approached nearly 907 mt of animal protein per year (Cobb 1905; Davidson et al. 2018; Teneva, Schemmel, and Kittinger 2018). These loko iʻa (fishpond aquaculture systems) represent another example of reciprocity-based management of biocultural resources that are made possible by the integration of Hawaiian worldviews, intimate relationships, and Knowledge of ʻāina (TEK). Native Hawaiians used this integration to develop Indigenous engineering practices and thereby create walled loko iʻa that harnessed natural processes and enhanced fish stocks to achieve ʻāina momona. In doing so, Hawaiians could have significantly large harvests while also providing protection to surrounding nearshore coral reefs from potential ecosystem disservices (Winter et al. 2020). Loko iʻa, like most aquaculture systems, requires a lot of care, observation, and stewardship. Sturdy barriers and healthy ecosystems within the system are needed to ensure fish are abundant outside and within the loko. The consequences of shifting away from Hawaiian reciprocity-based management systems into a system in which land and resources are seen as economic commodities has clearly resulted in a loss of native habitats, sustainability, and self-sufficiency (Beamer et al. 2021; Gon et al. 2018). Today, many loko iʻa have been destroyed by development, or left in disarray due to environmental degradation and legal and financial barriers (Keala, Hollyer, and Castro 2007; Pizarro 2021). The few loko i'a that remain today are largely maintained by many different education, visitor, and volunteer programs that work to reinvigorate TEK, aloha to place, and reciprocal place-based management (Wyban 2020).

KAHU MANŌ—SHARK KEEPERS

The genealogy (mo'okū'auhau) of our family ('ohana) includes the burden of responsibility (kuleana) for taking care of patron sharks (kahu manō). Traditionally, each locality along the coast had kahu manō whose practice resulted in intimate understandings of individual sharks and their appearances, behaviors, mo'okū'auhau, and home ranges (Beckwith 1917; Emerson 1892; Nakachi 2021). Our practices of care (mālama) allowed for coexistence and benefits that extended beyond just mutual gifts. For example, the ecosystem services that healthy shark populations provide (Barley, Meekan, and Meeuwig 2017; Sandin et al. 2008) were understood and achieved through intimate reciprocal Traditional Hawaiian practice of kahu manō. However, the practice of kahu manō, the abundance of shark populations, and the relationship between man and manō and the TEK gained from it have been affected by colonization, imperialism, capitalism, extractive tourism, and environmental degradation (Friedlander and DeMartini 2002; Nakachi 2021).

Traditionally, 'āina momona was achieved and maintained through continued practices of aloha 'āina such as, but not limited to, the examples above, as well as careful moku management on landscape and seascape scales (Winter et al. 2018). With 'āina momona, it is possible to generate a surplus of abundance that is more than enough for the People to thrive while not degrading the natural environment. While it is certainly desirable to recapture 'āina momona on a pae'āina (archipelago-wide) scale, several factors have imposed themselves over the last 240 years of post-contact history that greatly complicate simple solutions.

OBSTACLES IN RECIPROCITY

There are many obstacles to maintaining reciprocity in Hawai'i, including increasing difficulties to just spend time in place, show aloha to place, and maintain practices of aloha 'āina. These obstacles stem mainly from foreign contact, influence, and continued impacts of settler colonialism. While there are many obstacles and impacts, for brevity, we highlight only a few in this section. Specifically, we discuss examples of environmental impacts, governance obstacles, and educational obstacles.

ENVIRONMENTAL IMPACTS

One serious impact has been the compounding and cascading environmental impacts and land changes that stem from development and invasive species. For example, the introduction of nonnative plants and animals brought by foreigners has influenced and impeded agricultural success via competition, predation, and pathologies (Gon et al. 2018). Irreversible land developments have displaced many areas of formerly rich ecosystems and/or agricultural production, leading to vulnerability and degradation with the continued trend of human overpopulation and the anticipated changes in climate (Gon et al. 2018). As briefly mentioned earlier, reciprocal management practices and aloha ʻāina practices are continually affected by environmental impacts and land changes. Loko iʻa restoration practices are hindered as they deal with removing invasive species and navigating development impacts (e.g., changing water flows, erosion, and sedimentation) (Keala, Hollyer, and Castro 2007; Pizarro 2021; Wyban 2020). As land changes and invasive species continue to dominate, the ancestral footprints of our Native Peoples, species, and our sources of TEK are literally being erased.

GOVERNMENTAL OBSTACLES

Modern management and governmental systems create an abundance of obstacles to Native Hawaiians. Many obstacles to Hawaiians, especially settler colonialism, continue to impact Hawaiians as we become a minority in our own lands, and social values and decisions of place are no longer reflecting our worldview. Furthermore, management and governance are now dominated by Anglo-American[1] worldviews that produce many social inequities (e.g., displacement, power imbalances, increased poverty, economic imbalances, and incarceration or ineffective carceral punishments (Bennett et al. 2021; de Silva 2022; Fisk 2021; McGill et al. 2022; Reyes 2018). Hawaiians are disproportionately affected by social inequities as the Hawaiian population is outnumbered by other ethnicities in Hawaiʻi, underrepresented in management, and endures higher rates of disease, poverty, under-education, and incarceration (Andrasik et al. 2022; Kaʻanehe 2020; Kanaʻiaupuni, Malone, and Ishibashi 2005; Moy, Sallis, and David 2010;

---

1 Anglo-American is a term that refers to American and European worldviews that are often referred to as "western." I learned this term from Kumu Kamana Beamer, who articulated the importance of place and relationality in a Hawaiian way of life. What lies west of Hawaiʻi are not the peoples or worldviews to which we are referring. Worldviews and peoples that are important to highlight as the root harms to Native Hawaiians are Americans and those with similar worldviews; as such I refer to them as Anglo-American.

Reyes 2018). In addition to perpetuating social inequities, contemporary governance systems hinder Hawaiian management of our own lands and our abilities to show aloha to place (Osorio 2001; Vaughan and Caldwell 2015). Hawaiians today are forced to fight in legal systems, which are dominated by foreigners and foreign ideals, for aloha ʻāina and to protect our sacred resources (Ahia 2020; Fisk 2021; MacKenzie et al. 2015; Osorio 2001; hoʻomanawanui 2013; Ayers, Kittinger, and Vaughan 2018; Vaughan and Caldwell 2015). In these systems, foreign values and self-interest are raised above TEK and the need for reciprocal practices.

EDUCATIONAL OBSTACLES

Further problematic are the obstacles that exist from Hawaiian places and stories being perpetuated by non-Hawaiian voices (de Silva 2022; hoʻomanawanui 2013) and how education is dominated by colonial structures and Indigenous erasure (de Silva 2022; Reyes 2018). Narratives of Hawaiian history or places being told by non-Hawaiians, particularly in public settings, lend credibility to the story and the source even if in situations when they are inaccurate (de Silva 2022; hoʻomanawanui 2013). Such situations create harm as these narratives and sources are pitted against Native sources and are often in formats or settings more digestible, accessible, or popularized because they are often aligned with Anglo-American values, sources, and methods (de Silva 2022; hoʻomanawanui 2013). As education systems are also suited to Anglo-American values, expectations, methods, and socialization processes, those with conflicting cultures have difficulty functioning within these systems (Kaʻanehe 2020). TEK, place-based education, and reciprocal practices are not popularized in public schools that instead normalize and shape students to serve the economic interests of the state (Kaʻanehe 2020). Educational difficulties make it more difficult to finish and continue school, limit opportunities, and add to the susceptibility of financial hardships.

Following foreign contact, many issues have arisen that have created obstacles to Hawaiian lifeways and our abilities to connect and perpetuate Hawaiian worldviews. Hawaiian lives and lifestyles have been threatened by foreign diseases, colonization, imperialism, capitalism, detrimental development, destructive tourism, and environmental degradation (Beamer 2014; Goodyear-Kaʻopua, Hussey, and Wright 2014; Kameʻeleihiwa 1992; Osorio 2001; Trask 1999). As foreign populations increase, development grows, tourists take up more space and resources, governance favors monetary ventures, and all of these subsequent harms make it more and more difficult for Native Hawaiians to connect with and maintain reciprocal practices with ʻāina. Showing aloha to place has become increasingly difficult as just access to place is hindered either from development, overuse of areas, or hazards (e.g., environmental degradation, pollution, and changes in climate). Additionally, Hawaiians remain susceptible to financial woes and high costs of living, which have resulted in many of our People moving away from the islands or having to work many jobs (which also create barriers to showing aloha to place). While obstacles continue to compound and increase, Hawaiians continually seek and fight for these places, practices, and relationships that are foundational to our spiritual survival.

Maintaining Reciprocity Today

Perpetuating or, in some cases, reinstituting Traditional aloha ʻāina practices in today's Hawaiian world have continued to successfully conserve biocultural resources. Coastal locations under community-based management with customary reciprocal stewardship practices in place have exhibited equal or higher fish biomass than no-take marine protected areas (Friedlander, Shackeroff, and Kittinger 2013). Hawaiian communities (e.g., Hāʻena, Kaʻūpūlehu, Miloliʻi, Heʻeia, Moʻomomi) continue to implement contemporary applications of Traditional reciprocal management practices with conservation measures and restoration projects and in various stages of planning (Ayers et al. 2018; Ayers and Kittinger 2014; Delevaux et al. 2018; Friedlander, Shackeroff, and Kittinger 2013; Vaughan and Caldwell 2015; Winter et al. 2018). Throughout Hawaiʻi, many Hawaiians maintain reciprocal practices and aloha ʻāina through formal (e.g., educational groups, restoration practices, co-management) and informal processes. Below, we discuss how our family works to maintain reciprocal practices and aloha ʻāina.

KA MOʻOLELO O MĀUA—OUR STORY

On a personal level, our family seeks to interact with ʻāina to connect to our ancestors, family, and spirituality. We have been taught by our various kumu (teacher/Knowledge source) that the ʻāina, the land we walk on, the rocks, sand, dirt, water, plants, and life that bloom and thrive from ʻāina hold our ancestors and keep the moʻolelo of place. ʻĀina remembers the footsteps that tread on the surface and the hands that touch them. To this day, ʻāina holds the energy and the mana (spiritual power) of those touches. One day, when we are long gone, 'āina will still remember us by our touches and footsteps. Holding such an understanding is why it is critical for us to think about intentions, mentality, and/or our head space when interacting with 'āina. Sometimes our intentions can be mindless, where we are just existing and maybe just passing through areas without giving them much thought or connection. But with experience, age, and understanding, we realize that in every interaction with 'āina, we should think about our intentions and what energy we are putting forward.

Growing up, interacting with 'āina, and being in place, our dad and our grandparents would remind us of our intentions and to be aware of our thoughts. For example, this could include the practices of not saying out loud that we are going fishing and not allowing our minds to think too much or too hard about catching fish: otherwise, the fish would know. Other examples extend into thinking about our energies and thoughts when interacting with the ocean and wildlife. Even too much excited energy could sometimes be felt as a negative force. We were taught from a young age about the importance of energy, intentions, and the reciprocity of our actions, knowing that 'āina could feel them and reciprocate by giving back the same to us. However, this didn't really sink in for us until after graduating college. This isn't because college gave us a profound understanding, but rather, after graduating college, we experienced a loss of kupuna living in place with us. This loss made our memories and the memories of 'āina that much heavier and more precious to us.

Continuing reciprocal practices and finding time to be present in 'āina connects us to those we have lost. We can feel the mana of those before us and we can pass our mana on to the place. We can continue the mo'olelo of place by taking time to understand the elemental forces that connect everything, learning how these processes are foundational to natural systems, learning to coexist and live within these systems, and taking time to learn stories of place and tell the stories of place (ho'omanawanui 2012; Kanahele-Mossman and Karides 2021).

Conclusion

Taking time to be in 'āina is important in allowing us to remember our memories, learn the mo'olelo of place, maintain our spirituality, and understand the sacredness of 'āina (Andrade 2013; ho'omanawanui 2012). In every interaction we have in 'āina, we are connecting to our kupuna, our ancestors, our akua, and our nonhuman 'ohana and ancestors. These interactions and our relationship with 'āina are threatened as development and land changes devastates ancestral footprints; mo'olelo are altered by foreign voices; tourism and capitalism ravage resources, impede practices and values; and malihini (newcomer) self-interest is elevated over reciprocity. Despite the constant threats, we find ways to maintain our relationships with 'āina and ensure reciprocity continues. While we continue to regain and/or add to TEK and draw inspiration from the Traditional practices and biocultural resource management systems born out of the Hawaiian worldview, we recognize that simply reinstituting them in a contemporary setting is not enough. The foundation of these practices and systems is the reciprocal and intimate relationship kānaka share with the land and sea, and successful reimplementation requires rekindling this relationship where it has been lost and regularly maintaining it in perpetuity. As we continue to find places or ways to continue elevating our TEK and our customary practices, we advocate for our places and our values, and we do whatever we can to perpetuate our culture and ensure Hawaiian survival.

13

RECIPROCAL SOVEREIGNTY
Traditional Ecological Knowledge and a Commonwealth of Ecological Dignity

JOSEPH GAZING WOLF

Positionality Statement

Maternal descendant of the Amazigh and Nubian communities of Egypt with paternal Lakota heritage of the Northern Plains; raised and lived on Amazigh and Nubian territories in Egypt and on the Standing Rock Sioux Nation in the Dakotas; Arizona State University, School of Life Sciences, Senior Global Futures Scientist; Heritage Lands Collective, Executive Director.

Introduction

In this chapter, I explore Indigenous reciprocity in ancestral ecologies as an act of recognition of collective sovereignty that includes plant and animal life and the forces that support them (i.e., water, soil, etc.). The recognition of collective sovereignty, in turn, acts as the foundation for the establishment of a commonwealth of ecological dignity. This is a perspective I have come to understand through my early experiences as a shepherd among my mother's Amazigh and Nubian communities in the Eastern Sahara and later among my father's Lakota community as a buffalo range rider and hunter in the North American Plains. My work as an activist and academic with Indigenous communities in Mexico, Peru, Japan, Thailand, and Ecuador has further elucidated this concept of ecological dignity. I use a mix of storytelling and critical analysis throughout the text.

The concept of dignity has typically been applied only to humans. Human beings are said to possess intrinsic worth that should reflect in the values, institutions, laws, and interactions among humans and their societies (Mattson and Clark 2011). Every individual is seen as an intrinsic and valued part of their community. Human dignity is predominantly embodied in the rights accorded to individuals in their societies and the responsibilities that institutions have toward those individuals. It is not surprising therefore that when it came to protecting forests and waters, Indigenous and non-Indigenous communities turned to the Rights of Nature concept as a viable framework.

In the discussion that follows, I expand on the understanding that human societies have dignity by demonstrating how some Indigenous communities have accorded intrinsic worth to nonhuman entities through acts of reciprocity. I argue that to address the climate catastrophe, simply codifying rights for different elements of nature (e.g., water, trees, etc.) will not do. Members of marginalized communities understand that just because something is a right does not mean it will be enforced. Moreover, any environmentalist can be convinced that a tree needs to be cut down if the stakes are high enough (e.g., profits), but it is much harder to convince someone to kill their brother when the same stakes are at play. Dignity, a concept that necessitates the interconnected valuation of both the individual and their community in the context of reciprocal relationality, more fully encompasses the manner in which some Indigenous Peoples relate to the world around them. I argue that ecological dignity, as exemplified by Indigenous communities for thousands of years, is the only appropriate response not just to current environmental problems but to our place in the world as human beings.

A VISION OF ECOLOGICAL DIGNITY

"Hola Elodia, mi amor," I said jokingly as I passed her. Elodia smiled shyly with a smile that at once communicated her playfulness and profound wisdom. The previous day, Elodia taught me how to make ceramic art in the Traditional Kichwa way. We went to find clay in the stream beds nearby; the Ecuadorian Amazon is filled with them. Elodia and her younger sister, Beljika, knew every twist and turn in the streams we visited and could tell exactly where to dig in the stream to find the clay that was necessary for the work ahead of us. To me, the clay they dug looked and felt similar (gray and slimy), but through their teachings, I learned that there were different types of clay that turned different colors when fired. These Kichwa women could tell clay apart by sight and feel.

Unsurprisingly, these highly skilled practitioners of Traditional Ecological Knowledge are master ceramic artists, with tools made only of sticks, which were shaped and sharpened with stones, and locks of their hair for painting. They used different types of tree sap for glazing and carefully constructed wood fire as an oven. It made me ponder how many generations of their ancestors it took to harness this Knowledge and these skills, and how those ancestors are present in these women's daily way of life. My attempts at making a simple bowl, on the other hand, were so grotesque to Elodia that she came over several times and crushed my bowl and told me to start over. I had made every mistake possible: adding too much water, not enough water, walls too thick or thin, and so on. Fortunately, she spoke Spanish, and so I was able to tell her what I thought of her: "Elodia, if you keep being mean to me, I'm going to fall in love with you." She laughed and brushed me off as the clown that I am. On my third abysmal attempt at a bowl, she came by to look at the product of my creation and, with a big smile on her face, said, "You lost my heart." At once I was struck to the core with the joy of her wisdom and love of life, and her reciprocation of my playfulness. She reminded me of my grandmother.

When they were not trying to train this circus monkey in how to make clay art, Elodia and Beljika would take me into the forest and teach me about the plants that they used for food and medicine. They also taught me about the plants they use to make poisoned darts for hunting. As an academically trained plant and animal scientist, I was in paradise and also overwhelmed by the incredible biodiversity and my ignorance of it. But this fascination with the living beings all around me paled in comparison to what I became aware of as I followed in Elodia and Beljika's footsteps. As a Lakota, I had witnessed this dance only when I followed in my grandfather's footsteps out on the mixed-grass prairie of the Northeastern Plains.

I had not had a vision in a long time. Elodia and Beljika were barefoot, walking ahead of me through the thicket, every step a mindful one. I was wearing muck boots because I was a coward and afraid of injuring my foot or getting bit by a snake. Suddenly, however, I no longer saw the world as it appeared, Elodia and Beljika walked as if they were on clouds. Every step they took radiated cosmic energy through the soil and into the surrounding plants. The trees in turn knew them and embraced them; they were familiar with each other's touch. The women knew every tree, so much so that they would point out spaces where a tree once stood and was cut down by poachers who illegally cut down profitable trees (e.g., rubber trees) to sell to western interests—something akin to kidnapping one's sister or child. Elodia gave me directions by describing how we were going to turn once we got to a certain tree that had a specific look and markings; she knew everyone. She would tell me about the life history of some trees that she knew throughout her comparatively short life. "An aerial root that was this thick [motions with her hands] once grew out of this tree, it was the thickest I've ever seen; Beljika climbed it," Elodia said about one of her brother trees.

We stopped at yet another tree. I noticed that every time we stopped, Elodia would take the back of her knife and tap it several times on each side of a tree. She said something in her Kichwa language. I assumed she was assessing something about the tree before harvesting some of its bark, leaves, or fruit; leave it to my scientific, analytical mind to think in such a shallow, unimaginative way. I finally asked her what she was doing, and she responded, "I tap on my brother to wake him up so he is not startled when I take some of his bark for medicine." Once again, for the thousandth time that day, I stood in awe of her and the place that surrounded us. Every time I saw Elodia or Beljika walking by, washing their hair in the streams, digging for clay, or climbing trees without a rope, an old poem came to mind: "She walks in beauty, like the night" (from "She Walks in Beauty" by Lord Byron, c. 1788-1824). What can I say? I am a romantic like my father was before me and my grandfather was before him. Toward the end of my stay with these women, I realized that the beauty I noticed when I first met them, and had now come to see in everything they did, reflected the profound dignity they held in their relationships with the forest. They embodied the universal dignity of Unci Maka (Lakota words for Grandmother Earth) and nurtured that dignity daily through mindful reciprocity for all their living relatives.

HUMAN DIGNITY

The International Bill of Human Rights (UN General Assembly 1948a) emphasizes the centrality of human dignity to a fulfilled life, and consists of the Universal Declaration of Human Rights (UN General Assembly 1948b), the International Covenant on Economic, Social, and Cultural Rights (UN General Assembly 1966b), and the International Covenant on Civil and Political Rights (UN General Assembly 1966a; see also Eckert 2002; Ritschl 2001; Weston 2008). This concept is central to national and international policies (Lasswell and Macdougal 1992), and peoples' notions of honor and respect across diverse cultures (Howard and Donnelly 1986; Donnelly 1989; Kamir 2002; Statman 2002). Humans are said to have intrinsic worth which is reckoned as dignity (Beyleveld and Brownsword 1998; Arieli 2001). According to this view, dignity is something that all people want, which indicates that it is seminal to human existence, linked to our evolutionary history and emergent consciousness, and is part of first principles[1] (Yalom 1980; Schachter 1983; Damasio 1999; Caulfield and Chapman 2005).

Human dignity includes two components: valuing the *individual* as an integral part of a supportive *community* (Kelman 1973). Both a unique identity and community are accorded to the individual simultaneously. Persons are valued as individuals with their own goals and values, who are part of an interconnected community with inalienable rights (McDougal, Lasswell, and Chen 2018), and who are ends in themselves and not means to something else (e.g., economy, labor, war, sex) (Kelman 1977). Institutional structures and practices are in turn appraised based on their degree of success in providing for healthy individuals who are integral to healthy communities that live in healthy environments. The key metrics of success are how individuals' lives transpire and whether their loss is considered irreplaceable, regardless of a person's social status, ability, appearance, or origin (Kelman 1977).

The daily shape and texture of human dignity arise from interactions of human nature with human nurture, or how our biology interacts with our environment (Honneth 1992; Chochinov et al. 2004). Internally, the individual experiences a daily sense of self-worth in the context of a stable sense of personal identity and community (Kelman 1977). Subjective well-being (SWB), which includes physical and psychological parameters (Oishi 2000), measures how we feel about our overall life circumstances (Diener and Suh 2000) and provides an appropriate metric for our experience of human dignity and its components, such as human rights (Park 1987; Triandis 2000). Higher SWB is linked to greater access to food, shelter, health, security, income, choice, and other basic physical necessities (Diener and Oishi 2000; Inglehart and Klingemann 2000). Once these elements are met, the continued growth of SWB is contingent upon living within a supportive family/community and working toward self-actualization via living a meaningful life in collective dignity (Mattson and Clark 2011). SWB is therefore a good metric for monitoring the outcomes of building a commonwealth of human dignity.

Externally, institutions and the broader society are evaluated in terms of how adequately they provide physical and social spaces for authentic

---

1 The First Principles is a philosophical and scientific concept that describes necessary and sufficient truths, a foundational proposition or assumption that one arrives at via reflection on one's experiences or simple observation (see Arieli 2001; Starck 2002).

individual identity expression in the context of a supportive community (Kelman 1977). This provisioning of a supportive community is essentially the pursuit of social justice, while the provisioning of authentic identity expression is the essence of individual freedom (Howard 2000; Franzese 2007). Once again, the necessities of food, housing, clothing, security, health care, and education must be provided equitably, since they serve as the foundation of any life, let alone a full life. Communities must be protected from disaster, disease, and violence, and institutions should be governed and monitored for their abilities to provide equitable access to these benefits of societal membership for all individuals. Ultimately, the institutions of societies that pursue human dignity maximize opportunities for self-development and self-expression within the boundaries of respecting the rights of other individuals in the community. Moreover, these institutions protect and foster widespread participation in policy-making and decision-making at all levels of governance (McDougal, Lasswell, and Chen 2018). This, too, is measurable.

Individuals and communities that suffer systemic inequitable access to the benefits of societal membership (i.e., nutrition, employment, sanitation, safety, education, etc.) are essentially excluded from existence on local and/or global scales. This is an obvious limitation on individual freedom and social justice because people are treated as means to achieving the ends of the societally benefited, with no individual or collective dignity afforded them. There is little to no chance for self-development and the pursuit of a fulfilled life, or the development of an authentic individual or group identity. These disenfranchised individuals/communities are typically unable to resist the trampling of their freedoms and rights, as well as their complete erasure from history, both literally and physically. The "lucky" ones may have access to societal benefits only if they rid themselves of personal/communal identity and culture (i.e., freedom). Therefore, the lack of society-level, equitable reciprocity between individuals, communities, and institutions has direct and deleterious impacts on the exercise of freedom and justice—the cornerstones of human dignity (Kelman 1977).

Here we can see that rather than being mutually exclusive, individual freedom and social justice are interdependent, and the integrity of both of these values determines the outcomes of the pursuit of human dignity (Lasswell and Macdougal 1992). Moreover, for human dignity to be sustained, freedom and justice must be pursued in local to global communities (McDougal, Lasswell, and Chen 2018), with a sober appraisal of cultural differences (Kronman 2007). Unci Maka provides us with the most obvious case for this: national borders do not prevent the impacts that ocean dumping, atmospheric pollution, species exploitation, or pandemics contribute to the global community. Both recent and more distant history have hopefully demonstrated to those paying attention that local imperialistic invasions between nations often have global impacts on food security and economies (e.g., the invasion and genocide against Ukraine by the Nazis and Russians). Therefore, freedom and justice, and human dignity for all, can be upheld only if and when individuals, communities, and nations (i.e., institutions) limit their own desires, rights, and freedoms in an act of reciprocal sovereignty or deference to the greater collective.

Despite its potential as a unifying concept for global community building, human dignity policy and discourse have been practically ineffective in improving the lives of those who need it most, let alone in developing a commonwealth of human dignity. For example, in the United States, the wealthiest nation-state in the world, the child poverty rate increased from 12.1 percent in December 2021 to 17 percent in January 2022 because of the absence of the Child Tax Credit (Parolin, Collyer, and Curran 2022). This is in large part due to the vast disagreements and debates that exist over the nature and application of human dignity (Macklin 2003, 2004; Weston 2008), rendering global discourse and action virtually ineffective (Freeman 1994; Ashcroft 2005; Caulfield and Chapman 2005), despite efforts to evaluate the concept in meaningful, pragmatic ways (Donnelly 1989; Freeman 1994).

THE RIGHTS OF NATURE

The pragmatic goal of creating a commonwealth of human dignity from the individual to the global requires a healthy environment that is a requisite for a full life (Kelman 1977; McDougal, Lasswell, and Chen 2018). To approach human dignity, therefore, requires societies to manage human behavior and its relationship to the environment. Science, policy, medicine, industry, and all other facets of a society are moral means of creating a commonwealth of dignity inclusive of nature, which requires that nature is accorded the two key values of freedom and justice (Lasswell, Brunner, and Willard 2003). However, conventional environmental laws have typically legislated environmental harm rather than benefits (Cullinan 2003; Margil 2014; Diaz et al. 2019). Moreover, environmental impact reports rarely affect development plans (Cashmore et al. 2004; Jay et al. 2007; Morgan 2012), and the principles of "green economy" and "sustainable development" have resulted in little change to the status quo locally and globally (Borràs 2016).

Global concern over climate change and biodiversity loss (Diaz et al. 2019) present an alternative paradigm of ecological governance that grants the natural world rights to existence, evolution and development, ecological function, and interconnectedness (Stone 1996; Cullinan 2003; Berry 2011; Koons 2011). Entire ecological jurisdictions have been granted rights in Bolivia, Uganda, and Ecuador (Kotzé and Calzadilla 2017), as well as specific ecoregions in Colombia, India, Bangladesh, and New Zealand (Maloney 2018; O'Donnell 2018; Pecharroman 2018; Eckstein et al. 2019). These attempts and the addition of many others across the world are driven to give "voice" to nonhumans, based on the notion that nature is a subject and not an object (Berry 1999; Maloney 2015; Borràs 2016). As such, humans owe it respect and reciprocity (Magallanes 2018). As with human dignity, nature has rights because it is inherently valuable (Laitos 2013).

This Rights of Nature (RoN) concept, and related laws and initiatives, have proliferated globally and have influenced other resolutions on climate justice, biodiversity, economics, technological progress, etc. (UN General Assembly 2002; United Nations 2015; Yarra River Protection Act 2017; Rights of Nature 2019). The International Union for the Conservation of Nature (IUCN) has also recognized the concept as an effective decision-making framework and a potential unifying principle of environmental civility (IUCN 2012). In 2010, a Universal Declaration of the Rights of Mother Earth was created to provide a framework for collective action on climate change and other global challenges (Global Alliance for the Rights of Nature 2010). In it, Mother Earth is said to be a living being made up of a global community of interrelated living beings, each one an integral part of the whole. Mother Earth has inalienable rights with all living beings having equal rights without distinction or differentiation. This holds humans accountable to certain obligations including conserving and restoring ecological systems and processes, restricting human behavior that may be damaging to ecosystems, and enforcing rectitude on those who cause damage.

With this vision of Mother Earth, since 2006, RoN approaches have achieved many environmental successes.[2] More than one hundred con-

---

2 The UN Harmony with Nature Programme compiles laws and court cases on RoN across the world at http://harmonywithnatureun.org/rightsOfNature/, last accessed August 3, 2022. The Community Environmental Legal Defense Fund compiles data on US court cases and an RoN timeline at www.celdf.org/, last accessed December 3, 2022.

stitutional amendments, laws, and court rulings in some thirty countries provide elements of the environment and entire ecoregions with varying rights. Rivers, wetlands, lakes, seas, reefs, springs, mountains, forests, and even scenic roads have received some form of protection. Individual and small groups of chimps, orangutans, trees, and others have had their rights argued in court. Indigenous Peoples have also won rights of access to water, food, a healthy environment, and cultural identity. These are substantial successes indeed, and the RoN paradigm has the potential for many more when led by an Indigenous framework (Jacobs et al. 2022a,b).

Despite these successes, RoN approaches and laws continue to vary considerably, making their application difficult (Kauffman and Martin 2018). As would be expected, it is difficult to define Nature's rights: what is "Nature," what part needs to be protected, what rights should be recognized, who speaks on Nature's behalf, who is responsible for protecting these rights, does Nature have responsibilities as well as rights, and so on. These questions are answered quite differently depending on the national, governmental, historical, and cultural contexts in which they occur. Because of these variable contexts, RoN approaches have had vast limitations in implementation (De Lucia 2013); a patchy history of pragmatic effectivity (Freestone 2012; Young 2016); have been difficult to enforce (Whittemore 2011); and, even when court outcomes are favorable, it has been difficult to translate the legal decision into outcomes on the ground (Daly 2012). Moreover, court cases in India (e.g., on July 7, 2017, the Supreme Court of India agreed with an appeal against the original case that protected the Ganges River, placing the river's protection in limbo) and Ecuador (arguably the RoN global epicenter; e.g., in 2017, the Ecuadorian government gave new concessions for mining exploration across 2.9 million hectares, an increase of 300 percent, on Indigenous territories that are biodiversity hotspots) have been overturned or ignored. This highlights the transitory nature of the RoN approach (O'Donnell and Talbot-Jones 2018) and its ineffectiveness in producing lasting change (Burdon 2012).

There are also bigger-picture issues with the RoN approach. Implementing rights notions mostly fails to produce a commonwealth of dignity and its resultant subjective well-being for all because it is the bottom-line means to a dignified end (Donnelly 1989, 2007). At best, rights serve to protect the most vulnerable from abuses, but have no positive, constructive value for society. Rights-based approaches are like trying to empower people to have vibrant physical and psychological health by legislating a right to band-aids. To address these issues, some people emphasize the importance of defining implementation measures and assigning institutional responsibilities to ensure that RoN standards are put into practice (Kotzé and Calzadilla 2017; Calzadilla and Kotzé 2018; Pecharroman 2018; Eckstein et al. 2019). This institutional, detached, acontextual approach has also failed in part because the definition of "nature" is highly contextual and culturally defined, and nonhumans cannot discharge rights-based obligations as is the norm in human legal systems (Schillmoller and Pelizzon 2013).

The RoN approach also fails in multiple ways when critiqued from an Indigenous values lens. First, it is yet another effort to apply Indigenous values such as reciprocity in and through western frameworks that are completely foreign to these values. The very fact of its existence is telling of the separation of man and nature inherent in its philosophy. As understood by a Traditional Indigenous value system, human rights and rights of nature are not separate ontological categories, let alone ones in legal opposition to one another, where nature needs protection from humans. Human rights are the rights of nature and vice versa. Second, the fact that some communities feel the immense urgency to find means to protect the very essence of life, the life force that flows through the hands typing this text and the eyes reading it, speaks of a grave derangement in the global human community and its institutions. This is like telling someone they can't burn their own house down because it is illegal and their house has rights, and then experiencing this as a success. Addressing the symptoms of a much graver disease (i.e., how deranged humans have become because of their relational separation from the very Nature that constitutes them) will not be successful in the long-term. Third, RoN approaches are predominantly culturally agnostic, unless they are proposed by and within sovereign Indigenous communities. RoN can easily become another Indigenous solution without Indigenous Peoples. Based on this alone, I wholly reject it. Finally, it is one thing to attempt to institutionalize new norms via education or law but quite another thing to elevate, strengthen, and embody ancient Indigenous norms through practice. Pretending that we can legislate thousands of years of intimate reciprocity between Indigenous communities and their ancestral lands is a collective delusion that can prove fatal. Definition, legislation, enforcement, and the like must all grow within and through Indigenous relationality to place via place-based communities. Only place-based communities in intimate long-term relationships with the places they steward can determine what is valuable, why it is valuable, and how to protect and nurture it across local to global scales (Ignatieff 2001).

DIGNITY THROUGH RELATIONALITY

I miss Bermuda, its pink sands, clear waters, and relaxed island life. Most of all, I miss the relationships, brief as they were, with the magnificent ocean beings I met and with whom I swam. I was pursuing a Scientific Diver Certification to assist coastal Tribal communities who are losing their cultural heritage and lands to sea level rise. During the certification process, a guest speaker of French descent who had worked with Indigenous communities in Australia spoke about what he had learned throughout his career and how it led him to what he does now: exploring shipwrecks as hotspots of cultural and biological value. He talked about the importance of understanding the story of ocean beings and not just focusing on their biology. When he mentioned that fish have a culture, the young white students (men and women alike) scoffed. Later that night, the students went out to a pub, and as we sat there, the same students who had scorned the idea of fish culture began to mock the guest speaker and his ideas.

However, the speaker explained fish culture well. Among many other examples, he stated that the overfishing of older fish can have negative intergenerational consequences on fish populations because the Elders teach the younger generations where to find food, shelter, and safety. Though the concepts of culture, social order, and individual differences are common knowledge across many fields of the biological sciences (Marmot and Sapolsky 2014), including ichthyology (i.e., the study of fish; Carpenter et al. 2014; Abril-de-Abreu, Cruz, and Oliveira 2015), it seems that the ability to accord nonhumans any form of individual or cultural dignity is beyond the limited capacity of some humans, even if their knowledge systems confirm it. This is a problem, not just with western ways of being and knowing, but with any mode of existence that is detached from place. Such ignorance highlights the importance of long-term experiential learning opportunities for students (Mann et al. 2021); as I have observed, the classroom is where relationality and reciprocity with nature go to die.

Shortly after my return from Bermuda, I visited the OdySea Aquarium in Phoenix, Arizona. In one exhibit, the prerecorded voice of the animal caretakers noted how they realized via years of direct caretaking that the animals they serve have different personalities and that different species of animals placed in the same space eventually form an exchange and understanding-based culture. For example, some sharks like to be touched while others do not (one was said to be like a lapdog), different giant groupers make such distinct guttural sounds that their caretakers can tell them apart by sound, and smaller schools of fish recognize their feeding time and location by mere habit. One particular case struck me: Rita, a green sea turtle, was born with a deformity that caused air to be trapped in her shell. The deformity makes her too buoyant to dive down from the surface like other turtles, something that would have certainly spelled her quick demise in the wild. However, at the aquarium, Rita thrives and even looks out for the well-being of her fellow tank dwellers. Through her courage and perseverance, and the acts of reciprocal sovereignty of some humans, she has become a protector, a leader. This is individual freedom and social justice in action. This is culture. This is dignity. It is therefore not surprising that these factors can be seen only by those who have direct and sustained relationships with these beings.

RECIPROCAL SOVEREIGNTY AND THE DIGNITY OF NATURE

Though I do not find it productive to speak of a being's value in terms of itself or in comparison to something else, perhaps a brief discussion of this is necessary for some readers. It may be difficult for some folks to understand that other beings' modes of functioning and expression are different from ours, but not any less real or consequential. If a tree does not say "ouch," and then immediately pull away from me when I cut into it, it must not have any consciousness of what is happening to it. Moreover, if it does not feel pain because it has no pain receptors, then anything I do to it has no moral consequence, which, in turn, reduces its intrinsic existential value. To speak of a tree as having relationality, rights, or dignity in this example is ignorance at best and religious insanity at worst. Of course, plant scientists have known for decades that plants know well when they suffer an injury, including grazing injury; they just "know" and "respond" differently than humans do (i.e., isolate the injury from the cambium, produce reactionary growth, send out chemical signals to ward off herbivores or warn neighboring plants, etc.) (Tompkins and Bird 2002).

Indeed, it would not be difficult to argue that the life of a tree is far more consequential than that of a human, especially when it comes to creating a commonwealth of dignity. If a tree is treated with indignity, as nearly every tree is in suburbia, it may easily fall over from weak roots, destroying property or killing humans. In fact, there are several lucrative careers one can make out of such liability claims. Moreover, when a tree loses its life, many other species lose their homes or simply die, which may disrupt their entire life cycle and have intergenerational reverberations. On the other hand, if I were to disappear, it would not disrupt the life cycle of any living beings other than myself because few, if any, living beings would suffer at all, and the ones who would suffer would reestablish normalcy in due time. Indeed, objectively speaking, the impact my disappearance would have is likely a positive one overall when it comes to the commonwealth of dignity for the natural world because I live a fairly modern, consumeristic, and environmentally detached lifestyle. In many ways, my modern lifestyle is the antithesis of that of a tree: we live as opposing forces, one of destruction and one of regeneration.

More importantly, the concept of the Dignity of Nature may provide us with a universal, global framework to address the complex realities of collective human and nonhuman life in an increasingly interconnected world (i.e., human rights, climate change, trade, economics, etc.). Like the notion of human dignity, it is the most inclusive universal good (Schachter 1983; Glover 2012; Schwartz 2007). However, for it to be so, we must avoid the pitfalls of ideological rigidity (i.e., the need to define and specify everything with absolute exactness and definitional closure, as is often required of legislation for it to be effectively enforced). It is a fool's errand to attempt to define a beautiful, loving relationship; one can only describe its effects. Therefore, we ought to rely on the principle of sufficiency to conceive of this complex and context-sensitive concept (Kaplan 1958; Shils 1958). Moreover, for it to have any pragmatic value, we must conceptualize the dignity of nature universally enough for it to be applicable everywhere, and underspecified enough for it to apply to vastly different contexts (Weston 2008). A universalist notion lends itself easily to humanistic and biospheric altruism (Schultz 2000, 2001), and so any conception of dignity afforded to nature must be universal. But let us also recognize that any discussion of dignity, and all it relates to, is a human one. Universal and natural forces have lived in relative balance for nearly fourteen billion years, but only humans are capable of sustained indignities.

Unlike the Rights of Nature, I understand the Dignity of Nature as an emergent concept; it begins, is defined, and is governed by local interrelationships between all the living beings and systems that support them in a particular place. It is founded on reciprocal deference of sovereignty between all species and their environment—a mutuality in the sharing of the benefits of integral presence in an ecosystem (i.e., membership in a "society," citizenship in a Tribe).

It is important to note that not all integral elements of a system are by nature native to that system. For example, for us Lakota People, the horse has become a relative whose presence is inextricably tied to our ways of life, and it is not a native to the North American prairie. For any of us to become an integral part of a place-based community requires that we see both the forest and the trees and that we value the individual being and her role in her community (i.e., ecological population) and the broader society (i.e., ecological community). This only becomes a real, visceral, sustained practice through daily relationships of reciprocity, via the giving of time, resources, observation, thought, touch, laughter, and so on; nothing else can be a substitute.

A COMMONWEALTH OF ECOLOGICAL DIGNITY

As I followed in Grandfather's footsteps, I noticed how he greeted the living beings that surrounded him. Strumming his fingers through the grass, patting the side of the sheep in the pen, kissing the flowing waters in the stream, chasing the herding dogs for play, singing to his horse, and silently staring at a buffalo matriarch standing watch before her herd. He was at once recognizing their individual identities and their collective sovereignty. He recognized the unique identity expressions and community value of those he considered relatives. There was Ina the motherly hen who adopted orphaned chicks, Witko the crazy bull who protected the herd when he was not running into trees, and Ishna the lone prairie wolf who found a welcoming pack with our herding dogs. All were welcomed and included so long as they did not overstep the rights of other individuals or the collective well-being of the community. Necessities were provided to all via the collective efforts of all members of the community (i.e., humans provided and harvested plants, fed animals, dead animals fed plants, water provided both with life, etc.). Each individual's life was valued, and its loss was seen as a loss to the whole community. Ceremonies of mourning and celebration reminded the human participants of these fundamental realities. Grandfather even wrote poems that he would read to me about what he observed and felt. He, and other Elders, gave me a vision of this commonwealth of ecological dignity. Now, legislate that!

Though some consider the RoN movement to be paradigm-shifting (Graham and Maloney 2019), per usual with environmental movements, it is absurdly derivative from a traditional Indigenous Person's perspective.

All of its underlying principles have been part of Indigenous philosophies, Indigenous Knowledges (e.g., Traditional Ecological Knowledge), and Indigenous cultural practices for tens of thousands of years (Sheehan 2013; Knauß 2018; Espinosa 2019; Graham and Maloney 2019). The emphasis on reciprocity to Mother Earth (Margil 2014) is what underlies the cultural norms and laws of many First Nations across the world (Graham and Maloney 2019). More importantly, what Elodia, Beljika, and our Indigenous Elders embody does not arise out of top-down legalistic instruction in the values and rights of the living beings with whom they interact. Nor did these Elders receive a world-class ecological education in a western university; indeed, one can easily and scientifically critique some of their interactions with the natural world as not ideal. However, they embody the principles of a commonwealth of ecological dignity because they move, breathe, and have their being in intimate reciprocity with the living environments they call home. Such intimate levels of reciprocity come via the respect, deference, and acknowledgment that grow over time in any healthy relationship. This commonwealth is therefore inextricably tied to other emergent realities, such as our consciousness and well-being, and is dependent on the well-being and vigor of the commonwealth itself. This conception of a commonwealth of ecological dignity is broad enough to relate to every context and specific enough to be applicable in individualistic and communitarian cultures (Kitayama and Markus 2000; Bowles, Choi, and Hopfensitz 2003). Because it emerges in place, it is applicable to every place. It is unsurprising, therefore, that the contexts in which the RoN principle have been applied successfully are where Indigenous communities were given the authority for oversight of implementation mechanisms, decision-making processes, and/or stewardship of protected and non-protected environments (Ley de Derechos 2010; Kauffman and Martin 2016; Bangladesh Decision 2017; Te Awa Tupua 2017; Calzadilla and Kotzé 2018; Supreme Court of Colombia 2018; Eckstein et al. 2019).

Indigenous cultures and their place-based, emergent value systems may also shine a light on how to develop a commonwealth of ecological dignity in non-Indigenous contexts. A value-based conception of a commonwealth of universal ecological dignity perhaps offers some conceptual understanding of the experiences of these Indigenous visionaries and may provide a stable global framework within which to engage in pragmatic discourse about dignity for all. In particular, an orientation toward the values of deferential respect and universalist rectitude (McDougal, Lasswell, and Chen 2018

Schwartz 2007) may be an effective starting point for a commonwealth of universal ecological dignity because these values most closely relate to our evolutionary anxieties over responsibility, meaning, isolation, and death (Yalom 1980). Respect is concerned with what the world owes us or, in the context of the Rights of Nature, what is owed to rivers, forests, and the like (Dworkin 1977; Dicke 2001). Receiving one's culturally perceived, entitled rights is a good measure of respect in any context (de Sousa Santos 2002; Gott 2002). Rectitude, on the other hand, pertains to demands that we place on ourselves as a duty or obligation to others, and which also has vast cultural nuance. When either of these two values are violated, we experience a direct impact to our experience of a dignified existence (Wilkinson, Kawachi, and Kennedy 1998).

A balance must therefore be struck, at the scale of the commonwealth, between the rights owed to individuals by institutions (i.e., respect) and the responsibilities those individuals have to the commonwealth (i.e., rectitude), all within culturally authentic parameters (Gewirth 1978; Donnelly 1982). These values, and the process of balancing them, are important because they, in large part, determine feelings of self-worth, which are central to our experiences of personal dignity and the realization of the commonwealth (Suh 2000). Balancing these two values is what I have come to call *reciprocal sovereignty*—recognizing the meaningful exchange of dignity that must take place for living beings to survive and thrive.

It is important to note that for many Tribal communities, reciprocal sovereignty is not reached through some philosophical or spiritual journey. It is not some romanticized, pseudo-spiritual, deep wisdom to which only cool hippies in the Tribe have access. Acknowledging and embodying the dignity of other living beings is simply something you do because it is reality. It is like brushing your teeth in the morning or making your morning cup of coffee, it is just something you do because it is a reality that is part of your daily life, which you and others in your community also remind you of via cultural practices.

Working Toward a Commonwealth of Ecological Dignity

If you are feeling overwhelmed, you should be. This is no easy task, and the journey will be long and painful. Focus on the first steps and begin locally. With everything that is wrong with the world today, where do we begin? Wealth inequality is perhaps the simplest and most meaningful place to begin to build a commonwealth of ecological dignity. Wealth pits people's values against their current existential needs. Poverty and the associated lack of access to food, shelter, and health care have drastic impacts on self-respect and self-worth and, therefore, personal dignity (Massey 1996; Wilkinson 2004). Our standard for a commonwealth bottom line should be equitable access to survival needs (Corning 2000, 2003), the lack of which profoundly impacts the dignity of the individual and the commonwealth (Kagan and Moss 1983; Sirgy 1986; Harper, Harper, and Stills 2003; Farmer 2004) because of its negative effect on the value of power (i.e., choice, freedom, autonomy; Veenhoven 2000). In short, one cannot imagine a commonwealth of ecological dignity developing in a context where some human communities have (1) been excluded from creating dignity-relevant policies and practices; (2) experienced every means of degradation; and (3) been chronically deprived of basic survival needs. Therefore, we must dedicate time and resources to providing basic necessities to our families and communities.

Individually, you can begin your journey toward realizing a commonwealth of ecological dignity by aligning your expectations with reality. My karate sensei once joked that everyone who drives slower than us is a jerk and everyone who drives faster than us is a maniac. If you live in a world where everyone needs to do your bidding and you must have access to everything, be prepared for chronic discontent, anxiety, and a severely miserable life of indignity (Ratzlaff et al. 2000). Our expectations for reciprocity of the values we prize must concur with what the world can actually provide: a tree is never going to grow money, most people will disagree with you at least some of the time, and if you equate respect with worship and perfection, everyone will disappoint you. A stable commonwealth is founded on healthy, socially and emotionally mature human individuals in reciprocal solidarity with each other's limitations. You can realize those limitations if you let your interactions with the natural world—that is you and is within you—teach you something about existence and your roles within it. For example, the next time a mosquito bites you, try not to follow the preordained human practice of becoming angry and annoyed. Try to realize that you have such little control over anything that a being that is hardly visible to the human eye may use you as a party favor and transmit microscopic beings into your bloodstream that can make you wish for death. You are not the master of anything, and this is a reality that should provide you with peace as you rid yourself of the tyrant in your head that wishes to control everything and have everything.

Finally, as much as I have followed in the footsteps of ecologically embedded Indigenous Peoples, it is clear that—given our current crisis-level environmental circumstances, Indigenous Peoples' past and present when it comes to environmental stewardship, and the shortcomings of human dignity and RoN approaches—the wisest path forward would seem to be to simply follow in the footsteps of Indigenous communities as they guide us through their life-enhancing relationality to nature. The interfacing of using Traditional Ecological Knowledge (TEK) for guiding relationality, with western science as a precision tool, seems to be no longer an option but a necessity. The complex, wicked problems of the "Anthropocene" will not be solved by top-down, ecologically detached, legislative, or retribution-based approaches. TEK and the emergent reciprocal sovereignty it embeds in the hearts and minds of its adherents, coupled with the problem-solving utility of western science, may provide the only hope for long-term, sustainable futures. No matter what, it will take communities whose lives, histories, livelihoods, thoughts, ceremonies, ancestors, progeny, and identity are tied to a place for those places to have a dignified existence. Those communities exist and have been around for thousands of years; they just need access and decision-making sovereignty over the ecosystems they once stewarded and continue to steward. Now, all that is left is the dismantling of colonial paradigms of governance, education, and research, and their replacement with Indigenous Knowledges guided by Indigenous communities and their allies. There is much work to be done.

Acknowledgments

The author would like to acknowledge the following people and entities for their unflinching support and guidance: his Lakota and Amazigh/ Nubian Elders and family, the Standing Rock Sioux community, the many Indigenous communities he has worked with all over the world (Kichwa and Waorani of Ecuador, Quechua of Peru, Nubi of Upper Egypt, Amazigh of the Eastern Sahara, among others), Arizona State University faculty (Drs. Arianne Cease, Melissa Nelson, Sara Brownell, David Manuel-Navarrete), and Dr. Susan Clark (Yale).

Funding

The author would like to thank the following funders for their support: National Science Foundation, Arizona State University, American Indian Science and Engineering Society, Ecological Society of America, the Global Locust Initiative, and the University of Washington, among others.

14

PYROEPISTOMOLOGY
Reclaiming and Reciprocity

PAULETTE STEEVES

Positionality Statement

I am Cree-Métis, I live and work in Sault Ste. Marie, Ontario, the homelands of Anishinaabe, Cree, and Métis communities.

Tansi

Tansi, Paulette Steeves. Hello, I am Paulette Steeves. I am a descendant of Cree and Métis Peoples. I was born in Whitehorse, Yukon Territories, and grew up in British Columbia. My teaching and research are framed in Indigenous methods and theories and Indigenous ways of Knowing, being, and doing. I intentionally introduce myself and discuss my place in this story in part to create a relationship with readers. Shawn Wilson (Cree) discusses the role of relationality in Indigenous research methods in his (2008) book *Research Is Ceremony: Indigenous Research Methods*. Relational accountability is central to Indigenous research methods, as are respect, reciprocity, and responsibility (Wilson 2008).

Indigenous scholars often present their research as storytelling, which reflects where the storytellers are in their lives (Wilson 2008). Raven Peltier Sinclair (Cree/Assiniboine/Saulteaux) stated that "location in Indigenous research as in life, is a critical starting point" (Sinclair 2003, 122). In sharing the details of who I am, I acknowledge my ancestors, claim my ancestry, and declare my position first as an Indigenous Person and second as a researcher. In sharing my place in this story and discussing my research as relational and applied, I identify, define, and describe the elements of Indigenist research (Rigney 1997). Euro-western educators in many academic institutions continue to ignore Indigenous Knowledges (e.g., Traditional Ecological

Knowledge; TEK), culture, and language, excluding everything Indigenous from their curricula. Therefore, for many Indigenous scholars, writing is framed to privilege Indigenous Knowledges. However, introducing my ancestors serves cultural purposes and protocols, privileging Indigenous voices and acknowledging ancestors.

Many Euro-western scholars have asked me where to start in Indigenizing curriculum and how to decolonize their teaching and courses. I tell them to do research to gain an understanding of what Indigenous Knowledges are and that these Knowledge systems are as diverse as the thousands of Indigenous communities around the world. I also advise them to begin to build relationships with Indigenous Knowledge holders and communities. Indigenous Knowledges include all Knowledge of a particular People/community and associated lands, which have been orally transmitted across generations (Daes 1993). Indigenous Knowledges also include all kinds of scientific, agricultural, technical, and ecological Knowledge, including cultigens, medicines and the use of flora and fauna (Daes 1993). What people have Traditionally been taught in educational institutions about Indigenous Knowledges and Traditional Ecological Knowledge (TEK) is often framed more by what they are not taught rather than by what they are taught. Academic discussions about the First Peoples from the lands we know today as the Americas continue to be framed in agnotology, defined as how knowledge has not come to be and how ignorance is produced through "neglect, secrecy, suppression, destruction of documents, unquestioned tradition, and cultural political selectivity" (Proctor and Schiebinger 2008, ix). Educational materials framed in agnotology support colonization of the mind, teaching people to think in ways acceptable to the nation-state, and to not question so-called western scientific authorities (Proctor and Schiebinger 2008).

Histories of Dehumanizing Indigenous Erasure

In Euro-western literature, Indigenous Peoples are often portrayed as sub-human and a part of "nature," not of culture (Deloria 1997). Indigenous Peoples are often discussed as simple hunter-gatherers lacking creativity, science, and intellectualism. Additional Eurocentric biases associate "Indigenous thought with the barbaric, the primitive, and the inferior" (Battiste 2005, 3). Settler scholars and archaeologists often discuss early Indigenous sites in the Americas as mysterious, their former inhabitants unknown, and the Indigenous Peoples as disappeared (Fine 1988). Such ideologies are an embedded form of Indigenous erasure, disconnecting early Indigenous Peoples from contemporary Indigenous communities and the land. Euro-western scholars in education work hand in hand with nation-states, churches, and colonizers to erase all things Indigenous from the land and social memory (Battiste 2005; Gnecco 2016). However, the Indigenous Peoples of the western hemisphere built great cities such as Cahokia and Teotihuacan that were as old as or older than and more technologically advanced than many cities of the Eastern Hemisphere; these are civilizations with deep histories that are held in the land that cannot be erased (Loewen 2008; Pauketat 2004; Denevan 1992).

Indigenous Knowledges

A wealth of Knowledge exists regarding Indigenous People's respect for and links to the land and the environment. Indigenous Knowledges are as rich and diverse as the environments Indigenous communities have called home since time immemorial, including the lands to which they were forcibly relocated (Nichols 1990; Steeves 2021). The areas, commonly known today as North and South America, are some of the most biologically diverse environments in the world. Furthermore, Indigenous Knowledges of the land and environment in the Americas are held in hundreds of Indigenous languages, as the Americas are the most linguistically diverse continents of the world (Steeves 2021). Indigenous language families make up over 50 percent of all of the known language families on a global scale (Nichols 1990). Despite extreme cultural diversity, Indigenous Peoples hold many commonalities in worldviews, cultural understandings, and practices. For example, some often-expressed Indigenous views of the world are that all beings are related, all have intelligence and spirit, and all are respected as relations. Anishinaabe scholar Richard Wagamese writes,

> I've been considering the phrase "all my relations" for some time now. It's hugely important. It's our saving grace in the end. It points to the truth that we are all related, that we are all connected, that we all belong to each other. The most important word is "all." Not just those who look like me, sing like me, dance like me, speak like me, pray like me or behave like me. ALL my relations. That means every person, just as it means every rock, mineral, blade of grass,

and creature. We live because everything else does. If we were to choose collectively to live that teaching, the energy of our change of consciousness would heal each of us and would positively impact climate change, species extinction, and ongoing and impending biodiversity collapse. (2016, 36)

Pyroepistomology, Healing, and Renewal

In any work, specifically in teaching and education, it is important to return to the beginning of the journey and become informed of how we arrived at our current social, political, and environmental place. If we are to survive the impending collapse of biodiversity, species extinction, climate change, and coastal erosion, we need to work on ending the destruction of the planet, and we need to work on ways to heal the environment for all of our relations. Healing cannot happen without truth, and truth requires us to review and understand the journey. As many Euro-western academics find the truth about colonial history extremely distressing, it is most often not centered in discussion or education. However, some Euro-western scholars have opened their hearts and minds and realized that TEK and Indigenous Knowledges weave paths to healing the environment and communities (Fernández-Llamazares et al. 2021). However, the critical missing piece of this education and healing process is fire.

Since time immemorial, many Indigenous communities have used controlled fire to heal and regenerate the environment and the lands. I refer to these practices as pyroregeneration, which employs fire to clean the land, burning away dense undergrowth and allowing sunlight to bring new life to the earth. Though cultural burning in Canada was banned in the early 1900s (Kehoe 2020), there has recently been a reemergence of cultural burning led by Indigenous communities using TEK to care for and heal the land and communities (Kimmerer and Lake 2001). As a tool for regeneration and healing, pyroregeneration practices can also be applied to healing western academia and the hearts, minds, and spirits of individuals who have been so violently affected by colonialism.

In 2012, I coined the metaphorical term **pyroepistemology**, which describes the work of critical Indigenous scholarship and the decolonizing work carried out by like-minded and informed peers and allies (Kimmerer and Lake 2001). Pyroepistemological practices are ceremonies that cleanse the academic landscape of discussions that misinform worldviews and fuel

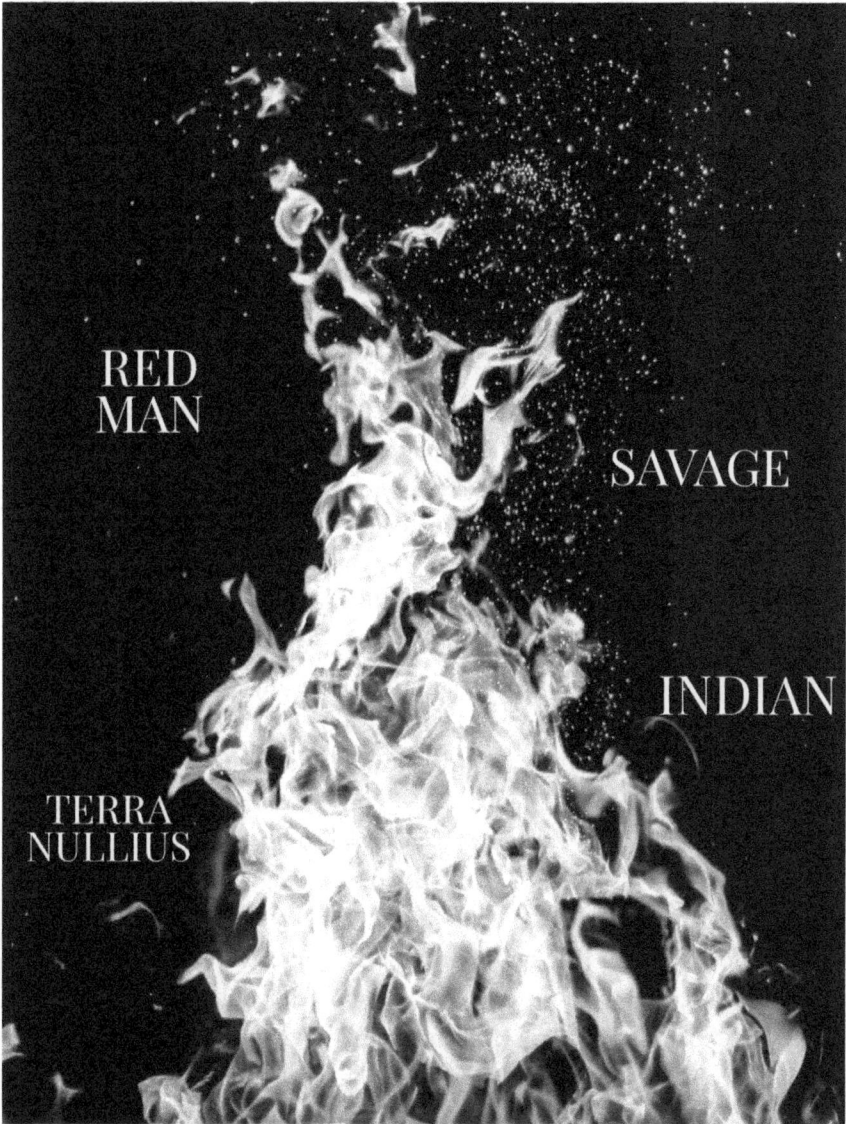

RED
MAN

SAVAGE

INDIAN

TERRA
NULLIUS

Figure 14.1. Pyroepistomology (Paulette Steeves 2022)

racism. Such forms of epistemological and literary burning and renewal clear the way for healthy growth in ways of knowing, doing, and being in academic fields of thought and the center of knowledge production (Steeves 2015). According to Marie Battiste (Mi'kmaq),

Whether or not it has been acknowledged by the Eurocentric mainstream, Indigenous [K]nowledge has always existed. The recognition and intellectual activation of Indigenous [K]nowledge today is an act of empowerment by Indigenous [P]eople[s]. The task for Indigenous academics has been to affirm and activate the holistic paradigm of Indigenous [K]nowledge to reveal the wealth and richness of Indigenous languages, worldviews, teachings, and experiences, all of which have been systematically excluded from contemporary educational institutions and from the Eurocentric knowledge system. (2002, 4)

Scholars have discussed research framed in Indigenous methodologies as counterstories and powerful forms of resistance (Brown and Strega 2015). Many Indigenous scholars seek to restore Knowledge of the Indigenous past, a place historically distorted, erased, and denied via western knowledge production (Gnecco 2016). Waziyatawin Angela Wilson (Wahpetunwan Dakota; 2004) discussed Indigenous Knowledge recovery as an anticolonial process fueled by the loss of lifeways, lands, and dreams of healing the future. She further states, "It springs from the disaster resulting from the centuries of colonialism's efforts to methodologically eradicate our ways of seeing, being, and interacting with the cosmos" (Wilson 2004, 359). The recovery of Indigenous histories works to revalue Indigenous cultures and histories that have been denied and denigrated "and revive that which has been destroyed" (Wilson 2004). Marie Kovach (Plains Cree and Saulteaux) explains what represents an Indigenous epistemology:

It includes a way of [K]nowing that is fluid and experiential (Little Bear 2000), derived from teaching transmitted from generation to generation by storytelling; each story is alive with the nuances and wisdom of the storyteller. It emerges from [T]raditional languages emphasizing verbs, not nouns. It involves a [K]nowing within the subconscious that is garnered through dreams and visions. It is the [K]nowledge that is both intuitive and quiet. Indigenous ways of [K]nowing arise with the human world, the spirit, and the inanimate entities of the echo system. Indigenous ways of [K]nowing to encompass the spirit of collectivity, reciprocity, and respect. It is born of the land and locality of the [T]ribe. . . . These ways of [K]nowing are both cerebral and heartfelt. As the [E]lders say, "If you have important things to say, speak from the heart." (2009, 27)

ORAL TRADITIONS, TEK, AND LISTENING

I have read many oral Traditions sharing Knowledge of spirits and spirit beings; everything has a spirit, not just humans but all beings, and all are to be respected. Anishinaabekew scholar Kathy Absolon (2022) writes that spirituality is at the heart of Indigenous epistemology. Leanne Betasamosake Simpson (Mississauga Nishnaabeg 1999) has discussed Aboriginal worldviews and Knowledge systems as spiritually based, and she has acknowledged that Indigenous Knowledge is spiritually derived. Knowledge comes from keen observation and experimentation and also from dreams, visions, ceremonies, and the spirit world. However, spirits, dreams, and visions are not a part of western knowledge or ways of knowing, being, and doing (Absolon 2022). In the western world, if you listen to thoughts or dreams, you may be considered to be suffering from a mental illness. Though some Euro-western scholars claim that thoughts are intuition, I would agree that thoughts are often spirits that carry messages. After growing up in both the western and Indigenous worlds, I had to retrain my mind and heart to listen to those spirits.

> Spiritually derived [K]nowledge is fully integrated into the consciousness of Anishinaabe [P]eople and contemporary [A]boriginal [P]eople who follow [T]raditional ways and into Anishinaabe Knowledge. . . . Given that the idea that [K]nowledge is spiritually derived is so well documented, . . . it is interesting that it is left out of most non-[A]boriginal definitions of TEK (Simpson 1999, 23; see also Absolon 2022).

Indigenous Knowledges, including TEK, have been passed through oral histories across thousands of generations. For thousands of years, before western scientists began to study human history and environments, Indigenous Peoples were sustainably managing their environments and practicing ways of honoring all beings. Knowledge of all our relations, the water, mountains, forests, crawlers, winged, rooted, four-legged and two-legged ancestors, and spirits are documented in oral Traditions, songs, dances, rock art, and cultural practices of respect and reciprocity.

Indigenous Knowledges have been discussed as our one hope for saving the planet. For example, some scholars write about how Indigenous Knowledges play a critical role in safeguarding the biological and cultural diversity of our world (Fernández-Llamazares et al. 2021). For Indigenous

Knowledges and TEK to begin the work of healing the planet, people must learn about Indigenous practices and ways of being, Knowing, and doing. That is the challenge. How do you reteach thousands of settler scholars who educate the general population that what they know about Indigenous Peoples and Knowledge comes from a biased western view? It has been my experience in teaching and working in academia that many settler scholars and members of the public can get very upset when you teach them that western education is based on a violent practice of dehumanizing Indigenous Peoples whose links to the land their ancestors and nation-states have worked to erase. I have found that some adult students and a few younger students experienced anxiety and stress when learning about violent acts of colonization and questioned the validity of challenging erasures of history. A vast majority of students have never learned of the impacts of colonization on colonized communities and are shocked to learn how violent residential schools were. However, some settler scholars have taken the time to become informed about the history of colonization and the impacts of western education and its ties to colonization: weaving Indigenous and western Knowledges together is a practice that is slowly creeping into all levels of education.

Understanding how to weave Indigenous Knowledges and TEK into all areas of education requires educators to start at the beginning to understand how and why Indigenous Knowledges and Peoples have been silenced and erased. This is a difficult and painful starting place for many settlers, but it is necessary to create a journey to a sustainable and just future for everyone. The Canadian government acknowledged a cultural genocide in 2008 (Dorrell 2009), and Pope Francis in 2022 acknowledged that taking Indigenous children away, and changing their race and culture, was a genocide in Canada (McKinney 2022). However, in 2018 and 2022, the Ford government of Ontario canceled the inclusion of Indigenous Knowledges in textbooks (Brant 2022). Thus, even while some progress is being made, we are still witnessing the erasure and silencing of Indigenous Knowledges in many areas of education and life.

Numerous publications and websites discussing Indigenous Knowledges and TEK stress the need to create respectful and mutually beneficial relationships between researchers and Indigenous Peoples (Fernández-Llamazares et al. 2021). However, few publications on cross-cultural education address how to achieve cross-cultural teaching and research relationships (Matsui 2015). One of the first steps is to become informed of Indigenous scholars and communities and the work they are doing to create paths to healing and rebuilding their communities. This can be done by fostering relationships with Indigenous communities to gain an understanding of their ways of Knowing, being, and doing and center research and education within Indigenous communities. Colonization and systems of apartheid in Canada and many areas of the world have kept the majority of Indigenous communities apart from settler communities: out of sight, out of mind, and often feared. Students have asked me to teach them about specific communities they would work in as social service and health-care providers. Even in British Columbia, where there are many Indigenous communities, settler students have told me they have never been to a First Nations community. They were afraid to do something offensive or wrong while working in Indigenous communities, as they knew very little about Indigenous Peoples. Weaving Indigenous Knowledges and creating classrooms where Indigenous Knowledge holders and community members lead processes of decolonizing education and teaching may support building all people's capacity to be cross-culturally and ethically competent.

Fernández-Llamazares and his coauthors appealed for urgent action to support Indigenous Peoples and communities in maintaining their "[K]nowledge systems, languages, stewardship rights, ties to lands and waters, and the biocultural integrity of their territories on which we all depend" (Fernández-Llamazares et al. 2021,145). In work to combat climate change and to protect biodiversity, we must support Indigenous communities and Peoples, and weave Indigenous Knowledges through education, policies, and processes.

Creating Decolonized Spaces in Academia

In 2021, I researched educational programs at universities on a global scale, focusing on cross-cultural studies. I found only one. In 2019, I began the process of creating a faculty body of cross-cultural (FCCS) studies at my institution, Algoma University, and planning processes for a school of global Indigenous studies. In July 2022, the FCCS at Algoma University became a reality. It was a very stressful undertaking: my like-minded faculty peers and I faced a lot of opposition. However, we prevailed. As we move forward in this new faculty of cross-cultural studies, we will continue to decolonize and Indigenize all curricula in the departments that are a part of the FCCS: sociology, anthropology, geography, geology, and land stewardship and community economic and social development. Faculty in FCCS consist of Indigenous Peoples and settlers who all have created relationships and partnerships with Indigenous communities. Our primary concerns are the environment and working to develop educational programs that support healing the natural and cultural environments in which we work and live.

Conclusion

In conclusion, when the general population becomes aware of and informed by the vast body of Indigenous Knowledges and the intellect and sciences of Indigenous communities across time, they begin to decolonize their minds and hearts. Decolonizing minds and hearts informs and challenges racism and discrimination. Anyone can begin to decolonize the spaces they live and interact in, creating paths to healing for all people. Thinking critically about what you are taught and what you read and experience is the beginning of the journey. Pyroepistomology is the fire within your spirit, the voices of ancestors that raise red flags and open spaces to cleansing and healing. Building networks of like-minded and informed people builds the fire; each voice adds one flame to cleanse colonized spaces, creating room for holistic growth and knowledge. Pyroepistomology weaves Knowledge from ancestral community fires and nurtures embers from Knowledge holders that feed heart and spirit, sending healing smoke across the land. Indigenous Knowledges and TEK weave paths to healing for all communities and the Earth. Much more than a tool of education, Indigenous Knowledges and TEK are ways of living and daily practices that are based on thousands of years of keen observation and worldviews in which all beings are related and respected.

15

A CARING UPHEAVAL
Transnational Abolitionism as a Pathway to More Reciprocal Futures

JONATHAN JAMES FISK

Positionality Statement

Taíno Boricua; born and raised on Tongva land, Ahwaanga, Long Beach, California; now living on Hawaiian lands, Kamōʻiliʻili, Oʻahu; University of Hawaiʻi at Mānoa

Introduction

Traditional Ecological Knowledge (TEK) as lived and embodied Knowledge (Simpson 2014) is a product of generations of Indigenous Peoples' intimate relations with the land. TEK is inseparable from larger paradigms—cultural epistemologies, ontologies, ideologies, and cosmologies—a component of larger "Knowledge-practice-belief complexes" that evolve as our knowledges, practices, paradigms, and surrounding social-environmental contexts change over time (Berkes 2018; Kimmerer 2013). For Indigenous communities, in particular, TEK is situated within kincentric ecological models wherein humans and the environment are not fully separate but instead entangled and interdependent with one another (Salmón 2000). Kincentric ecology describes how many Indigenous Peoples understand ourselves "as part of an extended ecological family that shares ancestry and origins" with other species and often the lands, waters, and air themselves (Salmón 2000, 1332). Such ontologies (ways of being and understandings of what is) and cosmologies (spirituality and understandings of the metaphysical) underscore how life is possible and abundant only when humans view the more-than-human life that surrounds us as kin, relatives, and cherished interconnected relations. Living in reciprocity with all of our relations is paramount to kincentric ecological ways of living: "Reciprocal relations underscore the mutual caretaking obligations held between and among nature and society, as intertwining entities that co-constitute one another" (Diver et al. 2019, 402).

Within many Indigenous lifeways, upholding reciprocal relations shapes everything from how and what we learn (Meyer 2004; Simpson 2014) to our deepest intimacies with each other and the land itself, with self and land often becoming indistinguishable (Kimmerer 2013; Osorio 2021). Cultural norms of reciprocity and the Indigenous Knowledges (e.g., TEK) born from reciprocal practices are vital to cultivating social-environmental resilience, a pressing concern as anthropogenic forces such as climate change, biodiversity loss, and defaunation harm our communities and loom over our futures (Diver et al. 2019; Salmón 2000). Furthermore, as movements toward decolonization—and therein the reinstitutionalization of TEK and surrounding paradigms (Fisk et al. 2021; Tuck and Yang 2012)—gain popularity and social traction, it's critical to inspect what honoring such reciprocal relations fully entails and what barriers inhibit living out such transformations. This is particularly important within contemporary, globalized, multicultural geographies and ecologies, in which a slew of different cultures and paradigms, particularly colonial paradigms, are often enmeshed with and dominate over Indigenous ways of living, reinforcing barriers to cultivating such social transformations toward Indigenous ontologies.

I write this chapter as a Taíno person born and raised in the diaspora in Long Beach, California, now living in Kamōʻiliʻili, Oʻahu. In this text, I uphold my responsibilities and intimacies with two lands I call home, genealogically and currently—Puerto Rico and Hawaiʻi, respectively. This is an important task, particularly given these lands' and Indigenous Peoples' shared histories of US colonialism and internal neocolonialism. As a diasporic Indigenous scholar, I highlight some of these shared struggles and futures, interweaving narratives rooted in these two lands to elucidate the overarching themes surrounding barriers toward achieving reciprocal relations, the material and ideological implications of attempting to cultivate reciprocal relations, and what these implications entail in terms of global politics and solidarities.

Given that I was not born and raised in Puerto Rico nor am I a Kanaka ʻŌiwi (Native Hawaiian), I do not want to focus on Indigenous cultural specificities too much, as that doesn't feel like my place to write about for this piece, instead inspecting the bigger picture of cultures, social systems, and food and material systems. Similarly, because of my positionality within

the diaspora as well as my organizing and kinship with Black family, I want
to devote special attention to the global nature of the worlds we inhabit,
especially how our very notions of kinship and reciprocity can expand such
that decolonization becomes a transnationalist project where all can be fed,
cared for, and find home. In particular, I focus on the materiality of our
contemporary social-environmental systems, especially our food systems,
within global contexts. In doing so, I highlight how existing material and
ideological systems are premised on the denial of reciprocity, domestic and
abroad, operating through ideals of extraction, exploitation, domination,
and neglect. By exploring the interconnectedness of material systems and
the systemic changes required to reinstitutionalize reciprocity in Puerto
Rico and Hawaiʻi, I trace how the political projects of abolitionism and
transnationalism are vital for cultivating reciprocity and shared liberation
for Indigenous communities and all of our relations.

SYSTEMS OF HARM

Accompanying colonialism, which dispossesses Indigenous communities of
our lands and lifeways, are interlocking material and ideological "systems of
harm" such as capitalism, (cishetero-)patriarchy (oppression and exploitation based on domains of gender and sexuality), imperialism, racism, and
ableism. The commonality shared among these systems is their logic of
domination and exploitation, wherein those explicitly or implicitly deemed
superior are granted social impunity in wielding power over and socially
abandoning othered classes, including the land, for the sake of maintaining
and deepening their relative power and profit (Kaba 2021; Povinelli 2020;
Walia 2021). Through their common logic, these systems reinforce and
shape the evolution of one another, mutually ensuring that their respective
striations of power and dominance persist such that the boundaries between
these systems are often indistinguishable (Osorio 2021; Povinelli 2020;
Walia 2021). Because of this interlocking nature, I use the term *systems of
harm* to encapsulate these systems and note the damage of their overarching impacts; although using this generalizing term, I also specify certain
systems by name to elucidate distinct dynamics within these systems.

One key impact of these systems of harm is their prevention and denial
of reciprocal relations, socially and environmentally, acting as fundamental
barriers toward reciprocity as a cultural norm (Osorio 2021; Salmón 2000).
This deficit of reciprocity is not an unintended by-product of these systems;
rather, their existence is premised on the structural denial of reciprocity

and on their accompanying power dynamics remaining entrenched and unchallenged. These systems of harm can persist only so long as reciprocal relations are forsaken and opposed.

The food and material systems in Puerto Rico and Hawai'i lay bare how these systems of harm necessitate and facilitate the denial of reciprocity. These distinct island chains are remarkably food insecure, importing about 85 percent of the foods consumed locally (Ginzburg 2022; Loke and Leung 2013). This high degree of dependency on imports is a historical product of colonialism and capitalism, particularly through the dispossession of land via direct land grabs and neoliberal cycles of socioeconomic displacement and privatization (Carro-Figueroa 2002; McMichael 2012; Morales 2019; Trask 1999). Facilitating this dispossession is the ongoing capitalist and (neo-)colonial seizure and consolidation of governing powers over food systems in the hands of the US federal government and large corporations. Through their entrenching of "corporate food regimes" (McMichael 2009) on the islands, these outside entities (e.g., US-based corporations such as Dole and Monsanto, now a subsidiary of Bayer) seek to maximize profits by keeping the islands dependent on their foods and products; thus, the precariousness of the islands' food systems becomes part of the profit model (Ginzburg 2022; Gupta 2015; McMichael 2012; Povinelli 2020).

Capitalism- and colonialism-induced food insecurity erodes systems of kinship and thereby disconnects us from our relations. Immediately, food insecurity creates disconnections from land and removals of agency to maintain reciprocity as Indigenous Peoples are displaced from their lands, forced to find jobs in non-agricultural and non-fishing sectors, and often pushed into urban centers or cast into diaspora for employment (Carro-Figueroa 2002; McMichael 2012; Vaughan 2018). Land becomes abandoned, rendered into a commodity sold in pursuance of survival. Further disconnections form between those who consume locally and those who produce elsewhere (e.g., those who farm, raise livestock, prepare and package foods and those who are exploited, forced into unsafe working conditions, and even killed for the sake of keeping the corporate food regime churning; Condra 2011; McMichael 2009). Subsequently, the foods we currently eat in Puerto Rico and Hawai'i are made available only by the extraction from lands and subjugation of communities invisibilized—a relationship wherein reciprocity is made impossible through intentional opacity.

Within the predominating corporate food regime, even local food production often bows to capitalist ideals, with the primary goal being profit maximization rather than local sustenance or ecological welfare. In the current structuring of food systems in Puerto Rico and Hawai'i, a significant portion of locally grown foods are produced solely for the sake of exporting rather than feeding local communities (over $500,000 annually for Hawai'i, and with no reliable statistics for Puerto Rico because of government neglect of data tracking), thus exploiting the favorable island climates and rich soils for the sake of profit within global markets while neglecting local peoples' needs and relations (Ginzburg 2022; Gupta 2015; Loke and Leung 2013; Ortiz Cuadra 2017). To compete in these global markets, destructive industrial agricultural practices reign supreme (e.g., monocropping "cash crops" in fields laden with toxic pesticides) and reduce lands and foods from kin to commodities and mere vehicles for profit.

Whereas TEK often emphasizes multigenerational sustainability to ensure that future generations experience abundance, industrial agriculture focuses on maximizing economic gains such that warping and extracting from the land until rendered barren becomes a normalized practice. With food no longer about communal and ecological welfare, but instead geared for the financial benefit of a relative few, these capitalist modes of food systems operate through the direct exploitation of workers throughout the supply chain (particularly migrant workers in the case of the United States, many of whom are Indigenous to lands now known as Latin America), the destruction of local environments through mechanisms like deforestation and biodiversity reduction, and the endangerment of nearby communities subjected to toxic runoff and pesticide exposure. When the foods we call kin are rendered into commodities, the relations we have with them that underly TEK are distorted at a foundational level and values of reciprocity and mutual care are replaced with the desire for capital and maximum efficiency, thus stripping our kin of any agency or perceived worth outside of the prices they can fetch. Within these capitalist food systems, kincentric Indigenous values are discarded and actively discouraged for the sake of capturing market potential.

To afford this gross dependency on imported foods, the corporate food regime dictates that Puerto Rico and Hawai'i have our economies (re-) structured on more tenuous but financially lucrative industries, particularly tourism, militarism, and manufacturing (Ginzburg 2022; Morales 2019; Trask 1999). These industries epitomize an absence of reciprocity by commercializing land and local communities to appease the idyllic fetishes of the tropics (Morales 2019; Trask 1999); razing and desecrating lands and communities under the guise of national security (Akaka et al. 2018; McCaffrey 2002); and abandoning the land and treating pollution as an unavoidable casualty for the sake of industrialism and the pursuit of infinite growth, wherein our kincentric ecologies have little to no value aside from the profits they might potentially yield (Beamer et al. 2021; Hunter and Arbona 1995; Liboiron 2021b).

The colonialist fetishization of our tropicality and cultures in Hawai'i and Puerto Rico hides how these industries that purport to appreciate, protect, and support our Peoples drive the displacement of local and Indigenous communities, in particular, from our islands (Trask 1999). Within the islands' dominant material systems, the economies that allow for continued food imports require the abject exploitation and neglect of lands and communities domestic and abroad, a global truncating of reciprocity for the profit of the corporate food regime and its collaborating industries. Through this exploitation and neglect of land and each other, our economies facilitate disconnection from our relations, ecologies, and intimacies with land, underlying TEK deemed unnecessary and counterproductive, and the time and care needed for cultivating and tending to relations with the land deemed distracting from supposed economic security. The material dependency on these industries reenforces capitalist lifeways wherein profit reigns as the supreme concern and local and Indigenous Peoples are coerced into these harmful economies for the sake of surviving within capitalism, further driving a caustic wedge between Indigenous communities and our abilities to live via our Traditional lifeways.

With the food systems of Puerto Rico and Hawai'i as the focal locus of our broader material and social systems, it becomes evident that the prevailing systems of harm, such as the corporate food regime, continuously deepen the deprivation of reciprocal relations on these lands and globally, too. Whether between the islands' Peoples and lands (particularly Kānaka 'Ōiwi and Taíno Peoples and our genealogical lands), local people and lands elsewhere ensnared in these systems of harm, or between the islands' people and other communities now coerced into relations of exploitation, reciprocity is corroded and denied, and kinship is remodeled into neoliberal market-based relations. Under these capitalist and colonialist paradigms, the intimacies of Indigenous food systems are stripped away to be replaced by marketability. The caring kincentric relations that inform our TEK are distorted by destruction, displacement, and coerced assimilation until our capacity to maintain our reciprocal relations with the land and each other dwindles, truncating our abilities to practice and perpetuate our Indigenous Knowledges, let alone ensure the intergenerational welfare of our human and more-than-human kin.

ABOLITIONISM TOWARD RECIPROCAL RELATIONS

Understanding that the existence of these systems of harm depends on and reinforces the denial of reciprocity, then reinstitutionalizing reciprocal relations must therefore entail the abolition of these systems. Concepts of abolition are often invoked in relation to specific structures, such as prison abolition and border abolition, denoting the dissolution of these systems and their underlying ideologies (Kaba 2021; Walia 2021). Given that systems of harm are materially and ideologically interlocked, this text evokes *abolitionism* to refer to the wholesale abolition of these interconnected systems and their common logic. I wield this broad-based term with the understanding that, because of their mutually reinforcing nature, no single system within these systems of harm could be fully abolished without the abolition of all of them, and that the continued existence of any one of them would entail the deferral of reciprocity (Kaba 2021; Tuck and Yang 2012; Walia 2021).

Abolition is certainly about the choice of what to raze or destroy, but even more so, it's about the worlds we want to create: an abject refusal of current systems and ideologies that are incompatible with more just, abundant, and reciprocal futures, as well as a meditation on what those futures could look like, how we can build them, and how we can live them in the present day (Kaba 2021; Kelley 2022). In this questioning of what we can construct, Traditional modes of reciprocity offer guidance.

Reciprocity offers a nucleus around which we can construct more just and abundant futures, particularly through re-institutionalizing kincentric ecologies as cultural modes—methods and norms through which we can understand and interact with ourselves and our relations in more caring and reciprocal ways (Diver et al. 2019; Salmón 2000; Simpson 2014). With ontological foundations in Indigenous paradigms, abolition and decolonization can become synergistic political projects that inform what we reject from present society (e.g., systems and ideologies that are premised on domination, deny reciprocity, and inhibit Indigenous lifeways) and what we can build together (e.g., futures that are predicated on communal care and responsibility, facilitate reciprocity, and are grounded in the histories and possibilities of Indigenous lifeways; Fisk et al. 2021; Tuck and Yang 2012). Where abolitionism prompts us to ask, "What can be?" reciprocity offers the tender reply, "This." In particular, TEK as lived Indigenous Knowledge systems offers place-based cultural modes outside of the ideologies propped up by systems of harm—lifeways that have been lived for innumerable generations by Indigenous Peoples and can become social norms once again to replace dominant ways of living with more caring and reciprocal alternatives. Furthermore, TEK as a lived process provides political and ecological guidance for how abolitionism can be carried out as a political project while ensuring we are acting in care and reciprocity toward our entangled tapestries of kin.

A monumental example of the potential born from the weaving of abolitionism with reciprocity and TEK is the Protect Kahoʻolawe ʻOhana (PKO), a group of Kānaka ʻŌiwi who, starting in 1976, occupied the island of Kahoʻolawe, putting their bodies on the line in an attempt to stop the US Navy from bombing the island (Akaka et al. 2018). A key feature of this group was the centering of Hawaiian culture and Hawaiian paradigms throughout their conduct and their goals, letting Traditional lifeways inform their path against the largest military in the world and create pathways toward futures where we live in better reciprocity with and care for the land. After nearly twenty years of protest, PKO was successful in getting the US military to agree to end their use of Kahoʻolawe, although efforts to restore the ecologies of this revered land are still ongoing after the decades of intensive bombings. A struggle that many had deemed an impossible battle, the fight to protect Kahoʻolawe not only centered Hawaiian culture in their vision for a free Hawaiʻi, but also directly informs and inspires generations of work to care for the land in reciprocity, freeing the islands of militarism and other such systems of harm, and ensuring that Hawaiian culture once again becomes the vibrant and unfettered norm in Hawaiʻi.

Given how insidiously and subversively systems of harm have been established and indoctrinated as inescapable norms, though, profound rigor is required to uproot these systems, their founding ideologies, and their common logics. What is and what can be must be critiqued down to the very foundation to ensure that reciprocity and kincentricity are the roots of our futures rather than branches grafted onto otherwise sickly trees. That is, it would be insufficient to focus on reforming current systems, even seemingly benign manifestations of systems of harm, while the underlying ideologies remain intact. Such reforms might achieve marginal betterment and opportunities for pockets of reciprocity amid otherwise violent terrains, but in leaving the larger systems unchallenged, they risk replicating and reproducing systems of harm. Even at their most efficacious, they risk being sabotaged by or appropriated into dominant systems.

To highlight the potential of weaving abolitionism with reciprocity, as well as the pitfalls of reformist engagements with reciprocity, I turn again to the food systems of Puerto Rico and Hawai'i. I focus here on small-scale agricultural initiatives as a locus of change to demonstrate the depth of rigor required to ensure reciprocity is the foundation of our futures. Across both island chains, numerous small-scale agricultural initiatives (e.g., community gardens, several-acre plots operated by nonprofits, and agricultural social enterprises) are sprouting up to counter the corporate food regime and work toward food security, food sustainability, and, ultimately, food sovereignty (Loke and Leung 2013; Carro-Figueroa 2002). Many of these efforts have been led by the Indigenous Peoples of our lands as a way to work toward food sovereignty and perpetuate our Traditional ways of relating with the land and our food systems, as is particularly the case with the restoration of lo'i kalo (wetland taro fields) in Hawai'i (Akutagawa et al. 2012; Goodyear-Ka'ōpua 2009). These efforts increase local food production and local power over food systems, and in doing so, they elucidate the potential for implementing kincentric paradigms as well as the unwitting risks of perpetuating dominant ideologies.

Market-based strategies are popular approaches for small-scale agricultural initiatives because of their promise of self-sustaining economics and potential for generating enough revenue to cover the costs and possibly facilitate the growth of such ventures (Loke and Leung 2013). However, these market-based strategies still operate within capitalistic frameworks, ultimately leaving capitalism unchecked, as a system and as a set of ideologies. Additionally, these approaches often pardon capitalism by only questioning how capitalism could look different while leaving the overall power dynamics and infrastructure untouched. A common line of thinking is that market-based strategies are a way to work *within* the system to *change* the system, but projects centered on internal reform raise questions about the efficacy, lack of reciprocity, and unintended harms caused by such approaches (Holt Giménez and Shattuck 2011). An example of a common market-based strategy in Hawai'i and Puerto Rico is the labeling of locally grown foods, as with the "Hawai'i Seal of Quality" program of the State of Hawai'i Department of Agriculture. These labeling initiatives aim to inform consumers such that they will be more compelled to buy from locally sourced foods and, through these consumer behavioral changes, shift the market in the favor of local growers such that their enterprises can expand (Holt Giménez and Shattuck 2011). Although this labeling of local foods can be valuable for some degree of consumer awareness, this strategy ultimately fails to address the overarching power structures of the corporate food regime, leaving the onus of food system transformation on consumer habits. Even further, reformist market-based strategies like the labeling of local foods raise questions about how far these approaches can take us toward food sovereignty and liberation, as well as the degree to which these approaches are compatible with Indigenous Knowledges and Traditional cultural modes.

In particular, what are the scalability and liberatory potentials of market-based approaches, and how deeply are these approaches rooted in Traditional lifeways and our ways of relating? Do we reasonably expect the institutions upholding the corporate food regime and market forces to bow out to market-based opposition, beaten at their own game? In discussing the dismantling of racist patriarchy, Audre Lorde notes that "the master's tools will never dismantle the master's house. They may allow us *temporarily* to beat him at his own game, but they will never enable us to bring about *genuine change*" (Lorde 2003, 112; emphasis added). Lorde highlights how the master's tools (in this case, the ideologies that serve as the foundation for racist patriarchy as well as the structures of power and ways of relating that sprout from racist patriarchy) will never themselves yield true liberation from the master (racist patriarchy) as they are inherently limiting in scope, and that dreaming and working outside these structures and systems is necessary to rid ourselves of the master. The master's tools not only have limits, but they can also be used to co-opt attempts to dismantle the master's house, instead refurbishing and remodeling the house to improve its appearance and palatability. In regard to food systems, this is readily seen in the commercial labeling of "sustainable" and "organic" products and the subsequent actions of corporate food regimes in corrupting these concepts into legal definitions deprived of their deeper intentions, prioritizing marketability over reciprocal relations with the land and those who tend it (McMichael 2009).

Furthermore, in relying on the master's tools, we risk perpetuating the master's ideologies; particularly, what it means to keep our food systems commercialized in the first place. Consider yuca (*Manihot esculenta*) and kalo (*Colocasia esculenta*), two of the most principal crops in Hawai'i and Taíno cultures that are paramount within our cosmologies, prized as abundant starchy staples that have fed our communities for countless generations, and also as a key focus of many of local agricultural initiatives (Goodyear-Ka'ōpua 2009; Ortiz Cuadra 2017). In trying to revitalize the place of yuca and kalo within our local food systems and rebuild our relations with them, what does it mean to relegate the statuses of our kin to commodities (e.g., Yucahú for yuca and Hāloa for kalo)? How does the commodification of our kin—our ancestors—premise our relationships with them on exploitation for profit (the bottom line for market-based approaches) rather than reciprocity decoupled from commercial value? By focusing on the fiscal viability of cultivating yuca and kalo, how are we failing to ask how food systems could operate without the commercialization of kin, without colonial separations of self from these plants, where food production and distribution aren't contingent on profit and affordability but instead mutual responsibilities to the land and others? Which aspects of our Traditional Knowledge systems and lifeways are we neglecting and which ones are we in conflict with when we contort our relations with our floral, faunal, and fungal kin for the sake of participating in market economies? How might such commodifications of these plants—these ancestors—distort our collective understandings of them as sacred and venerated kin with whom we have responsibilities to care for and live in reciprocity?

Additionally, how might market-based approaches to food systems transformation lead us to unwittingly maintaining unsavory components within the peripherals of our food systems? For example, how might the pressure for profit lead to a reliance on monoculture to meet a market niche versus an emphasis on multiscale biodiversity to facilitate ecosystem-level abundance? What are the impacts of the various resources being used for these agricultural initiatives, such as gasoline that contributes to emissions, tractors that compact the soil, and pesticides that devastate bug ecosystems and soil microbiology, nearly all of which are likewise extracted and imported via corporations from elsewhere? How does our use of these resources impact our ecologies, our Indigenous Knowledges of our ecologies and how to live in reciprocity with them, and our broader kinship networks regarding their production and consumption? Does our use of these resources uphold reciprocal relations with those producing the resources, or are we reliant on inputs derived from exploited labor and lands, particularly in the Global South (Galeano 1997; Nkrumah 1970; Rodney 2018)?

Finally, on the topic of land, the focus on small-scale agricultural initiatives beckons the question of whether small-scale efforts, even if they
proliferate, could ever match the scale of local food needs and larger socioeconomic forces, let alone facilitate the return of the lands of Hawai'i and
Puerto Rico to Indigenous Peoples in the face of the scale of such socioeconomic forces. What does it mean to create and maintain refugia when
the majority of the lands on our islands remain dispossessed, exploited,
and under mounting degradation? How might the prioritization of refugia
within food systems perpetuate dynamics where those in our communities with fewer resources or access to social capital are passively refrained
from cultivating reciprocal relations with foods and the land? Refugia are
certainly invaluable spaces, but they still leave our ecosystems of relations
and responsibilities fragmented while systems of harm and their ideologies
maintain power over Indigenous Peoples' land. What scale of land reclamation is necessary to ensure that the full expanse of our ecologies and
kin can experience reciprocal relations? How can such land reclamation in
Puerto Rico and Hawai'i be achieved in ways that don't rely on the master's tools, particularly market-based approaches and capitalist ideologies?
How can TEK and our Traditional relations with the land be the methodology through which we reclaim our ancestral lands, ensuring reciprocity
throughout the process and for innumerable generations to come?

These lines of questioning aren't meant to devalue small-scale agricultural initiatives or downplay their role in fostering reciprocal relations
with the land, particularly in urbanized settings where many of us have
been indoctrinated and conditioned to not understand our lands as kin,
nor to live in good, reciprocal relations with the land. As someone who
regularly participates in such agricultural endeavors, I've felt their potential for personal transformation in how we understand our relations with
our kincentric ecologies. These initiatives have helped teach me the names
and rhythms of countless plants, given me access to seeds, seedlings, and
cuttings to raise and care for in my apartment (including yuca and kalo),
and continually stoked my curiosity around these floral, faunal, and fungal
kin and how I can facilitate their abundance and live more intimately with
them. I've witnessed these programs empower community members, across
generations and cultural backgrounds, with resources and Indigenous
Knowledges so they can become more intimate with their foods, live in
greater reciprocity with their ecologies, and change their everyday practices to be in closer alignment with TEK. Rather, these lines of questioning

highlight the relative limits and harms of common approaches, particularly when they unwittingly perpetuate the ideologies of systems of harm, as well as how efforts toward food systems transformation and food sovereignty can be made more generative. Interweaving the politics of abolitionism and reciprocity can allow for a more rigorous assessment of the futures we're building and how we're building them, offering guidance in our actions toward re-institutionalizing reciprocal relations and achieving collective liberation. Through this interweaving, we're better equipped to discern how exactly TEK, rather than the ideologies of systems of harm, can be the means through which we cultivate a future where reciprocity and Traditional lifeways once again become the unfettered social norm.

Conclusion and Transnationalism

Interlocking systems of harm maintain Indigenous Peoples' dispossessions and the ruling class hegemony, particularly through the denial of reciprocal relations with the land. In addition to the outright harms birthed and perpetuated by these systems, their underlying ideologies complicate and hinder the restoration of reciprocity, especially for our material systems, such as food systems, where prevailing ideologies might not be readily apparent. However, abolitionism offers a political framework for dissolving these systems of harm and their ideologies—a necessary endeavor for reinstitutionalizing reciprocity, decolonizing our cultural and material systems, and cultivating Indigenous sovereignty, particularly through the restoration of TEK and the ways of relating with each other and the lands that uphold our lifeways.

Grounding abolitionism in Indigenous paradigms of reciprocity and kincentric ecologies requires looking beyond our immediate geographies. Just as the food and material systems of Puerto Rico and Hawai'i are dependent on resources and labor from outside of the islands, globalization has ensnared us within international webs of exploitation and neglect (Galeano 1997; McMichael 2009; Nkrumah 1970; Povinelli 2020). Recognizing the global nature of systems of harm means that a transnationalist approach is necessary to achieve mutually assured liberation: reciprocity in one geography requires supporting reciprocal possibilities everywhere, and understanding that all lands and peoples are worthy of abundance and reciprocity.

In particular, a transnationalist approach to engendering reciprocity entails abolishing our borders, rejecting border nationalism that divides our geographies and communities along contrived and rigid lines, and creating shared economies of kinship to establish local, regional, and global systems of reciprocity with the land and each other (Walia 2021). The ecologies we're in kinship with and the material systems we inhabit stretch far beyond our national borders, and so, too, do our understandings of community and kinship. Who we should strive for reciprocity with shouldn't be confined to the national borders dissecting our lands and relations.

The transnationalist implications of the interplay between the abolition of systems of harm and reinstitutionalizing reciprocal relations raise potent questions around paths to Indigenous sovereignty. How can decolonization prioritize restoring Indigenous governance over our lands without replicating the logics of ethnonationalism wherein tenuous inclusion is premised on the exclusion of those deemed as *Other*? How can Indigenous paradigms be restored and reinstitutionalized while allowing for their evolution, for multiplicities within and across cultures? How can our senses of kinship and reciprocal belonging overcome colonial logics of blood quantum and biological racism? Particularly, how can our senses of kinship (re-)expand to encompass our broader tapestry of relations, particularly for Black Natives who face lateral violence within our communities and for our broader Black kin who are often socially relegated as having no "true" land to call home? Likewise, how can our senses of kinship hold those within diasporas such that communities of different origins can still find belonging and a sense of place, live under Indigenous paradigms wherever they are without having to shed their respective cultures, and cultivate reciprocal relations with each other and the land?

The answers to the questions raised here will be culturally specific and evolve with time, but they are powerful questions worth exploring as we think of ways through which we can cultivate more abundant, intimate, and liberated futures together through reciprocity.

Acknowledgments

Although too many to list by name, I'd like to thank all of the people who have fed me over the years and taught me what it means to be in intimate relations with our environment, especially the foods we consume and can grow for one another. In particular, mahalo nui to all of the kalo farmers, fishers, limu gatherers, and stewards across Hawai'i who have shared your lands and your kin with me and have guided me in cultivating and continuously critiquing the reciprocal relations I seek to build with Hawai'i. I would also like to thank my PhD committee—Mehana Vaughan, my adviser; Noelani Goodyear-Kaʻōpua; Kirsten Oleson; Malia Akutagawa; and Clay Trauernicht—for all of your guidance during my PhD tenure, without which this analysis wouldn't have been possible. Last, I would like to thank all of my friends and family, blood and chosen, and particularly my parents, for supporting me throughout all these years.

The author of this chapter acknowledges funding from the National Science Foundation (grant number 2018254693).

16

A CRITICAL DECLARATION OF DECOLONIZATION AND INDIGENIZATION FOR SCIENTIFIC RESEARCH AND THE ACADEMY

BY LARA A. JACOBS, CHERRY YEW YAMANE, JESSICA HERNANDEZ, TARA MCALLISTER, ANDREW KALANI CARLSON, JONATHAN FISK, KAT MILLIGAN-MCCLELLAN, JOSEPH GAZING WOLF, LYDIA L. JENNINGS, JENNIFER GRENZ, CORAL AVERY

Positionality Statements and Land Acknowledgments

Jacobs. See Introduction for positionality statement.

Yamane. Kanaka ʻōiwi (Hawaiian), Uchinanchu (Okinawan); Moku o Waiʻanae hometown; now living on Potawatomi lands; University of Washington

Hernandez. Maya Chʼortiʼ and Binnizá (Zapotec) now living on Duwamish lands; University of Washington

McAllister. Te Aitanga a Māhaki (Māori) hapū (subtribe) Te Whānau a Taupara; raised on the ancestral lands of Ngāti Awa and Ngāti Raukawa; Te Wānanga o Aotearoa

Carlson. See chapter 8 for positionality statement.

Fisk. See chapter 15 for positionality statement.

Milligan-McClellan. Inupiaq; from Qikiktagruk; now on the territory of the Mohegan, Mashantucket Pequot, Eastern Pequot, Schaghticoke, Golden Hill Paugussett, Nipmuc, and Lenape Peoples; University of Connecticut

Gazing Wolf. See chapter 13 for positionality statement.

Jennings. Pascua Yaqui (Yoeme) and Huichol (Wixárika); raised in Tewa lands of Northern New Mexico; now living in Tohono O'odham and Pascua Yaqui lands of Southern Arizona; University of Arizona

Grenz. See chapter 25 for positionality statement.

Avery. Shawnee Tribal Citizen of Shawnee and mixed-European Heritage; Kispoktha ancestral town; raised on Kumeyaay Lands; now living on Kalapuya, Cowlitz, Siletz, Grand Ronde, and Atfalati Lands; Portland State University

Introduction

Though many forms of colonialism operate in society today (including but not limited to settler colonialism and neo-imperialism, etc.), each form shares common characteristics. "Colonialism is more than the intent, identities, heritages, and values of settlers and their ancestors. It's about genocide and access" (Liboiron 2021b, 9). Colonialism functions through domination and exploitation to control individuals or groups in the pursuit of land, labor, and resources. Colonialism is about genocide and access and operates as a persistent "societal structure, not just an historical event or origin story for a nation-state" (Liboiron 2021b; Tuck and Ree 2013, 642). Settler colonialism is "comprised by a triad, including a) the Indigenous inhabitant, present only because of her erasure; b) the chattel slave, whose body is property and murderable; and c) the inventive settler, whose memory becomes history, and whose ideology becomes reason" (Tuck and Ree 2013, 642). Settler colonialism deliberately intends to replace and remove Indigenous Peoples, languages, cultures, epistemologies (ways of knowing), ontologies (ways of being), axiologies (value systems), and rights; in contrast, decolonization offers a solution to rectify such harms through liberating practices that center Indigenous futures and #LANDBACK efforts.

Scholars from around the world have described and theorized decolonization processes, and have outlined decolonial methodologies that aid in liberating colonized peoples from colonizers and systemic colonial structures (see, to start, de Oliveira Andreotti et al. 2015; Fanon 1961; Smith 2021; Cintrón, Corcoran, and Bleeden 2021; Tachine and Nicolazzo 2023; Mignolo 2021). There are many forms of decolonization and distinctions within decolonial theory, more than we can reasonably cover in one chapter, so in this chapter we provide a generalized understanding of the core forms. While decolonization is viewed by some as the reversing of European imperial expansion processes and all of its associated consequences (Von Bismarck 2022), others recognize decolonization as an unsettling and violent process that de-centers colonial norms and acts through liberation to replace the colonizers with the colonized (Fanon 1961; Risam 2018). Frantz Fanon, a foundational philosopher of decolonization, wrote that decolonization is "always a violent event," and the "substitution of one 'species' of mankind by another" (Fanon 1961, 1). He also reminds us that decolonization implicitly carries a necessity to challenge the colonial situation to a point in which "the last shall be first" (1961, 2).

For hundreds of years, colonial regimes have positioned the needs and realities of Indigenous Peoples as the last priority, even though they are the First Peoples of the lands now occupied by colonizing institutions and settlers (Molloy 2019). In an Indigenous context, placing the last as the first requires the process of Indigenization, which is available only to Indigenous Peoples. Indigenous scholars acknowledge how Indigenizing processes are copacetic with decolonization because both work toward the same objectives, especially by creating spaces for Indigenous Peoples to live, be, and embrace their Indigeneity without compromise, complicity, or assimilation (Pete, Schneider, and O'Reilly 2013; Fellner 2018; Ng and AyAyQwaYakSheelth 2018; Phillips 2022). We also explicitly emphasize that Indigeneity is inclusive of Black Indigenous Peoples globally, and across a spectrum of complex and overlapping identities that have arisen from colonial violence, such as forced displacement and enslavement (Mays 2021a). While we broadly discuss Indigenization in a way that is inclusive of and relevant to Black Indigenous Peoples, it is important to clearly acknowledge that there are additional, unique, and structural components of anti-Black colonialism that must be addressed in pursuit of full decolonization and Indigenization (Mays 2021b). Any attempts to Indigenize and decolonize that do not address anti-Black racism are fundamentally flawed. Moreover, we insist that sovereign Indigenous futures must also be co-created with Black Peoples whose Indigeneity may have been violently stolen from them and those who may not have Indigenous homelands to which they can return (Sharma 2021; King 2019). The struggles for decolonization, Indigenization, Indigenous sovereignty, and Black liberation are therefore impossible to disentangle.

Indigenization privileges, centers, and amplifies Indigenous Knowledges (IK—which include Traditional Ecological Knowledges or TEK) and perspectives. Indigenization requires anti-imperial relations that dismantle and replace dominant colonial knowledge systems with the locally grounded, place-based worldviews of IK (Pitawanakwat and Pedri-Spade 2022; Watermeyer and Yan 2022). Indigenization is the decolonial process of unsettling colonial norms and spaces by replacing them with Indigenous Peoples, Indigenous values, epistemologies, ontologies, and axiologies

(Gaudry and Lorenz 2018). Essentially, when guided only by Indigenous leadership, Indigenizing processes place the last as the first and meet the needs of decolonial objectives.

The general concepts of colonialism, decolonization, and Indigenization are central to academic research that involves Indigenous Peoples and our IK. Many Indigenous academics have put Fanon's idea of placing the last as the first into practice by advancing the meanings and theories of decolonization, including Ngāti Awa and Ngāti Porou (Māori) scholar Linda Tuhiwai Smith. In 1999, Smith wrote the pivotal book *Decolonizing Methodologies: Research and Indigenous Peoples* as a guide for unsettling imperial western knowledge and research practices in contexts that involve Indigenous communities. Since then, a plethora of scholars continue to employ decolonizing methods in the frameworks of their research praxes. However, as Turner (2022) writes, colonial power dynamics are built into university settings and academic discourse. The use of the language of decolonization in these settings, especially by non-Indigenous academics, has therefore been critiqued as superficial, metaphorization, and settler moves to innocence (Tuck and Yang 2012).

Superficial adoptions of decolonization do not work toward Indigenous Peoples' liberation and instead take more of an inclusionary model in which Indigenous Peoples and their Knowledges are welcomed into colonial spaces, situations, and research projects that meet colonial objectives. By employing inclusion discourse, the academy uses Indigenization to increase the numbers of Indigenous bodies in academic spaces (Gaudry and Lorenz 2018)—but including the excluded in colonial structures does not liberate them from the colonial powers that be nor allow for Indigenous sovereignty. Inclusion is not an act of Indigenization, but rather a shallow adaptation that drives Indigenous Peoples deeper into assimilative colonial systems that seek their replacement. Inclusion is a type of soft-reform in which there is no acknowledgment or disruption of the power dynamics that determine whose voice is heard, listened to, and perceived as intelligible, comfortable, and desirable (de Oliveira Andreotti et al. 2015). As an inherently violent and sometimes chaotic process, decolonization is not about including Indigenous Peoples to diversify ongoing colonial structures. Instead, decolonial objectives replace and challenge the dominance of non-Indigenous and white researchers and research systems, which are similar aims of Indigenization. This requires rejecting the positioning of non-Indigenous and white settler researchers at the center or within the central proximity of Indigenous research practices, which should be led only by Indigenous Peoples and communities.

Indigenizing and decolonizing methods require researchers to place Indigenous leadership at the forefront of all parts of the research process, from project development to methods creation and facilitation, data analysis, and long-term data storage. Truly dismantling and disrupting settler colonial systems requires intentional and active efforts that go beyond normalized practices of stating positionalities, issuing surface-level land acknowledgments, and reflecting on how identity politics afford some individuals certain powers and privileges more than others. Without implementing these intentional practices under the leadership of Indigenous communities, researchers wittingly or unwittingly maintain colonial systems that continue to oppress, marginalize, and weaponize settler supremacy and Euro-centric dominance against Indigenous Peoples.

Furthermore, individuals who do not dismantle and replace these colonial structures engage in a system of *performative decolonization* that embodies what Tuck and Yang (2012) deem the metaphorization of decolonization. Overcoming shallow, performative decolonization requires an unsettling process that replaces settler colonial structures and erases practices of centering whiteness and performative fragility. White fragility here is not perceived as a weakness but as a form of racial violence and a performance wherein white discomfort socially requires the subsequent validation and protection of white people from People of Color who are cast as the culprits of friction (Applebaum 2017). Therefore, performing white fragility centers white emotion, problematizes People of Color, and thereby functions as an act of power that shields white people and whiteness, giving such a performance the alternative name of "performance of invulnerability" (Applebaum 2017). Academic matters relating to decolonization and Indigenization must foreground Indigenous Peoples as authorities of our own IK, thereby placing settler colonial interests and actors last and eventually eliminating and dismantling the powers of colonial interests and values altogether.

The authors of this thought piece are Indigenous scholars from across multiple disciplines whose communities and ancestral lands are located in various global geographies. We reflect on how colonialism and the associated pervasively dominant colonial norms work against Indigenous Peoples within the current landscape of academia and how we can make stronger moves to decolonize and Indigenize these terrains in non-performative ways. We reflect on decolonization, Indigenization, and the Indigenous value system of reciprocity as liberating functions that can free Indigenous research (especially projects focused on IK and TEK) from colonial restraints. This chapter creates a pathway for researchers to consider when working with Indigenous communities. We do not present it as the only way forward, but rather as a starting point that requires constant evolution to rid education and research practices of colonial ideologies.

This chapter begins with a reflection on centering the Other, in which we consider how the colonial concept of Otherness works as a tool against Indigenous Peoples but can also be used by Indigenous Peoples as a weapon for liberation. We also merge decolonization with the Indigenous value system of reciprocity and discuss how this transformative practice creates *Indigenously Other* places when facilitated by Indigenous Peoples. Then, we provide a discussion on the possibilities of non-Indigenous collaboration with Indigenous communities and conclude with a declaration on decolonization and Indigenization for research and the academy. When researchers consider, engage with, and enact the contents of each section, they may subsequently employ tools of liberation that work toward the benefit of Indigenous communities by placing them as the first at all parts of the research process instead of engaging in performative decolonization.

Centering the Other

Smith (2021) sets forth an agenda for decolonizing research practices that make positive differences for Indigenous Peoples by centering Indigenous ways of Knowing and providing requirements for non-Indigenous researchers to understand and reflect on their positionalities and participation as they work with Indigenous communities. Other scholars note that decolonizing the research process should include exercising critical reflexivity; reciprocity and respect for self-determination; embracing "Other(ed)" ways of knowing; and embodying a transformative praxis (Thambinathan and Kinsella 2021). Decolonization praxes should center Indigenous Peoples as experts and leaders throughout the research process, honor Indigenous value systems of reciprocity, and thereby avoid replicating settler colonial dynamics of power. Unfortunately, critical reflexivity and embracing Other(ed) ways of knowing alone do not require such protocols.

THE CENTER OF CRITICAL REFLEXIVITY

Critical reflexivity tasks researchers with addressing the ethical and political questions shaping the research process and the sociopolitical and cultural contexts in which the production of knowledge is entrenched (Palaganas et al. 2017). However, in situations where non-Indigenous peoples engage with Indigenous research, the power of addressing, analyzing, and reflecting on the roles that colonialism plays in centering non-Indigenous norms is typically held by non-Indigenous researchers and their institutions. This dynamic upholds power structures deeply ingrained in western and colonial infrastructures, such as centering whiteness, white supremacy, and settler authority, which normalize extraction from Indigenous communities and analyses by non-Indigenous peoples. Therefore, the methodological praxis of critical reflexivity is not inherently decolonial on its own. Rather, centering non-Indigenous perspectives and non-Indigenous expertise on Indigenous communities and our Knowledges is a dangerous form of colonialism that maintains settler power and authority in the academy and elsewhere. Non-Indigenous epistemologies originate from western and colonial understandings and processes, which always separate and *Other* forms of Knowledge that originate from non-westernized peoples. As Bratman and DeLince (2022) detail, this long-standing power dynamic leads to the publication of historic inaccuracies, misrepresentations of Indigenous Peoples, and appropriation—and indeed, often proves problematic in research projects that include TEK and other forms of IK.

The advent of academic and institutional diversity, equity, and inclusion programs and the Biden administration's recent calls for including IK into federal land management practices (Exec. Order No. 14008 2021) underscore a social revolution that intends to embrace Other(ed) ways of knowing, especially TEK. However, these recent moves are criticized for maintaining colonial understandings of IK as Other(ed) and situating such Knowledges as external epistemologies that need to be embraced into the current dominant colonial understandings of the world. This further underlines the existing colonization of knowledge by western science as the authority on what can and should be included in western knowledge production. The sudden rush of interest in IK is also seen as part of colonial efforts to access, know, control, and commercialize Indigenous ways, thereby assaulting our Knowledge-based heritages and threatening epistemological sovereignty (Battiste and Henderson 2000).

EPISTEMOLOGICAL COLONIZATION AND COLONIAL METHODOLOGIES

The problem with the rush to include IK is that such practices ultimately uphold epistemological colonization via the colonial desire to bring IK into spaces in which they have historically never belonged and from which they are persistently excluded. Gordon (2011) highlights how Indigenous Peoples exist within a paradoxical world (in this case, academia) in which we do not ultimately belong and our existence (and embodied Knowledges) functions as illegitimate and Other. Furthermore, there is a historical pattern wherein colonizers try to bring together different forms of knowledge under their control, thus coalescing (or merging) knowledges into a dominant colonial center. This coalescing process leads to the suppression and colonization of Indigenous Knowledges that have existed independently outside of colonial centers since time immemorial. Therefore, we view efforts by the academy and non-Indigenous peoples to access our IK, especially our TEK, as another form of suppression, exploitation, and colonization (Stevenson 1998). The dangers of collapsing and absorbing IK into the center of the dominant colonial domain should be carefully considered and critiqued for potential harm before we ever consider our readiness to braid, weave, or integrate our IK with western epistemologies.

Recent moves toward epistemological colonization contrast the many generations in which western scientists and colonial entities discarded IK because our understandings and sciences were too different and not in line with western standards, because everything about us is Other(ed) and questioned by colonialism and non-Indigenous people. The academy only considers IK and sciences as valid when they support and/or benefit settler colonial scholarship, agendas, and claims. As Fúnez-Flores (2022b) states, the western academy is the "standard yardstick" by which non-western knowledges (or in this case, anything Other(ed)) are measured. This can be seen in the long history of western scientists ignoring Indigenous ways of Knowing, dismissing them as anecdotal, appropriating them as a convenient "mystical metaphor," and degrading them to a symbol of inferiority until western scientists could objectively "prove" or support our epistemologies and ontologies using western tools and methods (Deloria 1997; Simpson 1999; Arvin, Tuck, and Morrill 2013; Nicholas 2018). Taking our communities' words for how we understand processes and phenomena through our own methods has never been enough nor considered valid in the academy without western tools of verification (Stevenson 1998; Hernandez and Vogt 2020).

Western science has many methods to validate and legitimize data. However, colonization exists in methodology, too (Fanon 2008). A good example of this is the way western scientists rely on triangulation, which requires multiple methods and sources of data to form comprehensive scientific understandings and test validity (Carter et al. 2014; Patton 1999). In western scientific frameworks, IK must be triangulated with other data and methods for verification and in pursuit of "objectivity" (Cheveau et al. 2008). These processes center colonial and western regulations and thereby consider our IK not valid on their own. In contrast, decolonial and Indigenizing approaches situate Indigenous data as the central and most dominant data source without relying on western requirements to triangulate validity. However, the root of the issue should not be focused on the verifiability or validity of IK but on how western scientific paradigms cannot be separated from colonialism because the colonial rule will not implement anything other than colonial understandings and methods for assessment.

Western science always questions what our Knowledges do not know and lacks the capacity to understand, prioritize, and care for our data. Subsequently, our data remain Other(ed) in western scientific paradigms, where they become siloed as external data used to support objectives of inclusion and are analyzed via triangulation. By design, triangulation in western scientific paradigms ignores the fact that Indigenous Knowledges already include a spectrum of data that are inherently triangulated. Our IK are a *lived science* that has been passed down from one generation to another, incorporating multiple sources and types of analyses that are verified by Elders, oral Traditions, and other forms of data keeping (Nicholas 2018). Therefore, the very premise of triangulation in western science is insufficient for capturing the depth and richness of Indigenous Knowledge systems.

Indigenous Sciences and practices are confirmed as superior ways of Knowing by the direct and evident realities of the wonderous ecosystems that settlers encountered upon their arrival to the Americas, and the inferior western paradigms that have since led to the current climate crisis and its many destructive reverberations. Questioning the validity of Indigenous sciences is disrespectful, disempowering, and colonial because such questions are premised on a need for colonial legitimization processes that have historically been and are currently being used as weapons against Indigenous Peoples to invalidate every aspect of our existence (e.g., blood quantum). As Cree scholar Shawn Wilson (2008) writes, Indigenous researchers should move beyond engaging in western research paradigms and instead use Indigenous methodological approaches to scientific inquiry.

RESEARCH WITHOUT COMPROMISE

Non-Indigenous researchers often question how to conduct research in and with Indigenous communities while respecting and honoring IK, without compromising the rigor of western methodologies (Huntington 2000). However, this questioning is problematic because it assumes that IK and Indigenous data must conform to western scientific standards, perpetuating the need for colonial legitimization. Instead, we should question how non-Indigenous researchers can conduct their work in and with Indigenous communities without compromising Indigenous ways of Knowing, being, and relating to the world and while they actively maintain colonial norms. Such questions are crucial because of the positionalities, colonial ideologies and epistemologies, biases, reliance on western methods for data extraction, and approaches to data analyses and interpretation of non-Indigenous researchers. Each of these factors can create harm in Indigenous communities and produce scientific compromises at the expense of our communities.

IK should not be exploited and appropriated by non-Indigenous peoples, nor used for their benefits. Our cultural traumas, health disparities, pain and loss, and sacred information should not be used as extractable commodities or as steppingstones that further the career trajectory of settler researchers (Resnicow et al. 2000; Okamoto et al. 2014). Such practices have been criticized because the exploitation of IK for academic purposes without proper recognition and collaboration with Indigenous communities is a form of epistemic violence (Resnicow 2000; Okamoto et al. 2014). Such practices maintain historical exploitation and colonization, attempting to explain a sense of "contemporary brokenness" in the pursuit of colonial compromise (Tuck 2009). These compromises merely support western scientific rigor instead of enhancing and privileging Indigenous communities' "cultural rigor" (Echo-Hawk 2019; Yamane and Helm 2022). Decolonization and Indigenization methods require a refusal to compromise (Simpson 2014) and the disruption and dismissal of western scientific standards as punitive and colonial. Accordingly, such methods necessitate a rejection of colonial data verification processes and data mining objectives so that Indigenous data do not bend to the will of others who remain outside of our communities.

Refusing to compromise is a form of disruption and disturbance: a function of decolonization that recognizes IK beyond the judgment of dominant, colonial values that extract and gatekeep. Refusal is necessary because colonial objectives have historically ensured that everything Indigenous Peoples bring to the table is perceived as worthy of destruction and dispossession, as Other(ed), abnormal, and historic (not present). Other(ed) narratives about IK and non-Indigenous moves toward "embracing" our Knowledges may continue the long history of pervasive harms that colonial forces have perpetrated on Indigenous communities, our identities, land rights, dispossessions, and IK (Reddi, Kuo, and Kreiss 2021). The readiness of the dominant colonial system to acquire and embrace our Knowledges, and potentially coalesce them into the dominant domain, should be met with curiosity, critique, and refusals to compromise.

Mignolo (2021) asserts that resisting and refusing such dominance and disobeying the expectations of colonial structures secures the continuation of non-colonial ways, modes of Knowing, and ontologies. Buffalo Tiger, of the Miccosukee Tribe of Indians of Florida, links such resistance with Indigenous survival: "We survive, because we go with nature, we can bend, we are still attached to the earth. Now your way of life is no longer working, and so you are interested in our way. But if we tell you our way, then it will be polluted, we will have no medicine, and we will be destroyed as well as you" (Sonnenblume 2016).

Mignolo and Buffalo Tiger emphasize the importance of resisting colonial demands to fold our Knowledges into the colonial center and the significance that disobedience and refusal can play in maintaining cultural continuity. When faced with non-Indigenous requests to research and access our Knowledges, resisting becomes a methodological safeguard to maintain our Knowledges for our communities and protect them from outsiders. Within the safety of our communities, we can enact additional forms of resistance (e.g., maintaining and reviving Indigenous cultural values and practices) that challenge colonialism.

To this point, we have discussed the "Othering" of IK as a negative, a way that colonial systems denigrate, destroy, and disregard non-western data and practice. But, as Jairo Fúnez-Flores (2022a) writes, Otherness has the capacity to become a condition of possibility that unsettles dominant notions of reality and knowledge. We argue that it is possible to use colonial Othering processes to our advantage by understanding how their maintenance ensures that IK are left under our communities' control and authority and are therefore unable to be folded and coalesced into the dominant domain of colonial science. We can also do this by understanding the dangers of folding our Knowledges into the center of western domains where the power of interpretation and understanding will no longer be up to our communities to hold as sacred and sovereign. Otherness of our Knowledges then becomes a tool of self-determination and decolonization that we can use as armor to refuse compromise, resist inclusion, maintain our cultures, and liberate our communities from epistemological genocide.

The proverbial Ivory Towers are painted white for a reason: they were not built with Indigenous Peoples in mind but built as colonial establishments on stolen lands that still contain our ancestors' bodies, and they desire to assimilate our Knowledges into colonial centers, all while assimilating Native bodies and family structures into uniform patriarchal order (Grande 2018; Million 2009). As individuals within such colonial institutions, settler researchers who participate in processes that maintain European dominance cannot step outside of their perspectives and positions of power to see our Knowledges as anything but Other in comparison to the dominant narrative. Yet, decolonizing processes require us to break apart the dominant western scientific and colonial powers that dictate what is normal and what is Other. This unsettling and replacing process requires us to reject inclusion requests, refuse to compromise, and ensure IK are maintained by our Peoples who *live* the science.

LIVING THE SCIENCE

We argue that those who see Indigenous Sciences as normal and not "Other(ed)" are Indigenous Peoples who have understood natural and cultural phenomena since time immemorial: those who have been *living* the science. Indigenous Peoples have been thinking *with* natural and cultural phenomena since time immemorial (Watts 2013). Unlike western science, Indigenous Sciences cannot be taught through colonial methods of disseminating information. For example, Indigenous Sciences cannot be fully learned by non-Indigenous students at a western academic institution because our sciences are so deeply ingrained into and disseminated through cultural protocols, Traditions, and intergenerational Knowledges, as well as our Indigenous languages, value systems, songs, histories, ceremonies, origin stories, and sacred practices that are not shared outside of our communities. Locating Indigenous Sciences or other fields of study inside specific Indigenous territories contextualizes the relationships between the land,

People, and specific settler colonial contexts, and holds the work accountable to specific communities (Barker 2017; Baldy 2018). Our diverse ways
of Knowing can never be learned and understood fully outside of the context of living with our communities. We cannot teach our colonizers what
it means to be us nor the interlinkages of our Knowledges with every fabric
of our cultures. Therefore, we should refuse to entertain such ideas.

Taking a university class that focuses on the generalizations of our
diverse IK will never make a student an expert in our ways or able to fully
comprehend the connective fibers through which our sciences are lived and
woven. Reading academic literature and conducting academic research will
never make someone outside of our communities an expert in our sciences
or cultural Traditions. This is because a person has to grow up in our communities, *live* our sciences, and be raised with our values, ceremonies, perspectives, and languages to fully understand the inherent cultural linkages
and framing. In instances where Indigenous Peoples are raised outside of our
Indigenous community centers, reconnecting to these expertise-based factors can be associated with multiple barriers and challenges because of their
geographic and sociocultural locations. Moreover, non-Indigenous peoples
can never be experts on Indigenous matters because they do not *live* and
embody our sciences, cultures, and Traditions: they are not us and are therefore capable only of repeating, reinterpreting, and repackaging data that has
been mined from experts within our communities. Beyond these localized
epistemic threats, non-Indigenous peoples lack community accountability
for the outcomes of research that can expose Knowledges or individuals to
media exploitation, threaten the physical safety of community members, and
impact governmental or grant funding for essential services (Smith 2021).

Western scientific paradigms also require Knowledge validation
through credential processes (academic degrees) that dismiss Indigenous
expertise (Hernandez and Vogt 2020). In contrast, the scientific experts
within our Indigenous communities are our Elders, medicine peoples,
ceremonial leaders, and other Keepers of the Sacred who have lived and
enacted our sciences through systems of reciprocity and responsibility since
time immemorial with land, water, community, and our more-than-human
kin. Indigenous Peoples' lived experiences, expertise, and scientific understandings are not commodities that can be harvested, bought, and then sold
by academic institutions via tuition costs for courses and subscriptions to
scientific journals because they are living data woven into the fabric of our
cultures. Therefore, our lived realities, which are inherent to our IK, are

not extractable, exploitable, or exportable. No western scientific project will ever understand the full capacity and nuances of our understandings, values, Knowledges, and ways of being. Holding graduate degrees or other colonial markers of expertise does not define the Indigenous processes our communities hold sacred for learning and living our sciences.

Decolonization and Indigenization methods recognize that IK cannot be learned or enacted outside of our communities and lands by people who do not carry or live our values, speak our languages, or embody our cultures and the wisdom from our Elders. Therefore, we must violently refuse the notion that western scientists can be experts in matters pertaining to Indigenous Science and our communities. Instead, we must uphold our communal obligations to recognize the true experts of our communities and underline the fact that western scientists can only be external observers who analyze our data through western colonial minds.

Indigenous scientists are not Others in research that employs Indigenous Sciences within our communities. Our leadership centers on critical reflexivity that includes and embodies our lived sciences as an unsettling process that may obstruct, disrupt, and dismantle western academic norms; thus, unsettling and decolonizing the dominant narrative of who is considered an "expert" as opposed to who is considered an "area of expertise" (Chandler and Reid 2020; Hernandez 2022). Additionally, Indigenous scientists require research to be facilitated in a respectful way that honors and privileges Indigenous epistemologies and remains accountable to community relations. Therefore, unsettling, Indigenizing, and decolonizing processes address whose Knowledges are valid while remaining accountable and responsible to such Knowledges and communities via systems of reciprocity. These processes also ensure that we employ politics of refusal (Simpson 2014) that reject settler colonial interference in Indigenous research and in decisions about who may count as experts and how research should be structured. Through such processes, reflexivity then may serve as a mechanism that leverages decolonial tools of refusal (Museus and Wang 2022) that work toward transformative and liberating objectives.

Decolonial Reciprocity

Whereas performative decolonization makes strides to bring IK into the infrastructure of the colonial regime, decolonization requires actors to address and destroy attempts for IK to be absorbed into colonial systems. Decolonization requires the absolute destruction and replacement of these systems. Moreover, decolonization ensures that Indigenous community oversight obstructs the needs and frameworks that support western scientific objectives and norms. So, why are settler scientists and colonial governments so quick to include IK into the same systems that seek to remove and replace us? Bringing our Knowledges into what Lorde (2003) refers to as "the Master's House" will not destroy that house: we cannot do decolonial work from the inside of these structures. And the "Master's Tools" (especially inclusion and performative decolonization) will also never help us bring down the master's house. Decolonization praxes also do not require a seat at the master's table; Indigenous Peoples already have our own tables (Hernandez 2022). At these Indigenous tables we stand outside of what has been deemed acceptable or common practice: we create what Simpson (2014) calls ethnographic refusal and begin to map our own survival, rather than perpetuating ahistorical narratives crafted by colonial desire. Embracing and including IK in the master's house (academia and governing entities) cannot be looked at as an act of liberation or an act of decolonization: it can only be seen as performative. Decolonization requires burning down the master's house, creating our own structures and Indigenous systems, and using our own tools to do the real work of Indigenization.

Yet, we still see so many researchers using the master's tools (in this case, western scientific tools and protocols) to validate IK and our various forms of science. We see them using critical reflexivity in situations in which they do not have the positionality necessary to reflect on our IK. These are not decolonial practices but merely performative decolonial tools that provide what Liboiron (2021b) refers to as the *infrastructure and maintenance* needed for colonial power structures to maintain authority over Indigenous Peoples and IK. But how can Indigenous Peoples unravel ourselves out of the knots we are so deeply tied into under the colonial system and the subsequent onslaught of performative decolonization? We suggest that one answer to this question is found by putting decolonization into action and embracing the Indigenous value system of reciprocity.

Reciprocity may include principles that dictate how we function with our human and more-than-human kin via cyclical obligations and processes of giving forth to others and receiving things back via equal exchanges (Kimmerer 2011). Corntassel (2012) and Jacobs et al. (2022a,b) highlight how intimately reciprocity is tied to Indigenous responsibilities to take care of all elements of the Earth, including our Indigenous communities (Museus and Wang 2022), which extends to our responsibilities to care for and safeguard our Knowledges. If we look at colonialism and western science in terms of what they have given to Indigenous communities, we must shine a light on the violence, harm, dispossession, and destruction that have been and continue to be inflicted onto our Peoples by both systems. When we merge the violence central to decolonial practices (Fanon 1961) with our understandings of reciprocity as an equal exchange practice that is responsible to our communities and kin, then *decolonial reciprocity* would require a form of Indigenization-based resistance that makes an equivalent response to colonial harm by unsettling and destroying colonial systems and structures (Jaramillo and Carreon 2014). Though decolonial reciprocity may be misunderstood here as solely a negative force because it intends to destroy western colonial structures, it should also be viewed as a positive force that works toward the mutual benefit of Indigenous communities to support our collective liberation.

Positive and negative forms of reciprocity can work toward different objectives. Positive reciprocity promotes cooperation and regifting generosity while negative reciprocity is a tool used for punishment (Shaw, Barakzai, and Keysar 2019). However, as a balanced positive and negative force, decolonial reciprocity creates a situation in which reciprocity becomes a tool of decolonization that can be used to break apart the colonial structures that have harmed Indigenous Peoples for hundreds of years, while at the same time being a liberating weapon against the systems and structures that maintain our oppressions today.

So, how do we mirror such actions when it comes to western scientific norms? One answer is that decolonial reciprocity rejects the notion that Indigenous Peoples' participation in research should be considered as a "gifting" process and a form of reciprocity (Tsosie et al. 2021). Another answer lies in rejecting and obliterating western scientific control, power, and authority at all levels of the research process and at any point when IK are involved or when topics pertain specifically to Indigenous communities' interests. In doing so, we can collectively tear down these systems through a powerful act of Indigenous resistance and decolonial reciprocity, thereby liberating IK from colonial structures and power systems.

INDIGENOUSLY OTHER TRANSFORMATIVE PRAXES

Another driver of decolonized research is the embodiment of transformative practices, which are by-products of multidimensional critical consciousness that focus on "reflecting and acting upon the world in order to transform it" (Freire 1968, 36; Maseko 2018). Transformation becomes an important aspect of decolonization when the goals aim for Indigenous liberation, dismantling colonial structures, advocating for #LANDBACK, opposing colonialism, asserting Indigenous sovereignty, and embracing an ethic of incommensurability (recognizing and respecting the inherent differences and incompatibilities between different cultures and Knowledge systems; Tuck and Yang 2012; Burkhart 2019). In their landmark essay "Decolonization Is Not a Metaphor," Eve Tuck and K. Wayne Yang write about the unsettling nature of decolonization. They state that transformational and decolonial practices need to prioritize being responsible and accountable to the futures of Indigenous Peoples, rather than to settlers or their futures. Therefore, decolonization may not be a friendly enterprise, and it "indeed requires a dangerous understanding of commonality that un-coalesces coalition politics" (Tuck and Yang 2021). Decolonization requires abandoning ideas that non-Indigenous peoples will be commensurable (having common standards and values that can be assessed on similar scales) to Native Peoples, including in research practices.

Tuck and Yang also point out that settler colonialism can be conceptualized as the "unbroke pace of invasion" and occupation of Indigenous lands, whereas the process of decolonization is established to rematriate land to Indigenous Peoples. In an academic context, colonial neoliberal logics invade and become entangled in the academy at a pace that does not allow for those inside the academy to divorce themselves from it (Museus and Wang 2022). Moreover, universities still occupy stolen Indigenous lands and work for colonial agendas. So, can we even decolonize such structures without being performative?

Decolonization is not meant to be applied to preexisting colonial frameworks and structures—it intends to unsettle and dismantle them. However, the creation of something new, something *Indigenously Other*, may provide a space in which we can enact decolonial reciprocity and ensure that power structures, control, and self-determination of research and education are rematriated fully to Indigenous communities. By rejecting the "patriarchal invasion of our stories," we reject narratives of incompetence and invisibility (Baldy 2018). These *Indigenously Other* spaces must be created and administered by only Indigenous Peoples within our distinct Indigenous communities—the spaces that remain as Other(ed) outside of the academy. These are places in which we continue to walk, live, and breathe life into our sciences. These spaces may already exist within our many sovereign Nations' boundaries yet should evolve in a way that creates sovereignty around research practices and violently rejects all forms of colonial control, settler attempts to collect Indigenous Knowledges, and the inclusion of our bodies and data into colonial systems as we "(re)write, (re)right, and (re)rite" within the context of community (Baldy 2018). *Indigenously Other* spaces, therefore, would rightfully maintain Indigenous realities as independent, or Other(ed) to settler colonial norms. In contrast, maintaining colonial control over Indigenous research continues a long history of invading Indigenous communities by centering whiteness, colonialism, and the goals of the colonial institution and non-Indigenous researcher. The creation of *Indigenously Other* spaces should unsettle and transform colonial norms and replace them with Indigenous Peoples' leadership, sovereignty, objectives, and needs. To be clear: this is not an inclusion process, this is a replacement process.

Decolonial reciprocity requires Indigenizing the research process from beginning to end and finding ways to unsettle, disrupt, and replace all elements of colonialism, including funding, research leadership, methods, knowledge systems, and so on. Under this model, principal investigators of Indigenous research projects are Indigenous community leaders, Indigenous governmental workers, and Indigenous scientists; research objectives are crafted by Indigenous communities; and all funding is delivered directly back to Indigenous communities to support their ultimate liberation. The funding piece is crucial because academic institutions use large amounts of research grants to cover indirect administrative costs that support the maintenance and power of the colonial academy. Ensuring that Indigenous communities receive such funding instead allows us to oversee the distribution of research monies on our terms without supporting colonial objectives. Each of these changes play a role in how we can decolonize research, create pathways for liberation that support Indigenous futurities, and thereby make strides in dismantling the infrastructure of the academy.

Decolonizing research practices through decolonial reciprocity and Indigenizing frameworks may bolster Indigenous futurities that are not based on colonial norms or practices. Mvskoke scholar Laura Harjo (2019) states, "The focus of futurity . . . holds promise for recuperating the unactivated possibilities of our ancestors." Harjo suggests two central tenets of Indigenous futurities: creating the conditions for these futures to happen; and maintaining a future, present, and past for Indigenous communities. Indigenizing the research process creates the conditions that Indigenous

Peoples need to enact self-determination and be able to guide all aspects of research with our communities without our work and IK being redirected to solely benefit colonial institutions and non-Indigenous Peoples. Additionally, Indigenizing the research process centers Indigenous Peoples, IK, Indigenous cultures, and multi-temporal dimensions (past, present, and future) in a world and multiple systems that strive to delegitimize them. Together, decolonial reciprocity, decolonization, Indigenization, and Indigenous futurities work toward the same goals: unsettling and replacing colonial structures while strengthening Tribal sovereignty and putting the needs, interests, perspectives, temporality, self-determination, and powers of Indigenous Peoples back into our hands. These methods also interrupt the colonial gaze that consistently sees our Peoples as (pre)historic relics instead of as present and future-based Peoples. When it comes to any type of Indigenous-focused research, we argue that each of these elements should be foregrounded within the research process.

DECOLONIAL VALUES OF COLLABORATION

Can collaboration between non-Indigenous peoples and Indigenous Peoples still take place in *Indigenously Other(ed)* spaces? Before answering this question, we must consider how collaborative work often does not uphold Indigenous values and instead works against Indigenous communities' interests. Non-Indigenous research remains exclusive and divorced from Indigenous Peoples and our value systems that are practiced and centered at the core of our communities. This is especially apparent in research collaborations that do not center decolonial methods, Indigenous data sovereignty, and Indigenous leadership. For generations, western scholarship has been done *to* and *on* Indigenous Peoples instead of for, with, and by us, inflicting various forms of harm that echo the colonial-induced cultural traumas Indigenous Peoples have faced since first contact (Dalton 2002; Tsosie et al. 2021; Smith 2021). Such unethical practices stem from colonial values that maintain a sense of disdain and disrespect for Indigenous Peoples (white supremacy). This is exemplified by generations of research projects that employ non-consensual research practices and result in non-Indigenous researchers stealing and using Indigenous data without permission and inflicting bodily harm on Indigenous communities (Pacheco et al. 2013; Fox 2020). In doing so, western scientists have conducted unethical research and demonstrated a lack of respect for Indigenous bodies, rights, sovereignty, and values. We contend therefore that Indigenous value systems should be folded into Indigenous research processes (which can only be done under the leadership of Indigenous Peoples) as a way to mitigate such harms from occurring in the future.

Indigenous scholars and practitioners have defined some Indigenous value systems, including respect, relevancy, reciprocity, responsibility, rights, reconciliation, redistribution, and relationships (Jacobs et al. 2022a,b). Though Indigenous communities may have distinct understandings of these values and philosophies or hold other values (Meissner 2022), these value systems can provide frameworks for research and collaboration between Native Nations and external entities that allow them to work together in a good way (Jacobs et al. 2022a,b). However, any practical applications of Indigenous value systems should always be conducted and led by Indigenous Peoples who understand how these operate within our communities and the subsequent actions such values require.

Collaborations are often situated in research relationships that are built on compromises that directly benefit those studying our Peoples as opposed to our communities. Often, non-Indigenous peoples who engage in Indigenous scholarship use collaborative processes to directly benefit themselves, exposing, exploiting, and using our communities' Knowledges and experiences as steppingstones for lines on their CVs and grant applications. But what direct benefits do Indigenous communities receive from such processes? Where are the values of reciprocity and relationships that should be guiding these processes?

To help mitigate such harms, various scholars have developed Indigenous values–based frameworks for building relationships with Indigenous communities and co-equity-based management processes. Indigenous value systems ensure that relationships and reciprocity remain intrinsic to all parts of engaging with Indigenous communities. Yet scholars rarely use such frameworks, and funding entities never require that they be used in Indigenous-based research. The colonial academic system inherently exists for western researchers to access, extract, and colonize our data into the dominant domain, while the extractive nature of non-Indigenous research ensures that reciprocity and relationships cannot be used and centered in ways that take care of our Peoples and Knowledges (Jacobs et al., 2022a, b; Tsosie and Claw 2020).

Collaboration in this context is inherently colonial, extractive, and exploitative, and collaborationist approaches that do not center Indigenous communities and value systems merely provide a polite fiction that hides the ongoing harm non-Indigenous researchers do in and to our communities. Colonialism intends to dispossess us of all things we care for—our lands, languages, children, Knowledges—and fold them into the central domain of colonial futurity. We question how collaborative research can be conducted through Indigenous values and ways of Knowing when so many research institutions are built on the literal bones of our ancestors and still store their bodies and artifacts in museums and storage areas (Smith and Bosman 2022). Grande (2018) writes that "Historically, the university functioned as the institutional nexus for the capitalist and religious missions of the settler state, mirroring its histories of dispossession." How can Indigenous communities be in good relations and work through reciprocity with non-Indigenous researchers when these institutions never divorced themselves from the long historical apparatuses of our genocide and dispossession and still serve as accessories to settler crimes against Black and Indigenous Peoples, occupy our lands, do not center our values or interests, and store, own, and refuse to return our ancestors' bodies (Wilder 2013; Grande 2018; Lee, Ahtone, and Pearce 2020; Ikeda 2020)? How can we stop the colonial extractions of our data and subsequent harm to our communities that privilege non-Indigenous Peoples? Why should we be amenable to our colonizers' needs and interests in collaborative research?

One answer to these questions exists in Simpson's (2014) ideas of a politics of refusal. Harnessing such politics allows us to refuse to admit non-Indigenous peoples into leadership spaces in Indigenous research endeavors and acknowledge that they may not be amenable to our interests. Opportunities for collaboration should be met only with Indigenous Peoples leading the entire process and dictating where and how non-Indigenous peoples and entities can support our endeavors. Collaboration must privilege our sovereignty and ensure our self-determination rights to liberate the health of our lands and our Peoples from colonial rule. This requires non-Indigenous peoples and funding entities to shift into a reality where Indigenous leadership, Indigenous futurities, and Indigenous communities' interests are paramount to research and funding approval processes. It requires replacing colonial interests with decolonial reciprocity so Indigenous communities can honor our ancestors by continuing to resist, persist, and foreground our value systems to guide our work. It also requires the liberation of our lands and Peoples and the presumed access to both by colonial empires maintained within academia at large and especially at land grant universities (Liboiron 2021b). It requires us to understand that the university is beyond reform and that such reformist strategies that enlist Indigenous Peoples, Knowledges, cultures, and histories into settler colonial futurities remain complicit in racism, genocide, dispossession, imperialism, and colonization (Grande 2018; Kelley 2016).

Grande further argues that we need commitments to collectivity, or refusing the individualistic project of the settler state and its associated institutions; reciprocity in a way that is answerable to communities; and mutuality, which focuses on developing social relations that aren't contingent on capital but refuse exploitation and assert connections (especially connections to land). These are not the only politics of refusal that should be considered, but examples that provide reflection points on how refusal can be enacted in collaboration. We encourage all Indigenous communities to reflect on how they can enact politics of refusal in any way that assists them in meeting their liberating objectives.

Conclusion and Final Declaration

In this chapter, we have addressed ways that decolonization and Indigenization can be woven into the fabric of Indigenous research. But how can we ensure that such practices are implemented? What steps must researchers take? What can and should all of this look like?

To address such questions, we end this paper with a critical declaration calling for decolonization and Indigenization in scientific research and the academy that can be used by grant entities to assess whether grant proposals meet such requirements; non-Indigenous researchers who want to work in collaboration with Indigenous communities; publication entities and peer reviewers to assess how Indigenous community involvement is centered in research projects; and Indigenous Nations and communities who need to establish decolonial research processes.

The declaration addresses how we can scrutinize academic publications, funding, and research processes in ways that unsettle, decolonize, and replace western scientific norms for conducting Indigenous-based research. By implementing the following protocols, we can provide transparency to multiple parts of the scientific research process, including the lenses through which research has been conducted; who is leading research processes; how decolonial reciprocity is incorporated into research and collaborations; and the ways in which decolonization and Indigenization are effectively used in research processes. This declaration is intended for use by those who are willing to move into the critical Indigenous futurities and decolonial and Indigenizing paradigms that Indigenous Peoples deserve. This declaration should continue to evolve via Indigenous leadership and through the prioritization of Indigenous communities' interests.

A Critical Declaration of Decolonization and Indigenization for Scientific Research and the Academy

ARTICLE I. RESEARCH DEVELOPMENT

1. Indigenous leadership, Indigenous communities' interests, and Indigenous sovereignty are the only factors directing the development of research objectives and questions, methodological approaches, data collection and storage processes, data analyses and interpretations, and authorship positions.

   A. Indigenous Nations, Indigenous scientists, including cultural practitioners, and Indigenous community members have oversight and authority to govern questions, research objectives, frameworks, interpretations, methodologies, authorship, and so on.

   B. Each factor is specified clearly in the methods sections of scholarly literature, technical reports, and other publications and discussions related to the project.

2. Indigenous expertise is not defined by colonial, elitist, educational merits or degrees, but by Indigenous communities' value systems and norms. Indigenous expertise is recognized in all parts of the research process and is defined by individual communities.

   A. Wherever possible, Indigenous Elders and cultural practitioners should be prioritized in definitions of expertise.

3. Indigenous research must engage with Critical Indigenous scholarship (including IK contained in oral histories and stories—scholarship is not limited to previously published or written work), rely heavily on Indigenous scholars' work and voices from Indigenous communities, demonstrate a clear understanding of non-westernized and decolonial approaches to research (centering work and methods grounded in the teachings and practices of individual Indigenous communities), and center objectives on Indigenous liberation.

   A. Critical Indigenous scholarship and Indigenous methodologies should be outlined and operationalized throughout publications.

      i. Authors identify how decolonization and Indigenization are operationalized and are not performative.

ii. The sharing of Critical Indigenous scholarship should follow community-defined guidelines and not bend to the needs of colonial entities.

iii. Long-term community impact should be ethically analyzed by the authors and Indigenous community partners, including how funding can be secured and maintained for the continuation of successful research projects, programs, or interventions.

B. Interpretations and implementations of such scholarship and methodologies should be led by Indigenous Peoples.

4. Indigenous communities leading the research process identify the Indigenous Peoples, places, and other living participants and nonliving entities and/or places from which data will be gathered.

5. Non-Indigenous scholars who desire to engage in any type of work with Indigenous communities should be required to demonstrate how they have developed intentional relationships of reciprocity with the communities they hope to serve via their research activities.

A. Direct and indirect service to the community of interest should be a prerequisite to research engagement. This service should be demonstrated via long-term efforts at respectful and reciprocal relationship building, and should be concrete and tangible.

ARTICLE II. RESEARCH FUNDING

1. Funding entities require a statement from Indigenous governments and/or communities that acknowledges that Indigenous leadership has been and will continue to be paramount to the project.

A. The acknowledgment statement should be derived from processes similar to Dr. Max Liboiron's (Métis) Community Peer Review Method to bring consent and self-determination into the sciences (Liboiron, Zahara, and Schoot 2018).

B. Terms of non-Indigenous collaboration should be outlined by Indigenous communities specifically about the roles and responsibilities of non-Indigenous contributors in all steps of the research process.

2. Funding should be distributed directly to the Indigenous sovereign Nation and/or to the Indigenous communities who are involved in the research.

A. Funding applications require specifications about how research funding will contribute to the liberation of Indigenous communities.

    B. Indigenous Nations and/or Indigenous communities have the authority to specify how and if funding is distributed to external partners (e.g., academics).

    C. Indigenous Nations and/or Indigenous communities oversee all parts of funding administration, including direct and indirect costs.

    D. Principal Investigator status is determined by Indigenous communities and not by western credentialism.

       i. Determination should be made using Indigenous and decolonial processes that center Indigenous practices, norms, and Traditions.

      ii. Principal Investigators do not need to hold any western degrees.

     iii. Principal Investigators must be Indigenous Peoples or individuals who work within sovereign Indigenous Nations and/or communities.

     iv. Wherever possible, Indigenous Elders and cultural practitioners should be prioritized as Principal Investigators.

3. Funding entities must have any Indigenous-related funding applications (e.g., utilizing Indigenous Knowledges) peer-reviewed by only Indigenous reviewers.

    A. Indigenous-related funding applications should be subject to additional/altered evaluation criteria that considers: cultural appropriateness; potential for Knowledge extraction; leadership of the project (Indigenous or non-Indigenous); experience of allies; nature of the relationships with Indigenous communities involved; catalyst for research (e.g., was research initiated by an Indigenous community); involvement of Indigenous Peoples in the research team; how resources will go to Indigenous communities; and sustainability of the project.

    B. Criteria for evaluation of any Indigenous-related funding applications should be at the discretion of the Indigenous reviewers.

    C. Funding applications that pass Indigenous peer reviews should not be subject to the same diversity, equity, and inclusion criteria as non-Indigenous applications, nor should they be subject to the evaluation of "research impact" that goes beyond the benefit of the Indigenous community where research is to occur.

    D. Final determination of whether Indigenous-related applications are funded should rest entirely on the decision of the Indigenous reviewers.

    E. Funding entities should work to support the creation of an Indigenous peer review circle, led by Indigenous Peoples, that can help to facilitate Indigenous peer review.

4. For Indigenous-targeted funding opportunities, funding entities must allow development, running, review, and evaluation of such programs to be led by Indigenous Peoples.
    A. These programs should not be accessible to non-Indigenous researchers.
    B. These programs should not be accessible only to colonial determinations of Indigenous communities (e.g., elected Tribal/Band Councils).
    C. These programs should be designed to have the flexibility required to fund community-based and community-designed projects that meet community-determined needs.

ARTICLE III. PUBLICATIONS AND RESULTS DISSEMINATION

1. In publications and presentations about the research, authors and collaborators include positionality statements that clearly explain the following factors that may be embedded within and guiding the research:
    A. Sociocultural locations, including Indigeneity, proximity to whiteness, analyses of power structures (e.g., colonialism and imperialism), and other relevant positionalities that create potentials for biases.
    B. Associated privileges non-Indigenous authors receive from the work that is being conducted.
    C. Authors identify and are transparent about all relationalities in the research process (e.g., relations with land, communities, and other living and non-living beings included in the project).

2. The ratio of Indigenous authors versus non-Indigenous authors should be heavily weighted to favor Indigenous Peoples.

3. Indigenous scientists, community leaders, and Indigenous community participants (especially Elders) take priority in authorship ordering.
    A. Non-Indigenous scientists are not given priority in authorship ordering and should position themselves at the last available authorship positions.

4. Publications should be made available and accessible via open access formats for Indigenous Nations and Indigenous Peoples who are outside of academic institutions.

ARTICLE IV. INDIGENOUS DATA SOVEREIGNTY AND INDIGENOUS DATA GOVERNANCE PROTOCOLS

1. Indigenous data (e.g., including, but not limited to, TEK) are not required to be triangulated with western methods or other forms of data.
   A. Indigenous data, in all their forms, are valued as stand-alone pre-validated and pre-triangulated data sets.
2. Non-Indigenous researchers and non-Indigenous entities do not own or store Indigenous data unless specifically requested by the involved Indigenous Nations and/or Indigenous communities and cannot charge for community access to such data.
   A. The terms and conditions of Indigenous data sovereignty and data governance are defined by the Indigenous Nation and/or Indigenous communities.
      i. Indigenous Nations and Indigenous communities have the agency to withdraw from, redefine, and re-consent to these terms and conditions at any point in time.
   B. Funding and publication entities must uphold Indigenous data sovereignty procedures and require authors to submit documentation from Indigenous Nations and/or communities that states that data sovereignty has been upheld throughout the project and publication.
3. A data governance plan that addresses the FAIR and CARE principles (Carroll et al. 2020) should be clearly outlined in any proposals made to Indigenous institutional review boards, funding proposals, and publications.

ARTICLE V. DECOLONIAL RECIPROCITY

1. Indigenous Nations/communities, institutions, and other individuals involved in research will have full and iterative autonomy as to their fair compensation, resource investment, degree of involvement and effort, ethical boundaries, and termination of research activities.
2. Any Indigenous communities that are involved in or may be affected by the proposed research must be involved in the research process from the beginning to the end. All grant proposals, research questions, theories, research design, data parameters, data storage, presentations/publications, conclusions, and research outputs shall be done in direct consultation and with the approval of all communities involved, and/or their representatives.

3. Compensation for participation is to be determined by Indigenous Nations and/or communities using community-oriented cultural value perspectives and/or other determining factors as they see fit (e.g., living wages and so on).

   A. Compensation should not be used for coercive recruitment.

   B. Disbursement of compensation should be coordinated in partnership with the organizing Indigenous community partners or group.

4. Indigenous Nations and community members choose the language(s) most appropriate for research projects, publications, presentations, and the like, and provide translations into Native languages whenever needed or requested.

   A. Scientific publications, technical reports, and presentations are translated and communicated in lay terms with the Indigenous community, using Native and other common languages spoken and/or preferred by the community.

   B. In situations where direct translations to Native languages are not possible, authors work with community members and Indigenous Nations to ensure that all parts of the research (objective setting, research planning, data analyses, results, etc.) are fully communicated to and completely understood by community members.

      i. Community forums, roundtable discussions, and other community-based approaches (e.g., culturally normative practices) to discussion are used to gauge the general consensus of community understanding.

NOTES

1. This declaration should be adapted to meet the needs, interests, capacities, and so on, of Indigenous Nations and communities.

2. Indigenous communities are not monolithic, especially considering the distinctions of settler governmental influences on the governance structures of Indigenous Nations. Therefore, we acknowledge that some of the articles of this declaration may not be perfectly aligned to meet the needs, capacity, and governing structures of Indigenous Nations and communities, including some Indigenous Nations and communities from the Global South. In instances where this occurs, the Indigenous Nation and/or community should be contacted to determine the best path forward for any research related enterprises.

3. This declaration provides one path forward but does not intend to be the only possible movement toward liberating Indigenous Peoples and other colonized Peoples from the harms of scientific research and academia. Therefore, we strongly encourage other colonized and minoritized Peoples to use this declaration and paper as a guide for creating parameters and declarations that work for their community's liberating interests and objectives.

Acknowledgments

We extend our gratitude to Jacquelyn Sparks and Tyler Tully for their time and the thoughts they provided to the authors on the contents of this chapter.

17

THE NATIVE AND UNIVERSITY PARADOX

LARA A. JACOBS AND CHERRY YEW YAMANE

Positionality Statements

Jacobs: See Introduction for positionality statement.

Yamane: Kanaka ʻōiwi (Hawaiian), Uchinanchu (Okinawan); Moku o Waiʻanae hometown; now living on Potawatomi lands; University of Washington.

They want to learn from us but not have our involvement in analyzing the data.

They want to hear our insights but not when those insights are disruptive to the colonial system.

They want to include our Knowledges but not our critiques of epistemic violence and genocide.

They want to use our sciences to create more diverse and inclusive classroom material, but they don't want us to be the teachers.

They want to include us, but they don't want to hire us.

They want us to teach them how to prevent environmental disasters but won't help us get our lands back so we can manage them.

They want to acknowledge the land and our Peoples, but they do nothing for our land and human rights.

They want cultural diversity but only as long as it doesn't create instances of white fragility or upset any preconceived notions about us.

They want us to bring our cultures to events but not into meetings.

They want our "red faces" but not enough of them to paint the Ivory Towers a different color.

They want to use us in DEI ad campaigns to get other Natives in their
    programs but won't support us once we are here nor work harder
    to make our experiences better.

They want us to be the noble, peaceful, flowery Native tropes, but not
    the warriors, nor the ones who want to change the system.

They want us to be seen but not heard.
They want us to comply with their systems but not disrupt nor
    unsettle them.
They want us to be colonial but not decolonial.
They want us to be whiter.

Where is the reciprocity?
Where is the responsibility?
Where are the relationships?
The university system maintains the absence of these essential
    value systems.

PART III

Responsibility

18
THE TREES AND THE SKY ARE MY TEACHERS
BY LUHUI WHITEBEAR

Positionality Statement
Enrolled Coastal Band of the Chumash Nation with Huastec and Cochimi ancestry; born in Coastal Chumash territory, raised in Coastal and Northern Chumash territory and in Siletz territory, now living in Kalapuya territory, Oregon State University, School of Language, Culture, and Society, Indigenous studies.

I. "Who was your first teacher?"
How do I tell you it was the trees
And water
And sky?
How do I tell you it was mothers
And aunties
And uncles
And Elders?
How do I tell you for you to understand?

II. Memories
The principal called my mom
"She keeps saying rocks are alive."
"She was taught they have a spirit too."
"Can you tell her to keep those thoughts to herself?"
Settler interruption of Indigenous teachings
Walking down cold hall
Sitting in cold seats

"No daydreaming out the window."
"Columbus was a hero."
"We study trees and rocks and water, they don't teach us."
Settler attempts to crush Indigenous Knowledge.

III. Teaching
At the bank of the Willamette I sit with my daughter
Coolness of spring breeze and smell of fresh rain
Splash of water on rocks and soil
"Listen to the water and the birds. See what they say."
"How do I know what they are saying, mommy?"
"Just listen and you will know. Listen and give thanks."
"Ok mommy. Thank you river for teaching me."

IV. Offerings
My children and I stand at the edge of the Pacific
Looking out across the channel to Limuw
Tobacco clutched in palms, carried away by salt air
An offering to our homelands
Cars passing by on Highway 101
"No matter where we are or who is around, we make time for this."
An offering of gratitude to earth and ocean and plants
An offering to the ancestors and our lands and waters
An offering passed down from Elders to my parents to me to my children to the future
In moments that stand still we understand

V. Returning
Some teachings are ours to give
And some teachings are ours to keep
Surrounded by story and braided into all we know
Some days I sit and wonder how many miss it all
In the every day hustle of capitalism
Some days I sit and wonder what I am missing
Then I remember that our stories are always there waiting
Carried by clouds
Curled into ferns

Drawn into stars
Dripping off leaves
Gathering into pools of water
Reflecting our teachings back to us when we are ready to return to
them.

19

INTERGENERATIONAL RESPONSIBILITY
What We Owe the Past, Present, and Future

JOANNA M. DEMEYER, MANDI HARRIS, DAVID INIGUEZ,
AND ANGELES MENDOZA

Positionality Statements

DeMeyer*: Cheyenne Arapaho Tribes of Oklahoma citizen; raised on Cheyenne and Arapaho Tribal lands and Washakie Bands of Shoshones lands (Wind River Indian Reservation); now living on Kalapuya, Siletz, and Grand Ronde lands; doctoral student, School of Psychological Science, Oregon State University.

Harris*: Cherokee Nation Citizen of Cherokee and mixed-European heritage; raised on Cow Creek Band of Umpqua Tribe of Indians lands; now living on Schitsu'umsh (Coeur d'Alene) lands; doctoral student, Information School, University of Washington.

Iniguez+: Mexica/Purepecha Ancestry, trained in Dakota Traditions/ spirituality. Raised in Tongva lands and currently resides in Tongva lands. Currently work with the US Forest Service, National Tech and Development Program as a natural resources specialist/assistant project manager.

Mendoza*: Masahua citizen, with mixed-European ancestry. Camotepec, Puebla, Mexico's ancestral town, living now on the ancestral territory of the Blackfoot Confederation, which is also the territory of Treaty 7 First Nations, in Alberta, Canada; IHE Delft Institute, Netherlands/White Eagle Sustainable Development.

Author Notes: *Authors contributed equally as a unified voice; +Author contributed equally up to the point of final submission.

> *We belong to the land, the land does not belong to us.*
> —Wes Martel, Eastern Shoshone,
> as quoted by E. Sherline (Franklin 2021).

Introduction

Responsibility contains many dimensions: as Indigenous Peoples, responsibility may span across the dimensions of time and space. Since time immemorial, we inherit from our Elders the responsibility to be caretakers of the land. In "The Statement of Manitoba Elders," Bineshiikwe and colleagues (2015) describe The Great Binding Law that the Great Spirit gave the People. This law is a sacred responsibility that ensures we leave future generations a world in which human and nonhuman beings care for each other in respectful relationships.

INDIGENOUS RELATIONS: HARMS OF COLONIALISM

The vitality of land, seed, life, and our cultures are indivisibly linked, even as we have been under attack for over four centuries from the far-reaching forces of colonialism. We have been forcibly removed from our lands, learning to eat a Euro-American diet consisting of carbohydrates, sugars, dairy, and chemical-laced foods and drinks; thus, un-centering our Peoples from our prior land-based diets of organic, fresh and dried meats, vegetables, nuts, and fruits. Despite these and other attacks on our Peoples, our Elders continue to impart the significance of taking care of our bodies and Mother Earth. Therefore, we encourage each other to remain connected to our lands, seeds, first foods, and cultures. We must become part of a good cycle that includes planting, growing, harvesting, eating, and connecting with our relatives—human and our more-than-human kin alike.

Mother Earth is made up of dynamic, living, and wise beings who allow us to learn valuable lessons that we can continue to share with each other and future generations. Oren Lyons, Faithkeeper of the Onondaga Indian Nation, relayed the history of the Haudenosaunee Peoples by stating, the Peacemaker told us to "make decisions on behalf of the **seven generations** coming. . . . We have a responsibility to them, to hold fast to our cultures, to hang on to our land, to follow the instructions, and to rebuild our nations" (Jorgenson 2007). Therefore, it is our responsibility to the seven generations coming to share our Knowledges and reclaim our healthy ways of living.

RESPONSIBILITY TO THE LAND

The losses of plant and animal biodiversity and Indigenous cultures and practices combined with future species-related losses due to climate change are some of the consequences of colonial interruption of Indigenous Peoples' caretaking responsibilities. Part of this interruption is facilitated by federal agencies that attempt to manage lands formerly tended by our Peoples. Such management attempts are directed at controlling "natural" places through a one-sided relationship: taking without giving and interrupting natural processes such as fire. In the centuries after colonization, colonial land managers have viewed fire as an enemy and have enacted Eurocentric fire suppression policies that have led to an unprecedented frequency and intensity of wildfires, causing a "catastrophic" destruction of lands and animals (Kimmerer and Lake 2001). Since time immemorial, many Indigenous Peoples have used fire as an effective tool to maintain our lands, health, and wellness (Hessburg et al. 2021; Lake et al. 2017). It is now our responsibility to help shift governing policies away from an outdated and unsustainable view of fighting fire to a holistic and Indigenous-centered view in which we reconnect with fire as our sacred relative and as a revered tool to keep the land's health.

Western fire and land management frameworks sometimes view the idea of the interactions between humans and nature as transactional. Land exists as a static thing to be occupied and harvested of resources, such as with mining and logging practices that benefit a select number of humans monetarily but irresponsibly damage the land by contaminating waterways and harming habitats. Indigenous Peoples offer a distinct worldview—one of sacred relationships built on foundations of reciprocity and responsibility. Many of our Traditional stories speak of the dangers of human irresponsibility, and our Elders recognize the need to be responsible for the consequences of our actions and maintain a balance between taking and caretaking. They often seek to guide us, as their descendants, through story work.

INDIGENOUS RESILIENCE ROOTED IN STORY AND TRADITIONAL ECOLOGICAL KNOWLEDGE

Jicarilla Apache philosopher Viola Cordova asks what it means to become human: "Of what memories and stories, relations and responsibilities . . . are we made?" (2007, 131). She inseparably links stories with responsibilities, relationships, and remembering—and all of these facets to our very existence, our fundamental makeup. Settler colonialism attempted to take our stories from us to suppress the Traditional Ecological Knowledge (TEK) contained within them, and to replace our Knowledges with western ideas. This resulted in the suffering of ecosystems, humans, and our more-than-human kin as our remembrances of responsibilities were forcibly erased.

In *Cherokee Stories of the Turtle Island Liars' Club*, Cherokee Elder Hastings Shade tells of a time when animal relatives sent sickness to punish humans for being disrespectful of our more-than-human relations (Teuton et al. 2012). The plant relatives stepped in with compassion and responsibility: for every illness sent to the humans, plants provide medicines for healing (Teuton et al. 2012). Our TEK, spiritual beliefs, and wisdom that accumulated over generations have been significantly affected by colonialism, but we remain unconquered. We are now in a time of Indigenous resurgence, a time in which we can and will bring back our Knowledges, values, and beliefs to restore broken relations with our Peoples and more-than-human kin. Our relatives, such as fire, have been falsely portrayed as our enemies. It is our responsibility to repair and restore this relationship. In this time, we all face a crisis like the one Cherokee Elders describe, yet the land, the water, and our many kin continue to hold up their responsibilities toward us. It is time for us to uphold our responsibilities toward them and all those who come after us.

Conclusion

As Indigenous Peoples we must work on the rematriation[1] of our Knowledges, Traditions and values, to nurture ourselves and our relationships with the land, the water, our many kin, and ourselves. We are responsible for building a new framework together with other peoples—both Indigenous and non-Indigenous—that is based on different systems of Indigenous Ways of Knowing, to revert the harm that colonialism has caused worldwide. This framework includes reestablishing our relationship with fire as a sacred relative and scientific tool for wellness. Upholding our responsibility to fire means critically analyzing governmental fire policies where we live and lobbying for the reestablishment of TEK in our areas.

We all are land custodians who must love, connect, and take care of each other. We are indebted to the past, present, and future generations. Such debt requires us to honor the responsibilities embedded within the Great Binding Law so our future seven generations can be blessed in perpetuity.

---

1 Rematriation is defined by Newcomb (1995, 3), as "to restore a living culture to its rightful place on Mother Earth," or "to restore a people to a spiritual way of life, in sacred relationship with their ancestral lands, without external interference."

Acknowledgments

We wish to express our gratitude to Lara A. Jacobs–Mvskoke (Creek) Citizen for her support during the preparation of this article. We want to also mention Dr. Luhui Whitebear–Coast Band of the Chumash Nation who was present at the initial idea session but subsequently was unable to participate.

20

THE DOCTRINE OF DISCOVERY STILL LIVES WITH US AND IT AIN'T GOOD

BY PAT GONZALES-ROGERS

Positionality Statement

I am the progeny of the Asian-Pacific (Chinese-Filipino-Samoan) diaspora to Hawai'i to support its colonial agricultural plantation interest in the late 1800s. Both my grandparents were chattel for corporate pineapple interests and worked in the plantations for over five decades. Further, they were from Mindanao of the Lumad people who were Indigenous to Mindanao.

Introduction

It may surprise most people to learn that our contemporary Indian law and policy is derived from a policy disseminated by the Catholic Church that had two broad goals: to evangelize the Catholic Church and acquire lands outside of Western Europe. These policies live with us today both domestically and internationally. When we consider the present-day landscape of conservation within our many Native communities, we might first take ourselves on a historical journey that returns us to the Vatican in late 1400s. Why must we travel back to a time more than seven hundred years ago, to address the contemporary? The simple answer is that we have been working from a historical construct that legally instructs, in a rigid manner, how and to what extent Tribes can operate in the here and now. This construct places most Native communities in a societal and institutional subordination and without a simple interest in the land that they have lived in for time immemorial. Without having a firm understanding of this piece of history, we operate with nary a cornerstone that affects both public policy and the basic standards of Indian law.

This chapter is divided into three parts. Part One discusses the history and impacts of the Doctrine of Discovery. Part Two provides an overview of the continued legacy of the Doctrine of Discovery as it pertains to Indian Country, including a focus on cooperative federalism, limitations on Tribal authority, and topics about the Environmental Protection Agency. Part Three provides a case study that brings into conversation Bears Ears National Monument with the legal struggles that have occurred through time to establish comanagement regimes between the US government and multiple Indigenous communities who have existed and stewarded these lands since time immemorial. This chapter provides readers with an understanding of how the Doctrine of Discovery is connected to modern law in the United States and how recent strides to incorporate Indigenous management (and Indigenous Knowledges such as Traditional Ecological Knowledge) in parks and protected areas have transpired over time. This is important because Tribal Nations in the United States have cultural responsibilities to manage their ancestral territories and should be uplifted into comanagerial positions.

Part One:
Francisco de Vitoria and the Doctrine of Discovery

Historians have been greatly intrigued by the forward-thinking ideas and vast knowledge of Francisco de Vitoria, a philosopher and theologian who belonged to the Roman Catholic tradition. Vitoria had many noteworthy accomplishments, including his scholarship and theories on international law and the basis and parameters for just war (Alves and Moreira 2009). In 1526, Vitoria founded the School of Salamanca—an intellectual movement steeped in humanist and Renaissance-based scholastic ideologies and Thomistic doctrine (Domingo 2022; Valenzuela-Vermehren 2013). The School of Salamanca held that the right of freedom applied to all people, which remains today as the cornerstone of most current western political philosophy.

As Europeans began exploring, the rationales and discussions permitting the Doctrine of Discovery did too, and the subsequent justifications for the actions taken on behalf of the Doctrine (e.g., land dispossessions) spanned centuries (Deloria 2010). However, Vitoria's commentary and posits on the freedom of commerce and the seas challenged these notions and subsequently remain relevant to this day, as many academics consider him to be one of the founders of modern international law, which later led to the formation of the United Nations (Pagden 1991). It is for his courageous and instructive insights into the intrinsic legal rights and basic dignity of Indigenous Peoples that he will serve as the protagonist of the beginning of this chapter and the symbolic light against the putative doctrinaire that changed the landscape for Indigenous Peoples over the past eight hundred years.

It is an exercise in simplification to merely say that the church allowed and instructed Catholics in Western Europe to colonize and evangelize the rest of the world. The real hammer to and subsequent repudiation of Indigenous Peoples' land entitlements occurred when Charles V, the Holy Roman Emperor, pursued the counsel of Francisco de Vitoria (Hernandez 1991) to explore the extent to which the Spanish could legitimately and ethically assert legal land interests (Anaya 2009). True to his constant moral nature and the inherent intent of the newly proclaimed Doctrine of Discovery, Vitoria refuted the pope, reasoning that Indigenous Peoples were the accurate possessors of their lands (Anaya 2009). His rationale was tethered to the idea that no one could maintain rights through the sole act of discovery, as this type of governmental exploitation could only be acceptable when such property was without obvious ownership (Anaya 2009). Felix Cohen, the seminal Indian law scholar, mirrored Vitoria's thoughts in his groundbreaking publication *Handbook of Federal Indian Law* (1941), writing that "even the Pope has no right to partition the property of the Indians, and in the absence of a just war, only the voluntary consent of the [A]borigines could justify the annexation of their territory. No less than their property the government of the [A]borigines was entitled to respect by the Spaniards" (Cohen 1941, 46).

To better understand Vitoria's contributions to Indigenous Peoples, it is worthwhile to provide a historical backdrop of the respective period, as it provides a direct nexus and platform for his writing and scholarship. Vitoria lived during the so-called Age of Discovery, which, while largely associated with the vast expansion of European mercantile interests and trade routes, can also be deemed as the start of what we now know as globalization and the decimation of agrarian and Indigenous societies. The Age of Discovery (also referred to as the Age of Exploration), began in the early fifteenth century and continued for more than three hundred years. During this time, many milestones and vanguard innovations were achieved, including the formation of previously unmapped routes to Africa; the West Indies; North, Central, and South America; India; Australia; New Zealand; Hawai'i, and the Pacific Ocean (Head 2018).

This period of prolific exploration was advanced by numerous break-throughs in technology, such as the development of the magnetic compass and more sophisticated ship designs, which, in turn, led to maps that were more accurate and depicted global geography previously unseen (Merson 1990). Such developments allowed for the trade and commerce of goods from different hemispheres and catapulted European entities into a period now known as the Age of Imperialism, wherein European countries became the political and economic masters of the world. However, perhaps the greatest impetus and license for the Age of Discovery was the Doctrine of Discovery. The objectives of increasing trade and commerce during the Age of Discovery are abundantly obvious; however no less important was the urgency of the church to expand its base and assimilate the unexplored global community. Unlike our contemporary political systems, there was very little separation between church and state at this time. Without these separations, the Doctrine of Discovery developed a multilayered matrix that included theological, political, and legal rationale, so that European explor-ers could colonize and take lands from non-Christians.

Vitoria's philosophy contrasted this matrix, which previously held precedent stemming from conclusions made by Pope Innocent IV. In 1240, Innocent wrote a legal commentary about the rights of non-Christians, in which he determined that invading the lands of Indigenous Peoples was a just cause in circumstances where invasions sought to defend Christianity and acquire lands previously owned by Christians (Miller and D'Angelis 2011; Muldoon and Peters 1977; Williams 1992). Innocent prioritized the legal and moral authority of Christians to dispossess non-Christians of *dominium* (sovereignty and ownership of lands), which helped provide cre-dence to the later-formed Doctrine of Discovery (Tierney 1992; Wheaton 1863; Miller and D'Angelis 2011).

More than two hundred years later, the Doctrine of Discovery contin-ued to grow out of the actions taken on behalf of Pope Alexander VI's issu-ance of the 1493 Papal Bull Inter Caetera, which was issued at the bequest of Spain. Spain and Portugal were equally concerned about conflicting own-ership of lands, which resulted in the demarcation of a line, from the North Pole to the South Pole and about 300 miles west of the Azores Islands, and granted Spain, under the authority of God, all lands discovered west of this line (Miller 2006). The Papal Bull justified the European ethos of colonization, which led to the ideological conquering of Indigenous Peoples and the settling of their lands under the guise of discovery (King 2021).

The Papal Bull also provided the representatives of these countries with the ability to discover new lands, claim them through the simple exercise of planting a flag on their soil, and then report back to their lords and rulers. Subsequently, by following this basic process, the land was then deemed in the hands of European interests.

The Doctrine of Discovery patently dismissed all views other than those of Judeo-Christian European rulers. In doing so, the embedded dominant ideology was based on the dehumanization of most other cultures. Some of the more egregious and morally pedantic elements of the Doctrine are outlined by Miller (2006):

First Discovery: The first European country that "discovered" lands previously unknown to that country gained property and sovereign property rights over the lands. Further, the mere act of discovery, even without actual physical possession of land, was sufficient to construct a legal title claim (Miller 2006).

Terra nullius: The literal translation of this phrase means a piece of land or Earth that has no worth and is null and void. Under the idea of terra nullius, when lands were not possessed or occupied by people or nations, or in circumstances when non-Europeans used them in a way that did not adhere to the European legal system's approval, then the lands were classified as empty and waste; thus, making them available for Discovery. European discoverers were quite liberal in their application of this principle and this criterion was used for hundreds of years, well into the western expansion of the United States (Miller 2006).

Christianity: Religion, particularly Christianity, played a central role in the Doctrine of Discovery. Non-Christians had lesser entitlements to land, sovereignty, and self-determination compared to Christians. These limited rights could be easily disregarded when Christians claimed the territories through the act of discovery (Miller 2006).

Civilization: European and later American explorers leveraged their specific definition of civilization as a reactive mechanism to initiate cultural and institutional superiority. At the core, was a belief that God directed them to introduce Eurocentric culture and education, via Christianity, to "conquered" populations. No doubt this resulted in and lent to the systemic paternalism and legal guardianship often associated with Native populations, even to this day. (Miller 2006)

After the Spanish *discovery* of the Americas, the Catholic Church sent many clergy to the New World. A seemingly small figure and asterisk to this period was Dominican Friar Antonio de Montesinos, who was a missionary on the island of what we now know as Haiti or the Dominican Republic (Bradstock and Rowland 2008). Montesinos was dismayed and alarmed by the treatment of the Indigenous Populations there, as the population had been decimated and was in a state of acute decline (Minister 2019). Most of the Native leaders had been killed, and the remaining People were given away as slaves to colonists: "A nobleman arriving with his wife could expect to be given 80 Native slaves and a soldier could expect 60" (Minister 2019). These conditions prompted Montesinos to act with conviction and courage, and on December 21, 1511, he gave a sermon that was at once scathing, impassioned, and an indictment on the church to do better for Indigenous Peoples:

> Tell me by what right of justice do you hold these Indians in such a cruel and horrible servitude? On what authority have you waged such detestable wars against these [P]eople who dealt quietly and peacefully on their own lands? Wars in which you have destroyed such an infinite number of them by homicides and slaughters never heard of before. Why do you keep them so oppressed and exhausted, without giving them enough to eat or curing them of the sicknesses they incur from the excessive labor you give them, and they die, or rather you kill them, in order to extract and acquire gold every day? (de Las Casas 1992, p. 66, quoted in Colón-Emeric 2017)

The sermon was not well received by the ruling government and the king (Ferdinand II) wanted Montesinos and others muzzled (Hussey 1932). The Dominicans responded by sending Montesinos to Spain to discuss his views with the king (Hussey 1932). Once in Spain, Montesinos and others were able to convince the king of the merits and integrity of their position. Subsequently, a commission was formed, and shortly thereafter the king enacted the Law of Burgos (Hussey 1932). The Law of Burgos was the first systematic codification of the required behavior of settlers in the New World, with a concentrated emphasis on their relationships with

Indigenous populations and human dignity (Hanke 1946; Iturbe 2012).

At this time, Vitoria was teaching at the University of Salamanca and was the elected prime chair of technology when he was made aware of the actions and progress made by Montesinos (Iturbe 2012). Perhaps, invigorated and inspired by the brave actions of the Dominican Friar, Vitoria initiated a path to address many of the same issues. So, while certainly the rights of Indigenous Peoples were high on his list of priorities, Vitoria chose to approach these topics more globally by setting the foundation for a new untried legal framework that acknowledged and respected the basic needs of every human being. As a devotee of Thomas Aquinas, Vitoria placed a special emphasis on criticizing the precepts of natural and divine law (Anghie 1996). To these ends was his sage realization that the discovery of the New World was not exclusively Eurocentric or even Spanish, but rather reflected a vast potential and possibility that should be shared by all people throughout the globe.

Vitoria's ability to discern and spiritually contemplate the existing Catholic theology juxtaposed against its secular framework allowed him to make bold statements and promulgations about the role of the church and its interaction with Indigenous Peoples. He candidly articulated the avarice of the church not just in its quest for lands and property, but also with its institutional proscription to convert new populations without their appreciable consent and cognizance. Vitoria held, "The upshot of all the preceding is this, then, that the [A]borigines undoubtedly had true dominion in both public and private matters, just like Christians, and that neither their princes nor private persons could be despoiled of their property on the ground of their not being true owners" (Rules of Warfare 2008).

By questioning ownership and property through natural and human law instead of primarily via divine law, Vitoria concluded that Indigenous Peoples were the rightful owners of their property and exercised their specific sovereignty (Anghie 1996). This extended to sovereignty claims made by the Pope and Charles V over discovered lands (Anghie 1996). Vitoria took this rationale to an entirely new level by also asserting that physical and violent acts were prohibited unless Indigenous Peoples had physically asserted themselves first against Spain. These words not only transcended modern Native rights by some five hundred years but also provided the first annunciation of his just war theory, as Vitoria thought none of the conditions and predicates for a "just war" were met and were "wholly lacking in the Indies" (Salas 2011, 331).

Vitoria's thoughts and opinions were held in great esteem and respect, while he was alive and still today. It is telling that Charles V, king of Spain, publicly requested his counsel on matters related to the treatment of Native Peoples and that Vitoria's thoughts on these matters draw a distinct parallel to the numerous apologies issued by many denominations for their respective involvement with the Doctrine of Discovery. Within the last fifteen years, at least twenty-three churches and religious communities have repudiated the Doctrine of Discovery, including Roman Catholic organizations, the Episcopal Church (USA), the Unitarian Universalist Association of Congregations, the United Church of Christ, the United Methodist Church, the World Council of Churches, the Community of Christ, the Presbyterian Church (USA), the Evangelical Lutheran Church in America, the Mennonite Church, and many others (Indigenous Values Initiative 2018). On March 20, 2023, the Vatican invoked the Christian mandate to respect dignity for all humans and stated, "The Catholic Church therefore repudiates those concepts that fail to recognize the inherent human rights of [I]ndigenous [P]eoples, including what has become known as the legal and political 'Doctrine of Discovery'" (Holy See Press Office 2023). The Vatican went on to detail that it stands with Indigenous Peoples and supports the international efforts that protect Indigenous Peoples' rights (such as the United Nations Declaration on the Rights of Indigenous Peoples). Despite the recent repudiations, the Doctrine of Discovery is alive and well today, especially in US law.

IMPACT OF THE DOCTRINE

The Doctrine of Discovery has had a significant and enduring impact of great magnitude. In 2012, the United Nations Permanent Forum on Indigenous Issues criticized and condemned the Doctrine of Discovery, recognizing that many of its member countries continue to experience the burdens imposed by this centuries-old doctrine. Among a litany of grievances, a specific note was made to delineate that the doctrine promoted terra nullis and "conquest," that it was "shameful," and had marginalizing and discriminatory impacts on all Indigenous Peoples (United Nations 2012a). The forum highlighted how the doctrine provided broad legal authority for the acquisition of land and cultivated and promoted ill-informed notions that Indigenous Peoples were "savages," "barbarians," and "inferior and uncivilized," notions that were core to the subjugation and exploitation of Indigenous Peoples and lands (United Nations 2012b).

The Doctrine of Discovery is also the original tenet and cradle of US federal Indian law, as it lays the groundwork for such contemporary concepts as the federal trust relationship, plenary power, and reserved rights. All these concepts share a common thread of institutional implications and instructions that position Tribes as subordinate to the interests and authority of the federal government, and, to some extent, state powers and sovereignty. Although the concept has gained recognition both domestically and internationally, its interpretation has been stretched to such an extent that it has become the foundation for numerous public policies that continue to marginalize and weaken the sovereignty and interests of Indigenous communities.

The doctrine still impacts all Indigenous Peoples in the United States to this very day. The Doctrine of Discovery is central to the federal trust relationship with all federally recognized Tribes and has played a role in many US Supreme Court decisions about these factors. For example, in 1823, the *Johnson v. M'Intosh* decision held that private citizens could not purchase from Tribes (Marshall and the Supreme Court 1823). Within the decision, Chief Justice Marshall makes a blunt articulation that, as the successor to Great Britain, the United States has an inherited authority over all previously claimed lands within Indigenous boundaries (Miller et al. 2010). Equally provocative is Marshall's analysis that the discovering country also gains the undivided right to extinguish the "right of occupancy" of Indigenous populations (Marshall and Supreme Court 1823; Miller et al. 2010). Effectively, this disallowed any Native claims to said lands. This same concept was adopted into American jurisprudence and utilized within westward expansion and Manifest Destiny.

As an effective concept of law, the impacts of the Doctrine of Discovery can be seen globally, as it was utilized as a legal rationale in the United States, Canada, Australia, and New Zealand (Miller et al. 2010). At present, it is still a valid precedent and is used by courts to decide property rights cases involving federally recognized Tribes against non-Natives. As recently as 2005, US Supreme Court Justice Ruth Bader Ginsburg cited the Discovery Doctrine in *City of Sherrill v. Oneida Indian Nation of New York* and decided against the Oneida. Justice Ginsburg held that the concerned land was legally transferred to European interests through the Doctrine of Discovery and that sovereignty, in this case, was an "ancient" and untenable concept.

Part Two: The Continued Legacy of the Doctrine of Discovery in Indian Country

To examine the Doctrine of Discovery under a modern lens, this section outlines two contemporary situations, in which, despite the great efforts and advocacy of Indian Country to educate and advance their inherent rights of sovereignty, it is clear to see this evolution is, at best, an institutional struggle. To this end, the following sections detail cooperative federalism and Tribal comanagement within the Bears Ears National Monument as primary examples. The two selected instances provide a stark contrast to the actions of the US federal government, in which one is acting within a status quo model and cosmetically checking the box whereas the other allows Native sovereigns real autonomy and formal recognition from the federal government.

COOPERATIVE FEDERALISM AND LIMITATIONS ON TRIBAL AUTHORITY

At its essence, the concept of cooperative federalism is essentially an aspirational dynamic where state, local, Tribal, and federal governments share governance responsibilities. This is most often seen in the operation of a federal regulatory schematic (such as in the governance of public lands). An implicit goal is to enhance the federal-state relationship by vesting and encouraging states to be affirmative actors in the implementation of federal law. Proponents assert that this framework lends to efficiency and collaboration while encouraging the state to be more creative and state-centric through its implementation. However, while practical on its face as to intergovernmental relations, cooperative federalism has its pronounced limitations, particularly when applied to specific constituencies, such as those within Indian Country.

At present, much of cooperative federalism is a dynamic in which the primacy of the role is exclusively occupied by the states. This prominence is counter to the actual history of Tribes and states, which is a long and bitter history. However, Tribes have long relied on the federal government to keep states at bay and to institutionally reiterate the government-to-government relationship, which is outside the scope of states, although recent movements in the Supreme Court may run counter to what was previously a legal idiom. To this point, as a basic legal tenet, states have no legal authority over Tribes and those Tribal members living within the confines of their respective reservations. However, starting in the mid-1980s, a series of environmental laws were amended to treat Tribes akin to states as applied to environmental statutes and regulations, otherwise known as treatment as states (TAS).

One of the goals of TAS was to acknowledge and incorporate the legal and political status of Tribes as domestic sovereigns. Despite the good intentions of TAS, and not unlike many other federal programs in Indian Country, TAS has not been entirely successful for two primary reasons: (1) unmet funding needs and (2) when non-Tribal members are affected, the extent of Tribal authority can be easily questioned. Further, from an organizational and cultural vantage, it's readily apparent that the more a Tribal program has features and affectations of a state program, the more likely it is to withstand legal challenges. Conversely, this effectively means that the more a Tribe tries to reflect its own culture, values, and precepts, the more it places itself in greater harm if it does not mirror similar state programs. Summarily, Traditional and customary Native programming are discounted and given nominal support.

Challenging Tribal authority is not just a challenge to cultural and organizational aspects, it is a challenge to the concept of Tribal sovereignty in and of itself. In some instances, Tribal programs and processes may look exactly like those of a state or the EPA. The challenge to Tribal authority comes in the form of the same arguments promoted in the Supreme Court criminal case, Oliphant v. Suquamish Indian Tribe (435 U.S. 191 1978), which held that non-Indians needed protection against Indian criminal systems and Tribal decision-making and that Congress intended to limit a Tribe's sovereign authority over non-Indians in a criminal context. In a civil context, in *Montana v. United States* (450 U.S. 544 1981), where Indian interests and non-Indian interests clashed over Tribal exercise of regulatory acts, the Supreme Court created a paradigm that made involuntary Tribal civil jurisdiction over a non-Indian nearly impossible to enforce. More recently, in the *Dollar General v. Mississippi band of Choctaw Indians* (579 U.S. 2016) matter, again within the civil context, the Supreme Court issued a 4-4 gridlock decision that barely upheld Tribal civil jurisdiction over a non-Indian seeking to enforce Tribal law.

The Dollar General dispute occurred within a context of what used to be the safest scenario for Tribes to exercise authority over a non-Indian: where a non-Indian voluntarily consented to Tribal jurisdiction within Tribally governed lands and conducted activity under that jurisdictional structure. In this case, the Mississippi Band of Choctaw's Tribal court not only resembles but exceeds its state counterparts in terms of function and performance; yet the non-Indian entity challenged the Tribal court's ability to assert jurisdiction, despite contractually and voluntarily consenting to Tribal court as a venue. Dollar General raised the long-perpetuated argument that non-Indians are subject to laws and customs to which non-Indians have no say; claiming non-Indians are subject to adjudication without representation. Despite the Tribe's readily accessible laws, Dollar General argued uncertainty as to law and forum.

Because challenging a Tribe's ability to assert its authority is a primary argument, many Tribes factor this threshold challenge to their authority into decisions of whether to seek TAS status for EPA programs, especially in the primacy context. The number of Tribes that have obtained TAS status is minuscule. In the Clean Water Act (CWA) context alone, while there are more than 567 federally recognized Tribes, fewer than 300 have Tribal lands eligible for TAS CWA programs (US GAO 2005). Of those eligible, the EPA authorized fifty-three Tribes to administer a water quality standards program, and only forty-two have EPA-approved water quality standards (US EPA nd).

In a more perfect system, having Tribes take on the responsibility of these regulatory tasks, in the same regard a state would partner with the EPA, would certainly integrate Tribal governments into the cooperative federalism that is now being promoted, but structural and cultural differences remain vast. Optimally, the federal government would establish the framework and the goals of the regulation, and the Tribe, similar to the federal-state model, would then articulate its process and method. While concerns exist about cooperative federalism between EPA and states, there's a similar concern about how the EPA can work with Tribes to achieve "true" cooperative federalism when Tribes are subjected to challenges simply because they are Tribal entities attempting to assert their sovereignty and establish potential regulations. Additionally, Tribes are also then subject to impacts on Tribal sovereignty because, for approval and funding, the EPA expects Tribes to implement programs that function and look familiar to the EPA.

To successfully implement cooperative federalism in Indian country, the EPA should responsibly understand that all Tribes are not equal concerning capacity, that most Tribal programs do not operate with the same organizational structure or support as states, and that the playing field or starting positions are different for each Tribe, especially when compared to states. Therefore, while cooperative federalism, as a policy term, may have the same ultimate goal for states and Tribes, in terms of practical implementation, cooperative federalism will have significantly different meanings and application starting points for each Tribal entity. For example, while the Navajo Nation may be programmatically and institutionally well-suited to work with the EPA to implement cooperative federalism ideas and concepts, many other Tribes, because of their lack of capacity and infrastructure, may not advance as quickly or be in a position to immediately emulate or imitate EPA's ideal cooperative federalism partner.

EPA FLEXIBILITY

There is a valid interest in standards and baselines and recognizing that the EPA is responsible for establishing baseline standards for human health, safety, and welfare, and, scientifically, that uniformity neither favors nor disfavors sovereignty. However, even in a more-perfect system, where Tribes determine both process and method to meet EPA's standards and regulation requirements, despite holding undisputed responsibility over tasks, Tribes would receive resources only after the EPA determines a Tribe's capability to mimic the EPA's program standards and methods. There appears little flexibility in the EPA's scope of standards or the method of their approval, yet EPA's approval of Tribal standards stems from EPA's regulations that identify how EPA will fulfill its congressional authorities. Those regulations may not include Tribal priorities. We lose the cooperative federalism essence further when a Tribe ultimately establishes standards that the EPA also understands under current models and expectations. If a Tribe establishes criteria beyond EPA expectations, in exercising its true Tribal sovereignty, those additional Tribal standards may be vulnerable because the criteria might exceed that of the EPA or EPA program.

Unlike most states, many Tribes do not have the depth of resources (financial or human) to occupy and promote the regulatory tasks that cooperative federalism presumes. Rather than merely push for Tribes to emulate states, and assume that role, the EPA can continue to work with Tribes to focus on capacity building and support Tribal sovereignty by working with and approving systems that operate within both the framework and goals that the EPA would establish, under a cooperative federalism perspective.

Like many other issues in Indian Country, funding and the institutional capacity of Tribes are critical elements of success. As the most encouraging models of success mirror reflections of the state models, it places Tribes in an ineffectual position. As we are currently experiencing in Indian Country, taking away Tribal jurisdiction always runs counter to both objectives of Tribes as well as their effectiveness.

Part Three: The Bears Ears National Monument and Comanagement

The Bears Ears Inter-Tribal Coalition (the Coalition) comprises five member Tribes (Hopi Tribe, Navajo Nation, Ute Mountain Ute Tribe, Ute Indian Tribe, and Pueblo of Zuni), who each refer to the area as "Bears Ears" in their Indigenous respective languages: Hoon'Naqvut (Hopi), Shash Jaa' (Navajo), Kwiyagatu Nukavachi (Ute), and Ansh An Lashokdiwe (Zuni; Biden 2021). In addition to more than a century of other efforts, the Coalition has readily advocated for the creation of the Bears Ears National Monument (BENM), culminating in President Obama's Proclamation No. 9558, 82 Fed. Reg. 1139, 1145 (January 5, 2017) in December 2016, which established the monument.

More than a century before the establishment of BENM, the Bears Ears region provided an impetus for the passage of the 1906 Antiquities Act to preserve the landscape and its unique cultural resources (Biden 2021). In 1904, advocates outlined for Congress the problematic issues of destroying historic and cultural sites in the Southwest and identified the Bears Ears area as a region that needed prompt protection (Biden 2021). However, no prompt actions were taken, and it took over a century of advocacy and efforts from a plethora of Indigenous Peoples, coalitions, scientists, and the like before such protections were granted (Biden 2021). One of the main drivers behind the change stemmed from the uniting of the five member Tribes into the Coalition, united by a common vision that advocated for the permanent protection of their Peoples' ancestral territories.

Proclamation 9558 describes the unique cultural histories of many Indigenous Peoples, historic sites, and the geology, biology, ecology, paleontology, and topography of the region, among other factors (Biden 2021). It also established the Bears Ears Commission to ensure that Tribal Nations were involved in and guided the management of the monument through their Traditional ways (Biden 2021). However, only a year after it was implemented, President Donald Trump issued Proclamation 9681, which effectively reduced the monument's protected areas by more than 1.1 million acres and removed protection from areas of historic and cultural interest

(Biden 2021). Trump's proclamation unlawfully attempted to revoke and replace the BENM with two, much smaller, monument units (an 85 percent decrease of the original monument size). In response to Proclamation 9681, the Coalition sued the Trump administration to have the revocation of the monument declared illegal as advanced by the Native American Rights Fund (NARF 2024).

Concurrent with the litigation challenging the illegal modification of boundaries by the Trump administration and in recognition of the fact that there are ever-growing needs for land management and conservation amid growing visitation to the Bears Ears landscape, the Coalition initiated work to develop a comprehensive land management plan for the 1.9-million-acre landscape that was depicted in the Coalition's original proposal to the Obama administration. The Coalition intended to develop a land management plan grounded in Native perspectives but also easily implemented into federal agencies' planning processes, led by the Bureau of Land Management (BLM) and the United States Forest Service (USFS). BLM's and USFS's expedited planning process reiterated the request that the agencies comply with the government-to-government relationship by engaging with the Tribes individually and allowing the Coalition the opportunity for input and collaboration, as encouraged in both the Obama and Trump proclamations.

The Coalition maintained that lands, natural resources, and scientific and cultural resources encompassing 1.9 million acres within the Bears Ears landscape need preservation and protection as a national monument. The need to structure long-term, sustainable land-management policies to protect and preserve lands and resources within the Bears Ears landscape implicates the federal government's role and strict adherence to the trust responsibility to consult with Tribes. The Coalition maintained the principles of the federal trust relationship be upheld by protecting the original intent of the monument declaration and requiring the lead agencies to meaningfully engage the Tribes in the management of the BENM (Chuipka 2022).

After Trump was voted out of office, his successor, the former vice president of the Obama administration, President Biden, issued Proclamation 10285 on October 8, 2021, which confirmed, restored, and supplemented Obama's proclamation, including the original protected areas (Biden 2021). In Proclamation 10285, Biden states,

Restoring the Bears Ears National Monument honors the special relationship between the Federal Government and Tribal Nations, correcting the exclusion of lands and resources profoundly sacred to Tribal Nations, and ensuring the long-term protection of, and respect for, this remarkable and revered region. Given the unique nature and cultural significance of the objects identified across the Bears Ears landscape, the threat of damage and destruction to those objects, their spiritual, cultural, and historical significance to Tribal Nations, and the insufficiency of the protections afforded in the absence of Antiquities Act protections, the reservation described below is the smallest area compatible with the proper care and management of the objects of historic and scientific interest named in this proclamation and Proclamation 9558" (Biden 2021).

Biden's proclamation was subsequently followed by a historic Inter-Governmental Cooperative Agreement less than a year later. On June 18, 2022, national, state, and local leaders of the Department of the Interior, BLM, US Department of Agriculture, and the USFS joined with members of the Bears Ears Commission to solidify the agreement, which covered the cooperative management of the federal lands and resources of BENM (Balles 2022). Agreement signatories included leaders from the BLM, USDA, Hopi Tribe, Navajo Nation, Ute Mountain Ute Tribe, Pueblo of Zuni, and Uncompahgre Band of the Ute Indian Tribe of the Uintah and Ouray and Ouray Reservation (Balles 2022).

BENM represents a new model and level of federal recognition of Tribal sovereignty, especially in parks and protected areas. The model affords institutional deference and cooperation, as it allows Tribes to be stewards and real managers of their ancestral homelands. This is strikingly new, because most US-based parks and protected areas situate sovereign Tribal Nations merely as stakeholders in management processes without any real management oversight or authority (Jacobs et al. 2022a,b; Fisk et al. 2021). Additionally, the successful advocacy for the monument declaration was unique and truly unprecedented. While historians, conservationists, scientists, archaeologists, and others have sponsored many requests for protection under the Antiquities Act, Tribes never previously congregated together to petition for a presidentially declared national monument. As a result, the differences between earlier monuments, other parks and protected areas, and BENM are many and deep. At BENM, the government acts as trustee for these five Tribes. Biden's proclamation acknowledges the Tribes as sovereign governments, with deep roots in the surrounding communities, and as entities who possess Traditional Ecological Knowledge that must be incorporated into the management of the BENM.

Furthermore, the signed cooperative agreement acknowledges that BENM is a place for cultural living for Tribal members, which holds the long histories of their Traditions and cultures in a location integral to their ceremonial practices, traditions, and other factors (Chuipka 2022). The agreement also recognizes the long histories that local Indigenous Peoples have honored in continually using the area since time immemorial, for purposes of healing, spirituality, prayer, rejuvenation, and connecting (Chuipka 2022). Additionally, a large emphasis of the agreement is placed on facilitating communication and understanding between Tribal Nations and federal land managers to protect cultural practices in the region and preserve and integrate Indigenous Peoples' Traditional Ecological Knowledges. As such, the purpose of the agreement is to ensure that Indigenous forms of Knowledge like Traditional Ecological Knowledge and Indigenous Peoples' expertise have meaningful influences on how the monument is managed by federal entities.

Traditional and cultural Knowledges of Tribes and their historical responsibilities as stewards of the land are now readily seen in pen to paper. In my opinion, this reflects a culmination of many years of efforts that are integral and valuable components relative to land management. This also opens the door for more qualitative approaches to land management that add to the context in which Tribes think about, relate to, and have responsibility for their lands.

As to the new cooperative agreement, Committee on Natural Resources Chair Raúl M. Grijalva (D-Ariz.) said,

> Giving the [T]ribes, the original inhabitants of our public lands, a
> say in how lands are managed and protected shouldn't be a radical
> idea. But for far too long, our federal government has treated it like
> one. Indigenous Peoples have a profound and unique understanding
> of their ancestral homelands, as well as a cultural connection
> to many of the sacred spaces on these lands. We should be
> honoring and elevating Indigenous [E]cological [K]nowledge in the
> stewardship of our lands, not silencing it, as we have so often done
> in the past. I'm grateful to the Biden administration for taking this

important step for both Bears Ears and for the [T]ribes who call the region home. (Press Pool 2022)

The sentiments and support of Natural Resource Chair Raul M. Grijalva are an important continuation and consistency of the full Committee on Natural Resources that held a historic oversight hearing on March 3, 2022, to examine the importance and benefits of Tribal comanagement of public lands (Grijalva 2022). At the hearing, Tribal witnesses shared testimony on the history of Indigenous land dispossession, opportunities to reverse course on that history, and existing examples of successful comanagement efforts. National Park Service Director Chuck Sams also discussed how the agency already has and will continue to expand the role of Tribal communities in federal land management.

Dr. Len Necefer captures the essence and core of why the Bears Ears National Monument is distinctly different from previous approaches by the federal government in his June 29 *Outside Magazine* article. He states that a cooperative management or comanagement approach between the federal government and Tribes has been enacted in other federal programs such as law enforcement, waste disposal, tax revenue, allocation of water rights, and the like. However, the BENM agreement is the first time in federal land management history in which the feds "treat [T]ribes as equals and experts, and not as [P]eople to be subjugated under a paternalistic policy." He emphasizes the importance of recognizing that BENM should not be casually regarded as a simple success story. It requires a deep understanding of the intricate jurisdictional complexities that have shaped the relationship between the federal government and Tribes, which has fluctuated between conflict and cooperation for centuries. The United States classified Tribes as "domestic dependent Nations," likening their relationship to that of a ward to a guardian. Even today, Congress retains complete authority over Tribes and holds the title for all Indian lands. So, the significance of the cooperation should be understood as it pertains to history, Tribal sovereignty, and federal Indian law.

The cooperative agreement to comanage BENM is a novel and vanguard approach to managing public and ancestral lands that at its primacy places Tribes with real and recognized authority to manage lands that are a critical part of their cultural heritage. It is a welcome departure from many of the attempts and activities of the last several hundreds of years that were ruled by the Doctrine of Discovery, as it places Tribes firmly at the table of decision-making while seeding them with resources and systematized inserts so they can weigh in and instruct the management of the monument in real time. Most of these objectives are reflected within the body and contents of the cooperative agreement.

The case for Tribal comanagement is straightforward and simple: Tribes have been passing down sacred forms of Knowledge about land, wildlife, and resource management since time immemorial and they have significant cultural responsibilities to enact their Knowledges through culturally informed management practices. Many have the willingness and expertise to comanage public lands effectively and have sacred places and legally recognized Treaty rights to hunt, fish, and gather on public lands; therefore, they have more than just a stake in their lands' effective stewardship.

To effectively protect sacred places, and to improve the stewardship of public lands, Tribes must be full partners in management praxes. It is a time of both great opportunity and validation for the five Tribes as it recognizes their ability to transfer their historical roles as stewards of the land in a modern context and operate side by side with federal agencies.

Finally, the Bears Ears, in my opinion, is both a fine and contemporary example of the advancement of Traditional Ecological Knowledge (TEK). When the Bears Ears Coalition first considered how to create a land management plan that would reflect the priorities of five distinct Tribes, it was both natural and pragmatic that all of the Tribes of the coalition seamlessly gravitated to their own respective Traditional and cultural practice as their directional compass (Bears Ears Inter-Tribal Coalition nd). This land management plan is very different from the rigid and formulaic documents usually created by the federal government. Rather, it considers the unique histories of each Tribe and their ancestral ties to the landscape by emphasizing Tribally led land management and returning lands for cultural and spiritual practices.

The Doctrine of Discovery had a detrimental impact on Native land practices, rendering them as ineffective and insignificant compared to western practices (Miller 2006). However, TEK allows Tribes to reconcile and reclaim their relationships and connections to the land. It's important to recognize that Bears Ears is not just a national monument designation or a conservation conscription; it is ultimately an altar and a place of worship for Native Peoples. Being the first Tribal comanagers of a national monument is a source of great pride. However, for Native Peoples, these changes restore and reestablish their ability to worship and honor the land, which is a fundamental aspect of our existence. The significance of this restoration cannot be overstated, as it allows Native Peoples to reconnect with spiritual Traditions and deeply revere the land. In other words, comanagement is arguably both an exercise of modern environmental justice and the return of sacred lands and Tradition. Ultimately, by incorporating TEK into their land management plan, it mitigates and counteracts many of the negative impacts stemming from the Doctrine of Discovery.

Conclusion

The history of Tribes in the United States is exceedingly more complicated than we view at the surface. The foundations of how we developed Indian law and policy are derived from the Doctrine of Discovery, which is now more than five hundred years old and instructs that Tribes are subordinated and do not have a right to own land. It allows the ruling sovereign, such as the United States, to act as a trustee of Indigenous communities, serving in a fiduciary capacity. However, recognizing the cultural responsibilities of Indigenous Peoples, especially those that pertain to their Traditional Ecological Knowledges, we must understand that Tribes are the original stewards and conservators of lands. We must also provide Tribal communities with sufficient credit for how they have managed lands through time and kept their sacred Knowledges alive and well throughout the processes of colonialism and the onslaught of policies and dispossessions granted by the Doctrine of Discovery.

Tribal communities have a proven track record, which in some instances is twenty to thirty times as long as the largest conservation groups; however, they get a fractional share of land assets, and often lack the opportunity to be in the room to articulate their solutions to land-management issues. Until very recently, the approaches to large-scale conservation efforts have been limited and narrow in scope. Today, especially with the repudiation of the Doctrine of Discovery, Tribes need to be the primary managerial decision-makers on their ancestral lands and not be denigrated into subordinated roles: Hard stop. Period.

21

FOOD-GROWER-GRIZZLY HELPS BEAVER COMMUNITY

JENNIFER GRENZ-NLAKA'PAMUX

Positionality Statement

See chapter 25 for positionality statement.

Blackbear Watches the Salmon

A MODERNIZED INDIGENOUS STORY TO TEACH LESSONS OF
FOOD SECURITY AND FOOD SOVEREIGNTY

Blackbear sat on a bridge over the river, dangling his feet over the edge. As he swung his legs back and forth, he peered down, into the sparkling water, catching glimpses of flashes of red backs darting here and there. Further upstream he could hear the splashes in the water of the sockeye salmon as they spawned in the gravel beds.

Blackbear's granddaughter, who had come along for a walk with her grandfather, growing bored, asked Blackbear why he sat and watched the salmon for so long. Reflecting on a conversation with his grandfather, Blackbear told his granddaughter that there was a time when there were so many spawning salmon in the rivers that there seemed to be more fish than water. It was as though you could walk on the backs of the salmon across the river. After the settlers arrived, they didn't know how to care for the fish and they harvested so many that they even left piles of fish, as high as a house, to rot on the banks of the river. Eventually, fewer and fewer fish came back. Blackbear told his granddaughter that when her mother was young, he and she would sit on that same bridge and watch the water, hoping to see the flash of the red backs of the sockeye salmon come spawning time, but some days they would not see a single one.

He said, "We grew hungry those days when the salmon disappeared. Sockeye is what we ate growing up. I grew up fishing with my family. We

271

would spend days at the river, harvesting. I never got to teach your mother to fish because there were no fish to catch."

"Well, what did you eat?" his granddaughter asked. Blackbear said, "Well, we did our best to eat our other foods, but it was difficult. Other protein sources were harder to come by. Many of us weren't very good at hunting other foods. People saw that we weren't looking very good."

He sighed and continued, "People from outside our community started giving us their food to eat. Some bears moved elsewhere and got jobs and earned money and bought food from the grocery stores. Us bears were sad. For thousands of years, we ate sockeye. It is part of our DNA. Then suddenly . . . No more. It was nice that there were other foods for us so we wouldn't starve but we weren't used to all of this new food. It was strange to us. Some bears felt sick eating the food, and started having health problems—health problems we bears had never had before. Health problems we still have to this day. We bears just weren't meant to eat that food, but . . . " He trailed off, sadness in his eyes as he stared at the water below.

Suddenly a fish jumped right below them and at least twenty fish swam together under the bridge toward the spawning beds. Blackbear smiled.

"The good news is that us bears worked very hard to help our salmon relations to grow in numbers again. Eventually, they started to come back. Many of my Elders were excited to start fishing again and be able to teach their sons and daughters at last, but the settler government said that we were not allowed to fish. And especially not in the ways we have always done."

Granddaughter bear looked perplexed. Her grandfather went on, "Well, the government felt that to get the fish numbers up high, we needed to let the fish rest, not catch them until there were enough. It's something us bears used to do long before the settlers came. We even have words for that in our language. We tried to tell the settlers about this resting before all the fish disappeared. They didn't listen to us. They learned a tough lesson and we suffered the most from their mistakes. As the fish started to come back, having learned these lessons, now they TELL US, the fish have to rest. That we can't fish. We understood that they wanted to do all they could to protect the fish. It just felt like all of a sudden they were protecting the fish FROM US." He shook his head and went on, "They forgot that we needed the fish to eat. That the fish are part of who we are. That we cared for the fish for thousands of years and managed to keep our bellies full at the same time.

But no. Still, they would not let us fish. And so we sat, just like this, on this bridge, for years, watching the fish pass us by."

"Are there enough fish to eat now grandfather?" granddaughter bear asked.

"Well, for us bears, yes. For all of the hungry settlers, probably not," he replied.

Granddaughter bear responded, "But now we can fish our way, right grandfather?"

The bear sighed. "Well, yes. The settler government is letting us fish again, mostly our way. So that's good."

"Why are so few bears fishing now grandfather?" granddaughter bear asked as she looked up and down the river.

"Well, many parents didn't learn how to fish our way. Like your mother. Remember, there weren't many fish when they were children. Now that fish have returned, some are learning again from the Elders. It is tough though. There still aren't very many fish, so that makes it harder. Many of the bears with fishing Knowledge have passed on. Many younger bears don't have time. The food from the store is easier to get. Bears are busy with their jobs. It takes a lot of time and effort to harvest fish. I understand that."

"I will learn. I want to learn," granddaughter bear said with great pride. She stood up abruptly, "I will also tell the government how to care for the salmon. Our way."

"Yes, my dear granddaughter. You will help us to reclaim our ways. You will help our salmon relations to flourish once more. There is still much work to be done, but I have hope in you and all of the young bears of your generation."

22

HONORING OUR RESPONSIBILITIES WHILE "DOING SCIENCE"
Indigenous Scientists' Perspectives

JESSICA HERNANDEZ, MELINDA M. ADAMS, VIVI VOLD, LYDIA
JENNINGS, MARGARET PALAGHICON VON ROTZ, ANGELO
VILLAGOMEZ, TARA MCALLISTER, LAUREN WENDELLE
YOWELUNH MCLESTER-DAVIS, VICTOR HERNANDEZ, EILEEN
JIMENEZ, BRANDIE MAKEBA CROSS, AND JOSEPH GAZING WOLF

Positionality Statements

Jessica Hernandez: See chapter 16 for positionality statement.

Melinda Adams: N'dee (San Carlos Apache); University of Kansas, Department of Geography and Atmospheric Science and Indigenous Studies Program.

Vivi Vold: Inuk from Kalaallit Nunaat; Ilisimatusarfik University of Greenland, SILA Department, Institute of Health and Nature.

Lydia Jennings: See chapter 16 for positionality statement.

Margaret Palaghicon Von Rotz: Tuwali Ifugao; Master of Laws (LLM) candidate in Environmental Law and Sustainable Development, School of Oriental and African Studies, University of London; Juris Doctor candidate at University of California, College of the Law.

Angelo Villagomez: Chamorro; Senior Fellow, Center for American Progress.

Tara McAllister: See chapter 16 for positionality statement.

Lauren Wendelle Yowelunh McLester-Davis:: Oneida Nation of Wisconsin; Tulane University Brain Institute.

Victor Hernandez: Maya Ch'orti' and Binnizá; University of Arkansas, School of Education.

Eileen Jimenez: Ñätho (Otomi); South Seattle College, College Transfer Division.

Brandie Makeba Cross: Afro-Indigenous (Choctaw/Chickasaw); California State University, Los Angeles, College of Natural and Social Sciences, Department of Biological Sciences.

Joseph Gazing Wolf: See chapter 13 for positionality statement.

We write this chapter as Indigenous scholars, scientists, community members, and advocates who have not made it this far in our careers by ourselves. We have been guided, supported, and mentored by Indigenous activists, community members, Elders, scholars, and scientists who have shaped the pathways for us to be able to conduct science for and by our communities while upholding our responsibilities as Indigenous Peoples.

Figure 22.1 An original linocut by Eileen Jimenez depicting three sets of hands, three generations, holding blooming and thriving flores de calabaza; it is the embodiment of our responsibilities to our work.

We acknowledge that we are but a few from a larger movement to bring Indigenous Science to the forefront of scientific research. We are working together to shift narratives that continue to dismiss Indigenous Knowledges and acknowledge the work that has been done thus far. We also come from different Indigenous Nations, communities, and Pueblos, and recognize that Indigenous Peoples are not a monolith, and that there is a great diversity of Indigenous thoughts and experiences. But across this diversity, there are probably more similarities than differences, just as small-town America shares values and cultures across its geographic diversity. Still, this chapter speaks solely to our personal experiences navigating our distinct responsibilities as Indigenous scientists.

Introduction

Indigenous Ways of Knowing (IWK) draw from generational Knowledges formulated since time immemorial and parallel what is considered a scientific discipline (Adhikari and Poudel 2022). IWK have been formulated through observations, hypotheses, close proximity and interactions with local environments, trial and error, and intergenerational transmission of discovery. While it does not follow the reductionist and linear ways of thinking that are the hallmarks of western science, IWK have been established with close study of the natural world (Johannes 1981; Goduka 2012; Birhane and Guest 2020; Kolopenuk 2020). IWK's establishment is inherited due to Indigenous communities' responsibilities. Although responsibilities differ among Indigenous communities, some of these responsibilities are rooted in reciprocal relationships with nature and local environments.

While Indigenous communities have the autonomy to determine whether they view their ways of Knowing as science, it is important to explain that Indigenous Knowledge systems exist in juxtaposition to what is viewed as science today. Western science is a manifestation of established dominant ways of knowing that arise from the colonial era (Menon 2022) and structure (Wolfe 2006). Many Indigenous thought leaders have referred to western science as "colonial science," given its involvement in colonization and upholding white supremacy. Historically, western science violently erased and dismissed IWK from all its existing frameworks (Lazrus et al. 2022). This violent erasure was facilitated by how western science bestowed and promoted throughout the globe specific ways of knowing and schools of thought throughout the European Enlightenment period and Industrial Revolution (da Costa Marques 2022).

Consequently, when both western sciences and Indigenous responsibilities are linked together, there is a need to merge relationality, reciprocity, re-membering, and futurity to ensure that western sciences do not harm IWK. While there is no set guide or way of doing this, as Indigenous scholars and scientists, we have to ensure science upholds our responsibilities within and beyond our communities. In this chapter, we provide reflections from Indigenous scholars and scientists, or *testimonios*, to present methods that uphold our responsibilities while doing science. While we share personal perspectives, projects, and research into how this is done, it is by no means the only way that Indigenous scholars and scientists can uphold our responsibilities.

RESPONSIBILITY TO OUR LAND AND COMMUNITY'S SPIRITUALITY

Within Indigenous communities, responsibilities dictate various norms that range from small scale to large scale. On an individual level, they can dictate who we are, and our places within our communities and the larger universe (Park and Bahia 2022). At larger scales, they can dictate Indigenous communities' responsibilities with one another, national entities, and so on. (Althaus 2022). Responsibilities emerge within a web of realities and norms that go beyond what can be described in words, which complicates our abilities to discuss the important nuances that Indigenous responsibilities embody, as they exist within parallel universes that not one person or one book chapter can fully detail. However, within our own distinct set of norms as Indigenous Peoples, we dive into some of the responsibilities that are indistinguishable within our distinct communities and demonstrate how we uphold them within our scientific research, projects, and scholarship.

Individual responsibilities include caring and stewarding our Lands and communities and serving as actors who uphold the larger scales of responsibilities that are bestowed on our communities (Tynan 2021). We have specific duties to our Mother Earth, one another, and other responsibilities to fulfill in this lifetime that project into the afterlife and beyond settler borders (Bannister 2020; Chua et al. 2019). For example, in the Zapotec community, everyone is responsible for maintaining a spiritual relationship with those who have transcended into the afterlife through altares (altars) that are set up and adorned in the person's tomb on the first and second days of November. Often referred to as Dia de Muertos, or Day of the Dead, this is the responsibility we uphold to our Ancestors and recently departed relatives (Chajon 2022; Lamrani 2022). Beyond settler borders, Zapotec People must maintain this Tradition by participating in ceremonies and other Traditions that commemorate our relatives and Ancestors in the spiritual world to bridge the divide between the human and spiritual world. While the Traditions and ceremonies differ, because of being displaced from our Ancestral Lands, they still hold on to the same sentiments and beliefs. This responsibility is also shared by other Indigenous communities; however, the cultural Traditions, ceremonies, and protocols differ among individual cultures. In Maya communities, Dia de Los Disfuntos (El Salvador) or Día de Todos los Santos (Guatemala) uphold the same responsibilities, but the ceremonies and Traditions are unique to each Maya community (Sosa 1985).

For Tuwali Ifugao, an Indigenous group in the Philippines, our responsibilities to one another extend into the afterlife and across borders as well. Though many in our communities engage in All Soul's Day Traditions for our atangs (altars), it is believed that our Ancestors communicate to us from the afterlife through multiple means. Such communication means that they are calling on us, no matter whether we are on our Ancestral Land or not, often to perform bogwa, or a cleaning of their bones, during which their burial blanket may be replaced, their grave is repaired, and other caretaking of their physical remains is performed. Furthermore, our creation stories indicate a reciprocal relationship with our gods and our environment; our stories indicate punishment for those who do not respect the lives of nonhuman species (i.e., those who needlessly kill). Our gods often take on nonhuman forms (e.g., our gods guide us with life-giving water in the form of a lizard). These metaphysical relationships are definitive aspects of the Ifugao. Our name is "People of the earth realm," thus we are charged with caring for the Earth as one of our own.

Maintaining a relationship with our Ancestors and relatives in the afterlife is a responsibility that is bestowed on us since the time of our birth. In order for us to truly continue our practices, we must uphold this responsibility within our homes, communities, and locations, even if that is beyond settler borders. This example of a Tradition that becomes a responsibility demonstrates how similar value systems of responsibility can be shared across Indigenous communities that now exist across settler borders—whether it is due to displacement or the creation of distinct nationhoods. Other responsibilities are intertwined with our Lands and communities, and these responsibilities are rooted in our relatedness and kinship to both our Lands and communities.

Our kinship and relatedness to our communities and our Land are all connected to our senses of self; from outside to inside our communities and ourselves, through systems of internal and external kinship. Everything is connected to this responsibility of being part of the community. For the Inuit community, this is a constant interrelatedness. For Inuit, the Land fluently speaks a language with no words. As the People of the Land, it becomes the Indigenous People's responsibility to learn and understand their Lands, seas, sky, animals, plants, and living beings. We have to learn the connection to the Land and that everything is connected through and with ourselves (Archibald et al. 2019). In relation, through Inuit Kalaallit kinship in Kalaallit Nunaat, individual responsibilities are vital for individuals and community members (Trondheim 2010). Additionally, through responsibility, Inuit get a sense of safety and understanding of how they are needed in the community and gain a spiritual sense of belonging and importance. Similarly, in other Indigenous communities, the elements of spirituality exist in a system of shared responsibility through which we know we are being taken care of, considered, and safe. In these spiritual responsibilities, a cycle of gratitude is created that serves as a constant reciprocal interconnectedness of great importance for the individuals' and communities' overall spiritual and mental health (Archibald et al. 2019).

To further demonstrate these connections, we reflect on Inuit Kalaallit concepts of Sila and Inua. Sila refers to weather and individual consciousness, which demonstrates how both are interrelated and connected to themselves and outside themselves; our inner worlds reflect our outer world. Furthermore, the way Inuit Kalaallit connect to IWK and memory is what Inuit Kalaallit call Inua. Inua is the spirit of the mountain, the grass, the sea, the stone, the animals, and the Knowledges that each element carries (Vold 2020).

We contend that as Indigenous scientists, it is our responsibility to ensure we carry such understanding with us in our work through a constant reciprocal understanding of connection. However, this does not speak for all Indigenous scientists, as morally, culturally, and so on, we differ in the ways we grasp these elements of responsibilities. In order for us to understand our Land, communities, and the Knowledges our Peoples carry, we must center our spirituality and understand the connections to our Sila and Inua, and the privileges we hold in our positions and places. Inuit Kalaallit strongly believe that the work that we do to understand and implement these factors, especially in science and research, are the responsibilities that we honor for our Ancestors.

For Māori, the Indigenous Peoples of Aotearoa New Zealand, we have distinct obligations to Papatūānuku (Mother Earth) that transcend generations. These relationships are determined by genealogy, which locates Māori within an environmental context, linking the intangible to the tangible. Māori are direct descendants of Papatūānuku and have an inherited responsibility to protect, sustain, and enhance our relationships with her. The intricate relationship between Māori and the environment is shown through the Māori language Some words have dual meanings that illustrate how our identity is inextricably linked to the environment. For example, whenua means Land and placenta, wai means water and who, and hapū means pregnant and sub-Tribe (McAllister, Hikuroa, and Macinnis-Ng 2023). Ancestral sayings like "mō tātou, ā, mō ngā uri ā muri ake nei," meaning for us and for our children after us, exemplify our intergenerational obligations to leave the environment in a similar or better state for future generations. Chamorros, the Indigenous Peoples of the Mariana Islands, have an intricate system of social responsibility called Chenchule', wherein obligations among families and individuals are affirmed through giving and receiving, especially during life milestones such as weddings, funerals, births, christenings, and birthdays. While these examples demonstrate our cultural responsibilities, upholding our responsibilities that are not intertwined with colonial structures (such as the academy and research) become more complex, especially in instances where our IWK are integrated into western science.

RESPONSIBILITY TO MAINTAIN OUR CULTURE AND IDENTITY

Maintaining and upholding our responsibilities throughout different complex systems, structures, and institutions that were created to exclude us becomes intricate, oftentimes resulting in the need to create various pathways for ourselves to be able to do so. For example, IWK and perspectives are often oversimplified, if not directly excluded from western science spaces that continue to devalue IWK, ethics, and community protocols that have been passed down through our communities for generations. The devaluing of IWK is inherently linked to white supremacy. Western academics typically view IWK as being supplementary to "real knowledge," which is why IWK are often relegated to being myths, legends, and anecdotes

(Kuokkanen 2011). Such supplementary "inclusion" of IWK into western systems often becomes a double-edged sword, wherein IWK quickly become a monolithic form of solving humanity's pressing environmental crises. For example, environmental advocates often "cherry-pick" Indigenous values, Traditions, and practices "as validation of support for a commonwealth in nature," rather than respecting Indigenous self-determination outright (Marshall 2019).

IWK, therefore, understand the diversity of Indigenous perspectives and lived experiences that inform our Knowledge production. Knowledge production is not an addendum to "real knowledge"; it is an epistemological (theory of Knowing) approach that lends itself to explaining our collective responsibilities to our communities and nonhuman relatives. It is an embrace of what Anishinaabe scholar Scott Richard Lyons argues is Indigenous modernity, where our Knowledge production exists within the modern world (such as embracing decolonizing methodologies) and is concurrently beholden to Indigenous community values as they exist today (Lyons 2010).

Recent research underlines how Indigenous Knowledges (e.g., Traditional Ecological Knowledge and Indigenous Science) improve western sciences (Bielawski 2020; Zidny, Sjöström, and Eilks 2020). However, Indigenous Knowledges are not integrated, because western sciences solely focus on Eurocentric understandings that acknowledge only European men as the founders of scientific disciplines (D'ignazio and Klein 2020). Indigenous Knowledges date back many millennia—before Europeans began studying us and our environments—and, arguably, have gone through the most rigorous peer-review processes of being confirmed across generations of Knowledge-holders (David-Chavez and Gavin 2018). Therefore, our first responsibility as Indigenous scientists is to ensure that our history is not erased, ignored, and silenced by the hegemonic (dominant) paradigms of western science. This is central to our Indigenous ways of living, our understandings of how we interact with one another, and our responsibilities to acknowledge and value our Ancestors' IWK. For example, evaluating oral histories of Indigenous Peoples should be considered the same as written text, since Indigenous Knowledges are often transferred by talking and/or "doing." Elders, with their accumulated education, experience, and wisdom, are regarded as the Knowledge-holders and educate the younger generations as part of a millennia-old lifestyle. Stories can range from historical recollections to scientific analyses of the Land (Iseke 2013). Storytelling as pedagogy and experience are deeply rooted in the Traditional engagement of Indigenous Peoples in research within our respective communities, whether it be family histories or understandings of the natural world.

Whether within Indigenous spaces, academic institutions, or other scientific spaces, our cultural responsibilities are intertwined with all of our relations. We are in relation with one another, including living and nonliving things (Hart 2010; Greenwood and Lindsay 2019). We are responsible for the community relations we build within research partnerships and for ensuring that we nurture the fruits of our labor beyond western and colonial metrics of success (e.g., publications, grants, etc.). Indigenous responsibilities are deemed unnecessary in western science because they do not necessarily translate to tangible materials (e.g., journal articles, technical reports, books, etc.) that determine success, productivity, prestige, and status in western institutions. These metrics of success have long been called sexist and racist, yet no changes have been achieved within academic systems to ensure that such oppressive structures are dismantled (Cell Editorial Team 2020; Davies et al. 2021; Chaudhury and Colla 2021).

It is no surprise that within the frameworks of western institutions, Indigenous scholars, scientists, and community members have to work twice as hard as their white counterparts and colleagues. Haar and Martin (2022) describe this as the "cultural double-shift," whereby Indigenous scientists experience an increased workload and have to fulfill two different roles: one as a scientist and one as an Indigenous scientist. As noted by Settles, Buchanan, and Dotson (2019), "Faculty of color experience a number of challenges within academia, including tokenism, marginalization, racial microaggressions, and a disconnect between their racial/ethnic culture and the culture within academia." This highlights the obstacles embedded within academia that spill over into western science and continue to disconnect Indigenous cultures and our associated responsibilities with various scientific disciplines. Indigenous Peoples have worked hard toward achieving self-determination in research, gaining more power in research decision-making, and attesting the need for culturally relevant data-sharing practices (Henri et al. 2022).

Responsibilities are important to Indigenous Peoples because they dictate and determine the work that we do, how we do it, and how we continue the work in the future. Whether we are working within our own communities or other Indigenous communities, we are responsible for upholding these kinships and reciprocal relationships in our methods and to the

Figure 22.2:
Responsibility praxis

communities we work with. For those of us in the diaspora, we remain responsible to the communities and the Places where we live. These responsibilities transcend our work as Indigenous scientists as they are embedded in the ways we navigate the relationships we uphold in the diaspora.

In retrospect, we keep ourselves accountable to our responsibilities and center Indigenous Knowledges by prioritizing relationality (relationships to the Land, more-than-human Relatives, and past, present, and future Ancestors); reciprocity (connectedness that positions individuals in a set of relationships with each other and with the Land); re-membering (collective and individual connection of bodies with place); and futurity (intergenerational exchanges; Archibald 2008; Smith 2021 [1999]; Wilson 2008; Montgomery and Blanchard 2021). Accountability, intentions, and impact serve as the main frameworks of our responsibility praxis (figure 22.2). These frameworks coexist with the pillars of responsibility; relationality, reciprocity, re-membering, and futurity (Smith 2021 [1999]; Baldy 2019; Harjo 2019; figure 2, concept in part from Adams et al. 2023).

This responsibility praxis offers key interventions that Indigenous scientists often employ and use in our work. For example, we consider these reflections crucial to scientific work with communities, which require researchers to take inventory of our intentions and positionalities (Smith

2021 [1999]). These interventions support decolonial approaches that aid Indigenous Peoples' efforts to retribute oppressive and colonial processes that research, projects, and processes often reciprocate (Varcoe and McKenzie 2022). Responsibility praxes disrupt western academic principles and guidelines, which permit us to hold conversations that address the above factors with community members, whether they be our communities or those in which we are guests. While some Indigenous communities evaluate and design specific principles to guide ethical research in their communities (David-Chavez and Gavin, 2018; Hayward et al. 2021; Carroll et al. 2022), this is not always the case, especially in communities that do not have nation-to-nation relationships established with other governments, such as Indigenous communities in the global south or non-federally-recognized Tribes.

Though diversity of Indigenous thoughts and experience exist, the following reflective questions may assist others with co-designing projects and research that align with the Indigenous community's interests. The questions listed in table 22.1 are what many Indigenous scientists reflect on before initiating projects, research, and the like. These questions are rooted on the three pillars of our responsibility praxis: accountability, intentions, and impact. They have been co-developed from the scholarship of Smith (1996), Wilson (2008), Smith (2019), Kovach (2021), and Quinless (2022).

These reflective questions serve as a preliminary guide for Indigenous-centered and Indigenous-led projects. We emphasize Indigenous-centered and -led projects because it is imperative that power is leveraged within Indigenous communities, thus research no longer has individual ownership, but rather a communal set of protocols. This will allow both Indigenous and non-Indigenous scientists to interrogate their ethics and value systems and ensure each is aligned with the Indigenous community's priorities.

RESPONSIBILITY TO UPHOLD ETHICS AND VALUES

Research harms have historically included and continue to include unethical practices, Knowledge extraction, Knowledge appropriation, lack of credit, and lack of consent (Warne and Frizzell 2014; Around Him et al. 2019; Brockie et al. 2022). Thus, in ethical research, it is imperative to initiate conversations with community members several stages before research commencement, and ensure that these conversations are ongoing throughout the research process (Jennings et al. forthcoming; Delgado-Serrano et al. 2015). It is the relationships and responsibilities to those

Table 22.1: Responsibility praxis reflective questions

Accountability	• What are the accountabilities scientists have and to whom or what are they accountable? • How can scientists relinquish their power and ensure that all power remains with the community? • How can scientists ensure deliverables are given to and directly benefit the community? • How can scientists demonstrate gratitude and reciprocity directly to the community (including nonhuman kin that are sometimes used as "subjects")?
Intentions	• Are the guiding intentions created with and/or by community members? • What voices can be elevated that are not necessarily elevated in western science or academia? • How can scientists' voices be decentered and prevented from becoming the dominant voice? • Who defines the definition of success and how and when is that success measured?
Impact	• How does the community access (required) shared benefits? How do such benefits serve community needs and priorities instead of those of colonial institutions? • How can scientists make sure their work primarily benefits the community and the benefits the scientist gains do not outweigh the community's benefits? • What is the potential for harm this work, project, or research can have on the community (including nonhuman kin)? • What opportunities are being provided to community members in analyses, reviews, and evaluations? • How are community members being compensated (whether monetarily or otherwise) for their time/energy/ Knowledges/expertise?

Note: Each question addresses scientific work, projects, and research with Indigenous communities.

relations that help reduce harm and build accountability within researchers and research practices. The leading global document for guidance on engaging with Indigenous Peoples and IWK is the United Nations Declaration on the Rights of Indigenous Peoples (UNDRIP; UN General Assembly 2007), which was created to protect Indigenous Peoples' rights globally and outlines the responsibilities that should be followed by researchers within Indigenous communities. However, there are no specific mechanisms of enforcement for free, prior and informed consent (FPIC) as UNDRIP is nonbinding on states, and many governments, such as the United States, have not ratified UNDRIP (Gómez Isa, 2019).

UNDRIP recommends obtaining FPIC from Indigenous Peoples as a prerequisite for any activity that affects Indigenous Peoples and their Ancestral Lands, territories, and natural resources (Hill and Lillywhite 2015). The international legal standard for FPIC is that it is temporary, meaning that at any stage of a project, the affected Indigenous group can veto a course of action; FPIC should be an ongoing process, not a one-time conversation (UN Human Rights Council 2018), and should be used to mitigate harm to communities.

Only one international treaty has a binding legal requirement for consent thus far, though it is not exactly FPIC. The International Labour Organization's Indigenous and Tribal Peoples Convention, 1989 (often cited as ILO 169) addresses the rights of Indigenous Peoples and creates merely a "duty to consult," meaning that consent is not required, but Indigenous Peoples must be spoken with. Though the duty to consent obligation is not as powerful as FPIC, not many countries ratified this agreement (only twenty-four signed, which were mostly in South America; ILO 2021). And while the Convention on Biological Diversity, another international treaty, does encourage states and relevant parties to obtain FPIC to gain access to IWK, the guidelines to do so are "voluntary" and are mostly associated with equitably sharing the benefits and use of IWK, particularly in conservation and biodiversity-related activities (Mo'otz Kuxtal Voluntary Guidelines 2016). Furthermore, some individual states may have specific enforcement of FPIC, and some international regional courts may enforce such requirements, such as when the Inter-American Court of Human Rights did so in *Saramaka v. Suriname* by applying OASDRIP (the Inter-American version of UNDRIP) and UNDRIP as reasons for ruling that FPIC must be obtained (Koorndijk 2019). But these are not the global trend, often leaving Indigenous communities on their own to ensure that outsiders are respecting their rights. However, a different way in which such responsibilities are bestowed onto researchers by Indigenous communities is through Indigenous data sovereignty and Indigenous data governance.

RESPONSIBILITY TO RESPECT INDIGENOUS DATA SOVEREIGNTY AND GOVERNANCE

Indigenous data sovereignty contrasts with mainstream definitions of data sovereignty, which is geographically bound and corporate-focused

(Carroll, Rodriguez-Lonebear, and Martinez 2019). Indigenous Data sovereignty, "[centers] any facts, [K]nowledge, or information about a Native [N]ation and its [T]ribal citizens, Lands, resources, cultures, and communities. Information ranging from demographic profiles, to educational attainment rates, maps of sacred Lands, songs, and social media activities" (Rainie, Rodriguez-Lonebear, and Martinez 2017; Walter et al. 2021). Unfortunately, research practices not accountable to data sovereignty may result in further harm to Indigenous communities, a practice that has been sustained for generations, even after UNDRIP was adopted in 2007.[1] As a result, Indigenous data sovereignty has been nonexistent and not the standard that researchers follow (Natonabah et al. 2020). Indigenous data sovereignty requires researchers to uphold and respect Indigenous Knowledge systems and Science and neither co-opt them nor repackage them as their own (McCartney et al. 2022; Reyes-García et al. 2022). Indigenous data sovereignty principles require nonextractive forms of research in which scientists learn from Indigenous Peoples (Williamson, Provost, and Price 2022).

Indigenous scientists know that once a research project has ended, we must still maintain community relations because of the responsibilities we inherit when working with one another and with Indigenous communities. This is why many of us push against "helicopter research" or "parachute science" (David-Chavez and Gavin, 2018; Minasny et al. 2020; Lewis 2021; Haelewaters, Hofmann, and Romero-Olivares 2021; de Vos 2022). Helicopter or parachute research is foundational to western science and continues to teach scientists to go into an environment, space, or community and extract in the name of research. Once these types of projects are completed, researchers leave, analyze, and publish data without community consultation, and never return to the community or area (Bharadwaj 2014; Gordon 2021). These practices fail to build capacity with community or amplify community expertise but, rather, demonstrate how such practices are rooted in what is valued within western science: numerical data, publications, and status. This stems back to individualism and extractive-based practices in which scientists are taught that they have the answers to pressing issues, despite not having any prior lived experience or a local lens to apply to the issue. Such individualistic practices are why many scientists,

---

1 It was adopted by the United Nations in 2007 with 144 countries adopting it, eleven abstaining, and four countries (Canada, the United States, New Zealand, and Australia) voting against it.

despite their good intentions, harm and erase Indigenous communities and voices.

Doing the opposite of "helicopter" or "parachute" research allows for the interrogation of how IWK can be incorporated and centered in the work, project, or research. IWK asks questions that help scientists understand the context of an ecosystem, culture, and community. It helps maintain the Knowledges within the community, where they are not only protected, but can also grow with other Knowledges or informed approaches. This is crucial because western methods require scientists to develop research questions and their own hypotheses, even when engaging in research with local Indigenous communities. This implies that scientists are capable of developing the best plans and frameworks for scientific endeavors before interacting with and learning from Indigenous communities. However, many Indigenous scientists and community members advocate for scientists to facilitate research with humility and understand that they may not have the best approaches for the community. They must recognize the limits of their expertise and unlearn this notion in order to understand how to responsibly work with Indigenous communities.

Unlike western science, Indigenous Sciences center all of our relations, human or nonhuman and those in between (e.g., spirituality), and all of our responsibilities. Indigenous Sciences make it possible for Indigenous Peoples to practice Science without having to lose our identities within western disciplines (e.g., ecology, environmental science, forestry, etc.). Indigenous People's responsibilities within Indigenous data sovereignty and data governance helps researchers ensure their work supports communities, and not just researchers, as western "colonial" science prioritizes.

RESPONSIBILITY TO CULTURAL PROTOCOLS

As Indigenous scientists and researchers, we are accountable for protecting our communities, first and foremost, and in a way that western practices do not always prioritize. Often, because western researchers and scientists view data and research in an extractive way, there are no limits on what should and can be researched. The institutional review board (IRB) process from universities determines only what is ethical and what should and can be researched, without consideration of sacred Knowledges, cultural protocols, and so on. Indigenous Scientists understand that there are specific Knowledges that should not be investigated and shared outside of our communities, even with IRB approval. These points also demonstrate why it is important for Indigenous Scientists to follow cultural protocols, which may also include following Tribal IRB processes, which are, in many cases, more extensive and provide more thoughtful guidelines for engaging with the community.[2] Colonized methodologies have created systems and power dynamics in which the holders of power and decision-makers determine what is ethical and appropriate relating to community research, especially for research with Indigenous Peoples. Contrasting this, Struthers (2001) discusses a cultural protocol in which researchers spoke to Elders, members of the community, and healers to gain research permission before any formal academic preparations were facilitated. Wilson (2008, 15) also supports this point that "Indigenous [P]eoples themselves decide exactly which areas are to be studied." These examples illustrate the importance of keeping Indigenous protocols and ways of being and Knowing at the center of research processes. Indigenous Knowledges and Indigenous Peoples' autonomy in research approaches are significant, especially as we continue navigating the effects of climate catastrophes.

RESPONSIBILITY TO CULTURAL LAND MANAGEMENT

In this section we turn more toward the application of our Knowledges while understanding the connections that such applications can have with research. Throughout the globe, virtually every metric related to forest fires is on the rise, ranging from the acres burned to the lives lost to the costs to fight the blazes (CalFire 2018). These recent trends are broadly consistent with other trends that are expected from anthropogenic climate change (Abatzoglou and Williams 2016). Climate change is inextricably linked to colonial practices, historically and in the present, as anthropogenic activities hinge on the dispossession of Indigenous Peoples' Lands and resources (Whyte 2018; Marino 2015; Wilson 2014; Cameron 2012). Since time immemorial, many Indigenous Peoples have conducted cultural fires as a spiritual and ecological approach to tending and caring for our Lands. Cultural burns are small area fires that center Traditional Ecological Knowledges (Long and Lake 2018; Aldern and Goode 2014) and Practices (Tom, Adams, and Goode 2023). These low-temperature burns improve the ecosystem and provide sociocultural medicines that activate healing

---

2 See, for example, https://extension.arizona.edu/sites/extension.arizona.edu/files/pubs/az1475.pdf; https://irb.unm.edu/library/documents/guidance/research-with-american-indian-communities.pdf; https://uttc.edu/about-uttc/our-leadership/institutional-review-board/.

and strengthen the intergenerational bonds between Indigenous community members (Aldern and Goode 2014). With colonization, government
agencies began suppressing and outlawing the use of cultural fires, and as
a result, practitioners and fire keepers have been unable to implement cultural burns. The loss of fire in landscapes is inextricably linked with many
historical policies of Indian removal and, subsequently, Indigenous Lands
were managed by settler governments (Aldern and Goode 2014; Williams
2000). In consequence, the appearance of many landscapes shifted tremen-
dously and became susceptible to prolonged drought seasons and vulnerable to catastrophic wild and forest fires (Greenlee and Langenheim 1990;
Stuart and Stephens 2006).

Recently, there has been a movement of Indigenous fire practitioners
throughout the globe (e.g., California, Oregon, and Australia) to reclaim
their land stewardship roles by conducting cultural burn demonstrations
(Hankins 2014; Lake et al. 2017; Long et al. 2016; Aldern and Goode 2014;
Marks-Block, Lake, and Curran 2019; Long and Lake 2019; Wilson 2020).
For example, the Karuk and Yurok communities in California conduct cultural fires, which has allowed Indigenous scientists to uphold their responsibilities with their communities, especially because these approaches come
directly from the Indigenous communities (Marks-Block and Tripp 2021).
An Indigenous science approach to fire ecology and wildfire science centers on Indigenous cultural fire revitalization and leads to inquiries such as,
what observations and lessons of Indigenous cultural burning can inform
ecological restoration of Lands (Adams et al. 2023), and what observations
and lessons of Indigenous cultural burning are transmitted via storytelling (Adams et al. 2023; Tom, Adams, and Goode 2023; Scott 2022). Such
work weaves together ecology and environmental science and is grounded
in Indigenous studies methodologies, including oral histories, storywork,
embodied Knowledges, and memory recall, as each activates and uplifts
Indigenous worldviews (Smith 2012; Archibald 2008; Wilson 2008).

These balances of scientific inquiry are rooted in Indigenous pedagogies
(methods and practices of teaching) and require respectful leadership that
enables people to educate and heal. Additionally, they are expected to lead
one small step toward self-determination: "Indigenous community development needs to be informed by community-based research that respects and
enhances community processes" (Smith 2021 [1999]). Cultural fire practices
and research are culturally grounded and relevant to Indigenous scientists
who come from communities that utilize this management approach to

steward their forests. These Land-keeping lessons elucidate responsibilities each community member holds because an ethic of care is prioritized prior to, during, and following each burn. Participants understand that, counter to western approaches to prescribed fire, cultural fire does not begin and end with fire. Rather, burners first prepare the Land to receive fire, so they are more attuned to weather, topography, and environmental conditions to ensure the safest possible demonstration. Following fires, burners have a responsibility to return to the Land to hand-mix ash into soils, replant, and maintain areas that have received fire (Mariani et al. 2022). These demonstrations directly identify stakeholders as Indigenous communities ("rights holders": an emerging term that Indigenous community members invoke, which means their inherent rights, as Indigenous Peoples, to steward Lands and waters) that are sharing Indigenous Knowledges through the practice of cultural fire. Scientific inquiries and projects such as the practice of cultural fires ultimately addresses root problems that commonly persist between researchers and community members when there is no reflection conducted to hold oneself accountable to research responsibilities (Kater 2022). Sustaining and reclaiming Traditions such as cultural fires are crucial within many Indigenous communities, especially as climate change impacts and conditions are leaving many environments, locations, and Indigenous communities vulnerable.

RESPONSIBILITY TO CLIMATE CHANGE

Cultural fires are an essential part of mitigating climate change impacts and by-products such as wildfires. While climate change does not directly cause wildfires, it impacts the environmental conditions that make forests more susceptible to extreme drought, which creates conditions for wildfires to persist (Mariani et al. 2022). Recently, we have experienced a huge increase in the "recognition" of the importance of Indigenous Knowledge systems and Indigenous Peoples as they relate to climate change mitigation and adaptation strategies. For example, the Intergovernmental Panel on Climate Change (IPCC) recognized Indigenous Knowledges as essential to climate change mitigation and adaptation efforts. This is because Indigenous Knowledges can support the reduction of climate risks within Indigenous communities and beyond (Zvobgo et al. 2022).

While it is promising to finally see IWK acknowledged as essential to climate change discourse, Indigenous scientists and Peoples do not seek validation from the same colonial entities that have dismissed, excluded, and silenced our voices and IWK. However, climate change deeply influences how many Indigenous scientists uphold our responsibilities, given the drastic and direct impacts it has on our human and nonhuman relations (Wildcat 2013; Vinyeta, White, and Lynn 2016; Shaffril et al. 2020). Climate change is an intersectional issue that Indigenous communities have long been observing and living through that is very important for the well-being of our communities. This is why Indigenizing climate change research is essential and important for us as Indigenous scientists. Indigenizing means creating an Indigenous-led approach in any research project or work, and shifting the colonial way of viewing Indigenous Peoples as "research subjects" and "areas of expertise" to a perspective that sees them as experts and researchers (Claw et al. 2018; Hernandez 2022). Claw et al. (2018) contend the need to have Indigenous Peoples as collaborators rather than research subjects because Indigenous Knowledges are inherited IWK that cannot be taught in classrooms or written in textbooks (Whyte, Brewer, and Johnson 2016; Simpson 2014). Indigenous Knowledges are place-based and transmitted through storytelling, artistic practices, and other ways of Knowing that are not aligned with western education or thought practices. Thus, while Indigenous Knowledges are acknowledged as important in climate change mitigation and adaptation efforts, this is something only Indigenous Peoples can practice, understand, research, and teach. This is why Indigenizing climate change research is important, as our communities have already survived the crises of settler colonialism, and we already know that our Knowledges play a vital role in surviving and adapting to extreme changes by ensuring we uphold our responsibilities.

Unfortunately, climate change impacts accentuate inequalities for Indigenous communities (Reyes-García et al. 2019). One inequity is the degree of responsibilities Indigenous Peoples hold as a result of climate change (Cajete 2020; Latulippe and Klenk 2020). Some of these responsibilities include adapting to climate change conditions, despite having little to do with greenhouse emissions, and creating solutions for food insecurity, especially as extreme weather events continue to occur. These degrees of responsibilities are not intended to paint Indigenous Peoples as victims, but rather to demonstrate that our responsibilities to Mother Earth are deeply ingrained and live within the consciousness of Indigenous Peoples. Thus, seeing how many Indigenous communities are suffering as a result of climate change motivates Indigenous scientists to continue working tirelessly toward meeting our responsibilities.

For Indigenous Peoples, there is no decision to make when it comes to climate change because protecting and healing Mother Earth and maintaining our relations with everything are responsibilities manifested through our Indigeneity. As a result, leading and co-leading the climate justice movement is not a trend Indigenous Peoples follow, but an inherited responsibility because it is often a life-or-death decision for our communities. Wildcat (2010) explains this relationality that pushes against climate change being viewed as an inconvenience, given that for Indigenous Peoples climate change is deadly. Through this relationality, Wildcat explains the responsibility we carry forward as Indigenous scientists.

Conclusion

As Indigenous scientists and scholars, we cannot simply do our scientific work without ensuring that our Indigenous responsibilities foreground all that we do. This is why we continue to advocate for the inclusion of Indigenous Peoples and communities in the climate change discourse and for Indigenous-led research. Our advocacy is infused with our individual responsibilities and can range from calls to action to publications and anything within a plethora of opportunities that center Indigenous voices and Knowledges. While we acknowledge that there is no right or wrong way to advocate, we center our unique, distinct, and indistinguishable responsibilities in our actions, reflections, and theories (e.g., responsibility praxis).

The authors of this chapter are deeply committed to ensuring that we carry our responsibilities in our work. While western science continues to uphold solely its theories, frameworks, and knowledge systems as the only truths (Schneider and Hayes 2020), we push back against this narrative. For many of us, Indigenous Knowledges cannot work in silos because we acknowledge that settler colonialism continues to grant western sciences the power and privileges to dictate the forms of scientific approaches and methods we must follow. Thus, we understand that oftentimes we have to weave or braid our Indigenous Knowledge with western science (Snively and Williams 2018) in order to uphold our responsibilities. We are living embodiments of Indigenous scientists doing our best to uphold our responsibilities to our communities, relatives, Land, and all of our relations. Honoring our relations to be good relatives is at the center of our work. Whether our work centers on soil or climate sciences, our inherited responsibilities are never forgotten, but rather uplifted in our projects, research, and protocols. This means that we have to work harder than our white colleagues and other scientists (Mohamed and Beagan 2019), but it is a work that has to be done as it is our responsibility.

Our collective stories, work, and *testimonios* in western sciences as Indigenous scientists tell a story of how our responsibilities to our communities go beyond what can be documented or evaluated within the western metrics of "success." Relationality, reciprocity, futurity, and re-membering are important pillars that help us uphold these sets of responsibilities, both collectively and individually. The responsibility praxis depicts what this looks like for us, while ensuring our accountability, intentions, and impacts are also integrated. It is important to reemphasize that our responsibilities require us to do work that does not necessarily end with by-products, and it goes beyond what western science dictates. This chapter is not intended to be a manual for non-Indigenous peoples on how to properly work with Indigenous communities, but rather for Indigenous scientists who are navigating their responsibilities in a world that centers individuality and success, and rewards unbalanced productivity. We end by thanking the Indigenous activists, community members, Elders, scholars, and scientists who have guided, supported, and mentored us. Their long-term work to shape pathways for us to be able to conduct science for and by our communities while upholding our responsibilities as Indigenous Peoples is unmeasurable.

23

RESPONSIBILITY WITH HEART
Protecting Indigenous Data Sovereignty and Traditional Ecological Knowledge

BY JENNIFER R. O'NEAL

Positionality Statement

Enrolled member of The Confederated Tribes of Grand Ronde (Chinook, Cree, Shasta, Modoc); raised and living on the Traditional homelands of the Kalapuya Peoples; assistant professor of Native American studies, University of Oregon, Department of Indigenous, Race and Ethnic Studies.

Information is a powerful tool. It can bring Indigenous communities either an immense amount of power, when it is within our control, or significant harm when used incorrectly or without our consent, causing misinformation and misuse of sacred Knowledges, cultures, and histories. Indigenous Peoples have been on Turtle Island since time immemorial, living and passing down Traditional Ecological Knowledge (TEK). Alongside that long history also exists the constant battle to protect our sacred information according to Tribal laws and protocols. During hundreds of years of colonization, salvage collecting, and the extraction of our Knowledges, resources, and cultures, Indigenous Peoples have continually fought to protect, defend, and return information to our communities, often expending extensive time and resources in the defense of Indigenous sovereignty. Since the Red Power movement era in the 1970s, there has been a resurgence in discourse and activism focused on the fight for Indigenous rights, control, and access to our Traditional Knowledges, cultures, and information, as well as land, resources, and property. Despite the long-term fight and ongoing historic injustices, over the past twenty years, Indigenous Peoples have increasingly fought back for restorative justice and for power to control our information through formal legal mechanisms, culminating with the United Nations

Declaration of the Rights of Indigenous Peoples (UNDRIP). UNDRIP is a nonbinding human rights instrument that was adopted by the United Nations General Assembly in 2007. The declaration affirms Indigenous Peoples' rights to self-determination as political entities and honors the principle of Indigenous control over Indigenous data, as well as protection of Indigenous Cultural and Intellectual Property Rights (ICIP) and Indigenous research ethics (Articles 14 and 31; Tsosie 2019; Davis 2016).

Most recently, self-determination and data activism led to the development of the global advocacy movement for Indigenous data sovereignty (IDS). Indigenous data is defined as data, information, and Knowledge, in various formats and mediums that are derived from or impact Indigenous Peoples, Nations, and communities at both the collective and individual levels and, most specifically, falls into these general categories: Peoples, languages, resources, environment, and Nations (Davis 2016). From a western perspective, some might think of data sovereignty mainly in the context of the digital age or connected to the nation-state; however, within this chapter, I contend that the definition of Indigenous data sovereignty should be expanded and considered as the protection of *all* information, including both intangible (song, dance, stories) and tangible (i.e., documents, objects, photographs) Traditional Knowledge and cultural heritage within and from Indigenous Nations. Rather than representing just numbers and digital information, Indigenous data sovereignty should be defined as the proper oversight, authority, and management of all information originating from and produced by sovereign Indigenous Nations.

Embedded within UNDRIP's call for the protection of collective rights and self-determinations is data sovereignty, which is Indigenous Peoples' rights "to maintain, control, protect and develop their cultural heritage, [T]raditional [K]nowledge[s] and [T]raditional cultural expressions, as well as their right to maintain, control, protect and develop their intellectual property over these issues" (Kukutai and Taylor 2016, xxii). UNDRIP reaffirms these rights and Indigenous data governance (the ownership, collection, control, analysis, and use of the data), then enacts those rights via specific "mechanisms grounded in Indigenous rights and interests that promote Indigenous values and equity, while providing a framework for addressing deeper historical issues" (Carroll et al. 2021, 1). IDS is then operationalized via Indigenous data governance, which utilizes Indigenous decision-making throughout data lifecycles and ecosystems to assert Indigenous rights and interests (Walter and Carroll 2021). Data governance is not just for existing data, but for access and control of the data for current and future governance (Smith 2016). Indigenous data governance provides a mechanism for honoring, protecting, and controlling Indigenous data, both internally and externally.

Over the past ten years, numerous national and international organizations and projects have formed that directly support and protect Indigenous data sovereignty and Traditional Ecological Knowledge (TEK), and utilize and implement Indigenous data governance.[1] These Indigenous-led advocacy, education, and research networks seek to address global concerns "to protect Indigenous data from misuse, ensuring Indigenous Peoples are the primary beneficiaries of the data and leveraging Indigenous data toward Indigenous aspirations" (Walter and Carroll 2021, 11). In September 2019, the recently developed Global Indigenous Data Alliance (2019) released the "CARE Principles for Indigenous Data Governance," which were produced by the Research Data Alliance International Indigenous Data Sovereignty Interest Group. The principles provide a data governance mechanism that is people- and purpose-oriented and addresses data concerns (e.g., collective benefit, authority to control, responsibility, and ethics). Highlighting the role of data and information in Indigenous self-determination, the principles direct, influence, and guide external data stakeholders and the secondary use of data. This then enhances and protects Indigenous Peoples' rights by providing much-needed direction to non-Indigenous data holders regarding the use of data and the important relationships that should be built with Indigenous Peoples to steward Indigenous information (Walter and Carroll 2021). Overall, the principles' main goal is to ensure that the use of Indigenous data "should result in tangible benefits for Indigenous collectives through inclusive development and innovation, improved governance and citizen engagement, and result in equitable outcomes" (Carroll et al. 2021, 2).[2]

---

1 The main Indigenous data sovereignty networks developed include (with formation year), Te Mana Rarauunga Maori Data Sovereignty Network (2015), United States Indigenous Data Sovereignty Network (2016), Maiam nayri Wingara Aboriginal and Torres Strait Islander Data Sovereignty Collective (2017), International Indigenous Data Sovereignty Interest Group at the Research Data Alliance (2017), and Global Indigenous Data Alliance (2019).

2 Many organizations and projects are already working to implement the principles into their systems and standards. This includes the Local Contexts project (https://localcontexts.org/), which is partnering with the Smithsonian Institution to develop Collections CARE Notices for Indigenous collection to provide guidance on how an item should be stewarded. This will extend the current Cultural Institution Notices developed by LC (2018), and the

In this chapter, I reflect on recent examples of collaborative partnerships with Tribal communities through the lens of two of the four core CARE principles—responsibility and ethics. The responsibility principles states, "Those working with Indigenous data have a responsibility to share how those data are used to support Indigenous Peoples' self-determination and collective benefit. Accountability requires meaningful and openly available evidence of these efforts and the benefits accruing to Indigenous Peoples" (RDAIDSIG 2019, 4). The principle of ethics states that "Indigenous Peoples' rights and wellbeing should be the primary concern at all stages of the data life cycle and across the data ecosystem," with a focus on minimizing harm and maximizing benefit to bring justice and representation from Indigenous communities (RDAIDSIG 2019, 5). Moreover, based on the values and principles of the communities, any potential future use or future harm must be taken into account and represented in metadata (i.e., provenance, purpose, limitations, or obligations; RDAIDSIG 2019, 4–5). Each guideline statement supports building positive relationships and expanding capability and capacity for Indigenous languages and worldviews.

To examine these two CARE principles, I use reflexivity and storytelling by critically reflecting on my past experiences working with Tribal Elders and highlighting specific interactions and collaborations. I use these reflection points to provide a critical thought piece for expanding the definition of Indigenous data sovereignty to include archival and museum collections, as well as how IDS should incorporate responsibility and ethics with heart. First, I provide an overview and argument that academics and research institutions have a responsibility of easing the burden that is often inflicted on Indigenous communities when conducting collaborative work. Second, I explore collaborative collection curation and curriculum development through a long-term partnership with Tribal Elder Myra Johnson Orange (The Confederated Tribes of Warm Springs), and recount specific stories representing the importance of minimizing harm and bringing justice to her family and Tribal community. Finally, I recommend solutions in Indigenous data sovereignty for minimizing harm and maximizing benefit to Indigenous communities by incorporating responsibility and ethics with

---

new Notices will reflect inherent relationships of care, responsibility and governance in collection stewardship within the institution. They will function as direct mechanisms to assist in management and decision-making consistent with CARE Principles (Carroll et al. 2020).

heart, specifically implementing and utilizing the framework of listening with our three ears by Jo-ann Archibald (Q'um Q'um Xiiem).

EASING THE BURDEN

As noted by Cheyenne scholar Desi Rodriguez, "Indigenous [P]eoples have long and rich histories of data collection and preservation, and these histories provide a solid foundation for the pursuance of Indigenous data sovereignty in contemporary settings" (Kukutai and Taylor 2016, 11–12). Taking this into perspective, while Indigenous data sovereignty as a formal concept is fairly new, the foundational activism has been occurring for many years beforehand through the efforts to protect Indigenous information, Traditional Knowledges, cultures, and collections at various non-Indigenous repositories, as well as in Indigenous communities. This is evident in the historic efforts to protect Indigenous human remains through the Native American Graves and Repatriation Act (NAGPRA), Indigenous archives at non-Tribal repositories via the Protocols for Native American Archival Materials (2006), and Indigenous Traditional Knowledge practices within various research fields. Most importantly, various Native Nations have proactively protected their history, Knowledges, and cultures by developing research procedures and protocols that must be followed when conducting research on their homelands. In addition, numerous Tribes have developed their own institutional review boards, protocols, and projects to give informational power back to Indigenous communities.[3] Much of this provides the foundational work that preceded the formal development of Indigenous Data Sovereignty and paved the way for more in-depth research to occur.

According to Māori scholar Tahu Kukutai and John Taylor, early expressions of Indigenous data sovereignty can be seen in Indigenous Oral Traditions, "which included a complex set of rights and responsibilities concerning the use of community-held information" (Kukutai and Taylor 2016,

---

3 A few examples of Tribal institutional review boards and research protocols include the Hopi Cultural Preservation Office, *Protocol for Research, Publication and Recordings: Motion, Visual, Sound, Multimedia and other Mechanical Devices* (https://www.hopi-nsn.gov/wp-content/uploads/2021/09/HCPO-Research-Protocol.REVISED.2021.pdf); Navajo Nation Human Research Review Board, https://nnhrrb.navajo-nsn.gov/aboutNNHRRB. html, accessed May 13, 2023; Karuk Tribe, *Protocol on Karuk Tribe's Intellectual Property Rights: Research, Publication and Recordings* (https://sipnuuk.karuk.us/system/files/atoms/file/ATALM17_KTResearchProtocol.pdf); and *Practicing Pikyav: Policy for Collaborative Projects and Research Initiatives with the Karuk Tribe* (https://sipnuuk.karuk.us/system/files/atoms/file/ATALM17_PracticingPikyav.pdf).

15). Essentially, this refers to and includes TEK, as well as Traditional cultural expressions, both of which include sacred information that must only be shared according to Indigenous Peoples' community and governmental protocols. While most of this information is passed down through generations orally, throughout history, such information has also been gathered, researched, and written down by outside researchers, often without Tribal prior and informed consent. Thus, presently, Tribal communities must spend significant time finding these collections, reconnecting with the displaced information, and then fighting and negotiating for increased control and protocols over their Traditional Knowledges that are now under the oversight of non-Indigenous people. Increasingly, local, state, and national repositories and collecting agencies have reckoned with their complex colonial collecting histories and are working to reconcile past actions by building relationships and partnerships with Tribal communities to ensure the co-stewardship of collections and data.[4] However, oftentimes this reconciliation comes with a physical, mental, and financial cost for Tribes.

Often, when institutions, repositories, or researchers have reached out to Tribal community partners to build collaborative relationships, work on a project, or begin conversations for reconciliation, too much of the burden is placed on the Tribal community. Tribal partners constantly have to be on the defensive, defending their histories, lifeways, and Traditions, and relive or be reminded of historic injustices that their ancestors lived through. They also have to expend extra labor to educate non-Natives about Tribal history and Traditions, even though much of that information can easily be found. This follows a long history in which Indigenous Peoples have been on the defensive for hundreds of years. However, now Tribal communities are finally moving to the offensive side by developing, controlling, and determining research protocols, compliance, data sovereignty, and curriculum within and outside their communities: this is Indigenous data sovereignty. This type of Indigenous offensive work must be done because of the

---

4 There are many examples from non-Indigenous institutions, both at a local and national level, with Indigenous collections that are actively collaborating with Indigenous communities. Here are a few example repositories: Library of Congress Folklife Center, National Anthropological Archives, Field Museum, Burke Museum, Eiteljorg Museum, Hood Museum, Washington State University Libraries, University of Wisconsin Libraries, University of California at Los Angeles American Indian Studies Center, University of Oregon Libraries and Native American and Indigenous Studies Program, Yale University, and Dartmouth Libraries. This is not by any means an exhaustive list but merely gives some examples of institutions engaged in collaborative project work with Indigenous communities.

current state of academic research that often privileges a university institutional review board (IRB) process over a Tribal Nation's research protocols, thus not honoring Tribal sovereignty or protecting Indigenous communities.[5] At the same time, so many organizations and institutions are finally acknowledging their problematic actions and are making strides to have Indigenous voices represented in research and collections. Yet the ongoing, frequent requests and work can also place an undue burden on Tribal communities, especially Tribal Elders, who must relive historic trauma. The increased burdens on Tribal communities are a side of the process that must be acknowledged before any work is conducted, and we must determine ways that these burdens can be mitigated so that they do not fall onto our most precious holders of Traditional Knowledge—our Elders. What follows are two stories from my work with a Tribal Elder I've worked with for more than ten years and the lessons she has imparted on this important topic.

THE HEART OF THE MAKER: TEK DATA SOVEREIGNTY IN COLLECTIONS

Over the past decade, I've had the honor of working with and building relationships with some of the most Knowledgeable and revered Tribal Elders from across Tribal communities in Oregon. In particular, I've worked most closely with Tribal Elders from The Confederated Tribes of Warm Springs and the Burns Paiute Tribe through the development of an Honors College course called "Decolonizing Research: The Northern Paiute History Project," which was taught from 2013 to 2017 in the Robert D. Clark Honors College at the University of Oregon, and co-instructed with Kevin D. Hatfield (2020).[6] Although I worked with numerous other Tribes over the years from my work at the National Museum of the American Indian, it was through working with Tribal Elders, developing the class,

---

5 University institutional review boards, also commonly referred to as IRBs, serve to protect the rights and welfare of the people participating in the institution's research according to federal and state policies. A formal IRB must be completed prior to any research that involves human subjects. However, these policies often fail to incorporate and honor Native American sovereignty and policies, which are often at odds with an institutional IRB or that privilege institutional data rather than Indigenous data sovereignty. For example, at most institutions, when research is conducted with grant funding all the data and intellectual property is then owned by the institution, unless the Native nations negotiate for an exception or petition to change the internal policies.

6 While the course is no longer taught, it has instead been restructured into two courses in the Department of Indigenous, Race and Ethnic Studies: ES410/510 Indigenous Research Methods (currently taught) and Tribal Community Fieldwork (forthcoming).

and listening to their stories that I learned more life and professional lessons than through anywhere else. Although that particular course has since concluded, I have been able to continue my relationships with many Tribal Elders through other projects on campus. During one of these projects, I experienced something so profound that forever changed me through the Knowledge that was shared and the lessons I learned. In partnership with the UO Libraries and the Museum of Natural and Cultural History (MNCH), Nathan Georgitis, archivist for Digital Collections, and I managed a grant to test the Mukurtu[7] collections management platform with various Tribal communities in Oregon, as well as repositories across campus that may want to use it as well. We had already been testing out the platform for some time with Tribal communities, but this was the first time we worked with objects from the MNCH repository.

As part of the project, we worked with Anthropology Collections Manager Elizabeth Kallenbach, who selected baskets from the repository that MNCH wanted to know more information about and that would greatly benefit from having curation by a Tribal Elder. I knew just the person with whom to connect her: Myra Johnson Orange, a Tribal Elder and expert basketmaker from The Confederated Tribes of Warm Springs (Wasco and Northern Paiute), with whom I worked since 2012 as part of the Honors College class. As part of testing the platform, we determined that the system could best be used to add Tribal Traditional Knowledge, which was often missing from the basic information about these cultural heritage items, as well as to determine the origin of the object, including the donor and Tribe. Elizabeth selected a list of baskets as ideal candidates that lacked necessary information that we hoped Myra could tell us more about to fill gaps in the data and share details that only Tribal community members and basketmakers might know. Unfortunately, we were trying to work on this project at the height of the pandemic, so we could not meet in person, but we met over Zoom and had an in-depth conversation about a few of the baskets.

In that conversation, we asked Myra to provide her Knowledge about a handful of baskets that we had added to the site from the MNCH collection.

---

7 Mukurtu is a free, mobile, and open-source platform built with Indigenous communities to manage and share digital cultural heritage. It empowers communities to manage, share, and exchange their digital heritage in culturally relevant and ethical ways, fostering relationships of respect and trust (https://mukurtu.org/). This project was part of the larger Mukurtu Hubs and Spokes grant that aimed to connect Tribal communities with the platform through providing training and connections through larger hubs.

After looking at the first few baskets, Myra asked us to bring up one that had caught her eye from the visual list. She was referring to a basket simply labeled as "basket," with virtually no other information (e.g., data of creation or collection or the like) attached to the record besides an attribution to the Warm Springs Tribe. Elizabeth noted that just because it was labeled as such indicated only that it was collected there at some point. We brought up the record so that she could see a larger version of the basket photograph. Myra then quickly indicated that she thought that this basket belonged to her grandmother and that it looked exactly like her grandmother's basket that had disappeared from her home. She noted that "it was my last basket that I had of my grandmother's and it was exactly like that." However, she conceded that it could also not be the same, but that it looked *exactly* like her grandmother's style of weaving, as well as Myra's mother's and paternal grandmother's styles. She reflected that "it just brought back so many memories because that was one of her last baskets. . . . When that basket disappeared it broke my heart because it was in perfect condition, just like that" (Johnson Orange 2020). Myra and Elizabeth then worked to determine a date of when it may have disappeared, nearly thirty years ago, and gathered additional information about the specific style of the basket, which was in such excellent condition. Myra found it odd to even see this type of basket, because normally when a Paiute person passes on they are buried with their belongings, especially their baskets. Earlier in the conversation, Myra noted that so many baskets were sitting in museums not being used as they were intended by her People. She said she cried for those baskets because, at one time, they belonged to a Tribal member, and these pieces have the heart of the maker in them. While I knew that this was a very common sentiment shared among Tribal members when I had met with them at various repositories, whether about objects, photographs, or textual items, little did I know just how connected Myra was to these specific baskets.

Having heard how heartbroken Myra was from seeing what was most likely her grandmother's basket, I wanted to find a solution to reuniting her with the basket. When we first envisioned this project, we ideally wanted to have Tribal Elders come and see the items in person, so I suggested having her come to the museum and spend time with the basket when health restrictions lifted so that she could see it. I suggested this solution knowing from past similar experiences that seeing an object in person is much more meaningful than simply seeing a photo online and that it provides a better connection with the object. While Myra appreciated the offer, she quickly noted that a visit to the museum would be too hard for her because of the bad feelings she had experienced when she had been to other museums to do similar consultation work. For her, it was too much to be reconnected with the basket and not be able to take it home where it belongs. My heart broke for Myra who, over and over again, relived this trauma from multiple museums. Yet, I was so grateful for her brutal honesty in letting us know that it was not best for her to see the object in person at the museum because of the additional pain it would cause her. At that moment, we talked through opportunities about what could be done to ensure that the basket could be reconnected with Myra and go back to Northern Paiute Traditional homelands. Elizabeth suggested the idea of taking the basket on a day trip and, later, a small traveling exhibit to the Warm Springs Museum on the reservation to honor and recognize where these baskets came from and reunite them with their People. While this will take some time to plan and execute, this is exactly the type of responsibility and restorative justice action that is needed for these objects that need to be reunited with their loved ones. Elizabeth and others at the museum hope to make this next step a reality in bringing healing to Tribal communities throughout Oregon.

There are many lessons learned from this interaction that can teach academics, teachers, collection managers, and community partners about Indigenous data sovereignty and TEK. Many educators and activists, both Native and non-Native, are working tirelessly to educate various groups about the basics of Tribal sovereignty and how the protection of Indigenous data and cultural Knowledges are central to honoring sovereignty. However, we must remember that Tribes simultaneously approach this work from two competing angles: the defensive and the offensive.

On the defensive side, Tribes are working to undo hundreds of years of colonization that have included "salvage collecting" (referring to the harmful practice of collecting and documenting of Indigenous communities in what many non-Indigenous peoples, usually anthropologists, archaeologists, and ethnographers, presumed was cultural decline) of Indigenous data, namely the information about our communities, Peoples, and cultures, and objects and items taken or stolen from those communities. As this happened to nearly every tribal community across North America, today the long-term effects of this extractive collecting is ever-present in the lives of Indigenous peoples as they actively seek to have their information, Knowledge, collections, and ancestors returned back to their communities. We are finally seeing some institutions, organizations, and individuals making significant changes to their research and collecting policies and reaching out to build productive and meaningful partnerships with Tribal communities. Yet, the work to undo hundreds of years of historic colonization will continue to take significant time and effort. While this work is much needed and must be done, it can also be traumatizing and exhausting for Tribal communities who have already lived through so much. Many are eager to do this work and will continue to do so, but for those organizations reaching out to and wanting to work with Tribal partners: please ensure that you are not causing undue trauma or inflicting more pain on individuals who have already lived through so much. Instead, entities must think of solutions to issues that are going to bring compassion and heal significant wounds that still exist today. This means not putting the responsibility on Tribal communities to just do this work or to provide all the answers to you. Rather, the onus should be on organizations, researchers, and educators to learn and understand more about the issues at hand and to find solutions that bring healing.

Sometimes the solutions are going to go against everything that your profession has taught you or that your organization says to do. Instead of following predetermined paths, be the first to take the big step by giving back collections that should have never ended up in your collection in the first place. Be the first to center Indigenous Traditional Knowledge in all aspects of your research. Be the first to give copyright privileges to Indigenous communities and Tribal Elders who are responsible for the Knowledge you receive in your research. Be the first to return collections home to the communities they came from and to the specific Peoples who should be caring for them. Be the first who leads by example to ensure that these types of new practices become the norm and that others after you see that it can both be done and should be our ideal practices in the academy and beyond.

STRIKING A BALANCE: TEK DATA SOVEREIGNTY IN CURRICULUM

When you make a basket it's so important to be connected to the piece, have good energy when you're working on the item, and understand your own self
—Myra Johnson Orange

Over the past five years, there have been increasing calls to include TEK in K–12 and higher education curricula. These calls stem mainly from the

recognition that Native American histories and Knowledges have historically been left out of standard curricula, especially in the humanities and
the sciences, and pressures from Tribal communities to include Indigenous
histories and cultures in education. In the Pacific Northwest, numerous
states, including Washington, Oregon, and Montana, have passed statewide laws to ensure that Native American histories are included in K–12
curricula at various grade levels.[8] Successful curricula require leadership
and development from Native American educators, experts, and Elders to
determine content, lessons, and implementation. In addition to history, law,
and policy, additional shifts in curricula now include information about
TEK, including topics such as Traditional cultural practices, food lifeways,
and environmental practices. While it is exciting to finally see this important information being centered in some curricula, Traditional Knowledge
Keepers and Tribal Elders caution educators and curriculum developers to
understand that the associated information and Knowledges must also be
balanced and protected. For example, in addition to the work she does with
basketry, Myra served as the former head of the Warm Springs Culture
and Heritage Department, as well as on the Tribal History, Shared History
statewide Tribal history curriculum committee in Oregon. When asked
about lessons learned from her time in these positions, she reflected that,
while it was so wonderful to see educators across the state of Oregon implementing the approved K–12 curricula developed by Tribal educators, she
also cautioned that a balance must be implemented concerning the content
Tribes share within the curricula.

Myra explained that when educators are teaching, learning, or researching TEK that "people really learn what it means to us and how we feel about
it . . . the goodness in it but also knowing when to step back if you're not
coming to the work from a good place." To strike a balance between including TEK in curricula while protecting sacred Knowledges, Myra noted
that the committee decided that they would include information about
Traditional Knowledge and lifeways, but not include specific details relating
to how or where to conduct these sacred Traditions in Tribal communities. For example, Myra specifically explained how she and others from her
community might talk about and build a curriculum around food lifeways,
but not provide information about the location of the foods or how they

8 Laws passed include Oregon, Senate Bill 13: Tribal History/Shared History, passed
in 2017; Washington, Since Time Immemorial: Tribal Sovereignty in Washington State,
passed in 2015; and Montana, Indian Education for All, passed in 1999.

are Traditionally processed. Such protective balances must exist to protect sacred Indigenous Traditional Knowledges for past, present, and future generations.

Myra applies this same principle when she teaches non-Native individuals basket weaving. While she is always eager to share her love for weaving and teach others the beauty of this cultural Tradition, she makes it clear when she teaches someone how to weave that the practice must be done in a good way and with a good heart. In addition, she ensures they understand that it is only for them and must not be used for commercialization purposes or for teaching others. So, each time she teaches someone new, she has to ensure they understand such cultural protocols before they begin their work. To Myra and her community, the practice of weaving and all that it brings with it are ways of life that are sacred and must be protected. More importantly, to Myra, the baskets come alive by the individuals who make them, who have the ancestry and a good heart. While this is often hard to convey to others, she reminds us that it is so important to educate outsiders while also protecting our sacred ways of Knowing. Similar to the basket making, she is both delighted to see Tribal history curricula finally being implemented in Oregon, yet she also wants to ensure that teachers are approaching the work in the right way and with the right feeling, not just going through the motions of teaching. Finally, while the term Traditional Ecological Knowledge is increasingly used and implemented in K–12 and higher education, in my ongoing work and conversations with Myra she makes very clear that she does *NOT* agree with the new terminology and chooses not to use the phrase in her work. Rather, as she rightly argues, she simply uses the term "Indigenous Knowledge."

WITH A GOOD HEART: LISTENING WITH OUR THREE EARS

During a conversation with Myra, we were joined by her granddaughter, Jazmine. Jazmine had previously worked on the Mukurtu platform at Washington State University, and we were lucky to have her as part of our grant project. We provided the opportunity for Jazmine to ask questions during the conversation. She asked Myra what would she want her to know about basket making and why it is so important. Myra noted that, "It is important to learn from family and learn how you're in touch with the basket, your feelings, and how to only work on it in a good mood, and if you're not in a good place knowing when to put it down. If you're tired and you're getting frustrated, put it away for a while so that you don't put those bad feelings in the basket" (Johnson Orange 2020). Whether teaching, learning, or researching, you must understand yourself and your connections to the work you are doing. Come at it with a good heart. "Know and understand the cultural values behind the work you do—this is the most important piece of learning" (Johnson Orange 2020). Therefore, it is so important to know who you are, where you come from, and those who came before you and passed on the Knowledges and feelings from many generations to the next. Basketry has the same symbolism.

After listening to Myra and hearing her recommendations for how to approach this work, it reminded me of the work of Stó:lō and Coast Salish scholar Jo-Ann Archibald (Q'um Q'um Xiiem). Archibald's work, *Indigenous Storywork: Educating the Heart, Mind and Spirit* (2008), provides an Indigenous theoretical, methodological, and pedagogical framework that includes seven storywork teaching principles, including respect, responsibility, reverence, reciprocity, holism, interrelatedness, and synergy. Similar to Myra's use of basketmaking to describe specific principles, Archibald also uses basket weaving throughout the book to make connections and explain these principles. Within these principles, she heeds the advice from her Elders that states we must listen with our three ears: "the two on the sides of our head and the one that is in our heart" (Archibald, Lee-Morgan, and de Santaolo 2019, 8). This approach has served as an important ethical and meaningful method, guide, and process for conducting research and underlines the important power of interconnectedness between intellectual, spiritual, emotional, and physical realms (Archibald, Lee-Morgan, and de Santaolo 2019; Christensen, Cox, and Szabo-Jones 2018).

While scholars and communities have created specific protocols, guidelines, and recommendations for protecting Indigenous data sovereignty and TEK, within and at the center of the work should be the responsibility of listening and working with a good heart and protecting Tribal members from harm. Some may say that this approach might be hard to teach since it deals with emotions and that we must instead focus on outcomes and data. Yet, information from our Elders shows us that bringing more heart and goodness into the work with data sovereignty and TEK will bring healing and repair. More importantly, if we want to be responsible when conducting our work, then we must approach it with a good heart. This means not just focusing on the Traditional academic outcomes of research (yes, those will always be there) but, instead, understanding the secondary outcomes that are just as, or even more, important to the project. For example, initially we wanted Myra to tell us some basic information about the baskets (e.g., the materials, basketmaker, Tribal identification, etc.). While she provided that information, we learned that an even more significant part of the project would be finding a way to reunite these baskets with Tribal community members on Tribal land. This experience, combined with many more I've had over the numerous years, exemplifies that we must be open to all solutions that bring the most healing, especially the solutions that are requested by the communities—this is our responsibility.

Conclusion

Mindful incorporation of the Indigenous data sovereignty CARE principles of responsibility and ethics to projects is key to supporting self-determination and the collective benefit of Indigenous Peoples. Following these core principles works to mitigate harm that can often accompany many well-intentioned collaborative projects and instead bring healing and restoration to Tribal partners. Those working with Indigenous data have a responsibility to share how those data are used to support Indigenous Peoples' self-determination and collective benefit. The stories shared in this chapter demonstrate how the principles of responsibility and ethics illustrate a pathway forward that others can also follow. Approaching the work with care and heart ensures that the needs of Indigenous Peoples' and communities are prioritized and centered first and foremost in how Indigenous data is managed, protected, and disseminated outside of Tribal communities. This means listening with an open mind, heart, and ears to the specific needs of the community, which oftentimes do not align with solutions or ideas that have worked previously. Listening and then implementing those suggestions—even when these solutions have never been done before—provides important restorative healing to Indigenous communities.

Acknowledgments

I wish to thank Myra Johnson Orange (Member of The Confederated Tribes of Warm Springs—Wasco and Northern Paiute) for her years of friendship, guidance, and unwavering gifts of her Knowledge. Working with her over all of these years has been the highlight of my career, and she has been one of the greatest teachers of Indigenous Knowledge, ways of Knowing, and understanding. I'm a better teacher, researcher, and human because of the lessons she has shared and taught me. This chapter is dedicated to her and all she does to center and preserve Northern Paiute history, lifeways, and

Traditions into education. I also wish to acknowledge Elizabeth Kallenbach, Anthropological Collections manager at the University of Oregon's Museum of Natural and Cultural History; and Nathan Georgitis, archivist for Digital Collections at UO Libraries, who have and continue to build strong connections and projects with Tribal communities in Oregon with displaced Tribal collections across campus.

24

TALOFAE, YOUR ANCESTORS ARE GOSSIPING ABOUT YOUR DATA MANAGEMENT PLAN

LEASI VANESSA LEE RAYMOND

Positionality Statement

Samoan and mixed heritage; raised on Wampanoag, Saudi, and Samoan lands; now living on Dena lands of the Lower Tanana, University of Alaska Fairbanks, Alaska Center for Energy and Power.

> Let our ancestors right into our world, come and dance with them in our world. We learn from them, through the continuity between us and them and also more importantly our distinct identity within the world system. With the depth of our history, we will bring our ancestors to us, carry our spirits, bring them forward to our world, willingly.
> —Hau'ofa 2001

Introduction

My ancestors are hilarious. I hear the saying "I'm my ancestor's wildest dreams," but me? I'm the butt of my ancestor's jokes. I'm their punchline, their talo fae (poor, pitiful one), the sucking of their teeth and the tsk-ing of their tongues. That doesn't mean they don't love me, or watch over me, or guide me. And it doesn't diminish their fierceness, or waver their intensity. It took me too long to understand that from the drop-dead hilarious to the deadly serious, my ancestors are with me. Once I did, it caused me to ask many questions about my life, my work, and my relationships.

As a result, this chapter explores data, culture, and the sacred through a relational framework. For me, as an afakasi, a person who walks in two worlds, a boundary spanner, these concepts are inextricably linked. My intellectual curiosity and my passion for good data management include a deep and yearning desire for data models, research practices, and software that can hold the immensity, beauty, power, and complexity of my culture and heritage. It stems from a desire to see myself, people like me, and, more importantly, what we know to be true, reflected in the processes, decisions, and tools used to tackle the big questions and challenges of this lifetime. It is a longing that bends toward the deep, the ancient, and the interconnected.

If we are to fully and deeply position ourselves in a world that centers our responsibilities of care and our relationships, how does that shift change our data work? How might we reflect our cultures and daily, interconnected sacredness into our data management activities? When Indigenous researchers acknowledge that our cultures incorporate relationships and an element of spirituality, ritual, and sacredness into our day-to-day activities, what is our responsibility to empower our work with these Knowledge systems and values?

In this chapter, I draw on examples from my understanding and interpretation of Samoan culture, an ancient and complex social system that intersects and interacts with Samoan Indigenous Knowledge, epistemology, governance, language, interpersonal relations, and all aspects of daily life. I highlight the ways that everyday actions exist within a spiritual framework that guide how our People and society operate. While translating concepts that do not exist in the English language and western world is always imperfect, throughout this chapter I do my best to elucidate non-western concepts using the imprecise vehicle of English.[1] These terms can never truly be understood outside of the Knowledge and cultural structure that is the Samoan language, and what will come across is, at best, an approximation of the true significance of these terms and concepts.

EVERYDAY SACREDNESS

Samoan relational ethicist Melani Anae describes the term teu le va as a "focus on secular and sacred commitments, guiding reciprocal 'acting in' and respect for relational spaces" (Anae 2016, 117). The phrase comprises two concepts, teu and va. Teu is a complex term describing a process for tidying, readying, smoothing, and preparing. One specific use of the term teu is in the preparation of pandanus leaves for use in weaving ie toga or fine mats, our most sacred and valued multigenerational/communally owned item. Va is a complex, multidimensional concept that incorporates space, time, and

---

1 The author is a Native speaker of English but does not speak Samoan. She humbly asks indulgence and forgiveness for any missteps.

relational ways of being. It is a foundational concept in Samoan culture, society, and Knowledge, describing how all things are related to each other and have their own proper position within time, space, and society. The spatio-temporal-relational va touches all aspects of Samoan life, from architecture (Simati 2011) to weaving (Tuagalu 2008), literature, interpersonal dynamics (Ng Chok et al. 2022), and governance structures (Anae 2016).

Anae (2016, 121) describes how "teu le va requires that one regards these (inter)actions as sacred in order to value, nurture, and if necessary tidy up the va—the social and sacred space that separates and yet unites in the context of va tapuia [sacred spaces], experienced in research relationships." Loosely translated, teu le va could mean to tidy or clean up the relations, but this translation loses the deeply interconnected and responsibility-laden implications of the term. Anae's work in research, ethics, and culturally relevant educational frameworks informs understandings of the everyday sacred and its role in data management. More specifically, teu le va has clear applications for our examination of sacred-informed data management as we seek to tidy, create relations, and respect our responsibilities to the universe around us.

INDIGENOUS CONCEPTS AND DATA

Data and Indigeneity are often seen as operating in separate spheres or, in some cases, in direct conflict with each other. Indigenous Peoples research, observe, and make sense of the world in distinct ways, often by incorporating values and ways of Knowing into their research practice. When Indigenous values are centered in research processes and, by extension, data activities, then we must acknowledge the sacred, multigenerational, human and nonhuman, present and past forces that have a vested interest in our present moment. Roxanne Struthers, an Ojibwe health researcher, describes the role her ancestors and guides played in shaping her practice:

> They just stood motionless, in silence and timelessness, peering
> closely upon her as she drifted in the sphere of the perpetual
> dream. The researcher celebrated the touch of her ancestors. She
> was profoundly affected by the past, the ancient, the very long ago.
> Instantaneously, she knew. She woke and sat straight up in bed.
> The dream was a message from the spirits. . . . They also directed
> her to write her thesis on women healers. . . . No absolute scientific
> process depicts how this type of [K]nowledge is transmitted. The

researcher embraced the sacred dream and its meaning. When you know, there is no questioning or pondering why. You just do as indicated by spiritual arrangement. (2001, 128–129)

To center Pasifika experiences in this topic of spiritual and ancestral involvement in our world through dreams and other methods of communication, we look to Gegeo and Gegeo, who share Solomon Island epistemology and Kawar'ae ways of Knowing to include the different types of lisi, or seeing, related to "seeing the unseen or invisible (eg, spirits), a gift or ability that extends the physical and temporal boundaries of physical seeing; . . . a communication of something to happen; and . . . psychic dreaming, which predicts a future reality and may come from an ancestral spirit or recently dead relative" (2001, 63). Sight and, more broadly, observations within their proper cultural and spiritual context include dreams and a variety of communication methods that western science and western data collection methods overlook.

Struthers (2001) and Gegeo and Gegeo (2001) reinforce how Indigenous sacred concepts are intertwined with Indigenous research practices by incorporating multi-temporal dimensions, dreams, and Indigenous values. Such factors are not typically included in western data practices. Table 24.1 describes western and Indigenous concepts used in data management, highlighting what counts as "data" within these conceptual frameworks, but also pointing out areas related to sacred or spiritual practice through the use of an asterisk (*) to denote concepts that may be sacred, inherently have sacred aspects, or are concepts related to something sacred. Table 24.1 merely provides examples; therefore, readers should recognize that all Indigenous cultures have unique and distinct informational and spiritual frameworks and not make generalizations. However, some commonalities and shared concepts exist across Indigenous communities that allow for such a table to be created.

Table 24.1 compares and contrasts western and Indigenous Knowledge structures via their informational frameworks. It is important to sit with and ask questions of the distance between these two ways of knowing and of conveying information about the world and our relationships to it. It is equally important to give Indigenous concepts their proper place, or va, and to respect the space and distance from western concepts. The high prevalence of sacred aspects related to Indigenous ways of Knowing underpins the premise of this chapter, that data management must be informed by

Table 24.1. Western and Indigenous conceptual frameworks for research

Observation Type	Western Concepts	Indigenous Concepts
Observations related to time *(temporal)*	Second, minute, hourly, daily, monthly, annually, decadal, seasonally, diurnal/ nocturnal	Millenia, generational/ancestral*, time marked by animals*, migration and animal behavior*, nonlinear/ multidimensional time/space*, reincarnation*, predictions and dreams*, seasonal, driven/directed by weather*, time marked by people's lives and time of living
Time examples	*Observation took place on 10/17/1995 at 1:43pm Eastern*	*During mango season, before my grandmother was born.*
Observations related to the physical world *(spatial, geospatial)*	Point, line, polygon, human population centers, national and regional boundaries, state and federal jurisdiction	Routes*, areas*, ecosystems*, habitats*, agreed-upon territorial boundaries, agreed-upon use boundaries*, Indigenous place names*, hunting and gathering places*, sacred sites*, gendered-use spaces*, seasonal-use spaces* celestial/star bodies and space phenomena*
Physical world examples	*Geolocated polygon describing our collection site*	*The stories we tell about stars we see along the route to my mother's village at the end of the rainy season*
Observations related to humans	Interviews, surveys, field recordings, oral histories, remains, audio, video, photo, culture, dance, Tradition, clothing/ regalia, tools, language, customs, tattoos, citizenship/ Tribal status, DNA, lab tests, BMI, weight, IQ	Relations*, family*, bones*, stories*, recordings*, audio*, video*, photo*, culture*, dance*, Tradition*, clothing/regalia*, tools, language, ritual and customs*, prayer*, tattoos*, sharing food and resources*, spending time*, respect of Elders*, respect of women*, respect of children*, preparation of food*, gift giving *, Traditional gender, sexual, and familial roles*, lineage*, role/title/other honorific*, personification/personhood of animals*, dreams/visions*, ritualized conversations, debate and discourse*
Human examples	*Sequenced genome*	*The songs my grandfather sang on the boat*

Table 24.1. Western and Indigenous conceptual frameworks for research (continued)

Physical items collected for analysis (specimens, samples)	Sample, plot, abundance, population counts, length/height, animal tracks, bones, scat, fossil, animal and plant "specimen," environmental samples	Animal smell*, animal taste*, qualities of animal pelt/skin/flesh such as color or thickness, timing of animal behavior, plant color, size, and location of growing, animal disease, stories told about the animals/plants*, stones*, stone/land formations*, specific water bodies and water formations*, specific trees*, plants*, lava fields*
Specimen examples	*Food contents of a salmon gut*	*Plant that revealed itself to me*
Observations collected from a distance (remote sensing)	Radar, satellite imagery, synthetic aperture radar, lidar	Dreams*, celestial navigation*, stories*, legend*, weather prediction*, Indigenous Knowledges, beach combing and things coming in with the tide, smells on the wind, qualities of the air/wind
Observation examples	*Satellite imagery*	*A smell in the wind*

cultural and sacred concepts in order to do proper justice to Indigenous ways of Knowing. The two sections below examine how different ways of Knowing relate to the sacred and, by extension, to data activities, in greater detail.

WHAT TRADITIONAL SOCIETAL ROLES TEACH US ABOUT PLANTS

In a Samoan context, to understand the healing and medicinal properties of a plant, one should know the legends about how our People and Gods came to be introduced to the plant, and the uses of the plant for ending possession by aitu, spirits and ghosts. A Samoan researcher may seek expertise from Elders, ask about the legends and stories surrounding the plant's origins, examine how the plant is used across Oceana, examine where the plant grows and what grows around it, and speak with Traditional healers. The researcher will spend time and sit with the Indigenous Peoples involved in the project, bringing proper gifts and demonstrating respectful protocols for all interactions. In such relational work, Samoan researchers may listen for stories about the plant and what procedures were performed by Traditional healers. When collecting specimens, the researcher would be careful to ask the plant permission before taking, never taking too much, and never disturbing the surrounding area unnecessarily. Samoan researchers would be exceedingly careful to avoid sacred sites or tapu (taboo) practices in their methodologies.

The Samoan researcher accepts that the spiritual and sacred are inextricably intertwined with the physical and thoroughly enmeshed with stories, languages, and cultures. As such, the plant and its healing qualities are intertwined with Traditional societal roles. Samoan culture posits that by living according to Traditional societal roles, or fa'a Samoa, the plant will be most likely to be discoverable or found (Ng Chok et al. 2022) in order to be used in a healing capacity. In Samoan healing practices, the plant heals a human as an honorific and out of respect and in honor of the righteousness of the individual. This Samoan healing framework stems from and relates to a highly interconnected world, and the larger fundamentals of va as well as Samoan cosmology (Ng Chok et al. 2022).

To separate the research of the plant from a Samoan healing framework is also, by extension, to exclude a very large body of work encompassing the origins of life, the universe, and, ultimately, the Gods. Moreover, the consequences of disrespectful or imbalanced research relationships may be quite severe. Anae writes that such consequences "will incur the wrath of the gods, the keepers of tapu, and positive successful outcomes will not eventuate; progress will be impeded, parties to the relationship will be put at risk, and appeasement and reconciliation will need to be sought" (2016, 122). Research done within a cultural and sacred context has both responsibility and consequences.

WHAT STONES TELL US ABOUT GOD

Whispers and Vanities: Samoan Indigenous Knowledge and Religion describes how, "We are forced to confront our ancestral spiritual world in which the sameness of stones and humans is considered fundamental trust and in which the tangible—*ma'a'* (stones)—and the intangible—*upu / tala* (words / stories) are comparable" (Sua'ali'i-Sauni et al. 2014, 32). The Samoan origin story describes an explosive schism between heaven and stone, the separation of the metaphysical and the physical. Our ancestors tell us that stones mixed with bacteria to form life and, ultimately, humans. Our ancestors explained the connection between humans and stones as that of kin, family, and relations (Powell and Fraser 1892). The authors of *Whispers and Vanities* describe the "equivalence between humans, animals, stones, rocks, earth, mountains, and all other material and cosmic life" (Sua'ali'i-Sauni et al. 2014, 34). In recent times, our ancestors' stories have been corroborated by western concepts such as the big bang theory, yet in the western ideological framing and retelling of this process, the familial relationship between humans and stones is lost.

Samoans and other Pasifika Peoples have not forgotten this kinship relationship. Take for example western data collection activities such as satellite imagery and remote sensing. This type of observation and way of knowing can never tell the sacred stories of the stones and sacred places, nor can it capture the multidimensionality of space-time that allow the river stone to be simultaneously the physical manifestation of the sacred (the stone is the Goddess), the historical memory (the stone reminds us of what happened to the Goddess), the sacred memorial site (we commemorate and honor the Goddess that became stone), and kin (the stone is ancestor). Likewise, the satellite imagery does not tell us how to properly engage (va) with proper respect, caution, and fa'a Samoa, or cultural Knowledge that would allow one to safely do so. The imagery cannot tell us what the Gods foresaw or predicted in this place, sacred information that informs how we can best protect it for the future. These examples show how Samoan ways of Knowing cannot and should not be separated from their layered and multidimensional parts that incorporate the sacred.

In a western research context, rivers, rocks, creek beds and other natural features are not generally considered sacred. Western researchers may have awe, reverence, and be humbled by natural forces they encounter in their work, but writ large there is a nonreligious tone to western research and discourse around data. Sacred practice is rarely explicitly included in western research and data management activities. As a result, the softwares and analytical tools used in research are not typically imbued with sacred protocols.

This absence stems from western notions about the purported objectivity of science, and morals related to the scientific method and what counts as proof: that which is observable, measurable, and reproducible. As alluded to in table 24.1, the data that western researchers collect and analyze are distinctly and intentionally considered non-sacred. In fact, to engage with sacred concepts in western research contexts (outside of religious studies) is often dismissed as pseudoscience. As a result, western data practices do not typically describe any explicitly sacred practice. If individual researchers engage in sacred practice as part of their work, then those actions are typically undocumented, and not mentioned in publications. More often than not, in western contexts, any sacred practice engaged in relation to research and data is considered a private and personal activity, as opposed to a foundational or prerequisite activity.

Gegeo and Gegeo frame this phenomenon within the context of subjective and objective Knowledge as it relates to Solomon Islands Kwara'ae epistemology:

> All [K]nowledge is subjective [K]nowledge in Kwara'ae: there can be no detachment of the [K]nower from the known as in mainstream Anglo-European epistemology, as exemplified in logical positivism with its focus on "objective knowledge," especially Karl Popper's concept of "knowledge without a knower" (1972). Thus the scientific notion of objectivity as classically defined in positivism does not exist in Kwara'ae. To the Kwara'ae [K]nowledge is socially constructed by communities of [K]nowledge-makers. (2001, 62)

A proliferation of discourse abounds about proper treatment and incorporation of Indigenous Knowledges within western research practices, including the 2022 White House Council on Environmental Quality (CEQ) and the White House Office of Science and Technology Policy (OSTP)'s *Guidance for Federal Departments and Agencies on Indigenous Knowledge*, which is "founded on the understanding that multiple lines of evidence or ways of knowing can lead to better-informed decision making" (Prabhakar and Mallory 2002b, 3). As encouraging as it is to see the Biden administration properly engage in nation-to-nation relationship-building that includes clear guidance on proper incorporation of Indigenous Knowledges, in practice there is much more work to do. To effectively engage Indigenous Knowledges requires acceptance and incorporation of sacred practices, Indigenous cosmologies (theories of the origin of the universe), and all that is imbued within Indigenous Knowledge systems. In research contexts, to truly engage with Samoan Indigenous Knowledges, or other Indigenous Knowledge systems, requires a reconceptualization of what counts as data, and an evolution of data activities including collection procedures, quality assurance and quality control, analytical practices, sharing and reuse activities, and all other aspects of the data life cycle. Similarly, the softwares designed to house and share these Knowledge objects need to be drastically restructured.

It is important to note that sacred-informed data activities should be treated as more than a "should," a "nice to have," or a box to check; they have sovereign accountabilities. Article 25 of the United Nations' Declaration on the Rights of Indigenous Peoples declares,

> Indigenous [P]eoples have the right to maintain and strengthen their distinctive spiritual and material relationship with the lands, territories, waters and coastal seas and other resources which they have [T]raditionally owned or otherwise occupied or used, and to uphold their responsibilities to future generations in this regard. (UNDRIP; UN General Assembly 2007, 19)

Engaging in Indigenous Knowledges and incorporating sacred practice into research and data activities improves decision-making in the face of climate change and honors human rights and the sovereign rights of Indigenous cultures worldwide.

ALL TIME IS NOW

With regard to western constructs of data collection, one of the foundational data collection tasks involves time and place, which are seen as straightforward and fundamental in the western world. However, Indigenous concepts of time and place vary greatly, and these differences are reflected in Indigenous descriptors and observations. European notions of time mark a linear before and after of a spiritual event (the birth of Christ), but have since largely been superseded by notions of time and timeliness driven by capitalism and the industrial revolution. Linda Tuhiwai Smith (2021, 55) writes in the seminal *Decolonizing Methodologies*, "Different orientations towards time and space, different positioning within time and space, and different systems of language for making space and time 'real' underpin notions of past and present of place and of relationships to land." To locate this within a Samoan context, Samoan poet and author Lana Lopesi's *False Divides* references Pasifika Peoples' concepts of nonlinear and deep time that "advances a more Indigenous sense of temporality, replacing basic conceptions of pre- and post-colonial eras" (2018, 10). Samoan worldviews place a primacy on the past that is accentuated and amplified by the simultaneously occurring present, sometimes described as walking backwards into the future. If we are to manage data respective of Indigenous Knowledges and frameworks, our softwares and other data management tools must be reconceptualized to hold different observational objects, and to account for data that stem from different epistemological frameworks, even as it relates to foundational data concepts such as time.

Gabbard's analysis of Pasifika cartography describes how "Maori cartographers from the 18th century [were] articulating physical space temporally, measuring space with time" (2017, 36), as opposed to European cartographers of the era who measured (and continue to measure) physical space without incorporating a reference to time. Gabbard describes in more detail concepts of "spiral time" and the Pasifika idea that "all time is now-time." (2017, 36). While time series data and temporal observations are taken as relatively straightforward concepts in western data management, time and spatial observations from non-western Traditional frameworks may be nonlinear, multidimensional, and contain other aspects, such as in Samoan Knowledge frameworks. Smith comments on the values underpinning western geospatial methods, as

a very specific spatial vocabulary of colonialism which can be assembled around three concepts: 1. The line, 2. The center, and 3. the outside. The "line" is important because it is used to map territory, to survey land, to establish boundaries and to mark the limits of colonial power. The "center" is important because orientation to the center was an orientation to the system of power. The "outside" is important because it positioned territory and [P]eople in an oppositional relation to the colonial center. (2012, 52)

While many of the fundamentals of temporal observation and observations about stones and physical landscapes have been touched upon by other Indigenous thinkers and writers, in this chapter I bring these concepts into context with data management plans and the data governance activities of researchers.

DATA MANAGEMENT PLANS THAT RECONCILE THE SACRED
Data management plans (DMPs) have become a requirement for academic funders and many resources exist to describe and create DMPs. Despite this, the data management plan is not a widely understood or particularly popular document. A study on perspectives of DMPs found that the most

commonly held perspective for the DMP was that it allowed researchers to make their data more FAIR (findable, accessible, interoperable, and reusable; Kvale and Pharo 2021; Wilkinson et al. 2016) for both humans and machines. In a different analysis looking at the content expectations for DMPs, "the only category that was addressed by the guidelines of all of the agencies was 'Access'—likely reflecting the underlying emphasis at the federal level for publicly available data—followed by 'Preservation'" (Thoegersen 2015, 1072). Perceptions of DMPs are that they describe how you access the data and share details about where the data are stored with the end goal of making data reusable, interoperable, and discoverable by researchers.

When we consider our data activities from a sacred-informed and Indigenous data sovereignty perspective, the emphasis on access and preservation takes on a distinctly different tone. Traditionally, access to information in Samoa would be passed through familial titular or hierarchical transmission lines. Samoan pedagogical structures place much value on Knowledge holders and custodians, with a deep cultural reverence for medicinal healers, orators, and matai (chiefs). It is distinctly and clearly not Knowledge that should be or could be accessed by anyone, and certainly not for all people in perpetuity. Tui Atua describes the transmission and sharing of Samoan Indigenous Knowledges, and its relation to the tapu:

> The passing on of [K]nowledge, especially tapu [K]nowledge, between one generation and the next is usually done within the confines of the family. This practice is tapu because such [K]nowledges are under the special guardianship of a [G]od—Atua or aitu, or spirit. The tapu [K]nowledge includes genealogical, house-building and fishing [K]nowledges and the transfer of these [K]owledges to outsiders would incur the wrath of the protecting Atua or aitu. (Efi 2005, 64)

Much Knowledge is encoded in Indigenous languages, and Samoa has languages for different societal roles, including a language reserved for high chiefs and other Peoples in respected roles. Cocreation of Knowledge through dialogic practice (practice of discussion, dialogue, discourse), or talanoa, is also a culturally appropriate method for Knowledge transmission (Matapo and Enari 2021). In order to reflect proper sharing of Knowledge from Samoan or other Indigenous Knowledges, further work is needed to create a data management plan that aligns with these values.

The DMP provides a unique opportunity for research teams to create a culturally aligned strategy for everything from research design to distribution of labor to data analysis activities. We can create new practices for ourselves that reflect our values. Below, I provide a template to guide data management planning including prompts and examples that will produce a culturally informed and responsible plan for research and associated data activities.

Template: Data Management Plan That Reconciles the Sacred Research Design

OBJECTIVE: To incorporate the sacred into research design

1. Describe what questions the research team's ancestors and guides want researched.
2. Has the research team connected with their guides?
3. Do the guides understand and approve of this research? If not, what questions do they have?
4. Describe how cultural and sacred protocols are observed and followed by members of the research team as part of the research design process.

Example: The research team consulted their ancestors and guides. They received positive feedback in the forms of dreams and other symbolic gestures that lead them to believe their ancestors encourage and support this work.

DATA COLLECTION

OBJECTIVE: To incorporate the sacred into the data collection activities

1. Describe the nature and depth of all researchers' relationship to and understanding of the place and the work being done. This is sometimes referred to as a positionality statement.
2. Describe the specific cultural protocols respected in the design and collection of these data.
3. Describe the ways in which plants, animals, bodies of water, rocks were spoken properly to / of, respected, and asked for permission before any research activity was conducted (Ng Chok et al. 2022).
4. Confirm and clearly state that the area where the data is being collected does not have special or sacred rules dictating how to act in that place (Ng Chok et al. 2022). If the area is governed by special or sacred rules, how were those respected and who were the sacred-informed People who facilitated the process with the research team?

5. Describe how researchers respect cultural values around taking and giving as part of the data collection activity. If culturally relevant, did researchers take only what was needed?

6. Did animals present themselves or intervene in any way during the collection activities, or was there a marked environmental change during the course of the data collection, indicating a possible omen or spiritual/guide communication?

7. Did any strange or unknown people appear during the data collection? Describe in detail and consult Elders, Knowledge holders, and guides on their significance.

8. Were People involved in the collection activity engaged in culturally accepted roles? For a Samoan example, was the collection done with permission from the Matai and assistance from village aumaga, each village's group for men without titles?

9. Was collection timing aligned with sacred or respected times of day / month / year? (Ng Chok et al. 2022).

Example: Men were engaged in the data collection activity. While collecting data in the forest, group members were quiet and respectful, and were properly attired. No singing, whistling, or boisterous behavior took place during specimen collection. There was a light drizzle that turned to sun very quickly while we worked. No collection happened during sa (spirit time), or under moonlight. Local guides and healers were involved in site selection and guided the team on the respectful handling of samples collected. An older man appeared in the forest as we were collecting data, our local guide greeted him respectfully and shared food with him. The man left shortly after that. Nothing was taken in excess so as to maintain balance. After analysis, specimens were returned to the same spot and proper words were spoken upon their return.

DATA QUALITY AND CLEANING ACTIVITIES

OBJECTIVE: To prevent cultural errors that can impact data quality.

The research team encountered the following cultural errors that may have affected the data quality (list and describe):

1. Were animals or other beings disrespected or spoken incorrectly of / to?

2. Were physical spaces or environments disturbed without proper prior communication or permission?

3. Was data collection conducted on sacred days, in sacred places, and/or during sacred times?

Example: The research team got lost on their way back to the village and were traveling through the jungle during sa. The team was quiet and respectful; however, they discovered an area where the plant they were seeking was growing plentifully. They picked a few leaves from several plants. Upon returning, the plants had withered and in addition to the time of day they were picked, the research team decided to discard them during the data quality process. The research team consulted village experts on how to address the situation and were guided back to the collection site at a better, more appropriate time.

DATA ANALYSIS

OBJECTIVE: To incorporate the sacred into data analysis activities.

1. Data analysis should be done by researchers with deep cultural Knowledge who have prior Knowledge of the place, culture, and area of research.
2. Researchers seek out rest and other restorative practices (e.g., such as consulting ancestors) when they are confounded or challenged by data analysis.
3. Data analysis questions will be discussed and resolved using culturally appropriate methods
4. Citation and attribution of data sources and original Knowledge sources will be recorded during the analysis and data reuse process to ensure proper citation as culturally appropriate and in accordance with cultural rules.

Example: The research team was composed of researchers with deep cultural understanding, and two of early (reconnecting) cultural understanding. The team involved Elders and Chiefs into the analysis effort by requesting an audience of the village Matai (chief) to discuss analysis questions. The research team was invited to a tea, and participated in Samoan oratorial and discursive process (discussion-based, face-to-face governance and decision-making models), involving listening, asking questions, paying close attention to words, references, and analogies used by Elders and Matai, and drinking tea and, when offered, kava. After several hours the research team retreated to their fale for rest.

DATA REUSE AND SHARING ACTIVITIES

OBJECTIVE: Sharing and reuse of data are governed by cultural and sacred values.

1. Culturally appropriate receivers of data should be identified by the Indigenous community.
2. Data are shared in culturally appropriate ways that align with Indigenous values around honor, respect, sharing, reciprocity, relationships, and responsibilities.
3. Indigenous Communities specify the people and/or organizations that may receive copies of data. Were cultural protocols respected with regard to sharing and also who has access going forward (and backwards) in time?

Example: Data were reused carefully and respectfully by researchers who have been identified by community members as having deep cultural Knowledge, who have prior Knowledge of the place, Peoples, culture, and area of research. Cultural protocols around attribution, sharing, and respectful use were incorporated into data reuse activities. Indigenous values were consulted and enacted through all of these processes.

DATA GOVERNANCE, PRESERVATION, AND ARCHIVAL ACTIVITIES

OBJECTIVE: How were cultural and sacred protocols reflected in the governance and decision-making of the data?

1. Describe the length or duration of preservation that is culturally appropriate in detail.
2. Which culturally appropriate archival methods were employed, such as oral transmission and social methods (e.g., gathering, sharing food, and storytelling)?
3. What methods were used to identify and work with designated Knowledge custodians and culturally appropriate Knowledge-holders for archiving the work as story, craft, convening, or incorporating it into other Traditional Knowledge sources?
4. Discussion and debate related to the data are performed in a culturally appropriate manner (Ng Chok et al. 2022).
5. The research team used consensus seeking activities, if culturally appropriate, to make decisions about the data. Regardless, decisions were made with respect to title holders, Elders, and honor respect protocols.

Example: Decisions about data governance were brought to the Matai and village Elders for discussion. The research team brought gifts and sat down when requesting an audience with the Matai. They sought the council of the Matai and listened as they discussed the decisions at hand, and then respected the final decision that the Matai made and implemented the specific directions within their data management activities.

DATA MANAGEMENT SOFTWARE AND FRAMEWORKS

Western concepts and values shape the logic of software and tech infrastructure. Socio-technologists and critical media studies researchers of all stripes from Marxist to feminist to Indigenous theorists have commented on the value systems engrained in large and minute ways in software and technology. Examples include Taina Bucher's exploration of the nonneutrality of APIs, wherein she describes how "bringing a software studies perspective to bear on data collection 'tools' like APIs, seems imperative if we want to understand what these 'tools' do and the politics and powers they entail, beyond helping to collect and provide access to the data" (Bucher 2013). New Design Congress's recent report "Memory in Uncertainty" describes ethical challenges related to archiving internet-based / web-based objects, "When tools are designed, they materialise with a baseline set of ethics "baked" into them. . . . For some, the belief of data permanence was an ideology that trumped issues of consent, invasion of privacy or other ethical considerations" (New Design Congress 2022). This colonizing and extractive logic extends across all technical spaces, including but not limited to data management software, data storage systems, and archival/presentation softwares. The ethical challenges to housing and storing Indigenous Knowledges within these colonized and colonizing software and infrastructural frameworks are ongoing.

The process of creating FAIR-compliant data makes it readable by both humans and machines, allowing it to be sifted, sorted, queried, shared, and delivered from one human to another using a machine. To do so, the data must be described and contextualized in specific ways that machines can understand, so machines can correlate one data source to another—that is, interoperable data objects and extensible (able to be used in different contexts) data processes. The FAIR data principles are meant for both human and machine ontological frameworks. This process of recontextualizing knowledge to make it interoperable and usable for machines requires a few steps to minimize complexity and create standardized data objects. These processes often default to long-established colonized power structures that govern language, knowledge, culture, and governance and, often, align with capitalist and imperialist influences. Ultimately the goal of creating granular (small) data objects that are easily shareable and usable outside of context may directly conflict with some Indigenous Knowledge systems and values. The fundamental premise of FAIR data can introduce an ethical conflict.

In *The Cost of Connection: How Data Is Colonizing Human Life and Appropriating It for Capitalism*, data colonialism and the relationship between data and capitalism describes how "the appropriation of data enables new ways of forming capital through the circulation and trading of informational traces (data)" (Couldry and Meijas 2019, 3). On the issue of data accessibility, authors describe the tendency of industry "to talk about data as though it was 'just there,' freely available for extraction and the release of its potential for humankind. . . . Data is assumed to just be there for the taking" (Couldry and Meijas 2019, 9). Likening the "taking" to concepts such as terra nullius (a Latin term meaning land belonging to no one and an international law that justified earlier methods of colonization and capitalist expansion across the Indigenous world), we understand that all aspects of collecting, sharing, and decontextualizing data and information must be undertaken with extreme caution.

Indigenous concepts, values, languages, histories, and sacred concepts governing Knowledge and sharing are largely not reflected in the software used in research and data management. Indigenous Peoples of the world successfully share Knowledges across our cultures and Traditions, and Indigenous sharing networks grow increasingly strong as advocacy and solidarity movements unite around self-determination and sovereignty movements. We know this is not a new phenomenon because of stories told by our ancestors, passed down through the generations. We know that, in the past, through our relationships we were able to share cultivation and stewardship practices, hunting and crafting methods, and transportation and navigation techniques. How might we revive the practice of sharing Knowledge across cultures and Traditions, while respecting values, responsibilities, and the sovereignty of the Knowledge holders and creators?

Table 24.2 examines how FAIR data principles and guidelines align with Samoan worldview as reflected in several concepts. Table 24.2 compares data principles with the Samoan concepts of fa'a Samoa, malamalama or enlightenment, sa and related sacredness and often tightly coupled with tapu or that which is taboo or forbidden, tatau or properness, and teu and va, described previously. These concepts were selected as playing a role in Samoan-informed research values, as identified by authors such as Melani Anae, Carolina Sinavaiana Gabbard, Lana Lopesi, Jacoba Matapo, Alfred Refiti, Benita Sharon Simati, I'uogafa Tuagalu, and Albert Wendt. While the

Table 24.2. FAIR data principles and Samoan concepts

FAIR Data Principle	fa'a Samoa (making/being Samoa)	malamalama (enlightenment, knowledge, comprehension)	sā (sacred, forbidden)	tatau (proper)	teu (ordering, cleaning, tidying up, preparing)	vā (spatiotemporal relational space)
Findable				Dictating proper order and proper placement of data objects	Expectation of tidiness and cleanliness applied to data, underpinning aspects of "findability"	Relational concept dictating who can find and how to find a data object, includi its proper place.
Accessible	Who has access to data governed by societal rules and hierarchy		Who has access to data governed by societal rules and hierarchy			Who has access to data governed by societal rules and hierarchy
Interoperable					Governing suitable use of data, ensuring items are ready for use	
Reusable						

goal of table 24.2 is to compare which data principles align with Samoan values, it also seeks to examine the role Samoan cultural values might play in governing data principles. This is a theoretical structure, proposed as a working hypothesis, designed to spark discussion around the ways in which specific cultural values can be drawn into data management and governance activities for ethical and culturally appropriate research. Last, but certainly not least, table 24.2 is held as a mirror to the western-informed data management structures that are influenced by a value structure so pervasive it is often hard to clearly see. By repositioning and recontextualizing, I hope to shine a light on the value systems currently at work. I expect this to spark debate, and welcome the critical and reflective processes that will come from this publication.

Conclusion

Drawing our cultures and values into our research and data practices is an act of intergenerational healing that involves our families, our diasporic and homeland communities, our ancestors, and our fellow Indigenous Peoples across the world. It allows us to shape and craft modes of inquiry that rectify the past with the present, and lets our wisdom, Knowledge, and millennia of guidance into the process of caring for this earth and caring for ourselves. Rooting research in restorative work lets the light in. It rights the world as our ancestors had designed it, creating relational ethics, spatial ethics, and temporal ethics, and reconnects us to the sacred, the ancient, and, by extension, a future in which they want to be part. Let these forces and this wisdom in.

Acknowledgments

I extend deep appreciation to the following Alaska Native, Inuit, Indigenous, and Indigenous data sovereignty leaders who speak on topics such as data, information, Indigenous Knowledge, decolonized archives, self-determination, ethical and equitable engagement, and sovereignty: Carolina Behe, Dr. Stephanie Rainie Carroll, Dr. Dalee Sambo Dorough, Kelly Eningowuk, Inuit Circumpolar Council, Anita Kora, Dr. Desi Rodriguez Lonebear, Margaret Rudolph, and James (Jimmy) Stotts. I also appreciate the support that Jack Ewers, Roreta Lee, and Lara A. Jacobs extended in providing insights to this chapter before submission.

25

THE RESPONSIBILITY OF RELATIONAL CONSIDERATION
Invasive and Nonnative Species in the Context of Indigenous Food Security and Food Sovereignty

JENNIFER GRENZ

Positionality Statement

Nlaka'pamux, of mixed ancestry; family are members of Lytton and Bonaparte First Nations; raised on the unceded territories of the scəẃaθən (Tsawwassen), xʷməθkʷəy̓əm (Musqueam), and other Coast Salish Peoples; now living on the lands of the Pentlatch-speaking People; assistant professor, Department of Forest Resources Management, faculty of Forestry and faculty of Land and Food Systems, University of British Columbia.

Introduction

If only we could see the wisdom of taking a meaningful pause as we walk through the forest. It is in that pause that we may look to our plant relations for important teachings about fulfilling our responsibilities to steward our lands in a changing climate. The responsibility of plant Knowledge Keepers to our Indigenous communities to ensure there are foods and medicines for all relations is not lost on any of us. While we work to reclaim our Traditional Ecological Knowledges, we find our walks through our forests today having been heavily influenced, purposefully or not, by western science and the culture that surrounds its application to ecological restoration. This influence has shaped our perceptions of plants such that we choose only to sit with species labeled as ours ("native") by our colonizers and vilify those they told us don't belong ("invasive"). This strategic othering allows us to limit our efforts to get to know those labeled as ecological enemies such that it makes easier our justifications for eradicating them.

But what of their lessons? If we do not take meaningful pauses to sit with them, we cannot learn from them. What might they be trying to tell us? Even species labeled "invasive" that justifiably require management to protect the values and needs of our relations and communities may still have important things to teach us if we ask them. Our ancestors survived changes in speciation on Turtle Island whereas we find ourselves today existing in an ecological restoration that may have hit the pause button on our ecosystems. This makes me wary of the certainty with which we have found ourselves labeling species to automatically determine their fates. The implications these labels have for Indigenous food security and food sovereignty may be counter to the very values these labels claim to uphold.

For whatever reason, I have always felt drawn to invasive plants. Perhaps these plants I knew so well from an almost two-decades-long career as an Invasive Species Specialist, yet treated as strangers, were calling out to me. Calls offering teachings they knew we were missing through our deliberate ignorance of them. Calls I couldn't hear over the colonial calls to action against them. Calls I could not ignore because our Earth Mother demanded that we do things differently before it was too late.

The question of species belongingness has become a central focus of our modern, Eden-based ecological restoration paradigm. The colonial nature of this focus has led to land-management practices based on a xenophobic dichotomy of invasive species as "bad" and native species as "good." This categorization within the field of ecological restoration continues to perpetuate colonial notions of who we are as Indigenous Peoples today and how our ancestors before us lived. The field of invasion biology was developed on a foundation of colonial history, making it difficult to reconcile with the true histories of our Peoples. This includes our presence and shaping of our lands since time immemorial and our relationships with the Peoples and lands of other Nations.

Even in a period of history when our Indigenous Knowledges are increasingly sought to inform ecological restoration, we continue to see colonial approaches to the management of species assemblages imposed on us by government agencies, non-Indigenous-led conservation organizations, and western scientific researchers. One such example a settler and ally friend involved in invasive plant management relayed to me was that a plant species deemed invasive by a colonial government agency was actively being treated with herbicide just outside of reserve lands. These same plants were present on reserve lands adjacent to where the herbicide treatment had occurred, and the government agency was putting pressure on the elected Indigenous government to allow them to treat the plants there. The Indigenous community was hesitant because of concerns about the use of herbicides, and it seemed that pollinators used those plants for food. Community members had described the plants as being "alive with bees." When this was communicated to the colonial government agency representative, the observations were immediately dismissed, and the dismissal was justified because the plants are invasive. Apparently, a community member had wisely responded to what was described by my friend as "an attempt to strong-arm the community into allowing herbicide treatment of the plants" by saying, "The bees don't know those plants are invasive." While it is true that there are invasive species that have clearly established negative impacts on the environment, economy, and human health, some that have been categorized as such do not, or the nature and/or extent of their impacts are largely unknown. The potential consequences of miscategorizing plants are particularly concerning as we face a changing climate that is disproportionately affecting the food systems of many Indigenous communities: a consideration not often given to the assessment of newly arrived or soon-to-arrive species from one geographic area to another. Being a People that have survived changes in speciation, we maintain a responsibility to (1) ensure that *all* of our relations (humans, animals, birds, insects, plants) are fed, into the future, and (2) give relational consideration to species from other geographic areas, rather than simply othering them. I define "relational consideration" as the fair and neutral evaluation of all relations, and the relationships of those relations, within a specific area for the purpose of land healing, which informs community-values-based actions to achieve a desired ecosystem balance. In this context, balance is dynamic, as it responds to changing factors such as community needs and climate.

While giving relational consideration to species categorized as invasive by colonial systems of land management may seem like an easy task, the culture that surrounds those engaged in invasive species management has led to the creation of a strict dogma that seemingly prohibits the practice of this type of consideration. This can likely be attributed to a colonial, static view of our ecosystems, the hyperbole so often attached to invasive species public education campaigns, and the perceived threat of undermining the field of invasion biology and its application. As a member of this professional community for nearly two decades, I find it interesting that there is very often an expressed desire by field practitioners to reapproach our assessment and management of species categorized as invasive or potentially invasive. Personal communications I have had with colleagues over the years attribute these sentiments to a lack of successfully eradicating species despite many years of management, the development of herbicide resistance, regulatory and procedural hurdles to managing native species that are behaving invasively, and observed ecological benefits of some invasive species, such as habitat value to insects, birds, and animal relations. Overcoming the culture of the field itself may present the greatest hurdle to adopting the practice of relational consideration. While some settler researchers and practitioners within the field have contributed similar rhetoric and been unsuccessful in their calls for change, Indigenous perspectives and the application of an Indigenous worldview to invasion biology may offer an acceptable path to reevaluating the dichotomously guided land healing we have collectively found ourselves practicing.

This chapter provides a reflection on how xenophobic approaches to the management of species on Turtle Island's ecosystems arose, Indigenous perspectives on invasive species and their management, and why we have a responsibility to our communities to give relational consideration to species often vilified by western science. As is consistent with the relational nature of many Indigenous worldviews, before looking to the future, we must first look to the past to understand how invasion biology has developed to this point in time, what contributions we wish to carry with us moving forward, and what our Indigenous axiology (beliefs and values), epistemology (ways of Knowing), and methodologies are up against as we work toward a future of caring for our lands and applying Knowledges beyond the confines of the singular, dominant worldview.

INVASION BIOLOGY: A COLONIAL HISTORY

Compared to other fields of science, invasion biology is relatively young. Its short history may help us to understand the controversy that surrounds it as a distinct area of study. Its "beginning" is recognized by many in the field as the 1958 publication of Elton's book, *The Ecology of Invasions by Animals and Plants*. Since that time, the research on biological invasions has arguably received more attention from ecologists and the public than any other ecological topic (Davis 2009). Elton's book did not get much attention until decades later. It was Elton's book, coupled with the 1985 creation of the Scientific Committee on Problems of the Environment, which was charged with focusing scientific attention on invasive species, that increased attention on the topic. In 1996, the publication of Williamson's book, *Biological Invasions*, became the catalyst for significant numbers of publications, books, conferences, and workshops on invasive species, which now extend into the thousands (Davis 2009).

Ecologists have long observed the presence of new species that have appeared to have negative ecological impacts (e.g., Fitch 1861; Drude 1896). Around the same time that Fitch and Drude were investigating such impacts, the United States Department of Agriculture sent biological explorers around the globe to find new plants of potential economic and aesthetic interest (Subramaniam and Schmitz 2016). In the early twentieth century, the "nativism paradigm" emerged after the recognition that many of the plant species brought to North America contained agricultural pests (Pauly 2008). The nativism paradigm is best understood as an ideology that regards native species as inherently more desirable than nonnative species (Chew 2006). However, the concept of nativeness stretches back farther in time, to 1835, when English botanist John Henslow first outlined the parameters of the concept in 1835 (David 2009). It was later, out of practicality, that the terms "native" and "alien" were applied from common law to define plants that were British in origin and those that were not (Alizadeh and Hitchmough 2019).

Decisions regarding the classification of native versus nonnative species are typically based on more than ecological rationale alone. For example, the decision-making behind these categories often fails to account for past climatically driven environmental changes or historical and prehistoric human impacts that substantially influenced the composition and functionality of ecosystems across much of the world, especially in the Late Quaternary period (2.58 million years ago to present) and onward through time (Crees and Turvey 2015).

The "nativism paradigm" holds a common assertion that the success of invasive species is due to their ability to perform better outside of their ecosystems of origin. One reason given to support this claim is that there are no natural predators such as diseases, insects, or animals that will keep their populations in check in the new range. Some species, such as Japanese knotweed (*Reynoutria japonica*), do affirm the fundamental assumption assertion of invasion biology, that most invasive species exhibit enhanced performance in their introduced range relative to their home range (Parker et al. 2013). This idea has resulted in numerous hypotheses explaining invasion success by virtue of altered ecological and evolutionary pressures. However, there is little data that test the underlying assumption that the performance of introduced populations, including organism size, reproductive output, and abundance, is enhanced in their introduced compared to their native range (Hufbauer et al. 2013). Findings by Parker et al. (2013) suggest that there is considerable uncertainty in assuming that invasive species are performing better in their new ranges and that most invasive species might be performing relatively similarly despite potentially large differences in ecological and evolutionary conditions (Hufbauer and Torchin 2007). While some species demonstrated general patterns of increased performance, substantial variation existed among taxa and species: roughly half of the species investigated showed little evidence of increased performance (Parker et al. 2013). Similarly, a different study by Firn et al. (2011) evaluated home and away abundances of twenty-six plant species across thirty-nine sites in eight countries and found no consistent increase in plant abundance. Parker et al.'s (2013) primary conclusion was that the "away-field advantage" for introduced species is likely driven by relatively few introduced species that exhibit strong differences and thus the phenomena may be relatively uncommon or fairly small in magnitude. Nevertheless, as Douglas (1966) contends, humans are preoccupied with "separating, purifying, demarcating, and punishing transgressions" to impose structure on an inherently untidy world. Perhaps it is this preoccupation that leads to the assumption that species should even be categorized in this fashion.

THE VILIFICATION OF SPECIES

The vilification of nonnative species likely began as the result of words used by Elton on a radio program that pre-dated his book, where he describes concepts of invasion biology using the phrase "biological explosions" (Davis 2009). Since that time, the use of militaristic language (e.g., invasion, explosions, target, etc.) (Janovsky and Larson 2019) and the extensive use of hyperbole (e.g., the common name of *Vespa mandarinia* being "murder hornets") in the field are standard vernacular. The use of this language is often explained as being a necessary part of the advocacy component that is so tightly linked to the field of study; helping elected officials to understand the importance of the invasive species "battle" to secure funding for eradication efforts is one of the main reasons it is used.

I am guilty of contributing to the vilification of species. I have designed several successful invasive species public education campaigns based on this concept. One such campaign, called "Alienbusters," was a *Ghostbusters*-inspired concept wherein each of the characters was an invasive plant species that was transformed into some sort of evil-looking character, and those eradicating them were given a hero-like appearance. The campaign was used to help gain a social license for the use of herbicides to control invasive species and to educate the public about these "bad" plants. If you ask my children what their mom does for a living, the response will often be, "she kills bad plants." I cannot argue that these techniques are ineffective because they have proven very effective in achieving their objectives: gaining political and public support and funding. Unfortunately, these types of characterizations create biases against species perceived as "bad," and these biases are often embraced by the public, policymakers, and those working in the field of invasion biology (e.g. conservationists, scientists, land managers, etc.) (Davis 2011).

Today, the successful indoctrination of invasive species in public education campaigns has created a pervasive assumption, particularly by the public, that nativeness is a sign of evolutionary fitness or a species having positive effects. However, this assumption is simply untrue, as there are examples of "native" species that have behaved invasively (e.g., *Dendroctonus ponderosae*, the "native" mountain pine beetle currently suspected of killing more trees than any other insect in North America; Davis 2011).

We cannot deny that some nonnative species are worthy of vilification. Species that cause measurable harm to ecosystems, the economy, and human health and safety may deserve such a label. For example, Japanese knotweed (*Reynoutria japonica*), which I have observed as a practitioner, alters hydrology, displaces native species, ruins road infrastructure, and has appeared in UK news as having caused the condemnation of homes. The trouble is that species with measurable negative impacts are few and far between, because these biases in plant evaluations have excluded most that end up in the "invasive" category from in-depth scientific study. Further, the use of militaristic language concerning these species could create biases against nonnative species and impact the objectivity of such evaluations.

Invasion biology has been plagued by generalizations of nonnative plant impacts, and much of this information has been repeated in the literature, in conference presentations, in invasive species management outreach, and in educational materials. A summation of these generalized principles that I have found through an analysis of invasive species management plans and educational materials that did not include supporting citations are

- Invasive species are the second greatest threat to biodiversity worldwide.
- Invasive species displace native species.
- Invasive species steal resources from native species.
- Invasive species lack predators in their new environment.
- Invasive species damage the local environment.
- Invasive species are more aggressive outside of their native range.

A couple of issues of concern should immediately arise from reading the above list. The first is that all species determined as invasive have the same impacts. The second is that the impacts listed are generalized and not specific. One of the greatest gaps in knowledge in invasive species management is the lack of understanding of the specific impacts of invasive species to the extent to which generalized theories can be applied.

Common citations are repeated in the literature to the extent that, over time, many of these citations are simply stated as facts without acknowledging the original author. Many of these have become boilerplate introductions and conclusions in research articles, proposals, and education materials (Davis 2009). Davis provides an example of the most commonly cited "fact":

> An example from invasion biology is the conclusion by Wilcove et
> al. (1998) that non-native species are the second greatest threat
> to the survival of species in peril. This statement has been cited in
> hundreds of scientific articles since its publication and countless
> research proposals, management documents, and college classes.
> By the early 2000s, it had become a common boilerplate for
> invasion literature, which provides evidence that those citing this
> information have likely not read the article. The authors of this
> article made clear that there were limitations to the data they used
> including the attribution of a specific threat to a species is usually
> based on the judgment of an expert source and may not be based on
> experimental evidence or even on quantitative data. Such data often
> do not exist. Data from this manuscript only dealt with species
> from the continental United States and Hawaii. (2009)

While there has been substantial research within the field of invasion biology, studies have most commonly been on the individual and population levels concerning impacts, whereas ecosystem-level impacts are less frequently reported and rarely quantified (Parker et al. 2013). For most invasions, no impact studies have been performed at all (Parker et al. 2013). For example, Forseth and Innis (2004) found that kudzu (*Pueraria montana*), a species known to be a poster child for the invasive species movement, lacked even the most basic metrics on ecological impacts. Additionally, experiments and even correlational studies of impacts are scarce for many other species known to be highly invasive (Ricciardi and Cohen 2007). Another limitation of existing impact studies is that they are often isolated local assessments.

It is difficult to understand why generalities and assumptions have been adopted within the field. One possible explanation is that erroneous generalities and assumptions regarding nonnative species' expansions have been made because of the rapid evolution of this growing discipline (Martin 2011). Davis describes the phenomena as "the ascendancy of preliminary claim to unquestioned lore" (2009). The question is, how do we bridge this gap? While the link between invasions and the extinction of natives remains widely accepted by scientists and conservations, available data to support this link are largely anecdotal, speculative, and based on limited observations (Gurevitch and Padilla 2004). For every introduced species that does cause negative impacts in an invaded ecosystem, dozens do not, and are instead adding to the species richness in what Martin (2011) referred to as "the inoculated ecosystem"—an ecosystem with an injection of additional species, increasing biodiversity. The impacts of most invasive species have not been quantified, and, when measured, those impacts are based on a limited number of response metrics, with the result being that the field of invasion ecology has been overwhelmed by speculation and bias regarding the ecological consequences of invasive plants (Barney 2013).

The recognition of this gap is starting to appear within the scholarly literature. Authors have begun to publish and cite an increasing number of studies demonstrating a lack of strong negative impacts from invasions on native ecosystems, assertions that challenge many of Elton's predictions and the paradigm status these invasion principles have acquired (Martin 2011). Martin (2011) asserted that the field's conventional wisdom is wrong and that biologists are more swayed by their emotions about invasive species than they care to admit. Brigg (2017) examined origin and biodiversity effects and concluded that exotic species that succeed in colonizing a native ecosystem rarely cause extinctions and are instead accommodated by the native species that occupy the appropriate niches or habitats. In terrestrial systems, such diversity generally gains results in a more stable system with higher productivity and greater resistance to invasion. This is true in marine environments as well.

An example of management based on assumptions can be found in the US attempt to eradicate tamarisk shrubs (*Tamarix* spp.) which were introduced from Eurasia and Africa into the country's arid lands in the nineteenth century. These drought-, salt-, and erosion-resistant plants were initially welcomed into the country, first as ornamental species for people's gardens and later as shade trees for desert farmers. Then, in the 1930s, when water supplies in eastern Arizona, central New Mexico, and western Texas ran short, they were indicted as "water thieves" and, later, during World War II, as "alien invaders." Beginning in 1942, they became the object of a seventy-year suppression project involving herbicides, bulldozers, and the picturesquely named LeTourneau Tree Crusher (Davis 2009). Ecologists have since discovered that tamarisks use water at a rate comparable to that of their native counterparts (Nagler et al. 2009). The plants are now the preferred nesting habitat of the endangered southwestern willow flycatcher, *Empidonax traillii extimus* (Paxton, Theimer, and Sogge 2011). Tamarisks survive under common water-management regimes that destroy native trees and shrubs and arguably play a crucial role in the functioning of human-modified riverbank environments (Davis 2009). Yet between 2005 and 2009 alone, the US Congress authorized $80 million to support ongoing tamarisk control and eradication (Davis 2009).

In my many years of working collaboratively with Indigenous communities on invasive species management initiatives, I have mostly experienced a hesitancy from land managers and staff, Knowledge keepers, and Elders to react as swiftly and decisively to manage invasive plants as I wanted. While such hesitancy at the time seemed frustrating, I recognize now that I was entrenched in the culture of the field of invasion biology. I did not question the categorization of species as invasive by our colonial government agencies. I see now the wisdom in such hesitancy as I have worked to apply an Indigenous, relational worldview: we need more species-specific research within specific contexts that fairly evaluates species impacts. This includes the evaluation of the positive impacts of these species, a category I have not yet encountered within species impact assessments created and used by government agencies. We also need research conducted beyond the limitations of western science, including research that is truly inclusive of Traditional Ecological Knowledge, the value systems of Indigenous communities, and the application of a relational worldview that focuses on the numerous relationships of potentially invasive species and all other relations that they may interact with both directly and indirectly—relational consideration research.

All of this is critical to better understanding the risks and benefits of species so we can ensure that limited resources are used wisely for the sake of managing healthy, functioning ecosystems that support all relations within the context of a changing climate. This could include embracing species that may be new to a geographic area and that could provide measurable benefits, or changing the classification of a species once deemed as invasive. Such a paradigm shift would require those who work with nonnative species to set aside their subscription to the native-invasive dichotomy and learn to recommit themselves to dynamic and practical management approaches focused on the needs of our changing planet (Davis 2011). Given the realities of climate change and the rapid redistribution of species around the globe, restoration ecologists must quickly adopt an objective approach to invasive species rather than automatically dismissing them (Brown and Sax 2004). Such objectivity is not an argument of full support for exotic species such that their spread should be fostered. Nor is it an argument for letting nature take its course and electing not to intervene in the dynamics of dispersal and extinction. It is to plead for more scientific objectivity and less emotional xenophobia. It is an argument for greater understanding of the impacts on biodiversity, ecosystem functions, and the economy. In my case, I will add a plea to fulfill the responsibility given to us by Creator to take care of our relations, which I consider as a willingness to apply our relational worldview and use Indigenous research methodologies to complete the picture for a field of study developed on a colonial foundation.

INDIGENOUS PERSPECTIVES

Many Indigenous communities have been modeling such a relational approach for thousands of years. The appearance of new species in some Indigenous Peoples' stories is often presented as a gift to community in a time of hardship: stories that seed an openness to new species that may face pushback from those who remain indoctrinated in the native versus nonnative dichotomy. Recently I heard a debate about the inclusion of nonnative species in the Indigenous garden at the University of British Columbia. The debate was over whether it was appropriate to include nonnative medicinal plants that have been used by local Elders for quite some time. Elders were confused about why a debate even existed because the plants contained medicinal benefits similar to their culturally important plants that have become difficult to find. Other species are demonstrating the ability to embrace nonnative species by evaluating them in their own right. For example, certain species of nonnative honeysuckles that were once banned by the USDA have increased the species richness of native bird species in Pennsylvania, and as a result, seed dispersal of native berry-producing plants is higher in places where nonnative honey suckles are most abundant (Davis 2011).

As I have worked to apply a relational lens to invasive plant management, I am observing interactions I had not noticed previously. For example, I found robin and hummingbird nests located in stands of Japanese knotweed (*Reynoutria japonica*) and have seen many species of pollinators on spotted knapweed (*Centaurea stoebe*) and orange hawkweed (*Pilosella aurantiaca*) along the sides of highways. I watched bears eating the Himalayan blackberry (*Rubus armeniacus*) on the edge of our farm. I am not using my observations to proclaim a "live and let live" philosophy for all species that behave invasively but am using these examples to underline the need for us to bring into focus that which we have been trained to overlook by the culture of invasion biology and give these relationships the attention and consideration they deserve. These relationships not only tell a story between two species, "native" and "invasive," but they can also tell stories about important issues such as the impacts of climate change. Such relationships could be important indicators of the health and availability of habitat values needed by those relations who have been place-based for a long time (aka "native" species).

While many people use western science as the justification for the concept of nativeness when categorizing plants, the concept itself points to a shift from science toward history and cultural values. A study by Trigger et al. (2008) showed the ambiguous nature of Australian ideas about what "belongs" ecologically and culturally across the Australian continent in a relatively young post-settler nation. In the United States, the ring-necked pheasant, which is the state bird of South Dakota, is not native to the great plains of North America but was introduced from Asia as a game bird in the latter half of the nineteenth century.

Many responses by Indigenous Peoples seek to embrace "exotic" plants, animals, and cultural forms (Trigger 2004). At the least, this is a complex matter rather than any simplistic divide in Traditional Indigenous thinking between natives and invaders. In some areas of Central Australia, cats are hunted for food and celebrated as spiritually significant with a dreaming route similar to those of native species (Cane 2002). Similarly, in the Gulf Country of northern Australia, the introduced water buffalo (*Bubalus bubalis*) has been historically celebrated with dances and songs mimicking the animal's features, just as with native species (Trigger 2004). If Indigenous Peoples in so-called Australia make intellectual room for nonnative species, recognizing their capacity to achieve a place in the environment and the nation, then what are the implications for notions of ecological restoration? This complicates any broad social assumptions that symbolically link "Indigenous Peoples" with an exclusively "native" ecology and any related view that simplistically equates things "native" with what is exclusively "natural."

We [Indigenous Peoples] have found opportunities in species that arrived after contact and now utilize them as both food and medicine just as we did with climate-driven changes in speciation over the thousands of years of our existence along the Salish Sea. Western red cedar (*Thuja plicata*) arrived approximately five thousand years ago in coastal British Columbia, which could have been considered an invasive species by modern-day species risk assessments, yet this species is foundational to our coastal Nations' identities. It is rooted in our stories, art, technologies, cultures, and medicines. However, its prevalence in the Pacific Northwest of Turtle Island came long after Indigenous Peoples to these lands. Clearly this species was given relational consideration during a time when Indigenous ecologies were lived. I cannot help but think that species newly arriving on lands back then were met with a genuine curiosity rather than the intense suspicion they are met with today. The differences in the very definitions of these words, curiosity and suspicion, clearly set different intentions in how species would be considered. "Curiosity" is defined as both a "desire to know" and, most interestingly, "one that arouses interest especially for uncommon or exotic characteristics" (*Merriam-Webster* nd, definition 1 and 3) whereas "suspicion" is defined as, "the act of an instance of suspecting something wrong without proof or on slight evidence" (*Merriam-Webster* nd, definition 1). It is not difficult to imagine the entirely different tacks of consideration that would be given, if the latter receives any consideration at all. A spirit of openness and curiosity is what should be behind the objectivity any species should be met with in truly giving relational consideration.

A story that demonstrates the fluid nature of our Indigenous worldview on belonging and one I spent many hours managing over the years was told to me by Elder Luschiim (Dr. Arvid Charlie; Cowichan Tribes) about Scotch broom, a species long known to be a pervasive invasive species on Vancouver Island, British Columbia. This story was shared with me and recorded with permission for the purposes of the research I did with Cowichan Tribes on invasive plant species and their impacts and the expressed permission of sharing of this story in publications related to that research. It is important to know that many stories cannot be shared outside of community. I also provide a direct transcript so as not to misinterpret the words of an Elder. Luschiim said,

> You know, how did we acquire the [K]nowledge about Scotch Broom? That's a very good medicine. It's beat medicines that the doctors gave. Some of the things that were bad that it was used for . . . [include] a fertilizer or what they put on strawberry plants. A lot of our [P]eople ended up, their skin just kind of melted away and weeping. And then it would spread. Just started weeping. My aunt, she's still here. She was picking berries when she was young. That's probably in the thirties. Twenties or thirties. And it [her skin] got really bad. It was weeping and she couldn't pick anymore. We used to go to the states, Washington, to pick berries. Strawberries or raspberries. So she got sent home cause she was just costing money when they're just feeding her. Money was really scarce. Everybody had to earn their keep. She wasn't earning her keep so they sent her home. So the grandpa, one of the grandpas, heard about it, his granddaughter been sent home. He come to see her. He looked at her. Went and got that Scotch Broom. Kept boiling water and cut that Scotch Broom put it there. Pour it. [motions with hands] Washed her up. Within a few days she, she started to heal. From that Scotch Broom. How did we find out? I don't know. I couldn't answer that. But there are many medicines like that. That came by, by sight, or a vision of some kind. A dream. How do you say that to somebody, like in a government? You know. Would they believe it? The things that some People can see. There is no explanation. Umm hmm.

It is not to say that we do not acknowledge the negative impacts that these species can have. Luschiim shared with me some of the negative impacts of species such as Scotch broom and daphne laurel, which have caused other medicines to disappear in specific areas. Within the same conversation, he went on to say,

> It's wiped out a lot of our natural vegetation such as a flower, some of the flowers that we use either as food or medicine. Um hmmm. Like up on Mount Tzouhalem. Where the onions and where the chocolate lily is. You know, there's no more there. And some of the places where balsam root used to grow, it's all just Scotch Broom. So yes, it does cause a lot of problems.

This Traditional Ecological Knowledge demonstrates the departure from a strict belongingness dichotomy and instead gives relational consideration based on the species' relationships in a specific place. This example demonstrates an Indigenous, relational worldview. It also provides a reminder that we, as humans, are part of ecosystems and that it is okay for us to influence them to meet the needs of all kin—human and more than human—within these locations. The construct of "naturalness" comes from and is a form of colonization that excludes the influence of humans shaping lands and waters. However, the legacy of Indigenous Peoples shaping lands through influencing plant species assemblages can be seen today within Indigenous food/technology/medicine growing systems being referred to as "Indigenous forest gardens." What remains of these systems, as they are reclaimed by Indigenous communities, directly challenges the colonial notions of species belongingness in forest ecosystems based on assumptions that "Indigenous [P]eoples must have 'happened upon' a naturally occurring abundance of resources" (McDonald 2005; Ames 2013, in Armstrong et al. 2021, 1). Such systems are identified throughout British Columbia and are distinct from other forested areas, as their species composition and densities are entirely different than immediately surrounding areas—an array of wetland crops, edible fruit and nut trees and shrubs, berries, and roots—all growing near archaeological village sites today (Armstrong et al. 2021). Yet these species assemblages would not be considered as "belonging" within modern-day forest ecosystem categorizations. While the species themselves may be considered "native" in modern-ecological contexts (e.g., Pacific crabapple, *Malus fusca*; saskatoon berry, *Amelanchier alnifolia*; salmonberry, *Rubus spectabilis*; and wild rice root, *Fritillaria camschatcensis*), the densities and combinations with which they are found suggest that the perception of forest communities is much more fluid and complex within an Indigenous Ecology.

As we work to reclaim, revitalize, and adapt our Traditional land stewardship practices (e.g., controlled burning), I cannot help but reflect on the freedom this provides to manage species considered "native" to ensure the thriving of desirable species in a specific area. I have been stuck working in the nonnative/native species dichotomously guided modern ecology for government agencies, where we were limited in our ability to manage species considered "native" that were dominating an area. Government policies, funding parameters, and, in some cases, regulations, prohibited us from managing species that needed management. "Native" species have become almost untouchable, even when they need to be reduced for the benefit of other desirable relations. My dissertation (Grenz 2020) describes how colonial notions of naturalness are the cornerstone from which ecological management occurs. Notions that ignore our purposeful shaping of lands. Some ecosystems require that human relationship, through the management of those species that "belong," to even exist. Canopy closure of grasslands and Garry oak ecosystems are perfect examples of this. Having lost the ability to use cultural fire in some places, we need to be able to replace those stewardship practices with other actions and tools to meet our goals, tools that are often regulated or controlled in such a way that they cannot be applied for native species such as tree and shrub species like Douglas-fir and snowberry.

When I think about relational consideration of species within the context of purposefully shaping our lands and waters, I cannot help but reflect on the contents of my harvest basket of medicines from our farm and the forests that surround it. Most recently, it carried yarrow (*Achillea millefolium*), Oregon grape (*Mahonia aquifolium*) roots, elderberry (*Sambucus racemosa* subsp. *pubens*) flowers, devil's club (*Oplopanax horridus*), calendula (*Calendula officinalis*), St. John's wort (*Hypericum perforatum*), narrow-leaved plantain (*Plantago lanceolata*), and comfrey (*Symphytum officinale*). I look at the collection of plants and their different colors and traits and think about the approximate periods they arrived on the lands I live on today—lands of the Pentlach-speaking Peoples. I look at them arranged together, looking peaceful. They do not appear to be fighting or hurling labels at each other. I think about the healing they bring when brought together to make medicines. I think about how these relationships have made me shape the lands I care for every day to provide for my family, community, birds, bears, deer,

Figure 25.1. Harvesting with relational consideration. Plants considered native, nonnative, and invasive.

and insects. I wonder what makes my basket different than the baskets of those who shaped our lands to serve the needs of our communities in the past. Perhaps the relations within the basket were different, but perhaps not entirely. Time separates us and yet we are united in the relational values that drive the filling of our baskets. Relational consideration has been within our harvest baskets on multi-temporal scales: before, now, and forever into the future.

The Knowledge Keepers who have taught me about the plants that are good for us did not categorize them as "native" or "invasive." They told me their stories and about their offerings to us. They told me how to care for them. They warned me about the ones I needed to keep an eye on and the consequences that they could run away. They taught me that caring for and paying attention to these medicines was part of fulfilling our responsibility of reciprocity for the gifts they offered. There was no differentiation in the respect for one species over another. All were worthy, even those that required "management." Relational consideration is not something new, it is simply something that is part of Indigenous Ecologies (e.g., Traditional Ecological Knowledge). Relational consideration is simply pausing to sit with the plants and getting to know them.

What We Are Up Against

I wish it could be easy for all those engaged in ecological restoration work to sit with and get to know those relations we have othered. However, authors such as Russell and Blackburn (2017) demonstrate how difficult it is for researchers within the field to venture outside of mainstream thinking and depart from the scientific dogma of invasive alien species. Their extreme viewpoints, in which they seem to equate skepticism with science denialism, and place skeptics of certain aspects of invasion biology on par with climate change deniers, show what anyone with an opposing viewpoint may face. Susanna Lidstrom's (2017) response to the article sums up the need to bridge the gap in knowledge by avoiding the creation of a dichotomy between evidence and values, as this dichotomy undermines science. She is a rare advocate for making space in science for differing perspectives, as well as co-designing and coproducing research so that we can have meaningful dialogue about our modern approaches to invasive species. She acknowledges the role that values play in ecological science and confronts the denialism surrounding that by pushing for an inclusive version of science equipped to navigate an ecology that includes people (Lidstrom 2017). Unfortunately, this response represents a minority within the field.

THE RESPONSIBILITY OF RELATIONALLY PREFERRED SPECIES

We all have a responsibility to our lands, waters, and communities to leave behind the use of dichotomies that vilify species through categorization processes with roots in colonialism. This responsibility includes being brave as we push back against colonial notions that guide the management of our ecosystems. Too much is at stake as we face a rapidly changing climate and the degradation and, in some cases, complete losses of our Traditional food systems. While many important species have been historically present within certain ecosystems, we must remember the dynamic nature of our ancestors and the planet. The presence of "native species" should no longer be the gold standard for measuring the success of ecological restoration nor should this be the north star for ecological actions.

As we work toward the reclamation of purposeful shaping of species assemblages in specific contexts, there will be species that we do and do not want, and everything in between. There may also be new species arriving at our doorsteps. While we must be cautious about the dissemination, spread, and widespread establishment of species with dominant characteristics through careful and thorough research inclusive of Indigenous Knowledges (e.g., Traditional Ecological Knowledge), our assessments must consider species in terms of their contributions toward the desired balance of a particular system. We can do this by considering their relationships with other relations as opposed to assigning them generally applied positive or negative labels.

This reminds me of what I was taught once in a parenting course: we should never label a child as good or bad. Instead, we assign an attribute to the action or behavior they are exhibiting. For example, stating Billy's behavior was bad describes the nature of the relationship between Billy and his action. Billy is not inherently bad nor is he a bad child. Perhaps Billy just tends to behave in certain ways in certain contexts. We need to apply a similar approach when it comes to species evaluations. When we apply labels to certain relations, it is difficult to see them as anything else. It is that simple. If Himalayan blackberry is a "bad plant" and you find it in your yard, you are more likely to think, "I need to get rid of that bad plant." When we are considering the ecological balance of systems, we need to shift toward more nuanced thinking that looks to the realities of our collective futures. This is why Himalayan blackberry are living on my farm in distinct patches. While I used to have a zero-tolerance policy for invasive plants, I decided I needed to learn to live with those I have othered for too long. My family likes the taste of Himalayan blackberry, our chickens like it, and the bears like it, so we maintain it where we want it to be now. I am finally getting to know a plant that I have managed for almost two decades.

Dichotomies make ecological restoration easier. However, land-based Knowledges and connections to community are essential to informing land healing. Unfortunately, many settlers do not experience place as Indigenous Peoples do. This has led well-meaning settlers to utilize cookie-cutter approaches to an ecological restoration based on colonial notions of nature that lack a food systems lens. While settlers now turn to us for our Traditional Ecological Knowledges to inform their ecological research and work on the ground, it is up to us (Indigenous Peoples) to ensure that they understand that our Knowledges are not limited to the past. Our Knowledge systems focus on managing our lands and waters for the next generations. In a modern context, we are only inhibited from doing this by settler understanding, approaches, regulations, and policies. Colonized ecology holds us back.

Xenophobic approaches to the management of species may take away our ability to adapt in the wake of a changing climate. Specifically, these approaches threaten our food security and food sovereignty. If we are losing our food, what next? The conversations around changes in speciation focus largely on stopping that change. One runs the risk of being accused of giving up by even suggesting that some change, such as the loss of certain species and the arrival of others, may need to be accepted. But what about adaptability? Plants are among our greatest teachers when it comes to adaptability: a trait often associated with species labeled "invasive." Thinking about how we adapt our food systems to a changing climate is not simply giving up, it reclaims the foresight of our ancestors to be adaptable and to reclaim the skills of giving relational consideration to species we have not previously met. I will not accept my newfound reality of telling Elders I could not find the medicines or foods for which they have asked. I am instead committed to using relational consideration to help those species that are struggling while at the same time using relational consideration to find new species to meet the needs of our communities.

Despite the professional risk, I have made a wholehearted commitment to learning from those species we have previously othered. I will listen to their stories and learn about their relations. I will see how they may help the other species we have come to rely on for foods and medicines. For those that may not contribute to the desired plant communities, I will take a pause and learn from them, before taking action to manage them. Are they calling for help for those who cannot do it themselves? I will try to see why they are bringing our attention to this system. Is someone else calling for help? I will work to train myself to be open to the arrival of new medicines and foods. I will work to reclaim the skills of finding and learning to care for them. I will be open to the idea of a harvest basket whose contents may change alongside our story upon our Earth Mother. I will work to make sure that our harvest baskets are always full for future generations.

If we all make such commitments, how then will we describe our relations within an ecological system without dichotomy? It's simple. We start by giving up the dichotomy. If we are giving relational consideration to species to establish a desired balance, then we shall shift terminology to describe species as those that are *relationally preferred*. I have begun referring to relationally preferred species as *relpref*, for short. The term *relationally preferred species* or *relpref* shall be defined as

> Species that are identified through a process of relational consideration and that contribute to the desired ecological balance of relations for a particular area at a particular time to meet the determined values and needs of communities.

It is difficult to ignore the responsibility that comes with an ecological restoration that embraces giving relational consideration to all species regardless of their place of origin. This takes away the simplicity that came with colonial notions of belongingness and the systematic restoration that accompanies it: a simplicity that leaves out the important and difficult conversations about what land healing is, in any place, in any community; a simplicity that makes it easy to leave out the critical voices of those who have had relationships with lands and waters since time immemorial; a simplicity that avoids conflict; a simplicity that relies solely on the singular, dominant worldview; and a simplicity that is no longer acceptable, given the urgency of the impacts of a rapidly changing climate on the food systems of all relations. So let us sit as communities in a circle inclusive of all voices, including the voices of those we have othered for too long. Let us listen to their stories and teachings and take up the immense responsibilities of having difficult conversations, making difficult decisions, and giving relational consideration to ensure all are fed into the future.

Acknowledgments

The author would like to acknowledge the support of Cowichan Tribes, as well as Elders Luschiim (Dr. Arvid Charlie) and Mena and Peter Williams, and Knowledge Keeper Harold Joe, who spent time with me on the land, sharing their stories, Knowledge, and perspectives. This project was partially supported by the Social Sciences and Research Council of Canada.

26

PUBLIC LANDS, TRADITIONAL ECOLOGICAL KNOWLEDGE, AND THE NEED FOR VNOKECKV (LOVE)

LARA A. JACOBS

Positionality Statement

See Introduction for positionality statement.

VNOKECKV

Research methods are guided by the worldviews and standpoints that scientists bring to their work, which is especially important in Indigenous research methods (Walter and Andersen 2016). I begin this chapter with my positionality, background, and standpoint to provide readers with information about the sociocultural and academic locations that guide my work and the current chapter.

I'm a Citizen of Muscogee (Creek) Nation and have Choctaw and mixed heritages. I'm a recreation ecologist who studies the ecological and pathogenic (e.g., diseases caused from bacteria) impacts of outdoor recreation on Tribal Treaty lands that are managed in trust by federal entities. I write this chapter at the end of my PhD program at Oregon State University, where I have expanded my expertise in recreation ecology, cellular and molecular biology/environmental engineering, marine science, Traditional Ecological Knowledge, federal Indian law, and parks and protected area policies. In many of my scholarly publications, I challenge the paradox of federal public land management policies and practices versus Tribal sovereignty and Indigenous Peoples' rights. This chapter follows suit.

As an Indigenous scientist, I inherited responsibilities from my ancestors to ensure that my Peoples and other Indigenous Peoples' rights and futures are centered in my work. I bring these responsibilities to my work as a western-trained scientist when I analyze policy through an Indigenous justice lens to find pathways that better the realities and futures of Indigenous Peoples and the Indigenous lands and waters available for outdoor recreation activities. I honor these responsibilities in the following sections by using a critical Indigenous justice lens to provide an overview of how (1) parks and protected areas were established in the United States and the resulting harms to Indigenous Communities; (2) current Indigenous justice-based deficiencies embedded within a crucial public land management framework used by federal agencies to manage visitor use; (3) potential new harms established by the Biden administration's latest policies for the inclusion of Indigenous Knowledges in federal management processes and the subsequent disconnect between the Biden administration's desires and the possibilities of implementing these desires into visitor use management contexts. This chapter highlights how Tribes have gained some rights in public land management contexts while also being subjugated by a visitor use management framework that places Tribes in roles that often denigrate the power of their voices and sovereignty. I also analyze the disconnect between the intentions of the federal government to include Indigenous Knowledges into federal management while federal land agencies are managed under frameworks that do not allow for such inclusion. I underline the decolonial need to replace current managerial paradigms with co-equity and #LANDBACK management agreements between Tribal Nations and the federal government. I argue that co-equity management and #LANDBACK agreements can rectify the issues with visitor use management frameworks while protecting Indigenous Peoples' rights in managerial processes that require their Indigenous Knowledges. Co-equity management agreements may also work toward the first step of decolonial processes that lead to Indigenous Peoples' liberation from all forms of colonial control.

In the Introduction of this book, I worked with several Citizens of Muscogee (Creek) Nation to define the Indigenous value system of responsibility as VNOKECKV, which, in our language translates to love. Muscogee concepts of VNOKECKV include every responsibility we must maintain to all our relations. This carries over to our responsibilities to our ancestors, current Peoples, and the future generations of MVSKOKVLKE (Muscogee Peoples). It also includes responsibilities for the protection of land, water, and our more-than-human animal and plant relations. To be responsible for all these relations means that we must practice love and foreground Indigenous Peoples' care and stewardship of all of the aforementioned factors, at all points of our work, and in every function of our lived realities. In the final section of this chapter, I analyze how the value system of VNOKECKV can be put into practice through the creation of co-equity management frameworks in which Tribes and the federal government equally share power over public lands and in situations where land is returned to the sole managerial authority of Indigenous Peoples. This chapter provides another piece of evidence on top of previous calls for why the federal government should paradigmatically shift into co-equal management frameworks with Tribes (Fisk et al. 2021; Jacobs et al. 2022a,b).

INDIGENOUS PEOPLES HISTORIES AND DISPOSSESSIONS

Indigenous Peoples have stewarded lands and waters on Turtle Island since time immemorial (Jacobs et al. 2022a,b). However, as the United States was created and became an occupying entity on Indigenous lands, an onslaught of colonial violence followed suit, including the establishment of a nation founded on white supremacy, the enslavement of Black and Indigenous Peoples, forced removals of Indigenous Peoples from their ancestral territories, land theft and settler colonial occupancy of Indigenous Peoples' lands, and additional policies that resulted in the largest genocide in world history (Jacobs et al. 2022a,b; Dunbar-Ortiz 2014; Koch et al. 2019). These are not just problems from the past: Indigenous Peoples have faced harm through all points of the United States' timeline (see the Introduction for more information), including from federal policies that forced Indigenous children to attend genocidal boarding schools that enacted forms of epistemicide (the killing of our Knowledge systems) to address the "Indian problem" and to "kill the Indian, and save the man" (Pratt 2013). The resulting harms of the colonial maintenance of trauma for more than five hundred years continue to challenge Indigenous Peoples today, even in parks and protected area contexts. For example, America's "best idea," the National Park System (NPS), contains a history of harm to Indigenous Peoples in which the national parks were created as tools of dispossession that resulted in the forced removals and relocations of Indigenous Peoples and, often, the forbiddance of their hunting, gathering, and ceremonial practices (Spence 1999; Dunbar-Ortiz 2014). Many of these harms still exist today due to the existence of parks and protected areas that occupy Indigenous Peoples' lands and the colonial processes in place that maintain barriers to Indigenous Peoples' accessing our cultural sites and Traditional plants and animals. Current colonial policies also limit the ability for Indigenous Peoples' perspectives and Knowledges to lead park management decision-making processes that focus on our ancestral territories. All of this establishes a reality in which colonial forces, such as parks and protected areas, maintain systems of dispossession through exclusionary, anti-Indigenous, and barrier-filled policies. As the next section shows, even inclusion practices that bring Indigenous Peoples to the colonial table of power (typically as stakeholders) also prove problematic.

INCORPORATING INDIGENOUS PERSPECTIVES IN FEDERAL DECISION-MAKING PROCESSES

On a general level, incorporating Indigenous perspectives into federal decision-making processes has been conducted through required Tribal consultation processes. However, no uniform policy exists describing how the federal government must consult with Tribal Nations (Mengden 2017). The United States Constitution, particularly Article I, bestows on Congress the exclusive power to handle matters concerning Tribal Nations and numerous Treaties between Tribal Nations and the United States acknowledge a government-to-government relationship, characterized by formal and informal consultations as well as diplomatic endeavors (Miller 2015). Historical laws, spanning back to 1787, reveal a long history of consultation processes between Tribes and the federal government and how the intentions of such processes do not always meet the needs of or benefit Tribal Peoples.

The Northwest Ordinance (1787) pledged that the federal government would engage in negotiations with Indian Nations to secure their consent for the acquisition of Tribal lands, stating, "the utmost good faith shall always be observed towards Indians; their land and property shall never be taken from them without their consent." This ordinance was written before countless Indigenous Peoples were forcibly relocated from our homelands, without consent, to Indian Territory, by President Andrew Jackson's Indian Removal Act of 1830. The ordinance paved the way for the US government to secure land for increased settlement and thereby promote westward expansion into Indigenous Peoples' territories, causing conflict between Indigenous Peoples and new European settlers. It also ensured that Indigenous Peoples' claims to land could be extinguished through consultation processes that led to US land acquisitions. For example, the "just and lawful wars" clause of the ordinance was used by US officials to authorize and practice war against Indigenous Peoples, thus legalizing genocide against those who resisted US demands for land dispossession (Ostler 2016).

Similarly, the Allotment Act, or the Dawes Act (1887) mandated that Tribal consent and consultation be sought prior to the allotment and purchase of reservations by the United States (Miller 2015). However, this act created much harm and was created to civilize and assimilate Indigenous Peoples, offering them US citizenship in exchange for leaving their Tribes (Otis 2014). The act was intended to eventually open Indigenous Peoples' reservation lands to white settlers under the guise of creating opportunities for harmony between Indigenous Peoples and settlers (Edlefsen 2018). But, in reality, it was a land grab and a calculated move to destroy Tribal sovereignty and diminish Indigenous Peoples' rights to their Treaty lands. Though consultation processes occurred, the act was a scheme of land dispossession that subjected Indigenous communities to losses of land, displacement and forced assimilation, fragmented Tribal territories, and many other harms (Edlefsen 2018).

Over time, the federal government began negotiating with Tribes through agreements, executive orders, and statutes (Mengden 2017). However, the necessity for the federal government to negotiate quickly diminished, resulting in a weakened emphasis on consent and negotiation. This shift is evident in significant unilateral statutes, such as other Termination Era laws, which were enacted without seeking Tribal input and greatly affected Indigenous Peoples (Mengden 2017). Miller (2015) and Mengden (2017) provide an overview of additional historic consultation policies between the federal government and Tribal entities, but readers of their work should carefully analyze the amount of harm that Indigenous Peoples endured because of these policies.

The need for Tribal consultation has historically been vocally supported by US presidents. For example, in 1970, during the ongoing Native American Rights movement, which exerted pressure on the federal government to enhance the rights of Indigenous Peoples, President Nixon addressed Congress on Indian affairs. His speech emphasized the need for federal Indian policies to acknowledge and leverage the capabilities and wisdom of Indigenous communities, stating, "It is long past time that the Indian policies of the Federal government began to recognize and build upon the capacities and insights of the Indian [P]eople" (Nixon 1970). Nixon expressed the importance of departing from the past and ensuring that the futures of Indigenous Peoples were shaped by our actions and choices. He advocated for empowering Indigenous communities to make decisions that would impact our lives, stating, "The time has come to break decisively with the past and to create the conditions for a new era in which the Indian future is determined by Indian acts and Indian decisions" (Nixon 1970). As a result of Nixon's speech, the 1970s witnessed notable advancements in Indigenous Peoples' rights, including the establishment of the Bureau of Indian Affairs Tribal consultation procedures in 1972, the enactment of the Indian Self-Determination and Education Assistance Act (ISDA), which mandated consultation with Indian organizations by the secretaries of the interior and of health, education, and welfare during the formulation of ISDA regulations, and the 1978 congressional mandate for Tribes to be involved in educational program planning and development. These developments reflected a growing recognition of the importance of consulting with Tribes and involving them in federal decision-making processes (Miller 2015).

Indigenous Perspectives and Public Lands

This growing recognition also filtered into public lands. According to the 1988 NPS Management Policies (5:11), specific Native American communities were permitted by law to "pursue customary religious, subsistence, and other cultural uses of park resources" for which they had Traditional heritage (US Department of the Interior National Park Service 1988). The NPS issued a policy directive (Director's Order #28) in 1998 (NPS 1998) that recognized Native American rights to access and use NPS lands for Traditional purposes. However, NPS consultation policies do not always prioritize Tribal rights. Some Tribes signed Treaties with the US government that allowed their Peoples to hunt and gather Traditional foods in Usual and Accustomed Areas that, today, typically exist in parks and protected areas. However, many Tribes, especially those first removed, such as my Tribe (the Muscogee (Creek) Nation), did not have such specifications in their Treaties. Legal rights of Tribes to hunt and gather in parks and protected areas have historically been subject to the individual Tribe and the Treaties they signed. For Tribes like mine that do not have legally defined Usual and Accustomed Areas that provide our People with legal access to our ancestral territories, we often face cultural barriers when we attempt to access our homelands for subsistence and cultural purposes (Fisk et al. 2021; Jacobs et al. 2022a,b). Some of these barriers are purposefully put into place by federal land management entities such as NPS, which create policies that require Tribes to surrender sacred data (such as Traditional Ecological Knowledges (TEK; see the Introduction for a definition of TEK) and information related to the ceremonial uses and significance of plants and Traditional sites) before we are able to obtain permits to gather plants (NPS 2016; Jacobs et al. 2022a). These permit processes require Tribes to make cultural compromises, because if they want to gather plants and then decide to complete permit applications, then they subsequently must allow the federal government permission to inventory, monitor, and research information related to Indigenous communities' TEK (Jacobs et al. 2022a; NPS 2016). Such requirements lead to the extraction of Indigenous Knowledges and ideologically embody the extractive nature and dispossession embedded within settler colonialism (Jacobs et al. 2022a,b). These types of extractive policies were not created with Indigenous Peoples' perspectives, rights, or best interests in mind, and Tribes are not consulted on how these policies impact them and dispossess them of their rights.

Concerning Tribal consultation in parks and protected areas, Executive Order 13175 of November 2000 requires federal agencies, including the NPS, to meaningfully consult and coordinate with Tribal governments on policy decisions that may affect their Peoples (Executive Order 13175 2000). However, Section 10 of the order states that it was created to improve internal management of the executive branch but does not create "any right, benefit, or trust responsibility, substantive or procedural, enforceable at law" by any party against the United States (Section 10). This means that the order provides no cause of action that may hold federal entities liable for poor and inadequate consultation procedures using the court system and thereby creates power imbalances in which Tribes cannot seek legal remediation (Mengden 2017). In 1996, Executive Order 13007 was issued, directing federal agencies to accommodate access to and ceremonial uses of Indian sacred sites while avoiding any harm to the sites' physical integrity. The order also emphasized the importance of engaging in Tribal consultation processes. However, similar to Executive Order 13175, it did not establish enforceable rights for Tribal Nations (Mengden 2017). The order merely requires federal agencies to "listen" to Tribal insights, without providing enforcement mechanisms or guarantees that agencies must act based on those insights.

In 2006, the NPS incorporated the requirement for NPS staff to consult with Tribes into its management policies. Under these guidelines, NPS must consult with Tribes in situations specifically related to the planning and management of park resources, cultural and historic resources, and sacred sites. The Department of the Interior (DOI; which contains many, but not all of the federal agencies responsible for land management) also established Tribal consultation policies in 2009 and, more recently, in 2022 committed to strengthening Tribal consultation policies (US DOI 2009, 2022). The updated guidelines aim to enhance the department's consultation policy by promoting early engagement, interactive dialogue, pre-decisional involvement, and transparency. They also seek to establish models for seeking consensus, mandate training for federal staff, require documentation of consultation activities, and more (US DOI 2009, 2022).

Though these consultation processes seem promising, it is important to acknowledge how Tribal consultation processes have a history of denigrating Tribes as merely stakeholders (Jacobs et al. 2022a,b). Tribal participation in stakeholder and Tribal consultation processes does not mean that Tribes consent to the subsequent federal management practices that take place after consultation concludes (Jacobs et al. 2022a). Federal agencies do not hold any responsibilities to enact all Tribal concerns and feedback, which results in situations where consultation processes become no more than just sounding boards in which Tribes provide feedback that is not guaranteed to be integrated into parks and protected area's management actions (Jacobs et al. 2022a,b). The newest policies from the DOI (US DOI 2022), mentioned above, seem to understand the need for consensus, but research will be needed to understand how the new consensus models incorporate Tribal perspectives. Arguably, seeing Tribes as stakeholders presents a particular challenge in public lands that have high volumes of outdoor recreation visitation that may create disturbance in lands and waters used by Indigenous Peoples for subsistence and cultural purposes—lands that many Indigenous Peoples maintain VNOKECKV with and that require our continued concern, care, and protection. As history has shown, Tribal consultation processes do not always result in benefiting Tribal Nations, especially when colonial policies maintain laws that work against Indigenous Peoples' rights. This history continues today through the frameworks used for managing visitor use in parks and protected areas or public lands.

MANAGING VISITATION IN PUBLIC LANDS: THE INTERAGENCY VISITOR USE MANAGEMENT FRAMEWORK

Before discussing how frameworks for visitor use management in parks and protected areas can create issues for Indigenous Peoples, it is important to understand the defining characteristics of visitor use management and the current framework used by the federal government to manage for visitor use. Visitor use management is practiced in parks and protected areas to ensure that managerial strategies and approaches optimize visitor experiences and safety and minimize environmental disturbance. Many federal land and water management agencies oversee visitor use and access to public lands, including the Bureau of Land Management, Forest Service, National Oceanic and Atmospheric Administration, National Park Service, US Army Corps of Engineers, and US Fish and Wildlife Service. Representatives from these federal entities serve on the Interagency Visitor Use Management Council with the support of technical advisers from additional agencies such as the US Geologic Survey and the US Department of the Interior (IVUMC 2019b). The council's purpose is multifaceted but includes a focus on developing interagency guidance for effective visitor use management (IVUMC 2019b). There are no Tribal Nations on this council, and the council does not state whether their processes include Tribal consultation. The council does not have any power over federal agencies and makes best-practice suggestions for federal entities to follow. The council created the Interagency Visitor Use Management Framework (IVUMF; figure 1), which provides an analytical process that US land and water managers can put into practice when making visitor use management decisions and, when necessary, supports their efforts in establishing visitor capacity regulations (IVUMC 2019b).

The IVUMF helps visitor use managers assess the effectiveness of park management actions in achieving and maintaining desired conditions by understanding the status and trend of conditions for selected indicators and providing information about how conditions compare with established thresholds (IVUMC 2019a,b). "Indicators are specific resources or experiential attributes that can be measured to track changes in conditions so that progress toward achieving and maintaining desired conditions can be assessed" (IVUMC 2019b, 25). Indicators can be established for social, ecological, or managerial conditions and should correlate directly with desired conditions. Indicators should make the desired condition descriptions translatable into measurable characteristics that can be tracked over time and used for evaluating changes in conditions. Thresholds describe the minimally acceptable conditions that are associated with specific indicators. Thresholds support managers in determining acceptable levels of change for specific indicators by establishing a point at which visitor effects on desired conditions may create enough concern for management actions to be implemented to maintain desired conditions (IVUMC 2019b). Thresholds

Table 26.1. Summary of the IVUMF's elements, steps, and outcomes (IVUMC 2019b). Note that VUM stands for "visitor use management."

Elements	Steps	Outcomes
Build the foundation	1. Clarify project purpose and needs 2. Review the area's purpose, legislation, policies, and other management directions. 3. Assess and summarize existing information and current conditions. 4. Develop a project action plan.	Understand why project is needed. Develop project approach.
Define the visitor use management direction	5. Define desired conditions. 6. Define appropriate visitor activities, facilities, and services. 7. Select indicators and thresholds.	Describe conditions to be achieved and maintained and how conditions will be tracked over time.
Identify management strategies	8. Compare/document differences between existing and desired conditions, and, for visitor-use-related impacts, clarify specific links to visitor use characteristics. 9. Identity visitor use management strategies and actions to achieve desired conditions. 10. Where necessary, identify visitor capacities and strategies to manage use levels within capacities. 11. Develop a monitoring strategy.	Identify strategies to manage visitor use to achieve or maintain desired conditions.
Implement, monitor, evaluate, and adjust	12. Implement management actions. 13. Conduct/document ongoing monitoring and evaluate the effectiveness of management actions in achieving desired conditions. 14. Adjust management actions, if needed, to achieve desired conditions, and document rationale.	Implement management strategies and actions and adjust based on monitoring and evaluation.

represent minimally acceptable conditions (not impaired conditions) but remain distinct from desired conditions, which park managers strive to achieve and maintain before conditions reach thresholds (IVUMC 2019b).

The IVUMF offers opportunities for collaborative development, implementation, and monitoring of management strategies and actions with the main objectives being to connect visitors with public lands and waters and provide quality visitation experiences while protecting cultural and natural resources (IVUMC 2019b; the IVUMF consists of four core elements: (1) Build Foundation; (2) Define Visitor Use Management Direction; (3) Identify Management Strategies; and (4) Implement, Monitor, and Evaluate) that require multiple steps that lead to specific outcomes (table 26.1 shows the general expected outcomes for each element and associated steps). Generally, the Building Foundation element provides information about the park's purpose and why it exists, to understand the need for the project and to develop a project approach. Such information is typically found in a park and protected area's planning documents (such as general management plans, trail plans, etc.) or other policies (such as the Wilderness Act) and legislation used to create the park or protected area.

The second element, Define Visitor Use Management Direction, builds on the first by clarifying the desired conditions and objectives for park areas and how such conditions will be assessed over time. Desired conditions may be defined in legislation used to establish parks and protected areas, parkwide planning documents, or other policies, but often, parks need to develop or update desired conditions as part of the planning process. Some park planning documents outline desired outcomes and indicators for each park area in terms of what resource conditions, visitor experiences and opportunities, facilities, and services the park will strive to achieve and maintain. But, similar to desired conditions, parks often need to develop or refine these in the planning process for specific visitor use scenarios, issues, and areas of analyses (geographic areas, specific features, or destination points that are the focus of the planning process).

The third element, Identify Management Strategies, continues to build off the first two elements by identifying how management strategies can achieve or maintain the previously defined desired conditions. The fourth element includes continuous implementation, monitoring of selected indicators, evaluation, and adjustments, which feed back into the overall framework through an iterative process by connecting back to the first element.

Monitoring is a process through which observations are made, or data is routinely and systematically gathered to assess resource conditions and visitor experience statuses (IVUMC 2019b). Monitoring requires three components: (1) the selection of indicators and the establishment of thresholds or objectives, and triggers; (2) routine and systematic observations or data collection of indicators over time; and (3) documentation and analysis of observations or data that relate to thresholds, triggers, or objectives (IVUMC 2019b). Managers select appropriate indicators and establish thresholds to achieve previously defined desired conditions and sustain data collection and observation processes about the indicators (IVUMC 2019b).

Before indicators are selected, managers must review the existing directions of the park; analyze the area's purpose, management direction, and project issues; and assess existing monitoring information (IVUMC 2019b). The process of selecting indicators occurs during element three of the IVUMF and includes identifying potential indicator topics (e.g., reviewing issues associated with the area of analysis and developing issue statements or monitoring questions), brainstorming and refining ideas for potential indicators, screening selected indicators, determining the appropriate unit of measurement, and testing indicators (IVUMC 2019b). Typically, indicators should be selected through the consultation and collaboration of an interdisciplinary team that includes the public and stakeholders (IVUMC 2019b).

Each element is influenced by law, policies, public involvement, and a sliding scale. The sliding scale uses issue complexity, impact risk, stakeholder involvement, and level of controversy as criteria to ensure that investments in time and resources for park projects align with the complexity and consequences of decisions (small impacts require lesser steps compared to larger impacts). The IVUMF provides an opportunity for parks and protected areas and various stakeholders, such as Tribes, to align their distinct perspectives into management priorities and define indicators, thresholds, and monitoring strategies.

PROBLEMS WITH THE IVUMF

Multiple issues for Tribes exist within the current IVUMF. The IVUMF provides situations in which Tribes may be included with other stakeholders to inform the management actions, indicators, thresholds, and desired conditions for a project. However, it does not center or allow Tribal values and Tribal feedback to lead these processes, which disregards Tribal sovereignty and Indigenous Peoples relations, responsibilities, and histories. Instead, the IVUMF allows for the culmination of perspectives from a large group of stakeholders (nonprofits, corporations, other governing entities, etc.) who may hold distinct values, perspectives, and priorities that inform the creation of indicators, thresholds, desired conditions, and management decisions. This is important because stakeholder perspectives are centered in the IVUMF, and their associated values and perspectives can be brought into the actual decision-making processes around how recreation will be managed. The IVUMF does not weigh or situate Tribal sovereignty as a heavy influence but works instead under the presumption that stakeholder knowledges and values may be commensurable (able to be measured on the same scale and combined) across groups and that commonalities may exist between stakeholders.

The IVUMF ignores the fact that Indigenous Peoples' rights, Knowledges, and values, which inform their perspectives, may not be commensurable to others, nor should they be measured on the same scales or combined with other communities' feedback. For example, nonprofit organizations focused on outdoor recreation and corporate entities might place higher importance on land use practices (such as off-road vehicles, including all-terrain vehicles) that have the potential to damage vegetation and areas with significant historical and cultural significance to Indigenous Peoples. In such a scenario, stakeholder feedback that informs the creation of desired conditions, thresholds, and indicators may ignore or downgrade Indigenous Peoples' concerns when a majority of other stakeholders have distinct perspectives geared toward maximizing use and not prioritizing specific species or sites on a culturally significant level. Some stakeholders may also exert disproportionate levels of influence during the park planning processes (Rose et al. 2022), which may create scenarios in which Indigenous Peoples' voices are therefore not incorporated.

The IVUMF reinforces colonial control over assessing which stakeholder perspectives are incorporated into managerial processes and which ones are not because, generally, Tribes hold no or little power beyond their Treaty rights in parks and protected areas. I consider the IVUMF's stakeholder policies for Tribes and most federal Tribal consultation policies as tools of colonialism that enact what Tuck and Yang (2012) refer to as "settler moves to innocence." Settler moves to innocence include practices (or in this case, policies) that relieve settler guilt and responsibility (to make sure Tribes have a seat at the colonial stakeholder table but have little power) without ever having to rectify issues such as land dispossession, colonial oppressions, and white supremacy (Tuck and Yang 2012).

The fact remains that non-Indigenous stakeholders will never have the same "stake" in Indigenous lands as Indigenous Peoples do, so using the same frameworks, such as the IVUMF, to solicit feedback from all stakeholders and Tribal Nations only serves colonial agendas to diminish the rights of Indigenous Peoples and to maintain land dispossessions. The larger stake exists because Indigenous Peoples sustainably managed our ancestral territories for tens of thousands of years before the United States was ever established. Our stakes involve our histories, values, Knowledges, and cultural Traditions, which include our responsibilities to land and our more-than-human kin (such as plants and animals) that exist in our ancestral territories. Our Knowledges and responsibilities to our lands have been discarded by our colonizers and not considered as valid ways of Knowing or reasonable responsibilities since the inception of the US government. Therefore, they are not used often to inform land and recreational management.

Though some researchers discuss social justice and equity as guiding factors for the IVUMF (Rose et al. 2022), I argue that any topic related to Indigenous lands and Tribal sovereignty cannot have an equity focus because equity is a colonial tool that reinforces settler rights to Indigenous lands. Instead, we need to move beyond equity conversations and instead choose to uphold an ethic of Indigenous justice. We need to advocate for Tribal sovereignty to be leading the management and discussions that take place around Tribal ancestral territories. Tribes can do this by bolstering an ethic of incommensurability (Tuck and Yang 2012) in any instance where their Knowledges, rights, and values are measured and assessed by colonial systems and in situations where the federal government seeks their feedback through stakeholder processes that do not prioritize Indigenous Peoples' feedback over other stakeholders (such as the IVUMF). An ethic of incommensurability implies an understanding of how competing values and perspectives cannot be reduced to a commonality or be compared on similar scales. It also requires the prioritization of Indigenous values, perspectives, and rights. Tuck and Yang (2012) state that such an ethic recognizes what is distinct and what is sovereign, especially in projects that relate to human and civil rights issues. Tribal Nations are sovereign entities, and any participation they have with federal agencies should be considered as government-to-government discourse between sovereign entities. According to the United Nations Declaration on the Rights of Indigenous Peoples, land dispossessions are a human and civil rights issue (UN General Assembly 2007), and Indigenous social justice requires activism directed at giving Indigenous Peoples the rights to live in and manage their ancestral territories. An ethic of incommensurability can be used by Tribes to ensure that their Knowledges, values, and perspectives are not folded into the mix of others (such as nonprofits and settlers) who do not have similar stakes and responsibilities to Indigenous lands. It can also be used to protest the

IVUMF, especially by recognizing the need for new frameworks to be created that address Tribal sovereignty, which would force parks and protected areas to move Tribal entities out of stakeholder positions and be treated rightfully as sovereign governments with the largest stake in lands compared to settler stakeholders. Recognizing Tribal sovereignty means that parks and protected areas would need to have pathways for the incorporation of Indigenous leadership into managerial frameworks.

However, the IVUMF does not currently have any pathway for Indigenous leadership to be incorporated in any of the steps or elements. This is because "the master's tools will never dismantle the master's house" (Lorde 2003, 2). Colonial governments will never create tools for colonized Peoples to gain power and control, especially over things that were taken from them, like land. Doing so disrupts the very structure of colonialism, which relies on policies and laws as the infrastructure that maintain colonial rule. Although the IVUMF may include Tribes as stakeholders during steps for multiple framework elements, there is little room, if any, for how Indigenous Knowledges, especially TEK, can be incorporated into managerial processes in non-extractive ways. This is because the IVUMF was created by federal entities that have historically operated under western epistemologies (ways of knowing) and western scientific norms and work in ways that maintain colonial power by excluding Indigenous Peoples' rights to occupy and solely manage our ancestral territories. The IVUMF typically relies on western science, especially the western field of ecology, for understanding levels of disturbance that inform the creation of desired conditions, indicators, and thresholds. However, western science is not always commensurable to Indigenous forms of science such as TEK, and therefore limits the ways in which TEK can inform stakeholder feedback processes for the creation of desired conditions, indicators, and thresholds that inform management actions and decision-making. Even in situations where TEK may be integrated into the IVUMF planning processes, parks and protected area managers are not equipped with the cultural Knowledges, beliefs, and practice systems to facilitate TEK-based management, nor should they attempt to do so. TEK is not a checklist of items that can be facilitated for management, and should be seen as a cultural responsibility of only Indigenous Peoples who have thousands of years of histories *living* their sciences through Tradition, ceremony, and genealogical processes that cannot be learned outside of our communities.

The IVUMF was not constructed in consultation with Tribes, and within the framework, Tribal Nations are still considered as merely stakeholders instead of as sovereign Nations that have a larger stake in land and visitor use management outcomes. Tribal Knowledges cannot be inputted into the IVUMF in ways that honor Tribal sovereignty and the responsibilities and cultural processes that are essential components to TEK. Therefore, similar to many Tribal consultation processes, the IVUMF remains deficient at meeting the needs of Tribal Nations and should be considered only as a colonial tool that limits Tribal rights, sovereignty, and the incorporation of Indigenous perspectives, values, and Knowledges. This is not unusual or unexpected because the federal government is a colonial entity that only exists because of the forced removals and dispossessions of Indigenous Peoples from their homelands. Federal land and water management entities act as colonial agents that maintain Indigenous Peoples' land dispossessions by enforcing policies (such as Tribal consultation and frameworks like the IVUMF that force Tribes into stakeholder positions) that maintain colonial rule and downgrade Tribal powers and our vested "stakes" in our homelands. These issues prove further problematic with recent developments by the federal government that instruct federal entities to incorporate Indigenous Peoples' TEK into management practices, especially when the current managerial frameworks, such as the IVUMF, have no pathway for this to occur.

TRADITIONAL ECOLOGICAL KNOWLEDGE AND FEDERAL AGENCIES

In 2021, the White House Office of Science and Technology Policy (OSTP) and the Council on Environmental Quality (CEQ) issued a memorandum that recognized Indigenous Knowledges as one of many important epistemologies that contribute to scientific, technical, and social advancements, as well as to the collective understanding of the environment (Lander and Mallory 2021). The memo also committed to advancing the relationship between the federal government and Tribal Nations to (1) advance equity for Indigenous Peoples; (2) ensure that federal agencies conduct regular and meaningful consultation processes with Tribes in the context of federal research, policies, and decision-making; and (3) develop a government-wide process for federal agencies on TEK in which TEK informs federal decision-making (Lander and Mallory 2021).

Over the following year, OSTP and CEQ convened an Interagency Working Group and sought feedback from Tribal Nations and Indigenous Peoples through Tribal Consultation and listening sessions and engaged with more than a thousand individuals and many Tribal Nations (Prabhakar and Mallory 2022a,b). I participated in one of the listening sessions as an attendee who provided critical feedback about the need for Tribal comanagement of parks and protected areas to protect Indigenous data sovereignty (the right of Tribal Nations and Indigenous communities to govern the collection, ownership, interpretation, and application of data about their Peoples; Carrol et al. 2021) of Indigenous Nations. In spring of 2022, I worked with OSTP and CEQ to moderate and facilitate a White House Listening Session at the 2022 National Traditional Ecological Summit, hosted by the Traditional Ecological Knowledge Club at Oregon State University (OSU TEKC 2022). During both sessions, I listened to the concerns of other Indigenous Peoples and understood that the aforementioned historic harms of the United States were central to the discussion. With over a year of feedback from Indigenous Peoples, in 2022, OSTP and CEQ published a memorandum and a guidance document for federal departments and agencies on Indigenous Knowledges (Prabhakar and Mallory 2022a,b). The memo and guidance documents underline the Biden-Harris administration's commitment to creating a new era of nation-to-nation engagement with Tribes and advancing equity and opportunity for Tribal Nations and Indigenous Peoples. They also provide guidance to support federal agencies in how to include Indigenous Knowledges in research, policy, and other decision-making processes (such as the IVUMF, which informs park planning for visitor use management).

In the forty-six-page "Guidance for Federal Departments and Agencies on Indigenous Knowledge" (Prabhakar and Mallory 2022b), OSTP and CEQ provide information for federal agencies on how they can begin incorporating Indigenous Knowledges (IK) such as TEK into the practical application of their work. The memo provides (1) an overview of IK; (2) a listing of federal statutes for which IK may be relevant (e.g., Endangered Species Act, National Environmental Policy Act, Marine Mammal Protection Act, Magnuson-Stevens Fishery Conservation Act, National Historic Preservation Act, Native American Graves and Preservation Act); (3) guidance on growing and maintaining relationships to support IK (including a focus on acknowledging historical context and past injustices; the need for early and sustained engagement; earning and maintaining trust; respecting different processes and worldviews; recognizing challenges; considering comanagement and co-stewardship structures and possibilities; and pursuing co-production of Knowledge); (4) applying IK (including promising practices to apply when considering IK in federal processes and opportunities to include IK in federal contexts). The appendices of the memo provide examples of IK applications and collaborations between federal agencies, Tribes, and Indigenous Peoples; select federal agency guidance documents on IK; provide an example approach to IK as source materials in highly influential scientific assessments under the Information Quality Act; list federal departments and agencies who contributed to the Working Group of IK; and provide additional references and resources for promising practices to apply when considering IK in federal processes.

A quick overview of the memo looks promising and underlines the Biden administration's commitment to moving into a new and more collaborative era with Tribal Nations in which IK are finally centered and included as valid sciences that inform federal policy and management practices. At the surface level, this is a strong contrast to the long history of discrimination Indigenous Peoples have experienced for generations in which western scientists refused to value, appreciate, or consider IK/TEK as valid forms of science. This progress is exceptional and, as other Indigenous scientists have pointed out, the climate catastrophe necessitates the re-centering of IK in environmental management scientific contexts (Hernandez et al. 2022). On a surface level, these new guidelines also look promising for how parks and protected areas can start centering Tribal leadership and TEK into management processes, such as the IVUMF.

However, the guidance documents also create a situation in which Indigenous data sovereignty may not be guaranteed. The memo establishes a situation in which Tribal collaboration (in which federal agencies collect or harvest TEK-based data from Tribes for federal application) in federal processes and the resulting sharing of information/data could potentially be released to the public under the Federal Release of Information Act (FOIA). The memo also establishes a need for interagency information sharing in which data that Tribes are sharing with one federal agency may also be shared with and transmitted to other federal agencies. However, such transmission processes may obscure Tribal involvement with and oversight of the data, which are crucial elements of Indigenous data sovereignty. An additional issue exists in terms of federal funding. When Tribes accept federal funding for any project that contains their sacred data, then they may be subject to federal mandates to make all data collected with federal dollars public and available (Marcum and Donohue 2022). Both of these issues pose many challenges to Indigenous data sovereignty and provide little incentive for Tribes to work collaboratively with federal agencies. Though the memo implies that the new processes will provide many benefits to Tribal Nations and communities, I have yet to find one specific benefit listed in the text. Instead, the document makes me pause and consider numerous important issues.

The memo works under the impression that once TEK data have been gathered by the colonial government that federal management entities will be able to apply TEK. This is especially ridiculous and concerning because TEK is not just a set of Knowledges that can be learned by reading and analyzing Tribal interviews, or by understanding the specific processes that lead to the implementation of our TEK-based practices. As the introduction to this book describes, TEK is a Knowledge-belief-practice system that incorporates much more than just ways of Knowing. It incorporates Indigenous value systems, spiritual belief systems, and ways of being that remain distinct from settler and colonial worldviews. TEK is not something that can just be learned through data collection and analyses, it is a *living science* that is embodied by Indigenous Peoples, who remain the only ones who can facilitate the sacred practices of *doing the science*. Additionally, the memo establishes a process wherein colonial agents may harvest TEK information from Tribal communities and thereby continue the long history of dispossessing Indigenous Peoples from everything we hold sacred. What benefits for Indigenous Peoples can possibly exist from such harvesting processes, especially when these processes are not centered on rectifying the historic and existing power imbalances through which colonial entities are the sole managers of Indigenous lands and waters? Similar to other colonial policies, I see the memo as only another settler move to innocence that refuses to rectify colonial legacies of harm and works ultimately under the guise of "inclusion." Similar to equity, inclusion practices are not geared toward the liberation of Indigenous Peoples, and are created to make colonial structures seem more diverse by the incorporation of non-settlers into colonial systems.

Furthermore, because parks and protected areas implement specific frameworks, such as the IVUMF, that do not create pathways for the incorporation of Indigenous leadership, perspectives, and TEK, I remain perplexed as to how they are supposed to incorporate this recent federal guidance into visitor use management practices. This seems like a classic example of putting the cart before the horse, in which the federal government created policies that do not match the current managerial frameworks (such as the IVUMF) of its colonial agents (such as federal land and water management entities). It seems further problematic that the Biden administration's recent push for the incorporation of TEK into federal management practices reinforces the need for Indigenous leadership through comanagerial approaches when frameworks like the IVUMF have no pathway for that to be incorporated and facilitated. How can parks and protected areas shift the IVUMF to match the Biden administration's directions? I argue that it might not be possible, and that instead, we need to replace the IVUMF with new solutions that are developed by and under the managerial responsibilities of Tribal entities.

Rectifying the Issues: Building VNOKECKV through Tribal Comanagement

Reflecting on Indigenous value systems, we must create policies that honor VNOKECKV and the associated responsibilities that Indigenous communities carry. However, current policies (such as the IVUMF, Tribal consultation approaches, and the Biden administration's recent guidance documents) and management paradigms do not allow for VNOKECKV to be realized because they continue to perpetuate systems of dispossession and Indigenous erasure that force Indigenous Peoples into positions with no power and minimal legal rights to honor their responsibilities. Yet, better and more effective approaches are available for addressing the many challenges discussed in this chapter. Such approaches do not rely on appropriating and exploiting Indigenous Knowledges or merely including Tribal Nations and communities as stakeholders in consultation processes pertaining to land, water, and visitor use management. Instead, they manifest through opportunities to move beyond inclusion politics into action-oriented frameworks that support decolonization efforts, help actualize the #LANDBACK movement (a social and political movement that recognizes the need for Indigenous Peoples to occupy and manage our ancestral territories), and strengthen Indigenous land governance and sovereignty (Fisk et al. 2021). To honor VNOKECKV, we need paradigm shifts and policies that work toward decolonial objectives—shifts that incorporate the liberation of Indigenous Peoples from the confines we've been bound to by the colonial state for centuries.

We need policies driven by managerial paradigm shifts that replace the sole colonial powers that exist in land, water, and recreation management contexts with shared, co-equal management paradigms in which Tribal Nations and communities are elevated to the same positions of power as federal management entities (Fisk et al. 2021; Jacobs et al. 2022a,b). If specific Tribal Nations are in positions with high capacity, then they may not need to share managerial powers with federal entities. In such circumstances, then Indigenous ancestral lands should be solely managed by the Indigenous sovereign Nation or community (Fisk et al. 2021; Jacobs et al. 2022a,b).

Furthermore, co-equity management and #LANDBACK paradigmatic shifts can help rectify the issues with the IVUMF and the Biden administration's new policies by creating new frameworks, developed by Indigenous Peoples that center their perspectives, values, and Knowledges in all points of the process. This would easily rectify the issues that Tribes face with consultation and stakeholder processes, and further ensure that IK are guided into management practices in non-extractive and non-exploitable manners. Instead of centering settler values and those of other stakeholders, Indigenous Nations can create novel visitor management frameworks guided by their perceptions of desired outcomes, thresholds, and indicators, or more culturally relevant management practices and concerns. This is especially important for Indigenous Peoples' sacred sites and Traditional animals and plants that are located within so-called public lands because no other stakeholder groups hold the same VNOKECKV, responsibilities, and cultural and historical ties to these elements. Indigenous management would inherently recognize that settler stakes are not commensurable to Indigenous Peoples' VNOKECKV and associated responsibilities and therefore should not be weighted at the same scales.

In shared managerial systems, Indigenous Peoples may choose to focus on specific areas, lands, and plants that have specific cultural significance, whereas the federal government may determine that other stakeholder perspectives could apply to park planning processes in areas without such Tribal significance. However, scenarios may also take place in which Tribal Nations have their perspectives centered in all areas of a park and protected area and other stakeholder interests may therefore be secondary. In areas that are solely managed under Tribal sovereignty, all decision-making processes will be subjective to the Indigenous Nation (Fisk et al. 2021).

With that said, it is important to recognize that there is not a one-size-fits-all solution that can guide the creation of policies in developing comanagerial or #LANDBACK opportunities. This is because Tribal Nations and communities are distinct and have different capacities, interests, values, responsibilities, and priorities for management. Therefore, these new paradigms will require a high level of subjectivism between Tribal Nations and Indigenous communities that should be navigated by Tribal leadership and interests that are elevated and centered in both comanagerial roles and #LANDBACK scenarios. Ultimately, the future of comanagement and #LANDBACK require Indigenous leadership and the prioritization of Tribal sovereignty, Indigenous values, IK, and VNOKECKV. Creating such realities would help rectify the many issues we have seen historically and contemporarily with Tribal consultation, stakeholder processes, visitor use management frameworks (such as the IVUMF), and federal government policies that intend to extract and dispossess Indigenous Peoples' from their sacred data in ways that will not benefit them (such as the Biden administration's TEK policies).

Conclusion

This chapter provides an Indigenous justice–based reflection on the existing issues with federal consultation and stakeholder processes, the IVUMF, and the Biden administration's new TEK guidance. I emphasize a significant need for paradigm shifts pertaining to land, water, and visitor use management to honor Indigenous values, Knowledges, and sovereignty. These shifts are necessary because the current policies we have in place (consultation, stakeholders, IVUMF, and TEK guidance) maintain colonial control and ultimately establish a disconnect between what is wanted by the federal government and what is possible through current visitor use management frameworks. Tribal consultation has presented many issues to Indigenous Peoples through time as have stakeholder processes. This is exemplified in the IVUMF's failures to center Tribal values, rights, and feedback, and its blatant disregard for Tribal sovereignty. The IVUMF perpetuates colonial control over decision-making processes about Indigenous lands and offers minimal, if any, ways to incorporate Indigenous leadership and Indigenous Knowledges into planning processes. Such frameworks add to the pervasive lack of recognition of Indigenous Peoples' responsibilities as the original stewards of all public lands. While recent federal guidance documents from the Biden administration acknowledge the importance of

IK and TEK, they also present challenges to Indigenous data sovereignty and are ultimately difficult, if not impossible, to infuse into the current IVUMF. To rectify these many issues, this chapter emphasizes a need to shift policies and management paradigms into realities that promote co-equal management and the #LANDBACK movement, thus elevating Tribal Nations to positions of power and ensuring that Tribal perspectives fully inform the desired conditions, indicators, and thresholds needed for visitor use management in parks and protected areas, without interference from stakeholders. Tribal sovereignty, Indigenous leadership, and the need for subjectivism are necessary components of developing comanagerial and #LANDBACK approaches. By centering the concept of VNOKECKV and honoring Indigenous Peoples' inherent responsibilities, we can create parks and protected area futures that are guided by Indigenous management, while rectifying some of the harms that Indigenous Peoples have experienced for more than five hundred years in this country.

REFERENCES

COMPILED BY ZENA GREENAWALD

Positionality Statement
Confederated Tribes of Siletz Indians Tribal member; descendant of Chinook, Euchre Creek, Kalapuya, Umpqua, Wasco bands, and Filipino ancestry.

Abatzoglou, John T., and A. Park Williams. 2016. "Impact of Anthropogenic Climate Change on Wildfire across Western US Forests." *Proceedings of the National Academy of Sciences* 113 (42): 11770–11775.

Abbott, Isabella Aiona. 1978. "The Uses of Seaweed as Food in Hawaii." *Economic Botany* 32 (4): 409–412.

Abbott, Isabella Aiona, and Eleanor Horswill Williamson. 1974. *Limu: An Ethnobotanical Study of Some Edible Hawaiian Seaweeds.* Kalāheo, Kauaʻi: Pacific Tropical Botanical Garden. https://georgehbalazs.com/wp-content/uploads/2019/04/1974-LIMU-EDIBLE-HAWAIIAN-SEAWEEDS.pdf.

Abril-de-Abreu, Rodrigo, José Cruz, and Rui F. Oliveira. 2015. "Social Eavesdropping in Zebrafish: Tuning of Attention to Social Interactions." *Scientific Reports* 5 (1): 1–14.

Absolon, Kathleen E. 2022. *Kaandossiwin: How We Come to Know: Indigenous Re-search Methodologies.* Nova Scotia: Fernwood.

Adams, Melinda M. 2023. "Storytelling through Fire: The Socio-Ecological and Cultural Reclamation of Indigenous Cultural Fire in Northern California." PhD diss., University of California Davis. escholarship.org/uc/item/4083f1gs.

Adams, Melinda, Pam Gonzales, Diana Almendariz, and Beth Rose Middleton. 2024 (under review). "Rematriating Fire: Practices and Protocols of Native Women Reclaiming Cultural Fire in California." In *LandKeeping: Restoring Indigenous Fire Stewardship and Ecological Partnerships in North America*, edited by J. Aldern and T. L. Gregor. Corvallis: Oregon State University Press.

Adhikari, Shalu, and Amir Poudel. 2022. "Indigenous Knowledge for Wetland Conservation and Resource Utilization: A Case Study of Ramsar Sites, Nepal." Nepal. May 8. https://papers.ssrn.com/sol3/papers.cfm?abstract_id=4103596.

Ahia, Māhealani. 2020. "Mālama Mauna: An Ethics of Care Culture and Kuleana." *Biography* 43 (3): 607–612.

Aikau, Hōkūlani K. 2019. "From Malihini to Hoaʻāina: Reconnecting People, Places, and Practices." In *The Past Before Us: Moʻokūʻauhau as Methodology*, edited by Nālani Wilson-Hokowhitu, 81–91. Honolulu: University of Hawaiʻi Press.

Aikau, Hōkūlani K., Noelani Goodyear-Kaʻōpua, and Noenoe K. Silva. 2016. "The Practice of Kuleana: Reflections on Critical Indigenous Studies through Trans-Indigenous Exchange." In *Critical Indigenous Studies: Engagements in First World Locations,* edited by Aileen Moreton-Robinson, 157–175. Tucson: University of Arizona Press.

Akaka, Moanikeʻala, Maxine Kahaulelio, Terrilee Kekoʻolani-Raymond, and Loretta Ritte. 2018. *Nā wāhine koa: Hawaiian Women for Sovereignty and Demilitarization.* Honolulu: University of Hawaiʻi Press.

Aken, Genevieve L. 2018. "Pōʻaiapuni O Kaʻaihonua: Using Voices of the Past to Inform the Present and Future." PhD diss. University of Hawaiʻi at Mānoa. https://scholarspace.manoa.hawaii.edu/items/403f7834-c599-4e68-acd3-c96c8197ca64/full.

Akutagawa, Malia, Lahela Han, Emillia Noordhoek, and Harmonee Williams. 2012. "Molokaʻi Agriculture Needs Assessment, A Molokai-pedia Project of Sustʻāinable Molokai." Molokai-pedia. https://doi.org/10.13140/rg.2.2.21407.41124.

Aldern, Jared Dahl, and Ron W. Goode. 2014. "The Stories Hold Water: Learning and Burning in North Fork Mono Homelands." *Decolonization: Indigeneity, Education and Society* 3 (3).

Alegado, Rosie. 2019. "Opponents of the Thirty Meter Telescope Fight the Process, Not Science." *Nature* 572 (7767): 7–8.

Alexander, Michelle. 2020 [2010]. *The New Jim Crow: Mass Incarceration in the Age of Colorblindness.* New York: The New Press.

Alizadeh, B., and J. Hitchmough. 2019. "A Review of Urban Landscape Adaptation to the Challenge of Climate Change." *International Journal of Climate Change Strategies and Management* 11 (2): 178–194. https://doi.org/10.1108/IJCCSM-10-2017-0179.

Althaus, Catherine. 2022. "Complementary Bureaucracy: Reimagining Weberian Impersonalism with Indigenous Relationality." *Perspectives on Public Management and Governance* 5 (2): 135–150.

Alves, André Azevedo, and Jose Moreira. 2009. *The Salamanca School.* New York: Bloomsbury.

Ames, K. 2013. "Complex Hunter-Gatherers." In *Encyclopedia of Global Archaeology,* edited by C. Smith. New York: Springer Science+Business.

Anae, Melani. 2016. "Teu le va: A Samoan Relational Ethic." *Knowledge Cultures* 4:117–130.

Anaya, S. James. 2009. *International Human Rights and Indigenous Peoples.* Boston, MA: Aspen Publishing.

Anderson-Fung, Puanani, and Kepā Maly. 2002. *Hawaiian Ecosystems and Culture: Why Growing Plants for Lei Helps to Preserve Hawaii's Natural and Cultural Heritage.* Honolulu: University of Hawaiʻi Press.

Andrade, Carlos. 2013. "A Hawaiian Geography or a Geography of Hawai'i?" In *I Ulu I Ka 'Āina: Land*, edited by Jonathan Osorio, 4–22. Honolulu: University of Hawai'i Press.

Andrade, Pelika, and Kanoe Morishige. 2022. "Huli 'ia: Every Place Has a Story . . . Let's Listen." *Parks Stewardship Forum* 38 (2).

Andrade, Pelika, Kanoe Morishige, Anthony Mau, Lauren Kapono, and Erik C. Franklin. 2022. "Re-imagining Contemporary Conservation to Support 'Āina Momona: Productive and Thriving Communities of People, Place, and Natural Resources." *Parks Stewardship Forum* 38 (2).

Andrasik, Michele P., Alika K. Maunakea, Linda Oseso, Carlos E. Rodriguez-Diaz, Stephaun Wallace, Karina Walters, and Michi Yukawa. 2022. "Awakening." *Infectious Disease Clinics of North America* 36 (2): 295–308. https://doi.org/10.1016/j. idc.2022.01.009.

Andrews, Kehinde. 2021. *The New Age of Empire: How Racism and Colonialism Still Rule the World*. London: Penguin UK.

Anghie, Antony. 1996. "Francisco de Vitoria and the Colonial Origins of International Law." *Social and Legal Studies* 5 (3): 321–336.

Applebaum, Barbara. 2017. "Comforting Discomfort as Complicity: White Fragility and the Pursuit of Invulnerability." *Hypatia* 32 (4): 862–875.

Applegate, Jesse. 1914. *Recollections of My Boyhood*. Roseburg, OR: Press of Review Publishing.

Archibald, Jo-ann. 2008. *Indigenous Storywork: Educating the Heart, Mind, Body and Spirit*. Vancouver: University of British Columbia Press.

Archibald, Jo-ann, J. B. J. Lee-Morgan, and J. de Santaolo, eds. 2019. *Decolonizing Research: Indigenous Storywork as Methodology*. London: ZED Books.

Archibald, Jo-ann, Jenny Lee-Morgan, and Jason de Santolo, eds. 2022. *Decolonizing Research: Indigenous Storywork as Methodology*. London: Bloomsbury Academic.

Archibald, Jo-ann (Q'um Q'um Xiiem), Shelly Johnson (Mukzva Musayett), Corrina Sparrow, and Andrea Lyall (Tlalillogwa). 2019. "Awakening the Spirit: Indigenous Culture and Language Revitalization through Land, Water, and Sky." *Canadian Journal of Native Education* 41 (1). https://ojs.library.ubc.ca/index.php/CJNE/article/view/196611.

Arieli, Yehoshua. 2001. "On the Necessary and Sufficient Conditions for the Emergence of the Doctrine of the Dignity of Man and His Rights." In *The Concept of Human Dignity in Human Rights Discourse*, edited by David Kretzmer and Eckart Klein, 1–17. New York: Kluwer Law International.

Armstrong, C. G., J. Earnshaw, and A. C. McAlvay. 2022. "Coupled Archaeological and Ecological Analyses Reveal Ancient Cultivation and Land Use in Nuchatlaht (Nuu-chah-nulth) Territories, Pacific Northwest." *Journal of Archaeological Science* 143. https://doi.org/10.1016/j.jas.2022.105611.

Armstrong, Chelsey Geralda, Jesse E. D. Miller, Alex C. McAlvay, Patrick Morgan Ritchie, and Dana Lepofsky. 2021. "Historical Indigenous Land-Use Explains Plant Functional Trait Diversity." *Ecology and Society* 26 (2): 6.

Arnott, James C., and Maria Carmen Lemos. 2021. "Understanding Knowledge Use for Sustainability." *Environmental Science and Policy* 120:222–230.

Arnott, James C., Rachel J. Neuenfeldt, and Maria Carmen Lemos. 2020. "Co-producing Science for Sustainability: Can Funding Change Knowledge Use?" *Global Environmental Change* 60:101979.

Arora, R. K., Sanjeev Sharma, and B. P. Singh. 2014. "Late Blight Disease of Potato and Its Management." *Potato Journal* 41 (1): 16–40.

Around Him, Deanna, Temana Andalcio Aguilar, Anita Frederick, Heather Larsen, Michaela Seiber, and Jyoti Angal. 2019. "Tribal IRBs: A Framework for Understanding Research Oversight in American Indian and Alaska Native Communities." *American Indian and Alaska Native Mental Health Research* 26 (2): 71–95.

Arvin, Maile, Eve Tuck, and Angie Morrill. 2013. "Decolonizing Feminism: Challenging Connections between Settler Colonialism and Heteropatriarchy." *Feminist Formations* 25 (1): 8–34.

Asase, Alex, Tiwonge I. Mzumara-Gawa, Jesse O. Owino, Andrew T. Peterson, and Erin Saupe. 2021. "Replacing 'Parachute Science' with 'Global Science' in Ecology and Conservation Biology." *Conservation Science and Practice* 4 (5): e517.

Ashcroft, Richard E. 2005. "Making Sense of Dignity." *Journal of Medical Ethics* 31 (11): 679–682.

Asiyanbi, Adeniyi P. 2016. "A Political Ecology of REDD+: Property Rights, Militarised Protectionism, and Carbonised Exclusion in Cross River." *Geoforum* 77:146–156.

Ayers, Adam L., and John N. Kittinger. 2014. "Emergence of Co-management Governance for Hawai'i Coral Reef Fisheries." *Global Environmental Change* 28:251–262.

Ayers, Adam L., John N. Kittinger, and Mehana Blaich Vaughan. 2018. "Whose Right to Manage? Distribution of Property Rights Affects Equity and Power Dynamics in Comanagement." *Ecology and Society* 23 (2).

Bahnke, Melanie, Vivian Korthuis, Amos Philemonoff, and Mellisa Johnson. 2020. "Navigating the New Arctic Comment Letter." https://kawerak.org/download/navigating-the-new-arctic-program-comment-letter/.

Bahnke, Melanie, Vivian Korthuis, Amos Philemonoff, and Mellisa Johnson. 2021. "NNA Follow Up Letter." https://kawerak.org/download/dec-2021-nna-follow-up-letter/.

Baldy, Cutcha Risling. 2018. *We Are Dancing for You: Native Feminisms and Revitalization of Women's Coming-of-Age Ceremonies.* Seattle: University of Washington Press.

Balles, A. 2022. "Federal and Tribal Leaders Formalize Agreement for Cooperative Management of Bears Ears National Monument." June 30. Bureau of Land Management. https://www.blm.gov/blog/2022-06-30/federal-and-tribal-leaders-formalize-agreement-cooperative-management-bears-ears.

Bangladesh Decision. 2017. Supreme Court of Bangladesh, "Turag Given 'Legal Person Status' Information." January 30. https://www.dhakatribune.com/bangladesh/court/2019/01/30/turag-given-legal-person-status-to-save-it-from-encroachmentandearthlawcentre.org.

Bannister, Kelly. 2020. "Right Relationships: Legal and Ethical Context for Indigenous Peoples' Land Rights and Responsibilities." In *Plants, People and Places*, edited by Nancy Turner, 254–268. Montreal: McGill-Queen's University Press. doi:10.1515/9780228003175-022.

Barker, Joann. 2017. *Critically Sovereign Indigenous Gender, Sexuality, and Feminist Studies*. Durham, NC: Duke University Press.

Barley, Shanta C., Mark G. Meekan, and Jessica J. Meeuwig. 2017. "Species Diversity, Abundance, Biomass, Size and Trophic Structure of Fish on Coral Reefs in Relation to Shark Abundance." *Marine Ecology Progress Series* 565:163–179.

Barney, Jacob N., Daniel R. Tekiela, Eugene S. J. Dollete, and Bradley J. Tomasek. 2013. "What Is the "Real" Impact of Invasive Plant Species?" *Frontiers in Ecology and the Environment* 11 (6): 322–329.

Barnhardt, Ray, and Angayuqaq Oscar Kawagley. 2005. "Indigenous Knowledge Systems and Alaska Native Ways of Knowing." *Anthropology and Education Quarterly* 36 (1): 8–23.

Bartlett, Cheryl, Murdena Marshall, and Albert Marshall. 2012. "Two-Eyed Seeing and Other Lessons Learned within a Co-Learning Journey of Bringing Together Indigenous and Mainstream Knowledges and Ways of Knowing." *Journal of Environmental Studies and Sciences* 2:331–340.

Battiste, Marie. 2002. *Indigenous Knowledge and Pedagogy in First Nations Education: A Literature Review with Recommendations*. Ottawa: National Working Group on Education.

Battiste, Marie. 2005. "Indigenous Knowledge: Foundations for First Nations." *WINHEC: International Journal of Indigenous Education Scholarship* 1:1–17.

Battiste, Marie, and James Youngblood Sa'ke'j Henderson. 2000. *Protecting Indigenous Knowledge and Heritage: A Global Challenge*. Vancouver: University of British Columbia Press.

Beamer, Kamanamaikalani. 2014. *No Mākou ka Mana: Liberating the Nation*. Honolulu: Kamehameha Publishing.

Beamer, Kamanamaikalani, Axel Tuma, Andrea Thorenz, Sandra Boldoczki, Keli'iahonui Kotubetey, Kanekoa Kukea-Shultz, and Kawena Elkington. 2021. "Reflections on Sustainability Concepts: Aloha ʻĀina and the Circular Economy." *Sustainability* 13 (5): 2984.

Bears Ears Inter-Tribal Coalition. nd. "Bears Ears Inter-Tribal Coalition: A Collaborative Land Management Plan for the Bears Ears National Monument." Accessed August 25, 2022. https://www.bearsearscoalition.org/beitc-land-management-plan.

Beckwith, Martha Warren. 1917. "Hawaiian Shark Aumakua." *American Anthropologist* 19 (4): 503–517.

Beckwith, Martha Warren, ed. 1972. *The Kumulipo: A Hawaiian Creation Chant*. Honolulu: University of Hawaii Press.

Bennett, Nathan J., Laure Katz, Whitney Yadao-Evans, Gabby N. Ahmadia, Scott Atkinson, Natalie C. Ban, Neil M. Dawson, et al. 2021. "Advancing Social Equity in and through Marine Conservation." *Frontiers in Marine Science* 8:711538.

Berkes, Fikret. 2012. *Sacred Ecology*. 3rd ed. New York: Routledge.

Berkes, Fikret. 2017. *Sacred Ecology*. Oxfordshire, UK: Routledge.

Berkes, Fikret. 2018. *Sacred Ecology*. 4th ed. Oxfordshire, UK: Routledge. http://ebookcentral.proquest.com/lib/ualberta/detail.action?docID=5015644.

Berry, T. 1999. *The Great Work: Our Way into the Future*. New York: Bell Tower/Random House.

Berry, T. 2011. *The Great Work: Our Way into the Future*. New York: Crown.

Beyleveld, Deryck, and Roger Brownsword. 1998. "Human Dignity, Human Rights, and Human Genetics." *Modern Law Review* 61:661.

Bharadwaj, Lalita. 2014. "A Framework for Building Research Partnerships with First Nations Communities." *Environmental Health Insights* 8:EHI-S10869.

Biden, Joe. 2021. "Proclamation on Bears Ears National Monument." October 8. https://www.whitehouse.gov/briefing-room/presidential-actions/2021/10/08/a-proclamation-on-bears-ears-national-monument/.

Bielawski, Ellen. 2020. "Inuit Indigenous Knowledge and Science in the Arctic." In *Human Ecology and Climate Change*, edited by David Peterson and Darryll Johnson, 219–227. London: Taylor and Francis.

Bineshiikwe, Oshoshko—Blue Thunderbird Woman, Osawa Aki Ikwe (Florence Paynter); Zoongi Gabowi Ozawa Kinew Ikwe—Strong Standing Golden Eagle Woman (Mary Maytwayashing); Nii Gaani Aki Inini—Leading Earth Man (Dave Courchene); Giizih-Inini—(Dr. Harry Bone); Zhonga-giizhing—Strong Day (Wally Swain); Naawakomigowiinin (Dennis White Bird); Kamintowe Pemohtet—Spirit Walker (D'Arcy Linklater); Mah Pe Ya Mini (Henry Skywater). 2015. "Ogichi Tibakonigaywin, Kihche'othasowewin, Tako Wakan: The Great Binding Law." Turtle Lodge. http://www.turtlelodge.org/2015/12/the-great-binding-law-statement-of-manitoba-elders.

Birhane, Abeba, and Olivia Guest. 2020. "Towards Decolonising Computational Sciences." *arXiv* preprint arXiv:2009.14258.

Borràs, Susana. 2016. "New Transitions from Human Rights to the Environment to the Rights of Nature." *Transnational Environmental Law* 5 (1): 113–143.

Bowles, Samuel, Jung-Kyoo Choi, and Astrid Hopfensitz. 2003. "The Co-evolution of Individual Behaviors and Social Institutions." *Journal of Theoretical Biology* 223 (2): 135–147.

Boyd, Philip W., Lennart T. Bach, Catriona L. Hurd, Ellie Paine, John A. Raven, and Veronica Tamsitt. 2022. "Potential Negative Effects of Ocean Afforestation on Offshore Ecosystems." *Nature Ecology and Evolution* 6 (6): 675–683.

Boyd, Robert. 1999. *The Coming of the Spirit of Pestilence: Introduced Infectious Diseases and Population Decline among Northwest Coast Indians, 1774–1874*. Seattle: University of Washington Press.

Boyd, Robert. 2021. *Indians, Fire and the Land in the Pacific Northwest*. 2nd ed. Corvallis: Oregon State University Press.

Bradstock, Andrew, and Christopher Rowland, eds. 2008. *Radical Christian Writings: A Reader*. Hoboken, NJ: John Wiley & Sons.

Brady, Laura M., Stephanie A. Fryberg, and Yuichi Shoda. 2018. "Expanding the Interpretive Power of Psychological Science by Attending to Culture." *Proceedings of the National Academy of Sciences* 115 (45): 11406–11413.

Brant, Jennifer. 2022. "Recalling the Spirit and Intent of Indigenous Literatures." In *Troubling Truth and Reconciliation in Canadian Education: Critical Perspectives*, edited by Sandra D. Styres and Arlo Kempf, 223. Edmonton: University of Alberta Press.

Bratman, Eve Z., and William P. DeLince. 2022. "Dismantling White Supremacy in Environmental Studies and Sciences: An Argument for Anti-Racist and Decolonizing Pedagogies." *Journal of Environmental Studies and Sciences* 12 (2): 193–203.

Bremer, Scott, and Simon Meisch. 2017. "Co-production in Climate Change Research: Reviewing Different Perspectives." *Wiley Interdisciplinary Reviews: Climate Change* 8 (6): e482.

Briggs, J. 2017. "Rise in Invasive Species Denialism? A Response to Russell and Blackburn." *Trends in Ecology and Evolution*. 32 (4): 231–232.

Brockie, Teresa N., Kyle Hill, Patricia M. Davidson, Ellie Decker, Lydia Koh Krienke, Katie E. Nelson, Natalie Nicholson, Alicia M. Werk, Deborah Wilson, and Deana Around Him. 2022. "Strategies for Culturally Safe Research with Native American Communities: An Integrative Review." *Contemporary Nurse* 58 (1): 8–32.

Brown, James H., and Dov F. Sax. 2004. "An Essay on Some Topics Concerning Invasive Species." *Austral Ecology* 29 (5): 530–536.

Brown, Leslie Allison, and Susan Strega. 2015. *Research as Resistance, 2e: Revisiting Critical, Indigenous, and Anti-Oppressive Approaches*. Toronto: Canadian Scholars' Press.

Bucher, Taina. 2013. "Objects of Intense Feeling: The Case of the Twitter API." *Computational Culture* 3.

Bullard, Robert D. 2018 [1990]. *Dumping in Dixie: Race, Class, and Environmental Quality*. Repr. New York: Routledge.

Burdon, P. D. 2012. "Environmental Protection and the Limits of Rights Talk." University of Adelaide School of Law. https://papers.ssrn.com/sol3/papers.cfm?abstract_id=2175967.

Burkhart, Brian. 2019. *Indigenizing Philosophy through the Land: A Trickster Methodology for Decolonizing Environmental Ethics and Indigenous Futures*. East Lansing: Michigan State University Press.

Cajete, Gregory. 2000. *Native Science: Natural Laws of Interdependence*. Santa Fe, NM: Clear Light.

Cajete, Gregory. 2004. "Philosophy of Native Science." In *American Indian Thought: Philosophical Essays*, edited by Anne Waters, 45–57. Malden, MA: Blackwell.

Cajete, Gregory. 2018. "Native Science and Sustaining Indigenous Communities." In *Traditional Ecological Knowledge: Learning from Indigenous Practices for Environmental Sustainability*, edited by Melissa K. Nelson and Dan Shilling, 15–26. Cambridge, UK: Cambridge University Press.

Cajete, Gregory A. 2020. "Indigenous Science, Climate Change, and Indigenous Community Building: A Framework of Foundational Perspectives for Indigenous Community Resilience and Revitalization." *Sustainability* 12 (22): 9569.

Cal Fire. 2018. 2018 Incident Archive. California Department of Forestry and Fire Protection (Cal Fire). https://www.fire.ca.gov/incidents/2018/. Accessed May 18, 2021.

Calzadilla, P. V., and L. J. Kotzé. 2018. "Living in Harmony with Nature? A Critical Appraisal of the Rights of Mother Earth in Bolivia." *Transnational Environmental Law* 7 (3): 397–424.

Cameron, Emilie S. 2012. "Securing Indigenous Politics: A Critique of the Vulnerability and Adaptation Approach to the Human Dimensions of Climate Change in the Canadian Arctic." *Global Environmental Change* 22 (1): 103–114.

Cancik, H. 2002. "'Dignity of Man' and 'Persona' in Stoic Anthropology. Some Remarks on Cicero, De Officiis I 105–107." In *The Concept of Human Dignity in Human Rights Discourse*, edited by David Kretzmer and Eckart Klein, 19–39. New York: Kluwer Law International.

Cane, S. 2002. *Pila Nuguru: The Spinifex People*. Fremantle: Fremantle Arts Center Press.

Carlson, Andrew Kalani. 2024. "AlterNatives to Blue Carbon Coloniality: An ʻŌiwi Perspective on Redirecting Funding to Indigenous Stewardship." In *Confronting Climate Coloniality*, edited by Farhana Sultana, 121–136. New York: Routledge. https://doi.org/10.4324/9781003465973-10

Carlson, Andrew Kalani, Takeshi Yoshimura, and Isao Kudo. 2024. "Kelp Dissolved Organic Carbon Release Is Seasonal and Annually Enhanced during Senescence." *Journal of Phycology* 60 (4): 980–1000. https://doi.org/10.1111/jpy.13483

Carpenter, R. E., K. P. Maruska, L. Becker, and R. D. Fernald. 2014. "Social Opportunity Rapidly Regulates Expression of CRF and CRF Receptors in the Brain during Social Ascent of a Teleost Fish, Astatotilapia burtoni." *PLOS One* 9 (5): e96632.

Carro-Figueroa, Vivian. 2002. "Agricultural Decline and Food Import Dependency in Puerto Rico: A Historical Perspective on the Outcomes of Postwar Farm and Food Policies." *Caribbean Studies* 30 (2): 77–107.

Carroll, Stephanie Russo, Desi Rodriguez-Lonebear, and Andrew Martinez. 2019. "Indigenous Data Governance: Strategies from United States Native Nations." *Data Science Journal* 18.

Carroll, Stephanie Russo, Ibrahim Garba, Oscar L. Figueroa-Rodríguez, Jarita Holbrook, Raymond Lovett, Simeon Materechera, Mark Parsons, et al. 2020. "The CARE Principles for Indigenous Data Governance." *Data Science Journal* 19 (43): 1–12.

Carroll, Stephanie Russo, Edit Herczog, Maui Hudson, Keith Russell, and Shelley Stall. 2021. "Operationalizing the CARE and FAIR Principles for Indigenous Data Futures." *Scientific Data* 8 (108).

Carroll, Stephanie Russo, Rebecca Plevel, Lydia L. Jennings, Ibrahim Garba, Rogena Sterling, Felina M. Cordova-Marks, Vanessa Hiratsuka, Maui Hudson, and Nanibaaʼ Garrison. 2022. "Extending the CARE Principles from Tribal Research Policies to Benefit Sharing in Genomic Research." *Frontiers in Genetics* 13:3152.

Carter, Nancy, Denise Bryant-Lukosius, Alba DiCenso, Jennifer Blythe, and Alan J. Neville. 2014. "The Use of Triangulation in Qualitative Research." *Oncology Nursing Forum* 41 (5): 545–547. doi:10.1188/14.ONF.545-547.

Cashmore, M., R. Gwilliam, R. Morgan, D. Cobb, and A. Bond. 2004. "The Interminable Issue of Effectiveness: Substantive Purposes, Outcomes and Research Challenges in the Advancement of Environmental Impact Assessment Theory." *Impact Assessment and Project Appraisal* 22 (4): 295–310.

Castellano, Marlene Brant. 2000. "Updating Aboriginal Traditions of Knowledge." In *Indigenous Knowledges in Global Contexts: Multiple Readings of Our World*, edited by George J. Sefa Dei, Dorothy Goldin Rosenberg, and Budd L. Hall, 21–36. Toronto: University of Toronto Press.

Caulfield, T., and A. Chapman. 2005. "Human Dignity as a Criterion for Science Policy." *PLOS Medicine* 2:736–738.

Cell Editorial Team. 2020. "Science Has a Racism Problem." *Cell* 181:1443–1444.

Chacón, Gloria Elizabeth. nd. "Zapotec Literature." *Oxford Research Encyclopedia of Literature*. https://oxfordre.com/literature.

Chah, Jane Mbolle, Esdras A. R. Obossou, Eromose E. Ebhuoma, Ifeoma Q. Anugwa, and Divine Ewane. 2022. "Enhancing Climate Change Adaptation through Indigenous Knowledge Systems and Local Governance in Sub-Saharan Africa: A Systematic Review." In *Indigenous Knowledge and Climate Governance: A Sub-Saharan African Perspective*, edited by Eromose E. Ebhuoma and Llewellyn Leonard, 165–179. Cham: Springer Nature.

Chait, Melanie. 1999. "Healing Hawai'i: The Recovery of an Island Identity." PhD diss., University of Oxford.

Chajon, A. 2022. "Transformaciones punitivas o voluntarias: personajes convertidos en piedra." *El Pez y la Flecha. Revista de Investigaciones Literarias Universidad Vericruzana* (uv.mx). https://elpezylaflecha.uv.mx/index.php/elpezylaflecha/article/view/121.

Chambers, Josephine M., Carina Wyborn, Melanie E. Ryan, Robin S. Reid, Maraja Riechers, Anca Serban, Nathan J. Bennett, et al. 2021. "Six Modes of Co-Production for Sustainability." *Nature Sustainability* 4 (11): 983–996.

Chambers, Lori A., Randy Jackson, Catherine Worthington, Ciann L. Wilson, Wangari Tharao, Nicole R. Greenspan, Renee Masching, et al. 2018. "Decolonizing Scoping Review Methodologies for Literature with, for, and by Indigenous Peoples and the African Diaspora: Dialoguing with the Tensions." *Qualitative Health Research* 28 (2): 175–188.

Chandler, David, and Julian Reid. 2020. "Becoming Indigenous: The 'Speculative Turn' in Anthropology and the (re) Colonisation of Indigeneity." *Postcolonial Studies* 23 (4): 485–504.

Chang, David A. 2019. "Where Is Hawai'i? Hawaiian Diaspora and Kuleana." In *Detours: A Decolonial Guide to Hawai'i*, edited by Hōkūlani K. Aikau and Vernadette Vicuña Gonzalez, 352–361. Durham, NC: Duke University Press.

Chaudhury, Aadita, and Sheila Colla. 2021. "Next Steps in Dismantling Discrimination: Lessons from Ecology and Conservation Science." *Conservation Letters* 14 (2): e12774.

Cheveau, Marianne, Louis Imbeau, Pierre Drapeau, and Louis Bélanger. 2008. "Current Status and Future Directions of Traditional Ecological Knowledge in Forest Management: A Review." *Forestry Chronicle* 84 (2): 231–243.

Chew, M. K. 2006. "Ending with Elton: Preludes to Invasion Biology." PhD diss., Arizona State University.

Chochinov, H. M., T. Hack, T. Hassard, L. J. Kristjanson and S. McClement. 2004. "Dignity and Psychotherapeutic Considerations in End-of-Life Care." *Journal of Palliative Care* 20:134–142.

Christensen, Julia, Christopher Cox, and Lisa Szabo-Jones, eds. 2018. *Activating the Heart: Storytelling, Knowledge Sharing, and Relationship.* Waterloo, CAN: Wilfrid Laurier University Press.

Chua, Ryan Yumin, Amudha Kadirvelu, Shajahan Yasin, Fahad Riaz Choudhry, and Miriam Sang-Ah Park. 2019. "The Cultural, Family and Community Factors for Resilience in Southeast Asian Indigenous Communities: A Systematic Review." *Journal of Community Psychology* 47 (7): 1750–1771.

Chuipka, Jason. 2022. "Bears Ears Inter-Tribal Coalition: A Collaborative Land Management Plan for the Bears Ears National Monument." July 5. Cortez, CO: Woods Canyon Archaeological Consultants. https://www.bearsearscoalition.org/wp-content/uploads/2022/08/FINAL_BENM_LMP_08252022.pdf.

Cintrón, Ralph, Casey Corcoran, and David Bleeden. 2021. "Thinking with/Not with Theories of Decolonization." *College English* 84 (1): 138–158.

Clancey, J., O. Saulters, and M. Shirley. 2019. "Leveraging Brownfields to Build Tribal Resilience." National Brownfields Conference, August 19–22, Palm Springs, California.

Clarkson, Linda, Vern Morrissette, and Gabriel Régallet. 1992. *Our Responsibility to the Seventh Generation: Indigenous Peoples and Sustainable Development.* Winnipeg: International Institute for Sustainable Development.

Claw, Katrina G., Matthew Z. Anderson, Rene L. Begay, Krystal S. Tsosie, Keolu Fox, and Nanibaa' Garrison. 2018. "A Framework for Enhancing Ethical Genomic Research with Indigenous Communities." *Nature Communications* 9 (1): 2957.

Cobb, John N. 1905. *The Commercial Fisheries of the Hawaiian Islands in 1903.* US Bureau of Fisheries. Doc. No. 590. Washington, DC: USGPO.

Cohen, F. 1941. *Handbook of Federal Indian Law.* Buffalo, NY: William S. Hein.

Cole, Douglas. 1995. *Captured Heritage: The Scramble for Northwest Coast Artifacts.* Vancouver: University of British Columbia Press.

Collins, Cary C. 2000. "The Broken Crucible of Assimilation: Forest Grove Indian School and the Origins of Off-Reservation Boarding-School Education in the West." *Oregon Historical Quarterly* 101 (4): 466–507.

Colón-Emeric, Edgardo A. 2017. "Microphones of Christ: Lessons from the Pulpit of Oscar Romero." *Homiletic* 42 (2).

Condra, Alli. 2011. "Balancing the Scales: Food 'Sovereignty' and Food Safety." *Food Safety News*, December 19. https://www.foodsafetynews.com/2011/12/balancing-the-scales-food-sovereignty-and-food-safety/.

Cordova, V. F. 2007. *How It Is: The Native American Philosophy of VF Cordova.* Tucson: University of Arizona Press.

Cordova, Viola Faye, Kathleen Dean Moore, Kurt Peters, Theodore S. Jojola, and Amber Corning. 2000. "Biological Adaptation in Human Societies: A 'Basic Needs' Approach." *Journal of Bioeconomics* 2:41–86.

Corning, P. A. 2000. "Biological Adaptation in Human Societies: A 'Basic Needs' Approach." *Journal of Bioeconomics* 2:41–86.

Corning, P. A. 2003. "The Basic Problem Is Still Survival, and an Evolutionary Ethics Is Indispensable." Paper presented to the Complexity, Ethics and Creativity Conference, September 17–18, London School of Economics.

Corntassel, Jeff. 2012. "Re-envisioning Resurgence: Indigenous Pathways to Decolonization and Sustainable Self-Determination." *Decolonization: Indigeneity, Education & Society* 1 (1): 85–101.

Costales, Mikayla. 2020. "Decolonizing Theory and Praxis: Principles for Collaboration between Native American Communities and Government Run Recreation." PhD diss., University of Colorado at Boulder.

Cote-Meek, Sheila, and Taima Moeke-Pickering, eds. 2020. *Decolonizing and Indigenizing Education in Canada.* Toronto: Canadian Scholars' Press.

Couldry, Nick, and Ulises A. Mejias. 2019. *The Cost of Connection: How Data Is Colonizing Human Life and Appropriating It for Capitalism,* Stanford, CA: Stanford University Press.

Crees, Jennifer J., and Samuel T. Turvey. 2015. "What Constitutes a 'Native' Species? Insights from the Quaternary Faunal Record." *Biological Conservation* 186:143–148.

CTKW (Climate and Traditional Knowledges Workgroup). 2014. *Guidelines for Considering Traditional Knowledges in Climate Change Initiatives.* Department of Interior Advisory Committee on Climate Change and Natural Resource Science. http://dx.doi.org/10.2139/ssrn.2555299.

Cullinan, C. 2003. *Wild Law: A Manifesto for Earth Justice.* Newark, NJ: Green Books.

da Costa Marques, Ivan. 2022. "Anthropophagy, European Enlightenment, Science and Technology Studies, and Responsible Knowledge Construction in Brazil." *Social Studies of Science* 52 (6): 812–828.

Daes, Erica. 1993. "Study on the Protection of the Cultural and Intellectual Property Rights of Indigenous Peoples." Paper presented at the Sub-Commission on Prevention of Discrimination and Protection of Minorities, Commission on Human Rights, United Nations Economic and Social Council, February 28.

Dalton, Rex. 2002. "Tribe Blasts 'Exploitation' of Blood Samples." *Nature* 420 (6912): 111–112.

Daly, E. 2012. "The Ecuadorian Exemplar: The First Ever Vindications of Constitutional Rights of Nature." *Review of European, Comparative, and International Environmental Law* 21:63.

Daly, Meaghan, and Lisa Dilling. 2019. "The Politics of 'Usable' Knowledge: Examining the Development of Climate Services in Tanzania." *Climatic Change* 157 (1): 61–80.

Damasio, A. 1999. *The Feeling of What Happens: Body and Emotion in the Making of Consciousness.* San Diego, CA: Harcourt.

David-Chavez, D. M., S. Valdez, J. Estevez, C. Meléndez Martínez, A. A. Garcia Jr., K. Josephs, and A. Troncoso. 2020. "Community-Based (Rooted) Research for Regeneration: Understanding Benefits, Barriers and Resources for Indigenous

Education and Research." *AlterNative: An International Journal of Indigenous Peoples* 16 (3). https://doi.org/10.1177/1177180120952896.

David-Chavez, Dominique, and Michael C. Gavin. 2018. "A Global Assessment of Indigenous Community Engagement in Climate Research." *Environmental Research Letters* 13 (12).

Davidson, Lesley, Jonathan James Fisk, Mia Iwane, Alohi L. Nakachi, and Kalani Quiocho. 2018. "Loko Solutions: Policy Analysis for Carbon Sequestration Potential of Aquaculture in Hawaiʻi." Prepared for State of Hawaiʻi Greenhouse Gas Sequestration Task Force. Project Final. University of Hawaiʻi at Mānoa.

Davies, Sarah W., Hollie M. Putnam, Tracy Ainsworth, Julia K. Baum, Colleen B. Bove, Sarah C. Crosby, Isabelle M. Côté, et al. 2021. "Promoting Inclusive Metrics of Success and Impact to Dismantle a Discriminatory Reward System in Science." *PLOS Biology* 19 (6): e3001282.

Davis, M. 2009. *Invasion Biology*. New York: Oxford University Press.

Davis, M. 2011. "Don't Judge Species on Their Origins." *Nature* 474:153–154.

Davis, Megan. 2016. "Data and the United Nations Declaration on the Rights of Indigenous Peoples." In *Indigenous Data Sovereignty: Toward an Agenda*, edited by Tahu Kuktai and John Taylor, 25–38. Canberra: Australian National University Press.

Dawson, Neil M., Brendan Coolsaet, Eleanor J. Sterling, Robin Loveridge, Nicole D. Gross-Camp, Supin Wongbusarakum, Kamaljit K. Sangha, et al. 2021. "The Role of Indigenous Peoples and Local Communities in Effective and Equitable Conservation." *Ecology and Society* 26 (3).

de Las Casas, Bartolomé. 1992. *Witness: Writings of Bartolomé de las Casas*. Maryknoll, NY: Orbis Books.

Delevaux, Jade, Kawika Winter, Stacy Jupiter, Mehana Blaich-Vaughan, Kostantinos Stamoulis, Leah Bremer, Kimberly Burnett, Peter Garrod, Jacquelyn Troller, and Tamara Ticktin. 2018. "Linking Land and Sea through Collaborative Research to Inform Contemporary Applications of Traditional Resource Management in Hawaiʻi." *Sustainability* 10 (9): 3147. https://doi.org/10.3390/su10093147.

Delgado-Serrano, Maria del Mar, Elisa Oteros-Rozas, Pieter Vanwildemeersch, Cesar E. Ortiz-Guerrero, Silvia London, and Roberto I. Escalante Semerena. 2015. "Local Perceptions on Social-Ecological Dynamics in Latin America in Three Community-Based Natural Resource Management Systems." *Ecology and Society* 20 (4).

Deloria, Vine. 1997. *Red Earth, White Lies: Native Americans and the Myth of Scientific Fact*. Arvada, CO: Fulcrum Publishing.

Deloria, Vine. 2010. *Behind the Trail of Broken Treaties: An Indian Declaration of Independence*. Austin: University of Texas Press.

Deloria Jr., Vine. 1988 [1969]. *Custer Died for Your Sins: An Indian Manifesto*. Repr. Norman: University of Oklahoma Press.

Deloria Jr., Vine. 1990. "Knowing and Understanding: Traditional Education in the Modern World." *Winds of Change* 5 (1): 12–18.

Deloria, P. J., K. T. Lomawaima, B. M. J. Brayboy, M. N. Trahant, L. Ghiglione, D. Medin, and N. Blackhawk. 2018. "Unfolding Futures: Indigenous Ways of Knowing for the Twenty-First Century." *Daedalus* 147:6–16.

De Lucia, V. 2013. "Towards an Ecological Philosophy of Law: A Comparative Discussion." *Journal of Human Rights and the Environment* 4 (2): 167–190.

Denevan, William M. 1992. "The Pristine Myth: The Landscape of the Americas in 1492." *Annals of the Association of American Geographers* 82 (3): 369–385.

de Oliveira Andreotti, Vanessa, Sharon Stein, Cash Ahenakew, and Dallas Hunt. 2015. "Mapping Interpretations of Decolonization in the Context of Higher Education." *Decolonization: Indigeneity, Education and Society* 4 (1).

de Silva, Kahikina. 2022. "Haʻu ka Waha i ka Nahele: Dissonance and Song in Kanaka Sites of Counter-Memory." *Space and Culture* 25 (2): 192–204.

De Sousa Santos, B. 2002. "Toward a Multicultural Conception of Human Rights." In *Moral Imperialism: A Critical Anthology*, edited by B. Esperanza Hernandez-Truyol, 39–60. New York: New York University Press.

de Vos, Asha. 2022. "Stowing Parachutes, Strengthening Science." *Conservation Science and Practice* 4 (5).

de Vos, Asha, and Mark W. Schwartz. 2022. "Confronting Parachute Science in Conservation." *Conservation Science and Practice* 4 (5).

Diaz, S., J. Settele, E. S. Brondízio, H. T. Ngo, M. Guèze, J. Agard, A. Arneth, P. Balvanera, K. Brauman, S. H. Butchart, and K. M. Chan. 2019. "Summary for Policymakers of the Global Assessment Report on Biodiversity and Ecosystem Services of the Intergovernmental Science-Policy Platform on Biodiversity and Ecosystem Services." https://files.ipbes.net/ipbes-web-prod-public-files/inline/files/ipbes_global_assessment_report_summary_for_policymakers.pdf.

Dicke, Klaus. 2001. "The Founding Function of Human Dignity in the Universal Declaration of Human Rights." In *The Concept of Human Dignity in Human Rights Discourse*, edited by D. Kretzmer and E. Klein, 111–120. Leiden: Brill Nijhoff.

Diener, Edward, and Eunkook M. Suh. 2000. "Measuring Subjective Well-Being to Compare the Quality of Life of Cultures." In *Culture and Subjective Well-Being*, edited by E. Diener and E. M. Suh, 185–218. Cambridge, MA: MIT Press.

Diener, E., and S. Oishi. 2000. "Money and Happiness: Income and Subjective Well-Being across Nations." In *Culture and Subjective Well-Being*, edited by E. Diener and E. M. Suh, 13–36. Cambridge, MA: MIT Press.

D'ignazio, Catherine, and Lauren F. Klein. 2020. *Data Feminism*. Cambridge, MA: MIT Press.

Dilling, Lisa, and Maria Carmen Lemos. 2011. "Creating Usable Science: Opportunities and Constraints for Climate Knowledge Use and Their Implications for Science Policy." *Global Environmental Change* 21 (2): 680–689.

Diver, Sibyl, Mehana Vaughan, Merrill Baker-Médard, and Heather Lukacs. 2019. "Recognizing 'Reciprocal Relations' to Restore Community Access to Land and Water." *International Journal of the Commons* 13 (1).

Djenontin, Ida Nadia S., and Alison M. Meadow. 2018. "The Art of Co-production of Knowledge in Environmental Sciences and Management: Lessons from International Practice." *Environmental Management* 61 (6): 885–903.

Dollar General v. Mississippi Band of Choctaw Indians, 579 U.S. 2016. https://supreme. justia.com/cases/federal/us/579/13-1496/.

Domingo, Rafael. 2022. "Rethinking the School of Salamanca—Reviewed: *The School of Salamanca: A Case of Global Knowledge Production*." *Journal of Law and Religion* 37 (3): 560–568.

Domínguez, Daniela G., Dellanira García, David A. Martínez, and Belinda Hernandez-Arriaga. 2020. "Leveraging the Power of Mutual Aid, Coalitions, Leadership, and Advocacy during COVID-19." *American Psychologist* 75 (7): 909.

Donnelly, Jack. 1982. "Human Rights and Human Dignity: An Analytic Critique of Non-Western Conceptions of Human Rights." *American Political Science Review* 76 (2): 303–316.

Donnelly, Jack. 1989. *Universal Human Rights in Theory and Practice*. Ithaca, NY: Cornell University Press.

Donnelly, Jack. 2007. "The Relative Universality of Human Rights." *Human Rights Quarterly* 29:281.

Donner, Kevin, Alagamił Nicole Norris, Hoku Ka'aekuahiwi Pousima, Blair Paul, and Melissa Poe. 2021. "The 7 R's of Integrating Tribal and Indigenous Partnerships into Aquaculture Literacy." NOAA, August 12. https://www.noaa.gov/office-education/stories/7-r-s-of-integrating-tribal-and-indigenous-partnerships-into-aquaculture-literacy.

Dorrell, Matthew. 2009. "From Reconciliation to Reconciling: Reading What 'We Now Recognize' in the Government of Canada's 2008 Residential Schools Apology." *ESC: English Studies in Canada* 35 (1): 27–45.

Douglas, M. 1966. *Purity and Danger: An Analysis of Concepts of Pollution and Taboo*. New York: Frederick A. Praeger.

Drude, O. 1896. *Manuel de geographie botanique*. Paris: Librairie Des Sciences Naturelles.

Dunbar-Ortiz, Roxanne. 2014. *An Indigenous Peoples' History of the United States*. Boston: Beacon Press.

Duran, Eduardo. 2006. *Healing the Soul Wound: Counseling with American Indians and Other Native Peoples*. New York: Teachers College Press.

Dworkin, Ronald. 1977. *Taking Rights Seriously*. Cambridge, MA: Harvard University Press.

Echo-Hawk, Abigail. 2019. "Indigenous Health Equity." *Native Americans and Philanthropy*, April 30. Urban Indian Health Institute. https://nativephilanthropy. issuelab.org/resource/indigenous-health-equity.html.

Eckert, Joern. 2002. "Legal Roots of Human Dignity in German Law." In *The Concept of Human Dignity in Human Rights Discourse*, edited by David Kretzmer and Eckart Klein, 41–53. New York: Kluwer Law International.

Eckstein, Gabriel, Ariella D'Andrea, Virginia Marshall, Erin O'Donnell, Julia Talbot-Jones, Deborah Curran, and Katie O'Bryan. 2019. "Conferring Legal Personality on the World's Rivers: A Brief Intellectual Assessment." *Water International* 44 (6/7): 804–829.

Edlefsen, David. 2018. "How the West Was Claimed: The Homestead Act and the General Allotment Act." Working Paper for the Western Political Science

Association Conference. http://www. wpsanet. org/papers/docs/WPSA_HtWwC. pdf.

Efi, Tui Atua Tupua Tamasese Taisi. 2005. "Clutter in Indigenous Knowledge, Research and History: A Samoan Perspective—Ministry of Social Development." *Social Policy Journal of New Zealand* 25.

Eicken, Hajo. 2010. "Indigenous Knowledge and Sea Ice Science: What Can We Learn from Indigenous Ice Users?" In *SIKU: Knowing Our Ice: Documenting Inuit Sea Ice Knowledge and Use*, edited by Igor Krupnik, Claudio Aporta, Shari Gearheard, Gita J. Laidler, and Lene Kielsen Holm, 357–376. Dordrecht: Springer.

Ellam Yua, Julie Raymond-Yakoubian, Raychelle Aluaq Daniel, and Carolina Behe. 2022. "A Framework for Co-production of Knowledge in the Context of Arctic Research." Ocean Best Practices. https://repository.oceanbestpractices.org/handle/11329/1943.

Ellis, Juniper, and Epeli Hauʻofa. 2001. "A New Oceania: An Interview with Epeli Hauʻofa." *Antipodes* 15 (1): 22–25. http://www.jstor.org/stable/41958724.

Emerson, Joseph S. 1892. *The Lesser Hawaiian Gods*. Vol. 2. Hawaiian Historical Society. https://books.google.com/books/about/The_Lesser_Hawaiian_Gods. html?id=XCCenQEACAAJ.

Emmons, George. 1841. "Journal of George Emmons, George F. Emmons Papers, 1841 July 25–Sept. 16." Beineke Special Collections, Yale University, New Haven, Connecticut.

Espinosa, Cristina. 2019. "Interpretive Affinities: The Constitutionalization of Rights of Nature, Pacha Mama, in Ecuador." *Journal of Environmental Policy and Planning* 21 (5): 608–622.

Executive Order No. 13175. 2000. 65 Fed. Reg. 67249-67252. November 9. https:// www.federalregister.gov/documents/2000/11/09/00-29003/ consultation-and-coordination-with-indiantribal-governments.

Executive Order No. 14008. 2021. 86 FR 7619 (7619-7633).

Fanon, Frantz. 1961. *The Wretched of the Earth*. Trans. Richard Philcox. New York: Grove Press.

Fanon, Frantz. 2004. *The Wretched of the Earth*. Trans. Richard Philcox. Repr. New York: Grove Press.

Fanon, Frantz. 2008. *Black Skin, White Masks*. New York: Grove Press.

Farmer, Paul. 2004. *Pathologies of Power: Health, Human Rights, and the New War on the Poor*. California Series in Public Anthropology, vol. 4. Berkeley: University of California Press.

Farrell, Justin, Paul Berne Burow, Kathryn McConnell, Jude Bayham, Kyle Whyte, and Gal Koss. 2021. "Effects of Land Dispossession and Forced Migration on Indigenous Peoples in North America." *Science* 374 (6567): eabe4943.

Fellner, Karlee D. 2018. "Embodying Decoloniality: Indigenizing Curriculum and Pedagogy." *American Journal of Community Psychology* 62 (3/4): 283–293.

Fernández-Llamazares, Álvaro, Dana Lepofsky, Ken Lertzman, Chelsey Geralda Armstrong, Eduardo S. Brondizio, Michael C. Gavin, Phil O'B. Lyver, et al. 2021. "Scientists' Warning to Humanity on Threats to Indigenous and Local Knowledge Systems." *Journal of Ethnobiology* 41 (2): 144–169.

Fine, Kathleen. 1988. "The Politics of 'Interpretation' at Mesa Verde National Park." *Anthropological Quarterly* 61 (4): 177–186.

Firn, J. 2011. "Abundance of Introduced Species at Home Predicts Abundance Away in Herbaceous Communities." *Ecology Letters* 14:274–281.

First Archivists Circle. 2006. *The Protocols for Native American Archival Materials.* Flagstaff: Northern Arizona University.

Fisk, Jonathan James. 2021. "Care, Not Incarceration: Exploring the Carcerality of Fisheries Enforcement and Potential Decolonial Futures in Hawaiʻi." *Heliyon* 7 (4): e06916.

Fisk, Jonathan J., Lara A. Jacobs, Brigitte Ululani Kekahiliokalani Russo, Erica Meier, ʻAlohi Nakachi, Kekaha K. P. Spencer, Kainoa Kaulukukui-Narikawa, Amber Waialea Datta, and Kalani Quiocho. 2021. "Cultivating Sovereignty in Parks and Protected Areas: Sowing the Seeds of Restorative and Transformative Justice through the #LANDBACK Movement." *Parks Stewardship Forum* 37 (3).

Fitch, A. 1861. "Sixth Report on the Noxious and Other Insects of the State of New York." *New York State Agricultural Society Transactions* 20:746–868.

Food and Agriculture Organization of the United Nations. 2016. "Free, Prior and Informed Consent: An Indigenous Peoples' Right and a Good Practice for Local Communities—Manual for Project Practitioners," 1–52. https://www.fao.org/3/i6190e/i6190e.pdf.

Forseth, I. N., and A. F. Innis. 2004. "Kudzu (*Pueraria montana*): History, Physiology, and Ecology Combine to Make a Major Ecosystem Threat." *Critical Reviews in Plant Sciences* 23 (5):401–413.

Fox, Keolu. 2020. "The Illusion of Inclusion—the "All of Us" Research Program and Indigenous Peoples' DNA." *New England Journal of Medicine* 383 (5): 411–413.

Fox, Robert, Nina Buchanan, Suzanne Eckes, and Letitia Basford. 2012. "The Line between Cultural Education and Religious Education: Do Ethnocentric Niche Charter Schools Have a Prayer?" *Review of Research in Education* 36 (1).

Franklin, Manasseh. 2021. Rephotographing Wind River Glaciers—Ed Sherline Q&A. *WildSnow*, June 11. https://wildsnow.com/29566/rephotographing-wind-river-glaciers-ed-sherline/.

Franzese, Alexis. 2007. "To Thine Own Self Be True? An Exploration of Authenticity." PhD diss. Duke University. https://people.duke.edu/~rcd2/Dissertation/D_Franzese_Alexis%20_a_200712.pdf.

Freeman, Michael. 1994. "The Philosophical Foundations of Human Rights." *Human Rights Quarterly* 16:491.

Freestone, David. 2012. "International Governance, Responsibility and Management of Areas beyond National Jurisdiction." *International Journal of Marine and Coastal Law* 27 (2): 191–204.

Freire, Paulo. 1968. *Pedagogy of the Oppressed.* London: Bloomsbury.

Freire, Paulo. 2018 [1968]. *Pedagogy of the Oppressed: 50th Anniversary Edition.* Trans. Myra Ramos. Repr. London: Bloomsbury.

Friedlander, Alan M., and Edward E. DeMartini. 2002. "Contrasts in Density, Size, and Biomass of Reef Fishes between the Northwestern and the Main Hawaiian

Islands: The Effects of Fishing Down Apex Predators." *Marine Ecology Progress Series* 230:253–264.

Friedlander, Alan M., Janna M. Shackeroff, and John N. Kittinger. 2013. "Customary Marine Resource Knowledge and Use in Contemporary Hawai'i." *Pacific Science* 67 (3): 441–460.

Fryberg, Stephanie A., and Arianne E. Eason. 2017. "Making the Invisible Visible: Acts of Commission and Omission." *Current Directions in Psychological Science* 26 (6): 554–559.

Fúnez-Flores, Jairo I. 2022a. "Decolonial and Ontological Challenges in Social and Anthropological Theory." *Theory, Culture and Society*: 02632764211073011.

Fúnez-Flores, Jairo I. 2022b. "Toward Decolonial Globalisation Studies." *Globalisation, Societies and Education* 21 (2): 1–21.

Gabbard, Caroline Sinavaiana. 2017. "Samoan Literature and the Wheel of Time: Cartographies of the Vā." *symplokē* 26 (1/2): 33–49.

Galeano, Eduardo. 1997. *Open Veins of Latin America: Five Centuries of the Pillage of a Continent*. New York: New York University Press.

Galindo, Ed. 2022. *Children of the Stars: Indigenous Science Education in a Reservation Classroom*. Corvallis: Oregon State University Press.

Garnett, Stephen T., Neil D. Burgess, Julia E. Fa, Álvaro Fernández-Llamazares, Zsolt Molnár, Cathy J. Robinson, James E. M. Watson, et al. 2018. "A Spatial Overview of the Global Importance of Indigenous Lands for Conservation." *Nature Sustainability* 1 (7): 369–374. https://doi.org/10.1038/s41893-018-0100-6.

Garrison, Rebekah. 2019. "Settler Responsibility: Respatialising Dissent in 'America' beyond Continental Borders." *Shima* 13 (2).

Gatschet, Albert. 1877. Calendar of the Atfalati. Original manuscript in the National Anthropological Archives, Southwest Oregon Research Project, University of Oregon Special Collections.

Gaudry, Adam, and Danielle Lorenz. 2018. "Indigenization as Inclusion, Reconciliation, and Decolonization: Navigating the Different Visions for Indigenizing the Canadian Academy." *AlterNative: An International Journal of Indigenous Peoples* 14 (3): 218–227.

Gegeo, Davis Welchman, and Karen Watson-Gegeo. 2001. "How We Know: Kwara'ae Rural Villagers Doing Indigenous Epistemology." *Contemporary Pacific* 13 (1): 63. doi:10.1353/cp.2001.0004.

Gewirth, Alan. 1978. *Reason and Morality*. Chicago: University of Chicago Press.

Ghosh, Amitav. 2021. *The Nutmeg's Curse*. Chicago: University of Chicago Press.

Gilio-Whitaker, Dina. 2019. *As Long as Grass Grows: The Indigenous Fight for Environmental Justice, from Colonization to Standing Rock*. Boston: Beacon Press.

Ginzburg, Shir Lerman. 2022. "Colonial Comida: The Colonization of Food Insecurity in Puerto Rico." *Food, Culture and Society* 25 (1): 18–31.

Global Alliance for the Rights of Nature. 2010. World People's Conference on Climate Change and the Rights of Mother Earth, Universal Declaration on the Rights of Mother Earth, February. https://www.garn.org/universal-declaration/.

Glover, Jonathan. 2012. *Humanity: A Moral History of the Twentieth Century*. New Haven, CT: Yale University Press.

Gnecco, Cristóbal. 2016. "Native Histories and Archaeologists." In *Indigenous Peoples and Archaeology in Latin America*, edited by Cristóbal Gnecco and Patricia Ayala, 53–66. London: Routledge.

Goduka, Nomalungelo. 2012. "From Positivism to Indigenous Science: A Reflection on World Views, Paradigms and Philosophical Assumptions." *Africa Insight* 41 (4): 123–138.

Gómez Isa, Felipe. 2019. "The UNDRIP: An Increasingly Robust Legal Parameter." *International Journal of Human Rights* 23 (1/2): 7–21.

Gon III, Samuel M., Stephanie L. Tom, and Ulalia Woodside. 2018. "'Āina Momona, Honua Au Loli'—Productive Lands, Changing World: Using the Hawaiian Footprint to Inform Biocultural Restoration and Future Sustainability in Hawai'i." *Sustainability* 10 (10): 3420.

Goodyear-Ka'ōpua, Noelani. 2009. "Rebuilding the 'Auwai: Connecting Ecology, Economy and Education in Hawaiian Schools." *AlterNative: An International Journal of Indigenous Peoples* 5 (2): 46–77.

Goodyear-Ka'ōpua, Noelani, Ikaika Hussey, and Erin Kahunawaika'ala Wright. 2014. *A Nation Rising: Hawaiian Movements for Life, Land, and Sovereignty*. Durham, NC: Duke University Press.

Gordon, Heather Sauyaq Jean. 2021. "Ethnographic Futures Research as a Method for Working with Indigenous Communities to Develop Sustainability Indicators." *Polar Geography* 44 (4): 233–254.

Gordon, Lewis R. 2011. "Shifting the Geography of Reason in an Age of Disciplinary Decadence." *Transmodernity: Journal of Peripheral Cultural Production of the Luso-Hispanic World* 1 (2).

Gott, Gil. 2002. "Imperial Humanitarianism: History of an Arrested Dialectic." In *Moral Imperialism: A Critical Anthology*, edited by Berta Esperanza Hernández-Truyol, 19–38. New York: New York University Press.

Graham, M., and M. Maloney. 2019. "Caring for Country and Rights of Nature in Australia: A Conversation between Earth Jurisprudence and Aboriginal Law and Ethics." In *Sustainability and the Rights of Nature in Practice*, edited by Cameron La Follette and Chris Maser, 385–399. Boca Raton, FL: CRC Press.

Grande, Sandy. 2018. "Refusing the University." In *Toward What Justice?*, edited by Eve Tuck and K. Wayne Yang, 47–65. New York: Routledge.

Greenlee, Jason M., and Jean H. Langenheim. 1990. "Historic Fire Regimes and Their Relation to Vegetation Patterns in the Monterey Bay Area of California." *American Midland Naturalist* 14 (2): 239–253.

Greenwood, Margo, and Nicole Marie Lindsay. 2019. "A Commentary on Land, Health, and Indigenous Knowledge(s)." *Global Health Promotion* 26, no. 3 (suppl): 82–86.

Grenz, Jennifer Berneda. 2020. "Healing the Land by Reclaiming an Indigenous Ecology: A Journey Exploring the Application of the Indigenous Worldview to Invasion Biology and Ecology." PhD diss., University of British Columbia.

Grijalva, R. M. 2022. "Natural Resources Committee to Hold First Congressional Hearing Examining Tribal Co-Management of Public Lands." https://naturalresources.house.gov/media/press-releases/natural-resources-committee-to-hold-first-congressional-hearing-examining-tribal-co-management-of-public-lands.

Grosenick, L., T. S. Clement, and R. D. Fernald. 2007. "Fish Can Infer Social Rank by Observation Alone." *Nature* 445 (7126): 429–432.

Grunow, Tristan R., Fuyubi Nakamura, Katsuya Hirano, Mai Ishihara, ann-elise lewallen, Sheryl Lightfoot, Mayunkiki, Danika Medak-Saltzman, Terri-Lynn Williams-Davidson, and Tomoe Yahata. 2019. "Hokkaidō 150: Settler Colonialism and Indigeneity in Modern Japan and Beyond." *Critical Asian Studies* 51 (4): 597–636. https://doi.org/10.1080/14672715.2019.1665291.

Gupta, Clare. 2015. "Return to Freedom: Anti-GMO Aloha ʻĀina Activism on Molokai as an Expression of Place-Based Food Sovereignty." *Globalizations* 12 (4): 529–544.

Gurevitch, J., and D. K. Padilla. 2004. "Are Invasive Species a Major Cause of Extinctions?" *Trends in Ecology and Evolution* 19 (9):470–474.

Haar, Jarrod, and William John Martin. 2022. "He Aronga Takirua: Cultural Double-Shift of Māori Scientists." *Human Relations* 75 (6): 1001–1027.

Haelewaters, Danny, Tina A. Hofmann, and Adriana L. Romero-Olivares. 2021. "Ten Simple Rules for Global North Researchers to Stop Perpetuating Helicopter Research in the Global South." *PLOS Computational Biology* 17 (8): e1009277.

Hahn, Steven C. 2004. "The Invention of the Creek Nation, 1670-1763." Lincoln: University of Nebraska Press.

Hall, Budd L., and Rajesh Tandon. 2017. "Decolonization of Knowledge, Epistemicide, Participatory Research and Higher Education." *Research for All* 1 (1): 6–19. doi:10.18546/RFA.01.1.02.

Halualani, Rona Tamiko. 2002. *In the Name of Hawaiians: Native Identities and Cultural Politics.* Minneapolis: University of Minnesota Press.

Hanke, Lewis. 1946. "Free Speech in Sixteenth-Century Spanish America." *Hispanic American Historical Review* 26 (2): 135–149.

Hankins, Don L. 2014. "Restoring Indigenous Prescribed Fires to California Oak Woodlands." In Proceedings of the Seventh California Oak Symposium: Managing Oak Woodlands in a Dynamic World. GTR PSW-GTR-251. Berkeley, CA: USDA Forest Service, Pacific Southwest Research Station.

Hauʻofa, Ellis, and Epeli Hauʻofa. 2001. "A New Oceania: An Interview with Epeli Hauʻofa." *Antipodes* 15 (1): 22–25. http://www.jstor.org/stable/41958724.

Harjo, Laura. 2019. *Spiral to the Stars: Mvskoke Tools of Futurity.* Tucson: University of Arizona Press.

Harper, Frederick D., Jacqueline A. Harper, and Aaron B. Stills. 2003. "Counseling Children in Crisis Based on Maslow's Hierarchy of Basic Needs." *International Journal for the Advancement of Counselling* 25:11–25.

Harris, LaDonna, and Jacqueline Wasilewski. 2004. "Indigeneity, an Alternative Worldview: Four R's (Relationship, Responsibility, Reciprocity, Redistribution) vs. Two P's (Power and Profit). Sharing the Journey towards Conscious Evolution."

Systems Research and Behavioral Science: The Official Journal of the International Federation for Systems Research 21 (5): 489–503.

Hart, Michael A. 2010. "Indigenous Worldviews, Knowledge, and Research: The Development of an Indigenous Research Paradigm." *Journal of Indigenous Social Development* 1:1A.

Hawai'i State Legislature. 1986. "Aloha Spirit." Hawai'i Revised Statute [§5-7.5].

Hayward, Ashley, Erynne Sjoblom, Stephanie Sinclair, and Jaime Cidro. 2021. "A New Era of Indigenous Research: Community-Based Indigenous Research Ethics Protocols in Canada." *Journal of Empirical Research on Human Research Ethics* 16 (4): 403–417.

Head, David, ed. 2018. *Encyclopedia of the Atlantic World, 1400–1900: Europe, Africa, and the Americas in an Age of Exploration, Trade, and Empires.* 2 vols. Santa Barbara, CA: ABC-CLIO.

Henri, D. A., L. M. Martinez-Levasseur, J. F. Provencher, C. D. Debets, M. Appaqaq, and M. Houde. 2022. "Engaging Inuit Youth in Environmental Research: Braiding Western Science and Indigenous Knowledge through School Workshops." *Journal of Environmental Education* 53 (5): 261–279.

Henry, Alexander, and David Thompson. 2015. *New Light on the Early History of the Greater Northwest.* Vol. 2. Cambridge, UK: Cambridge University Press.

Hernandez, Jessica. 2022. *Fresh Banana Leaves: Healing Indigenous Landscapes through Indigenous Science.* Berkeley, CA: North Atlantic Books.

Hernandez, Jessica, and Kristiina A. Vogt. 2020. "Indigenizing Restoration: Indigenous Lands before Urban Parks." *Human Biology* 92 (1): 37–44.

Hernandez, Jessica, Julianne Meisner, Lara A. Jacobs, and Peter M. Rabinowitz. 2022. "Re-Centering Indigenous Knowledge in Climate Change Discourse." *PLOS Climate* 1 (5): e0000032.

Hernandez, Jessica, and Michael S. Spencer. 2020. "Weaving Indigenous Science into Ecological Sciences: Culturally Grounding Our Indigenous Scholarship." *Human Biology* 92 (1): 5–9.

Hernandez, Ramon. 1991. "The Internationalization of Francisco de Vitoria and Domingo de Soto." *Fordham International Law Journal* 15:1031.

Hessburg, Paul F., Susan J. Prichard, R. Keala Hagmann, Nicholas A. Povak, and Frank K. Lake. 2021. "Wildfire and Climate Change Adaptation of Western North American Forests: A Case for Intentional Management." *Ecological Applications* 31 (8): e02432.

Hill, Christina, and Serena Lillywhite. 2015. "The United Nations 'Protect, Respect and Remedy' Framework: Six Years On and What Impact Has It Had?" *Extractive Industries and Society* 2 (1): 4–6.

Hoagland, Serra Jeanette. 2017. "Integrating Traditional Ecological Knowledge with Western Science for Optimal Natural Resource Management." *IK: Other Ways of Knowing* 3 (1): 1–15.

"Hoihi—Wehe²wiki² Hawaiian Language Dictionaries." nd. Accessed November 18, 2022. https://hilo.hawaii.edu/wehe/?q=hoihi.

Hokowhitu, Brendan. 2020. "Introduction." In *The Routledge Handbook of Critical Indigenous Studies*, edited by Brendan Hokowhitu, Aileen Moreton-Robinson, Linda Tuhiwai-Smith, Chris Andersen, and Steve Larkin, 1–5. London; Routledge.

Hokowhitu, Brendan, Aileen Moreton-Robinson, Linda Tuhiwai-Smith, Chris Andersen, and Steve Larkin, eds. 2020. *The Routledge Handbook of Critical Indigenous Studies*. New York: Routledge.

Holt, John. 1995. *On Being Hawaiian*. 4th ed. Honolulu: Ku Paʻa Publishing.

Holt Giménez, Eric, and Annie Shattuck. 2011. "Food Crises, Food Regimes and Food Movements: Rumblings of Reform or Tides of Transformation?" *Journal of Peasant Studies* 38 (1): 109–144.

Holy See Press Office. 2023. "Summary of Bulletin: Joint Statement of the Dicasteries for Culture and Education and for Promoting Integral Human Development on the 'Doctrine of Discovery.'" https://press.vatican.va/content/salastampa/en/bollettino/pubblico/2023/03/30/230330b.html.

Honneth, Axel. 1992. "Integrity and Disrespect: Principles of a Conception of Morality Based on the Theory of Recognition." *Political Theory* 20 (2): 187–201.

hooks, bell. 2014 [1994]. *Teaching to Transgress*. New York: Routledge.

hoʻomanawanui, kuʻualoha. 2012. "Hanohano Wailuanuiaho ʻāno: Remembering, Recovering, and Writing Place." *Hūlili: Multidisciplinary Research on Hawaiian Well-Being* 8 (1): 187–243.

hoʻomanawanui, kuʻualoha. 2013. "Displacing Place: 'Translating' Pele in Cyberspace." *Settler Colonial Studies* 3 (3/4): 395–413.

hoʻomanawanui, kuʻualoha. 2019. "Theorizing Moʻokūʻauhau as Methodology in an Indigenous Literary Context." In *The Past Before Us: Moʻokūʻauhau as Methodology*, edited by Nālani Wilson-Hokowhitu. Honolulu: University of Hawaiʻi Press.

Horvath, Ronald J. 1972. "A Definition of Colonialism." *Current Anthropology* 13 (1): 45–57.

Howard, Allen M. 2000. "Mande Identity Formation in the Economic and Political Context of North-West Sierra Leone, 1750–1900." *Paideuma* 46:13–35. https://www.jstor.org/stable/40341781.

Howard, Rhoda E., and Jack Donnelly. 1986. "Human Dignity, Human Rights, and Political Regimes." *American Political Science Review* 80 (3): 801–817.

Hufbauer, R., and M. Torchin. 2007. "Integrating Ecological and Evolutionary Theory of Biological Invasions." *Biological Invasions: Ecological Studies* 193:79–96.

Hufbauer, R. A., Alexis Rutschmann, Bruno Serrate, Hervé Vermeil de Conchard, and Benoit Facon. 2013. "Role of Propagule Pressure in Colonization Success: Disentangling the Relative Importance of Demographic, Genetic and Habitat Effects." *Journal of Evolutionary Biology* 26 (8): 1691–1699.

Hunter, John M., and Sonia I. Arbona. 1995. "Paradise Lost: An Introduction to the Geography of Water Pollution in Puerto Rico." *Social Science and Medicine* 40 (10): 1331–1355.

Hunter-Ripper, Coyote Marie. 2022. "Understanding/Embracing Death and Dying." In *Restoring the Kinship Worldview: Indigenous Voices Introduce 28 Precepts for Rebalancing Life on Planet Earth*, edited by Wahinkpe Topa and Darcia Narvaez, 43–48. Berkeley, CA: North Atlantic Books.

Huntington, Henry P. 2000. "Using Traditional Ecological Knowledge in Science: Methods and Applications." *Ecological Applications* 10 (5): 1270–1274.

Hussar, B., NCES, J. Zhang, S. Hein, K. Wang, A. Roberts, J. Cui, et al. 2020. "Characteristics of Postsecondary Faculty." In *The Condition of Education 2020*, 150–153. Washington, DC: National Center for Education Statistics.

Hussey, Ronald D. 1932. "Text of the Laws of Burgos (1512–1513) Concerning the Treatment of the Indians." *Hispanic American Historical Review* 12 (3): 301–326.

Ignatieff, Michael. 2001. "Human Rights as Idolatry." In *Human Rights as Politics and Idolatry*, edited by Amy Gutmann, 53–98. Princeton, NJ: Princeton University Press.

ʻĪʻĪ, John Papa. 1959 [1866–1870]. *Fragments of Hawaiian History*. Translated by M. K. Pukui. Edited by D. B. Barrère. Honolulu: Bishop Museum Press.

Ikeda, Mitsuho. 2020. "Repatriation of Human Remains and Burial Materials of Indigenous Peoples in Japan: Who Owns Their Cultural Heritages and Dignity?" *Co*Design* 7:1–16.

Indigenous Values Initiative. 2018. "Repudiations by Faith Communities." Doctrine of Discovery Project. July 30. https://doctrineofdiscovery.org/faith-communities/. Updated September 2, 2021.

Inglehart, R., and H. D. Klingemann. 2000. "Genes, Culture, Democracy, and Happiness." In *Culture and Subjective Well-Being*, edited by E. Diener and E. M. Suh, 165–183. Cambridge, MA: MIT Press.

Inglis, Julian, ed. 1993. *Traditional Ecological Knowledge: Concepts and Cases*. Ottawa, CAN: IDRC.

International Labour Organization. 1989. "Ratifications of Convention (No. 169) Concerning Indigenous and Tribal Peoples in Independent Countries." June 27. 1650 U.N.T.S. 28383, Article 38.

Inuit Circumpolar Council—Alaska. 2015. "Alaskan Inuit Food Security Conceptual Framework: How to Assess the Arctic from an Inuit Perspective." Anchorage, AK: Inuit Circumpolar Council-Alaska.

Iseke, Judy. 2013. "Spirituality as Decolonizing: Elders Albert Desjarlais, George McDermott, and Tom McCallum Share Understandings of Life in Healing Practices." *Decolonization: Indigeneity, Education & Society* 2 (1).

Ishihara, Mai. 2019. "The Stolen History of Ainu 'Liminars.'" Discussion paper for workshop, Settler Colonialism and Indigeneity in Modern Japan and Beyond, March 15, 2019. University of British Columbia.

Iturbe, Mariano. 2012. "The Natural Law in the Times of St. Francis Xavier: Francisco de Vitoria (1492–1546)." https://core.ac.uk/download/pdf/83578286.pdf.

IUCN. 2012. WCC-2012-Res-100-EN "Incorporation of the Rights of Nature as the Organisational Focal Point in IUCN's Decision Making." Decision of the IUCN World Conservation Congress." https://portals.iucn.org/library/sites/library/files/resrecfiles/WCC_2012_RES_100_EN.pdf.

IVUMC. 2019a. *Visitor Capacity Guidebook: Managing the Amounts and Types of Visitor Use to Achieve Desired Conditions*. Lakewood, CO. Accessed May 16, 2023. https://visitorusemanagement.nps.gov/VUM/Framework.

IVUMC. 2019b. *Monitoring Guidebook: Evaluating Effectiveness of Visitor Use Management.* Lakewood, CO. Accessed May 16, 2023. https://visitorusemanagement.nps.gov/VUM/Framework.

Jacobs, Lara A., Coral B. Avery, Rhode Salonen, and Kathryn D. Champagne. 2022a. "Unsettling Marine Conservation: Disrupting Manifest Destiny-Based Conservation Practices through the Operationalization of Indigenous Value Systems." *Parks Stewardship Forum* 38 (2).

Jacobs, Lara A., Serina Payan Hazelwood, Coral B. Avery, and Christy Sangster-Biye. 2022b. "Reimagining US Federal Land Management through Decolonization and Indigenous Value Systems." *Journal of Park and Recreation Administration* 40 (1).

Jacobs, Melville. 1945. Kalapuya Language field journals, Jacobs Collection, University of Washington.

Jacobs, Melville, Leo Joachim Frachtenberg, and Albert Samuel Gatschet. 1945. *Kalapuya Texts.* Seattle: University of Washington Press.

Janovsky, Rachel M., and Eric R. Larson. 2019. "Does Invasive Species Research Use More Militaristic Language Than Other Ecology and Conservation Biology Literature?" *NeoBiota* 44:27–38.

Jaramillo, Nathalia, and Michelle Carreon. 2014. "Pedagogies of Resistance and Solidarity: Towards Revolutionary and Decolonial Praxis." *Interface: A Journal for and about Social Movements* 6 (1): 392–411.

Jay, Stephen, Carys Jones, Paul Slinn, and Christopher Wood. 2007. "Environmental Impact Assessment: Retrospect and Prospect." *Environmental Impact Assessment Review* 27 (4): 287–300.

Jennings, Lydia, Talia Anderson, Andrew Martinez, Rogena Sterling, Dominique David Chavez, Ibrahim Garba, Maui Hudson, Nanibaa' A Garrison, and Stephanie Carroll. 2023. "Applying the 'CARE Principles for Indigenous Data Governance' to Ecology and Biodiversity Research." *Nature Ecology and Evolution* 7 (10): 1547–1551.

Johannes, Robert Earle. 1981. *Words of the Lagoon: Fishing and Marine Lore in the Palau District of Micronesia.* Berkeley: University of California Press.

Johnson Orange, Myra. 2020. Interview with Jennifer O'Neal and Elizabeth Kallenbach, December 8.

Jorgensen, Miriam, ed. 2007. *Rebuilding Native Nations: Strategies for Governance and Development.* Tucson: University of Arizona Press.

Kaʻanehe, Rebecca J. I. 2020. "Ke Aʻo Mālamalama: Recognizing and Bridging Worlds with Hawaiian Pedagogies." *Equity and Excellence in Education* 53 (1/2): 73–88.

Kaba, Mariame. 2021. *We Do This 'Til We Free Us: Abolitionist Organizing and Transforming Justice.* Edited by Tamara Nopper. Chicago: Haymarket Books.

Kagan, Jerome, and Howard A. Moss. 1983. *Birth to Maturity: A Study in Psychological Development.* New Haven, CT: Yale University Press.

Kahanamoku, Sara, Rosie 'Anolani Alegado, Aurora Kagawa-Viviani, Katie Leimomi Kamelamela, Brittany Kamai, Lucianne M. Walkowicz, Chanda Prescod-Weinstein, Mithi Alexa de los Reyes, and Hilding Neilson. 2020. "A Native Hawaiian-Led Summary of the Current Impact of Constructing the Thirty Meter Telescope on Maunakea." *arXiv*, January 3. https://arxiv.org/abs/2001.00970.

Kamakau, Samuel M. 1976. "Na hana a ka poe kahiko [The Works of the People of Old]." Bernice P. Bishop Museum Special Publication 61. Honolulu: Bishop Museum Press.

Kameʻeleihiwa, Lilikalā. 1992. *Native Land and Foreign Desires: Pehea lā e pono ai?* Honolulu: Bishop Museum Press.

Kamelamela, Katie L., Hannah Kihalani Springer, Roberta Kuʻulei Keakealani, Moana Ulu Ching, Tamara Ticktin, Rebekah Dickens Ohara, Elliott W. Parsons, Edith D. Adkins, Kainana S. Francisco, and Christian Giardina. 2022. "Kōkua aku, kōkua mai: An Indigenous Consensus-Driven and Place-Based Approach to Community Led Dryland Restoration and Stewardship." *Forest Ecology and Management* 506.

Kamir, Orit. 2002. "Honor and Dignity Cultures: The Case of Kavod and Kvod Ha-Adam in Israeli Society and Law." In *The Concept of Human Dignity in Human Rights Discourse*, edited by David Kretzmer and Eckart Klein, 231–262. Leiden: Brill Nijhoff.

Kanahele, George. 1986. *Kū Kanaka, Stand Tall: A Search for Hawaiian Values.* Honolulu: University of Hawaiʻi Press.

Kanahele, Pualani Kanakaʻole. 2011. *Ka Honua Ola: ʻEli ʻEli Kau Mai.* Honolulu: Kamehameha Publishing.

Kanahele-Mossman, Huihui, and Marina Karides. 2021. "Papakū Makawalu and Grounded Theory: A Combined and Collective Analysis for Hawaiʻi Land Stewardship—Honuaiākea." *AlterNative: An International Journal of Indigenous Peoples* 17 (4): 449–459.

Kanaʻiaupuni, S. M., N. J. Malone, and K. Ishibashi. 2005. "Income and Poverty among Native Hawaiians: Summary of ka huakaʻi Findings." Kamehameha Schools–PASE. https://www.semanticscholar.org/paper/INCOME-AND-POVERTY-AMONG-NATIVE-HAWAIIANS-Kana-Malone/f3c9c068f1a7e81d5c7b192dbebe4ede7518599b.

Kanakaʻole Kanahele, P., K. Kealiikanakaoleohaililani, H. Kanahele-Mossman, K. Nuʻuhiwa, K. Kanahele, J. Kauahikaua, M. Takabayashi, et al. 2017. *Kīhoʻihoʻi Kānāwai for Restoring Kānāwai for Island Stewardship.* http://nomaunakea.weebly.com/uploads/1/0/2/2/102246944/kanahele_kihoihoi_kanawai_final.pdf.

Kaplan, Abraham. 1958. "American Ethics and Public Policy." *Daedalus* 87 (2): 48–77.

Kater, Ilona. 2022. "Natural and Indigenous Sciences: Reflections on an Attempt to Collaborate." *Regional Environmental Change* 22 (4): 109.

Kauanui, J. Kehaulani. 2008. *Hawaiian Blood: Colonialism and the Politics of Sovereignty and Indigeneity.* Durham, NC: Duke University Press.

Kauffman, C. M., and P. L. Martin. 2016. "Testing Ecuador's Rights of Nature: Why Some Lawsuits Succeed and Others Fail." Paper presented at the International Studies Association Annual Convention, Atlanta, Georgia, March 18. http://files.harmonywithnatureun.org/uploads/upload471.pdf.

Kauffman, Craig M., and Pamela L. Martin. 2018. "Constructing Rights of Nature Norms in the US, Ecuador, and New Zealand." *Global Environmental Politics* 18 (4): 43–62.

Keʻala. 2020. In discussion with Ululani Kekahiliokalani Brigitte Russo Oana, May.

Keala, Graydon "Buddy," James R. Hollyer, and Luisa Castro. 2007. *Loko I'a: A Manual on Hawaiian Fishpond Restoration and Management*. Mānoa: University of Hawai'i, College of Tropical Agriculture and Human Resources.

Kealiikanakaoleohaililani, Kekuhi, Natalie Kurashima, Kainana S. Francisco, Christian P. Giardina, Renee Pualani Louis, Heather McMillen, C. Kalā Asing, et al. 2018. "Ritual+ Sustainability Science? A Portal into the Science of Aloha." *Sustainability* 10 (10): 3478.

Keane, Moyra. 2008. "Science Education and Worldview." *Cultural Studies of Science Education* 3:587–621.

Keaulumoku. 1700. *Kumulipo: A Hawaiian Creation Chant*. https://ulukau.org/ulukau-books/?a=d&d=EBOOK-BECKWIT2.2.9.1&e=-------en-20--1--txt-txPT-----------.

Kehoe, Alana K. 2020. "Fanning the Flames of Disaster: The Role Colonialism Plays in the Impact of Wildfire on Indigenous People in Northern Alberta." MA thesis, University of Western Ontario.

Kelley, Robin D. G. 2016. "Black Study, Black Struggle." *Ufahamu: A Journal of African Studies* 40 (2).

Kelley, Robin D. G. 2022. *Freedom Dreams: The Black Radical Imagination*. Boston: Beacon Press.

Kelman, Herbert G. 1973. "Violence without Moral Restraint: Reflections on the Dehumanization of Victims and Victimizers." *Journal of Social Issues* (Fall): 25–61. https://doi.org/10.1111/j.1540-4560.1973.tb00102.x.

Kelman, Herbert C. 1977. "The Conditions, Criteria, and Dialectics of Human Dignity: A Transnational Perspective." *International Studies Quarterly* 21 (3): 529–552.

Kikiloi, Kekuewa, Alan M. Friedlander, 'Aulani Wilhelm, Nai'a Lewis, Kalani Quiocho, William 'Āila Jr., and Sol Kaho'ohalahala. 2017. "Papahānaumokuākea: Integrating Culture in the Design and Management of One of the World's Largest Marine Protected Areas." *Coastal Management* 45 (6): 436–451.

Kikiloi, Kekuewa, and M. Graves. 2010. "Rebirth of an Archipelago: Sustaining a Hawaiian Cultural Identity for People and Homeland." *Hūlili: Multidisciplinary Research on Hawaiian Well-Being* 6:73–114.

Kilian, Alexandra, Tyee Kenneth Fellows, Ryan Giroux, Jason Pennington, Ayelet Kuper, Cynthia R. Whitehead, and Lisa Richardson. 2019. "Exploring the Approaches of Non-Indigenous Researchers to Indigenous Research: A Qualitative Study." *Canadian Medical Association Open Access Journal* 7 (3): E504–E509.

Kimmerer, Robin Wall. 2002. "Weaving Traditional Ecological Knowledge into Biological Education: A Call to Action." *BioScience* 52 (5): 432–438.

Kimmerer, Robin. 2011. "Restoration and Reciprocity: The Contributions of Traditional Ecological Knowledge." *Human Dimensions of Ecological Restoration: Integrating Science, Nature, and Culture*, edited by Dave Egan, Evan E. Hjerpe, and Jesse Abrams, 257–276. Washington, DC: Island Press.

Kimmerer, Robin. 2013. *Braiding Sweetgrass: Indigenous Wisdom, Scientific Knowledge and the Teachings of Plants*. Minneapolis: Milkweed Editions.

Kimmerer, Robin Wall, and Frank Kanawha Lake. 2001. "The Role of Indigenous Burning in Land Management." *Journal of Forestry* 99 (11): 36–41.

King, Farina. 2021. "The Complications of Columbus and Indigenous Identity at BYU." *Dialogue: A Journal of Mormon Thought* 54 (2): 105–108.

King, Marsha. 2008. "Tribes Confront Painful Legacy of Indian Boarding Schools." *Seattle Times*, February 3.

King, Tiffany Lethabo. 2019. *The Black Shoals: Offshore Formations of Black and Native Studies*. Durham, NC: Duke University Press.

Kitayama, Shinobu, and Hazel Rose Markus. 2000. "The Pursuit of Happiness and the Realization of Sympathy: Cultural Patterns of Self, Social Relations, and Well-Being." *Culture and Subjective Well-Being*, edited by E. Diener and E. M. Suh, 113–161. Cambridge, MA: MIT Press.

Knauß, Stefan. 2018. "Conceptualizing Human Stewardship in the Anthropocene: The Rights of Nature in Ecuador, New Zealand and India." *Journal of Agricultural and Environmental Ethics* 31 (6): 703–722.

Koch, Alexander, Chris Brierley, Mark M. Maslin, and Simon L. Lewis. 2019. "Earth System Impacts of the European Arrival and Great Dying in the Americas after 1492." *Quaternary Science Reviews* 207:13–36.

Kolopenuk, Jessica. 2020. "Miskâsowin: Indigenous Science, Technology, and Society." *Genealogy* 4 (1): 21.

Koons, J. E. 2011. "Key Principles to Transform Law for the Health of the Planet." In *Exploring Wild Law: The Philosophy of Earth Jurisprudence*, edited by Peter Burdon, 45–59. Kent Town, S AUS: Wakefield Press.

Koorndijk, Jeanice L. 2019. "Judgements of the Inter-American Court of Human Rights Concerning Indigenous and Tribal Land Rights in Suriname: New Approaches to Stimulating Full Compliance." *International Journal of Human Rights* 23 (10): 1615–1647.

Kotzé, Louis J., and Paola Villavicencio Calzadilla. 2017. "Somewhere between Rhetoric and Reality: Environmental Constitutionalism and the Rights of Nature in Ecuador." *Transnational Environmental Law* 6 (3): 401–433.

Kovach, Margaret. 2009. *Indigenous Methodologies: Characteristics, Conversations, and Contexts*. Toronto: University of Toronto Press.

Kovach, Margaret. 2021. *Indigenous Methodologies: Characteristics, Conversations, and Contexts*. Toronto: University of Toronto Press.

Kronman, Anthony T. 2007. *Education's End: Why Our Colleges and Universities Have Given Up On the Meaning of Life*. New Haven, CT: Yale University Press.

Kuákari, H. 2021. *Kaxúmbekua*. Trans. J. Flores. Analitica Design.

Kuhn, Thomas S. 1996. *The Structure of Scientific Revolutions*. Chicago: University of Chicago Press.

Kukutai, Tahu, and John Taylor. 2016. "Data Sovereignty for Indigenous Peoples: Current Practice and Future Needs." In *Indigenous Data Sovereignty: Toward an Agenda*, edited by Tahu Kukutai and John Taylor, 1–24. Canberra: Australian National University Press.

Kūlana Noiʻi Working Group. 2021. *Kūlana Noiʻi v.2*. Hawaiʻi Sea Grant, Honolulu, Hawaiʻi. https://seagrant.soest.hawaii.edu/wp-content/uploads/2021/09/Kulana-Noii-2.0_LowRes.pdf.

Kuokkanen, Rauna. 2011. *Reshaping the University: Responsibility, Indigenous Epistemes, and the Logic of the Gift*. Vancouver: University of British Columbia Press.

Kurashima, Natalie, Jason Jeremiah, A. Nāmaka Whitehead, Jon Tulchin, Mililani Browning, and Trever Duarte. 2018. "'Āina Kaumaha': The Maintenance of Ancestral Principles for 21st Century Indigenous Resource Management." *Sustainability* 10 (11): 3975.

Kurashima, Natalie, Lucas Fortini, and Tamara Ticktin. 2019. "The Potential of Indigenous Agricultural Food Production under Climate Change in Hawaiʻi." *Nature Sustainability* 2 (3): 191–199.

Kvale, Live Håndlykken, and Nils Pharo. 2021. "Understanding the Data Management Plan as a Boundary Object through a Multi-Stakeholder Perspective." *International Journal of Digital Curation* 16 (1). https://doi.org/10.2218/ijdc.v16i1.746.

Lacy, Linda Hogan. 2007. "How It Is: The Native American Philosophy of V.F. Cordova." In *How It Is: The Native American Philosophy of V.F. Cordova*, edited by Kathleen Dean Moore, Kurt Peters, Theodore S. Jojola, and Amber Lacy. Tucson: University of Arizona Press.

Laitos, Jan. 2013. "Rules of Law for Use and Nonuse of Nature." In *Rule of Law for Nature: New Dimensions and Ideas in Environmental Law*, ed. Christina Voight, 209–221. Cambridge, UK: Cambridge University Press.

Lake, Frank K., Vita Wright, Penelope Morgan, Mary McFadzen, Dave McWethy, and Camille Stevens-Rumann. 2017. "Returning Fire to the Land: Celebrating Traditional Knowledge and Fire." *Journal of Forestry* 115 (5): 343–353.

Lamrani, Myriam. 2022. "The Ultimate Intimacy: Death and Mexico, an Anthropological Relation in Images." *American Ethnologist* 49 (2): 204–220.

Lander, Eric S., and Brenda Mallory. 2021. "Memorandum for the Heads of Departments and Agencies." Memorandum, November 15. https://www.whitehouse.gov/wp-content/uploads/2021/11/111521-OSTP-CEQ-ITEK-Memo.pdf

la paperson. 2017. *A Third University Is Possible*. Minneapolis: University of Minnesota Press.

Large, Ernest Charles. 1940. *The Advance of the Fungi*. New York: Henry Holt.

Lasswell, H. D., and M. S. Macdougal. 1992. *Jurisprudence for a Free Society: Studies in Law, Science, and Policy*. Vol. 1. Leiden: Martinus Nijhoff.

Lasswell, Harold D., Ronald D. Brunner, and Andrew R. Willard. 2003. "On the Policy Sciences in 1943." *Policy Sciences* 36 (1): 71–98.

Latulippe, Nicole, and Nicole Klenk. 2020. "Making Room and Moving Over: Knowledge Co-Production, Indigenous Knowledge Sovereignty and the Politics of Global Environmental Change Decision-Making." *Current Opinion in Environmental Sustainability* 42:7–14.

Lawrence, Jane. 2000. "The Indian Health Service and the Sterilization of Native American Women." *American Indian Quarterly* 24 (3): 400–419.

Lazrus, Heather, Julie Maldonado, Paulette Blanchard, M. Kalani Souza, Bill Thomas, and Danial Wildcat. 2022. "Culture Change to Address Climate Change: Collaborations with Indigenous and Earth Sciences for More Just, Equitable, and Sustainable Responses to Our Climate Crisis." *PLOS Climate* 1 (2): e0000005.

Lee, Robert, Tristan Ahtone, and Margaret Pearce. 2020. "Land-Grab Universities." *High Country News*, March 30. https://www.hcn.org/issues/52.4/ indigenous-affairs-education-land-grab-universities.

Lemos, Maria Carmen, James C. Arnott, Nicole M. Ardoin, Kristin Baja, Angela T. Bednarek, Art Dewulf, Clare Fieseler, et al. 2018. "To Co-produce or Not to Co-produce." *Nature Sustainability* 1 (12): 722–724.

Letters from the Oregon Superintendent of Indian Affairs, National Archives Records Administration RG 75, M2. Letters Received by the Office of Indian Affairs, 1824–1881, Correspondence of the Oregon Superintendency, Washington, DC.

Letters from the Oregon Superintendent of the Indian Affairs, National Archives Records Administration RG 75, M234 microfilm series. Letters Received by the Office of Indian Affairs, 1824–1881, Correspondence of the Oregon Superintendency, Washington, DC.

Lewis, David G. 2015. "Natives in the Nation's Archives: The Southwest Oregon Research Project." *Journal of Western Archives* 6 (1): 4.

Lewis, David G. 2021. "Missing Pages: Additional Signatory Tribes to the Willamette Valley Treaty." *Quartux Journal*, May 25. https://wp.me/p2ENjV-2r2.

Lewis, David Gene. 2009. *Termination of the Confederated Tribes of the Grand Ronde Community of Oregon: Politics, Community, Identity*. Corvallis: University of Oregon Press.

Lewis, David. 2016a. "Indian Fishing Rights on the Grand Ronde-Siletz Indian Agency." *Quartux Journal*, December 4. https://wp.me/p2ENjV-Pn.

Lewis, David. 2016b. "Sickness Issues from the Trumpet: Health Conditions at the Early Western Oregon Reservations." *Quartux Journal*, October 24. https://wp.me/ p2ENjV-KR.

Lewis, David. 2018. "Promise of Citizenship and Informal Allotment at the Grand Ronde Reservation." *Quartux Journal*, October 8. https://wp.me/p2ENjV-1Hp.

Lewis, David. 2021a. "Draining Lake Labish." *Quartux Journal*, December 19. https:// wp.me/p2ENjV-2Dw.

Lewis, David. 2021b. "Draining Wapato Lake." *Quartux Journal*, December 24. https:// wp.me/p2ENjV-2EV.

Lewis, David. 2023. *Tribal Histories of the Willamette Valley*. Portland, OR: Ooligan Press.

Lewis, Jordan. 2021. "Community-Engaged Research with Indigenous Communities to Improve Elder Health and Well-Being." *Innovation in Aging* 5, no. 1 (suppl): 232.

Ley de Derechos de la Madre Tierra—Estado Plurinacional de Bolivia. 2010. December 21. https://bolivia.infoleyes.com/norma/2689/ ley-de-derechos-de-la-madre-tierra-071.

Liboiron, Max. 2021a. "Decolonizing Geoscience Requires More Than Equity and Inclusion." *Nature Geoscience* 14 (12): 876–877.

Liboiron, Max. 2021b. *Pollution Is Colonialism*. Durham, NC: Duke University Press.

Liboiron, Max, Alex Zahara, and Ignace Schoot. 2018. "Community Peer Review: A Method to Bring Consent and Self-Determination into the Sciences." *Preprints*, June 7. doi:10.20944/preprints201806.0104.v1.

Lidstrom, S. 2017. "An Interdisciplinary Perspective on Invasive Alien Species." *Official PLOS Blog*, October 18. https://theplosblog.plos.org/2017/10/an-interdisciplinary-perspective-on-invasive-alien-species/.

Lili'uokalani (Queen of Hawai'i). 1978 [1897]. *The Kumulipo: Translated from Original Manuscripts Preserved Exclusively in Her Majesty's Family*. https://www.higp.hawaii.edu/~scott/GG104/Readings/Liliuokalani_1897.pdf.

Lili'uokalani. 1898. *Hawai'i's Story by Hawai'i's Queen*. Boston: Lee and Shepard.

Lindberg, David C. 2010. *The Beginnings of Western Science: The European Scientific Tradition in Philosophical, Religious, and Institutional Context, Prehistory to AD 1450*. Chicago: University of Chicago Press.

Little Bear, Leroy. 2000. "Jagged Worldviews Colliding." *Reclaiming Indigenous Voice and Vision* 77.

Local Contexts. 2018. "Cultural Institution Notices." https://datascience.codata.org/articles/10.5334/dsj-2020-043#B27.

Lock, Mark John, Faye Beverley McMillan, Bindi Bennett, Jodie Martire, Donald Warne, Jacquie Kidd, Naomi G. Williams, Paul Worley, Peter Hutten-Czapski, and Russell Roberts. 2022. "Position Statement: Research and Reconciliation with Indigenous Peoples in Rural Health Journals." *Australian Journal of Rural Health* 30 (1): 6–7.

Loewen, James W. 2008. *Lies My Teacher Told Me: Everything Your American History Textbook Got Wrong*. New York: The New Press, 2008.

Loke, Matthew K., and PingSun Leung. 2013. "Competing Food Concepts: Implications for Hawai'i, USA." *Food and Energy Security* 2 (3): 174–184. https://doi.org/10.1002/fes3.33.

Lomawaima, K. Tsianina. 1993. "Domesticity in the Federal Indian Schools: The Power of Authority over Mind and Body." *American Ethnologist* 20 (2): 227–240.

Long, Jonathan W., and Frank K. Lake. 2018. "Escaping Social-Ecological Traps through Tribal Stewardship on National Forest Lands in the Pacific Northwest, United States of America." *Ecology and Society* 23 (2).

Long, J. W., M. K. Anderson, L. Quinn-Davidson, R. W. Goode, F. K. Lake, and C. N. Skinner. 2016. "Restoring California Black Oak Ecosystems to Promote Tribal Values and Wildlife." Albany, CA: USDA Pacific Resource Research Station. https://www.fs.usda.gov/psw/publications/documents/psw_gtr252/psw_gtr252.pdf.

Long Tom Watershed Council. 2021. "Indigenous Fire Trainees Carry Out Prescribed Burn." October 19. https://www.longtom.org/indigenous-fire-trainees-carry-out-prescribed-burn/.

Lopesi, Lana. 2018. *False Divides*. Vol. 70. Wellington, NZ: Bridget Williams Books.

Lorde, Audre. 2003. "The Master's Tools Will Never Dismantle the Master's House." *Feminist Postcolonial Theory: A Reader* 25:27.

Lorde, Audre. 2012 [1984]. *Sister Outsider: Essays and Speeches.* Berkeley, CA: Crossing Press.

Loughridge, Robert McGill, and David M. Hodge. 1890. *English and Muskokee Dictionary.* St. Louis, MO: Printing House of JT Smith.

Lövbrand, Eva. 2011. "Co-producing European Climate Science and Policy: A Cautionary Note on the Making of Useful Knowledge." *Science and Public Policy* 38 (3): 225–236.

Luckey, J. 1995. "Native and Non-Native Perspectives on Aboriginal Traditional Environmental Knowledge." Unpublished major paper, Faculty of Environmental Studies, York University, Toronto.

Luschiim, Dr. Arvid Charlie. 2016. Elder and Plant Knowledge Keeper, Cowichan Tribes. Invasive species and Indigenous perspectives. Personal communication. March 25. Lands of the Cowichan People.

Lyons, Scott Richard. 2010. *X-Marks: Native Signatures of Assent.* Minneapolis: University of Minnesota Press.

Mach, Katharine J., Maria Carmen Lemos, Alison M. Meadow, Carina Wyborn, Nicole Klenk, James C. Arnott, Nicole M. Ardoin, et al. 2020. "Actionable Knowledge and the Art of Engagement." *Current Opinion in Environmental Sustainability* 42:30–37. https://doi.org/10.1016/j.cosust.2020.01.002.

MacKenzie, Melody Kapilialoha, Susan K. Serrano, D. Kapuaʻa Sproat, Ashley Kaiao Obrey, and Avis Kuuipoleialoha Poai, eds. 2015. *Native Hawaiian Law: A Treatise.* Honolulu: Kamehameha Publishing.

Macklin, Ruth. 2003. "Dignity Is a Useless Concept." *BMJ* 327 (7429): 1419–1420.

Macklin, Ruth. 2004. "Reflections on the Human Dignity Symposium: Is Dignity a Useless Concept?" *Journal of Palliative Care* 20 (3): 212–216.

Madrigal, T. 2015. "Partial Proceedings of the First Forum in Defense of Water." *Karani,* February 12. https://karani.wordpress.com/2015/02/12/partial-proceedings-of-the-first-forum-in-defense-of-water-yaqui-territory-community-of-vicam/.

Magallanes, Catherine J. 2018. "From Rights to Responsibilities Using Legal Personhood and Guardianship for Rivers." *Responsibility: Law and Governance for Living Well with the Earth,* edited by B. Martin, L. Te Aho, and M. Humphries-Kil, 216–239. London: Routledge.

Malo, Davida. 1951 [1903]. *Hawaiian Antiquities (moʻolelo Hawaiʻi).* Vol 2. Trans. Nathaniel Emerson. Honolulu: Hawaiian Gazette Company.

Maloney, Michelle. 2018. "Environmental Law: Changing the Legal Status of Nature: Recent Developments and Future Possibilities." *LSJ: Law Society Journal* 49:78–79.

Maloney, Thad C. 2015. "Thermoporosimetry of Hard (Silica) and Soft (Cellulosic) Materials by Isothermal Step Melting." *Journal of Thermal Analysis and Calorimetry* 121:7–17.

Maly, Kepā, and Onaona Maly. 2003. *Ka Hana Lawaiʻa a Me Nā Koʻa o Na Kai ʻewalu: A History of Fishing Practices and Marine Fisheries of the Hawaiian Islands.* Hilo, HI: Kumu Pono Associates.

Mann, Jeff, Tonia Gray, Son Truong, Pasi Sahlberg, Peter Bentsen, Rowena Passy, Susanna Ho, Kumara Ward, and Rachel Cowper. 2021. "A Systematic Review

Protocol to Identify the Key Benefits and Efficacy of Nature-Based Learning in Outdoor Educational Settings." *International Journal of Environmental Research and Public Health* 18 (3): 1199.

Marcum, Christopher Steven, and Ryan Donohue. 2022. "New Guidance to Ensure Federally Funded Research Data Equitably Benefits All of America." *OSTP Blog*, May 26. https://www.whitehouse.gov/ostp/news-updates/2022/05/26/new-guidance-to-ensure-federally-funded-research-data-equitably-benefits-all-of-america/.

Margil, Mari. 2014. "Building an International Movement for Rights of Nature." In *Wild Law—In Practice*, edited by Michelle Maloney and Peter Burdon, 149–160. New York: Routledge.

Mariani, Michela, Simon E. Connor, Martin Theuerkauf, Annika Herbert, Petr Kuneš, David Bowman, Michael-Shawn Fletcher, et al. 2022. "Disruption of Cultural Burning Promotes Shrub Encroachment and Unprecedented Wildfires." *Frontiers in Ecology and the Environment* 20 (5): 292–300.

Marino, Elizabeth. 2015. *Fierce Climate, Sacred Ground: An Ethnography of Climate Change in Shishmaref, Alaska*. Fairbanks: University of Alaska Press.

Marks-Block, Tony, Frank K. Lake, and Lisa M. Curran. 2019. "Effects of Understory Fire Management Treatments on California Hazelnut, an Ecocultural Resource of the Karuk and Yurok Indians in the Pacific Northwest." *Forest Ecology and Management* 450:117517.

Marks-Block, Tony, and William Tripp. 2021. "Facilitating Prescribed Fire in Northern California through Indigenous Governance and Interagency Partnerships." *Fire* 4 (3): 37.

Marmot, M. G., and Robert Sapolsky. 2014. *Of Baboons and Men: Social Circumstances, Biology and the Social Gradient in Health*. Washington, DC: National Academies Press.

Marr, C. J., and A. Fernando. 2013. "Between Two Worlds: Experiences at the Tulalip Indian Boarding School, 1905–1932."   https://www.hibulbculturalcenter.org/Base/File/HCC-PDF-Explore-AboutTulalipPeople-BetweenTwoWorlds.

Marshall, John, and Supreme Court of the United States. 1823. *U.S. Reports: Johnson v. McIntosh* 21 U.S. 8 Wheat. 543. Library of Congress Periodical. https://www.loc.gov/item/usrep021543/.

Marshall III, Joseph M. 2002. *The Lakota Way: Stories and Lessons for Living*. London: Penguin.

Marshall, Virginia. 2019. "Removing the Veil from the 'Rights of Nature': The Dichotomy between First Nations Customary Rights and Environmental Legal Personhood." *Australian Feminist Law Journal* 45 (2): 233–248.

Martin, C. W. 2011. "Shifting Paradigms in the Field of Invasion Ecology." *Journal of Ecosystem and Ecography* 1:e101.

Martin, Jack B., and Margaret McKane Mauldin. 2000. *A Dictionary of Creek/Muskogee*. Lincoln: University of Nebraska Press.

Maruska, K. P., A. Zhang, A. Neboori, and R. D. Fernald. 2013. "Social Opportunity Causes Rapid Transcriptional Changes in the Social Behaviour Network of the Brain in an African Cichlid Fish." *Journal of Neuroendocrinology* 25 (2): 145–157.

Marx, Karl, and Friedrich Engels. 1970. *The German Ideology*. Vol. 1. New York: International Publishers.

Maseko, P. B. Neo. 2018. "Transformative Praxis through Critical Consciousness: A Conceptual Exploration of a Decolonial Access with Success Agenda." *Educational Research for Social Change* 7 (SPE): 78–90.

Massey, Douglas S. 1996. "The Age of Extremes: Concentrated Affluence and Poverty in the Twenty-First Century." *Demography* 33:395–412.

Matapo, Jacoba, and Dion Enari. 2021. "Re-Imagining the Dialogic Spaces of Talanoa through Samoan Onto-Epistemology." *Waikato Journal of Education* 26:79–88. Special Issue: Talanoa Vā: Honouring Pacific Research and Online Engagement. https://doi.org/10.15663/wje.v26i1.770.

Matsui, Kenichi. 2015. "Introduction to the Future of Traditional Knowledge Research." *International Indigenous Policy Journal* 6 (2).

Mattson, David J., and Susan G. Clark. 2011. "Human Dignity in Concept and Practice." *Policy Sciences* 44 (4): 303–319.

Maunakea, Summer. 2019. "'Nē huli ka lima i lalo piha ka 'ōpū': 'Ōiwi Agency and Outcomes of 'Āina-Based Education." PhD diss., University of Hawai'i at Mānoa.

Mawhinney, Janet Lee. 1998. "Giving up the Ghost, Disrupting the (Re)production of White Privilege in Anti-Racist Pedagogy and Organizational Change." MA thesis, Ontario Institute for Studies in Education of the University of Toronto. https://tspace.library.utoronto.ca/bitstream/1807/12096/1/MQ33991.pdf.

Mays, Kyle. 2021a. "A Provocation of the Modes of Black Indigeneity: Culture, Language, Possibilities." *Ethnic Studies Review* 44 (2): 41–50.

Mays, Kyle. 2021b. *An Afro-Indigenous History of the United States*. Boston: Beacon Press.

McAllister, Tara, Daniel Hikuroa, and Cate Macinnis-Ng. 2023. "Connecting Science to Indigenous Knowledge: Kaitiakitanga, Conservation, and Resource Management." *New Zealand Journal of Ecology* 47 (1): 3521.

McCaffrey, Katherine T. 2002. *Military Power and Popular Protest: The US Navy in Vieques, Puerto Rico*. New Brunswick, NJ: Rutgers University Press.

McCartney, Ann M., Jane Anderson, Libby Liggins, Maui L. Hudson, Matthew Z. Anderson, Ben TeAika, Janis Geary, Robert Cook-Deegan, Hardip R. Patel, and Adam M. Phillippy. 2022. "Balancing Openness with Indigenous Data Sovereignty: An Opportunity to Leave No One Behind in the Journey to Sequence All of Life." *Proceedings of the National Academy of Sciences* 119 (4): e2115860119.

McDonald, James. 2005. "Cultivating in the Northwest: Early Accounts of Tsimshian Horticulture." *Keeping It Living: Traditions of Plant Use and Cultivation on the Northwest Coast of North America*, edited by Douglas Deur and Nancy Turner, 240–271. Seattle: University of Washington Press.

McDougal, Myres S., Harold D. Lasswell, and Lung-chu Chen. 2018. *Human Rights and World Public Order: The Basic Policies of an International Law of Human Dignity*. Oxford: Oxford University Press.

McGill, Bonnie M., Stephanie B. Borrelle, Grace C. Wu, Kurt E. Ingeman, Jonathan Berenguer Uhuad Koch, and Natchee B. Barnd. 2022. "Words Are Monuments: Patterns in US National Park Place Names Perpetuate Settler Colonial

Mythologies Including White Supremacy." *People and Nature* 4 (3): 683–700. https://doi.org/10.1002/pan3.10302.

McGregor, Davianna Pōmaikaʻi. 2007. *Nā Kuaʻāina: Living Hawaiian Culture*. Honolulu: University of Hawaiʻi Press.

McGregor, Davianna Pōmaikaʻi, Noa Emmett Aluli, and Rosanna ʻAnolani Alegado. 2020. "Lessons from Aloha ʻĀina Activism." In *The Value of Hawaiʻi 3: Hulihua, the Turning*, edited by Noelani Goodyear-Kaʻōpua, Craig Howes, Jonathan Kay Kamakawiwoʻole Osorio, and Aiko Yamashiro, 210–217. Honolulu: University of Hawaiʻi Press.

McGregor, Davianna Pōmaikaʻi, Paula T. Morelli, Jon K. Matsuoka, Rona Rodenhurst, Noella Kong, and Michael S. Spencer. 2003. "An Ecological Model of Native Hawaiian Well-Being." *Pacific Health Dialog* 10 (2): 106–128.

McGregor, Deborah. 2005. "Traditional Ecological Knowledge: An Anishinaabe Woman's Perspective." *Atlantis: Critical Studies in Gender, Culture and Social Justice* 29 (2): 103–109.

McGregor, Deborah. 2006. "Traditional Ecological Knowledge." *Ideas: The Arts and Science Review* 3 (1): 1–6.

McGregor, Deborah. 2008. "Linking Traditional Ecological Knowledge and Western Science: Aboriginal Perspectives from the 2000 State of the Lakes Ecosystem Conference." *Canadian Journal of Native Studies* 28 (1): 139–158.

McKinley, L., dir. 2014. *Campesino*. Vimeo video. https://vimeo.com/94948238.

McKinney, Stephen J. 2022. "'… and Yet There's Still No Peace': Catholic Indigenous Residential Schools in Canada." *Journal of Religious Education* 70:327–340.

McMichael, Philip. 2009. "A Food Regime Genealogy." *Journal of Peasant Studies* 36 (1): 139–169. https://doi.org/10.1080/03066150902820354.

McMichael, P. 2012. "The Land Grab and Corporate Food Regime Restructuring." *Journal of Peasant Studies* 39 (3/4): 681–701. https://doi.org/10.1080/03066150.2012.661369.

Meissner, Shelbi Nahwilet. 2022. "Teaching Reciprocity: Gifting and Land-Based Ethics in Indigenous Philosophy." *Teaching Ethics* 22 (1): 17–37.

Mengden, Walter H. IV. 2017. "Indigenous People, Human Rights, and Consultation: The Dakota Access Pipeline." *American Indian Law Review* 41 (2): 441–466.

Menon, Minakshi. 2022. "Indigenous Knowledges and Colonial Sciences in South Asia." *South Asian History and Culture* 13 (1): 1–18.

Menzies, Charles R., ed. 2006. *Traditional Ecological Knowledge and Natural Resource Management*. Lincoln: University of Nebraska Press.

Menzies, Charles R., and Caroline Butler. 2006. "Introduction: Understanding Ecological Knowledge." In *Traditional Ecological Knowledge and Natural Resource Management*, edited by Charles Menzies, 1–17. Lincoln: University of Nebraska Press.

Merk, Emily M. 2019. "A Growers Guide to Quality Potato Seed." *Creative Components* 411.

Merriam-Webster. nd. Curiosity. *Merriam-Webster.com Dictionary*. Accessed October 5, 2022. https://www.merriam-webster.com/dictionary/curiosity.

Merriam-Webster. nd. Suspicion. In *Merriam-Webster.com Dictionary*. Accessed October 5, 2022. https://www.merriam-webster.com/dictionary/suspicion.

Merson, John. 1990. *The Genius That Was China: East and West in the Making of the Modern World*. New York: Overlook Books.

Meyer, Manulani Aluli. 2004. *Hoʻoulu: Our Time of Becoming: Collected Early Writings of Manulani Meyer*. Honolulu: ʻAi Pōhaku Press/University of Hawaiʻi Press.

Meyer, Manulani Aluli. 2008. "Indigenous and Authentic: Hawaiian Epistemology and the Triangulation of Meaning." In *Handbook of Critical and Indigenous Methodologies*, edited by Norman K. Denzin, Yvonna S. Lincoln, and Linda Tuhiwai Smith, 217–232. Thousand Oaks, CA: Sage.

Midzain-Gobin, Liam. 2019. "Decolonizing Borders." January 12. https://www.e-ir.info/2019/01/12/decolonizing-borders/.

Mignolo, Walter D. 2021. "Coloniality and Globalization: A Decolonial Take." *Globalizations* 18 (5): 720–737.

Mihesuah, Devon Abbott, ed. 1998. *Natives and Academics: Researching and Writing about American Indians*. Lincoln: University of Nebraska Press.

Miller, R. J. 2006. *Native America, Discovered and Conquered: Thomas Jefferson, Lewis & Clark, and Manifest Destiny*. New York: Bloomsbury.

Miller, Robert J. 2015. "Consultation or Consent: The United States' Duty to Confer with American Indian Governments." *Notre Dame Law Review* 91:37.

Miller, Robert J., and Micheline D'Angelis. 2011. "Brazil, Indigenous Peoples, and the International Law of Discovery." *Brooklyn Journal of International Law* 37:1.

Miller, Robert J., Jacinta Ruru, Larissa Behrendt, and Tracey Lindberg. 2010. *Discovering Indigenous Lands: The Doctrine of Discovery in the English Colonies*. Oxford: Oxford University Press.

Million, Dian. 2009. "Felt Theory: An Indigenous Feminist Approach to Affect and History." *Wicazo Sa Review* 24 (2): 53–76.

Minasny, Budiman, Dian Fiantis, Budi Mulyanto, Yiyi Sulaeman, and Wirastuti Widyatmanti. 2020. "Global Soil Science Research Collaboration in the 21st Century: Time to End Helicopter Research." *Geoderma* 373:114299.

Minister, Christopher. 2019. "Biography of Antonio de Montesinos, Defender of Indigenous Rights: A Voice Crying in the Wilderness." August 20. https://www.thoughtco.com/antonio-de-montesinos-2136370.

Mitchell, Todd A., Nicole J. Casper, Lindsay T. Logan, Erin M. Colclazier, and Karen J. R. Mitchell. 2024 (in press). "Using Traditional Ecological Knowledge to Protect Wetlands: The Swinomish Tribe's Wetland Cultural Assessment." *Ethnobiology Letters*.

Mitchell, Todd A., and Rebecca Kobel. 2024. *Our Ways Book 2, Testimonies of the Swinomish Way of Life, Swinomish Tribal Community, LaConner, WA*. Available from and located in the Swinomish DEP collection.

Mitchell, Todd A., Debra Lekanoff, and Fern M. Schultz. 2011. *Our Ways, Testimonies of the Swinomish Way of Life, Swinomish Tribal Community, LaConner, WA*. Available from and located in the Swinomish DEP collection.

Mitchell, Todd A., Karen J. R. Mitchell, Shannon B. Stewart, Heidi M. Bock, and Nicole J. Casper. 2024 (in preparation). Water Level and Water Quality Responses to Increased Tidal Flux after Installation of Self-Regulating Tidegates.

Mohamed, Tameera, and Brenda L. Beagan. 2019. "'Strange Faces' in the Academy: Experiences of Racialized and Indigenous Faculty in Canadian Universities." *Race Ethnicity and Education* 22 (3): 338–354.

Mohatt, Gerald V., Kelly L. Hazel, James Allen, Mary Stachelrodt, Chase Hensel, and Robert Fath. 2004. "Unheard Alaska: Culturally Anchored Participatory Action Research on Sobriety with Alaska Natives." *American Journal of Community Psychology* 33 (3/4): 263–273.

Möhlenkamp, Paula, Charles Kaiaka Beebe, Margaret A. McManus, Angela Hi'ilei Kawelo, Keli'iahonui Kotubetey, Mirielle Lopez-Guzman, Craig E. Nelson, and Rosanna 'Anolani Alegado. 2018. "Kū Hou Kuapā: Cultural Restoration Improves Water Budget and Water Quality Dynamics in He'eia Fishpond." *Sustainability* 11 (1): 161.

Molloy, Luke. 2019. "The Ideas of Frantz Fanon and Practices of Cultural Safety with Australia's First Peoples." In *Frantz Fanon's Psychotherapeutic Approaches to Clinical Work*, edited by Lou Turner and Helen Neville, 183–196. New York: Routledge.

Montana v. United States. 1981. 450 U.S. 544.

Montgomery, Michelle, and Paulette Blanchard. 2021. "Testing Justice: New Ways to Address Environmental Inequalities." *Solutions Journal*, February 17.

Montgomery, Monica, and Mehana Vaughan. 2018. "Ma Kahana ka 'Ike: Lessons for Community-Based Fisheries Management." *Sustainability* 10 (10): 3799.

Mo'otz Kuxtal Voluntary Guidelines. 2016. Conference of Parties to the Convention on Biological Diversity, Decision XIII/18. U.N. Doc. CBD/COP/DEC/XIII/18. https://www.cbd.int/doc/c/e2f2/d701/a0b64957a0c70ed531c5d542/cop-13-dec-18-en.pdf.

Morales, Ed. 2019. *Fantasy Island: Colonialism, Exploitation, and the Betrayal of Puerto Rico.* New York: Bold Type Books.

Moreton-Robinson, Aileen, ed. 2016. *Critical Indigenous Studies: Engagements in First World Locations.* Tucson: University of Arizona Press.

Morgan, Richard K. 2012. "Environmental Impact Assessment: The State of the Art." *Impact Assessment and Project Appraisal* 30 (1): 5–14.

Morishige, Kanoe'ulalani, Pelika Andrade, Pua'ala Pascua, Kanoelani Steward, Emily Cadiz, Lauren Kapono, and Uakoko Chong. 2018. "Nā Kilo 'Āina: Visions of Biocultural Restoration through Indigenous Relationships between People and Place." *Sustainability* 10 (10): 3368.

Morrow, David R., Michael S. Thompson, Angela Anderson, Maya Batres, Holly J. Buck, Kate Dooley, Oliver Geden, et al. 2020. "Principles for Thinking about Carbon Dioxide Removal in Just Climate Policy." *One Earth* 3 (2): 150–153.

Moy, Karen L., James F. Sallis, and Katrine J. David. 2010. "Health Indicators of Native Hawaiian and Pacific Islanders in the United States." *Journal of Community Health* 35:81–92.

Muldoon, James, and Edward Peters, eds. 1977. *The Expansion of Europe: The First Phase.* Philadelphia: University of Pennsylvania Press.

Muscogee Creek Nation. nd. a. "Muscogee (Creek) Nation History. Muscogee Nation. Accessed November 13, 2021. https://www.muscogeenation.com/culturehistory/.

Muscogee Creek Nation. nd. b. "Mvskoke History: A Short Course for Muscogee Nation Employees." State of Oklahoma. Accessed November 13, 2021. https://sde.ok.gov/sites/ok.gov.sde/files/Mvskoke_History_Powerpoint.pdf.

Museus, S. D., and A. C. Wang. 2022. "Refusing Neoliberal Logics in Research Design." In *Weaving an Otherwise: In-Relations Methodological Practice*, edited by Amanda R. Tachine and Z. Nicolazzo, 15–28. Sterling, VA: Stylus Publishing.

Mustonen, Tero, Sherilee Harper, Gretta Pecl, Vanesa Castán Broto, Nina Lansbury, A. Okem, A. Ayanlade, et al. 2022. "Cross-Chapter Box INDIG: The Role of Indigenous Knowledge and Local Knowledge in Understanding and Adapting to Climate Change." In *IPCC Climate Change 2022: Impacts, Adaptation and Vulnerability. Contribution of Working Group II to the Sixth Assessment Report of the Intergovernmental Panel on Climate Change*, edited by H.-O. Pörtner, D. C. Roberts, M. Tignor, E. S. Poloczanska, K. Mintenbeck, A. Alegría, M. Craig, et al., 2713–2807. https://www.researchgate.net/publication/362432216_The_Role_of_Indigenous_Knowledge_and_Local_Knowledge_in_Understanding_and_Adapting_to_Climate_Change.

Mwampamba, Tuyeni H., Benis N. Egoh, Israel Borokini, and Kevin Njabo. 2022. "Challenges Encountered When Doing Research Back Home: Perspectives from African Conservation Scientists in the Diaspora." *Conservation Science and Practice* 4 (5): e564.

Nadasdy, Paul. 2003. *Hunters and Bureaucrats: Power, Knowledge, and Aboriginal-State Relations in the Southwest Yukon*. Vancouver: University of British Columbia Press.

Nagler, P. L., K. Morino, K. Didan, J. Erker, J. Osterberg, K. R. Hultine, and E. P. Glenn. 2009. "Wide-Area Estimates of Saltcedar (*Tamarix* spp.) Evapotranspiration on the Lower Colorado River Measured by Heat Balance and Remote Sensing Methods." *Ecohydrology* 2 (1): 18–33.

Nakachi, Kaikea I. 2021. "Heeding the History of Kahu Manō: Developing and Validating a Pono Photo-Identification Methodology for Tiger Sharks (*Galeocerdo cuvier*) in Hawai'i." Master's thesis, University of Hawai'i at Hilo.

Nally, David. 2008. "'That Coming Storm': The Irish Poor Law, Colonial Biopolitics, and the Great Famine." *Annals of the Association of American Geographers* 98 (3): 714–741.

NARF. 2024. "Protecting Bears Ears National Monument." https://narf.org/cases/bears-ears/.

Natonabah, Serena, Brianne Dewani Lauro, Dominique M. David-Chavez, and Stephanie Carroll. 2020. "How Are We Supporting Indigenous Data Stewards? Aligning Indigenous and Federal Environmental Science Research Ethics Guidelines." *AGU Fall Meeting Abstracts* 2020: SY020-0010. https://ui.adsabs.harvard.edu/abs/2020AGUFMSY0200010N/abstract.

Necefer, L. 2022. "The Comanagement of Bears Ears Is an Important Step in Tackling Climate Change." *Outside Online*, June 29. https://www.outsideonline.com/outdoor-adventure/exploration-survival/co-management-bears-ears-tribes/.

Neeganagwedgin, Erica. 2013. "Ancestral Knowledges, Spirituality and Indigenous Narratives as Self-Determination." *AlterNative: An International Journal of Indigenous Peoples* 9 (4): 322–334.

Nelson, Melissa K. 2014. "Indigenous Science and Traditional Ecological Knowledge: Persistence in Place." In *The World of Indigenous North America*, edited by Robert Warrior, 214–240. New York: Routledge.

Nelson, Melissa K., and Daniel Shilling, eds. 2018. *Traditional Ecological Knowledge: Learning from Indigenous Practices for Environmental Sustainability.* Cambridge, UK: Cambridge University Press.

Newcomb, Steven. 2015. "PERSPECTIVES: Healing, Restoration, and Rematriation." *Indigenous Law Institute, News and Notes* (Spring/Summer): 3. http://ili.nativeweb.org/perspect.html.

New Design Congress. 2022. "Memory in Uncertainty: Web Preservation in the Polycrisis." New Design Congress Report, November 11, p. 35. https://newdesigncongress.org/en/report/2022/memory-in-uncertainty/.

Newland, Bryan. 2022. "Federal Indian Boarding School Initiative Investigative Report." Washington, DC: US Department of the Interior.

Ng, Wendy, and J'Net AyAyQwaYakSheelth. 2018. "Decolonize and Indigenize: A Reflective Dialogue: Viewfinder: Reflecting on Museum Education." *Medium*, June 12. https://medium.com/viewfinder-reflecting-on-museum-education/decolonize-and-indigenize-a-reflective-dialogue-3de78fa76442.

Ng Chok, Sefo Tuumatavai, Iokapeta Ng Lam, Roreta Lee, and Ruta Ng Chok. 2022. In discussion with author Leasi Vanessa Lee Raymond, October 31.

Nicholas, George. 2018. "It's Taken Thousands of Years, but Western Science Is Finally Catching Up to Traditional Knowledge." *The Conversation* 15.

Nichols, Johanna. 1990. "Linguistic Diversity and the First Settlement of the New World." *Language* 66 (3): 475–521.

NICWA (National Indian Child Welfare Association). nd. "About ICWA." Accessed December 1, 2022. https://www.nicwa.org/about-icwa/.

Nixon, R. 1970. "Special Message to the Congress on Indian Affairs." Public papers of the presidents of the United States, Richard Nixon, containing the public messages, speeches, and statements of the president. https://www.presidency.ucsb.edu/documents/special-message-the-congress-indian-affairs.

Nkrumah, Kwame. 1970. *Class Struggle in Africa.* London: Panaf Books.

Norström, Albert V., Christopher Cvitanovic, Marie F. Löf, Simon West, Carina Wyborn, Patricia Balvanera, Angela T. Bednarek, et al. 2020. "Principles for Knowledge Co-Production in Sustainability Research." *Nature Sustainability* 3 (3): 182–190. https://doi.org/10.1038/s41893-019-0448-2.

Northwest Ordinance. 1787. July 13, 1787, 1 Stat. 50. https://constitutioncenter.org/the-constitution/historic-document-library/detail/the-northwest-ordinance#:~:text=Summary,slavery%20in%20the%20new%20territories.

Norton, W. H. 2013. "Toward Developmental Models of Psychiatric Disorders in Zebrafish." *Frontiers in Neural Circuits* 7:79.

NPS (National Park Service). nd. "Muscogee (Creek) Removal." Accessed November 13, 2021. https://www.nps.gov/ocmu/learn/historyculture/upload/Accessible-Muscogee-Creek-Removal.pdf.

NPS (National Park Service). 1998. Director's Order #28: Cultural Resource Management. Approved: Robert Stanton, Director, National Park Service. Effective Date: June 11. https://www.nps.gov/policy/DOrders/DOrder28.html.

NPS (National Park Service). 2016. "Rule No. 2016-16434." Federal Register 81, no. 133 (July 12): 45024–45039. https://www.federalregister.gov/documents/2016/07/12/2016-16434/gathering-of-certainplants-or-plant-parts-by-federally-recognized-indian-tribes-for-traditional.

NPS (National Park Service). 2019. "St. Paul's Mission." https://www.nps.gov/places/mission-point.htm#:~:text=continuous%20human%20presence.-,St.,to%20the%20public%20year%20round.

NSF (National Science Foundation). 2018. "NSF 19-511 Navigating the New Arctic (NNA)." https://new.nsf.gov/funding/opportunities/navigating-new-arctic-nna/505594/nsf19-511/solicitation.

Nuʻuhiwa, Kalei. 2019. "A Methodology and Pedagogy of Understanding the Hawaiian Universe." In *The Past Before Us: Moʻokūʻauhau as Methodology*, edited by Nālani Wilson-Hokowhitu, 39–49. Honolulu: University of Hawaiʻi Press.

O'Donnell, Erin L. 2018. "At the Intersection of the Sacred and the Legal: Rights for Nature in Uttarakhand, India." *Journal of Environmental Law* 30 (1): 135–144.

O'Donnell, Erin L., and Julia Talbot-Jones. 2018. "Creating Legal Rights for Rivers." *Ecology and Society* 23 (1).

Oishi, S. 2000. "Goals as Cornerstones of Subjective Well-Being: Linking Individuals and Culture." In *Culture and Subjective Well-Being*, edited by E. Diener and E. M. Suh, 87–112. Cambridge, MA: MIT Press.

Okamoto, Scott K., Stephen Kulis, Flavio F. Marsiglia, Lori K. Holleran Steiker, and Patricia Dustman. 2014. "A Continuum of Approaches toward Developing Culturally Focused Prevention Interventions: From Adaptation to Grounding." *Journal of Primary Prevention* 35 (2): 103–112.

Oliphant v. Suquamish Indian Tribe. 1978. 435 U.S. 191.

Oliveira, Katrina-Ann R. 2014. *Ancestral Places: Understanding Kanaka Geographies*. Corvallis: Oregon State University Press.

Oliveira, Katrina-Ann R., and Erin Kahunawaikaʻala Wright. 2016. *Kanaka ʻŌiwi Methodologies: Moʻolelo and Metaphor*. Honolulu: University of Hawaiʻi Press.

Oliveira, R. F. 2012. "Social Plasticity in Fish: Integrating Mechanisms and Function." *Journal of Fish Biology* 81 (7): 2127–2150.

Oluo, Ijeoma. 2019. *So You Want to Talk about Race*. New York: Seal Press.

O'Neal, Jennifer, and Kevin Hatfield. 2020. "Decolonizing Research: The Northern Paiute History Project." *Western Humanities Review* (Fall).

Orange, Myra Johnson. 2020. Interview with Jennifer O'Neal and Elizabeth Kallenbach. December 8.

Oregon State University's Traditional Ecological Knowledge Club. *2022 Traditional Ecological Knowledge Summit: White House Presentation and Public Listening Session*. YouTube video, 1:25:27. May 2022. https://www.youtube.com/watch?v=LEpnJgYe83c.

Ortiz Cuadra, Cruz M. 2017. *Eating Puerto Rico: A History of Food, Culture, and Identity*. Trans. Russ Davidson. Chapel Hill: University of North Carolina Press.

Osorio, Jamaica Heolimeleikalani. 2021. *Remembering Our Intimacies: Moʻolelo, Aloha ʻĀina, and Ea*. Minneapolis: University of Minnesota Press.

Osorio, Jonathan Kamakawiwoʻole. 2001. "'What Kine Hawaiian Are You?': A Moʻolelo about Nationhood, Race, History, and the Contemporary Sovereignty Movement in Hawaiʻi." *Contemporary Pacific* 13 (2): 359–379.

Ostler, Jeffrey. 2016. "'Just and Lawful War' as Genocidal War in the (United States) Northwest Ordinance and Northwest Territory, 1787–1832." *Journal of Genocide Research* 18 (1): 1–20.

Otis, Delos Sacket. 2014. *The Dawes Act and the Allotment of Indian Lands*. Vol. 123. Norman: University of Oklahoma Press.

Pacheco, Christina M., Sean M. Daley, Travis Brown, Melissa Filippi, K. Allen Greiner, and Christine M. Daley. 2013. "Moving Forward: Breaking the Cycle of Mistrust between American Indians and Researchers." *American Journal of Public Health* 103 (12): 2152–2159.

Pagden, Anthony. 1991. *Vitoria: Political Writings*. Cambridge Texts in the History of Political Thought. Cambridge, UK: Cambridge University Press.

Paki, Pilahi. 1962. Hawaiian Civic Club of Wahiawā Meeting Minutes, Oʻahu, Hawaiʻi. November 9. https://hoikaha.org/key-tenets-of-aloha/.

Paki, Pilahi. 1984. Speech to the International Society of Ministers at Mauna Kea, Hawaiʻi. January 23. https://hoikaha.org/key-tenets-of-aloha/.

Palaganas, Erlinda C., Marian C. Sanchez, Visitacion P. Molintas, and Ruel D. Caricativo. 2017. "Reflexivity in Qualitative Research: A Journey of Learning." *Qualitative Report* 22 (2).

Palmer, Joel. 1854. "Letter of March 27, 1854," 1854. Documents relating to the Negotiation of an Unratified treaty March 25, 1854, with the Kalapuya Indians. Records of the Oregon Superintendency of Indian Affairs, 1848–1873, Microfilm series M-2, Reel 4.

Park, Augustine S. J., and Jasmeet Bahia. 2022. "Examining the Experiences of Racialized and Indigenous Graduate Students as Emerging Researchers." *Sociology of Race and Ethnicity* 8 (3): 403–417.

Park, Han S. 1987. "Correlates of Human Rights: Global Tendencies." *Human Rights Quarterly* 9:405.

Parker, J. D., M. E. Torchin, R. A. Hufbauer, N. P. Lemoine, C. Alba, D. M. Blumenthal, O. Bossdorf, et al. 2013. "Do Invasive Species Perform Better in Their New Ranges?" *Ecology* 94 (5): 985–994.

Parolin, Zachary, Sophie Collyer, and Megan A. Curran. 2022. "Absence of Monthly Child Tax Credit Leads to 3.7 Million More Children in Poverty in January 2022." *Poverty and Social Policy Brief* 6 (2). www.povertycenter.columbia.edu/publication/monthly-poverty-january-2022.

Pascua, Pua'ala, Heather McMillen, Tamara Ticktin, Mehana Vaughan, and Kawika B. Winter. 2017. "Beyond Services: A Process and Framework to Incorporate Cultural, Genealogical, Place-Based, and Indigenous Relationships in Ecosystem Service Assessments." *Ecosystem Services* 26:465–475.

Patton, Michael Quinn. 1999. "Enhancing the Quality and Credibility of Qualitative Analysis." *Health Services Research* 34 (5) Pt 2: 1189.

Pauketat, Timothy R. 2004. *Ancient Cahokia and the Mississippians*. No. 6. Cambridge, UK: Cambridge University Press.

Pauly, P. J. 2008. *Fruits and Plains: The Horticultural Transformation of America*. Cambridge, MA: Harvard University Press.

Paxton, E. H., T. C. Theimer, and M. K. Sogge. 2011. "Tamarisk Biocontrol Using Tamarisk Beetles: Potential Consequences for Riparian Birds in the Southwestern United States." *The Condor* 113 (2): 255–265.

Pecharroman, Lidia C. 2018. "Rights of Nature: Rivers That Can Stand in Court." *Resources* 7 (1): 13.

Pete, Shauneen, Bettina Schneider, and Kathleen O'Reilly. 2013. "Decolonizing Our Practice: Indigenizing Our Teaching." *First Nations Perspectives* 5 (1): 99–115.

Phillips, Laura. 2022. "Teaching Decolonizing and Indigenizing Curatorial and Museum Practices." *Museum Worlds* 10 (1): 112–131.

Pielke Jr., Roger A. 2007. *The Honest Broker: Making Sense of Science in Policy and Politics*. Cambridge, UK: Cambridge University Press.

Pierotti, Raymond, and Daniel Wildcat. 2000. "Traditional Ecological Knowledge: The Third Alternative (Commentary)." *Ecological Applications* 10 (5): 1333–1340.

Pitawanakwat, Brock Thorbjorn, and Celeste Pedri-Spade. 2022. "Indigenization in Universities and Its Role in Continuing Settler-Colonialism." *Janus Unbound: Journal of Critical Studies* 1 (2): 12–35.

Pizarro, Mohammad. 2021. "Loko I'a Fishponds, Story of Hawai'i Communities Restoring Fisheries and Traditional Food System." *Community Fisheries* (blog). February 20.

Porter, James J., and Suraje Dessai. 2017. "Mini-Me: Why Do Climate Scientists' Misunderstand Users and Their Needs ?" *Environmental Science and Policy* 77 (December): 9–14.

Poudyal, Mahesh, Bruno S. Ramamonjisoa, Neal Hockley, O. Sarobidy Rakotonarivo, James M. Gibbons, Rina Mandimbiniaina, Alexandra Rasoamanana, and Julia P. G. Jones. 2016. "Can REDD+ Social Safeguards Reach the 'Right' people? Lessons from Madagascar." *Global Environmental Change* 37:31–42.

Povinelli, Elizabeth A. 2020. *Economies of Abandonment: Social Belonging and Endurance in Late Liberalism*. Durham, NC: Duke University Press.

Powell, T., and J. Fraser. 1892. "The Samoan Story of Creation: A Tala." *Journal of the Polynesian Society* 1 (3): 164–189.

Prabhakar, Arati, and Brenda Mallory. 2022a. "Implementation of Guidance for Federal Departments and Agencies on Indigenous Knowledge." Memorandum, November 30. Washington, DC: Office of Science and Technology Policy, Council on Environmental Quality.

Prabhakar, Arati, and Brenda Mallory. 2022b. "Guidance for Federal Departments and Agencies on Indigenous Knowledge." Washington, DC: Office of Science and Technology Policy, Council on Environmental Quality. https://www.whitehouse.gov/wp-content/uploads/2022/12/OSTP-CEQ-IK-Guidance.pdf.

Pratt, Richard H. 2013. "The Advantages of Mingling Indians with Whites." In *Americanizing the American Indian*, by Francis Paul Prucha, 260–271. Cambridge, MA: Harvard University Press.

Press Pool. 2022. "Chair Grijalva Celebrates Historic Tribal Co-Management Agreement for Bears Ears National Monument: Bureau of Land Management, U.S. Forest Service, and Five Tribes Making Up Bears Ears Commission Sign Inter-Governmental Cooperative Agreement." News Release, June 22. Democrats on the House Natural Resources Committee. https://democrats-naturalresources.house.gov/media/press-releases/chair-grijalva-celebrates-historic-tribal-co-management-agreement-for-bears-ears-national-monument.

Proctor, Robert N., and Londa Schiebinger, eds. 2008. "Agnotology: The Making and Unmaking of Ignorance." Stanford, CA: Stanford University Press. https://philarchive.org/archive/PROATM.

Prucha, Francis Paul. 2014. *American Indian Policy in Crisis: Christian Reformers and the Indian, 1865–1900*. Norman: University of Oklahoma Press.

Pukui, Mary. 1983. *'Ōlelo No'eau: Hawaiian Proverbs & Poetical Sayings*. Honolulu: Bishop Museum Press.

Pukui, Mary Kawena, and Samuel H. Elbert. 1986. *Hawaiian Dictionary: Hawaiian-English English-Hawaiian Revised and Enlarged Edition*. Honolulu: University of Hawai'i Press.

Puniwai, Noelani. 2020. "Pua ka wiliwili, nanahu ka manō: Understanding Sharks in Hawaiian Culture." *Human Biology* 92 (1): 11–17.

Puniwai, Noelani, Steven Gray, Christopher A. Lepczyk, Aloha Kapono, and Craig Severance. 2016. "Mapping Ocean Currents through Human Observations: Insights from Hilo Bay, Hawai'i." *Human Ecology* 44:365–374.

Pyne, Stephen J. 2015. *Between Two Fires: A Fire History of Contemporary America*. Tucson: University of Arizona Press.

Quinless, Jacqueline M. 2022. *Decolonizing Data: Unsettling Conversations about Social Research Methods*. Toronto: University of Toronto Press.

Rainie, Stephanie Carroll, Desi Rodriguez-Lonebear, and Andrew Martinez. 2017. "Policy Brief: Data Governance for Native Nation Rebuilding (Version 2)." Tucson: University of Arizona, Native Nations Institute. http://nni.arizona.edu/application/files/8415/0007/5708/Policy_Brief_Data_Governance_for_Native_Nation_Rebuilding_Version_2.pdf.

Ramos, Seafha C. 2018. "Considerations for Culturally Sensitive Traditional Ecological Knowledge Research in Wildlife Conservation." *Wildlife Society Bulletin* 42 (2): 358–365.

Ratzlaff, C., D. Matsumoto, N. Kouznetsova, J. Rarque, and R. Ray. 2000. "Individual Psychological Culture and Subjective Well-Being." In *Culture and Subjective Well-Being*, edited by E. Diener and E. M. Suh, 13–36. Cambridge, MA: MIT Press.

RDAIDSIG (Research Data Alliance International Data Sovereignty Interest Group). 2019. "CARE Principles for Indigenous Data Governance." The Global Indigenous Data Alliance. September. https://www.rd-alliance.org/app/uploads/2024/03/CARE20Principles20for20Indigenous20Data20Governance_OnePagers_FINAL20Sept2006202019.pdf.

Reddi, Madhavi, Rachel Kuo, and Daniel Kreiss. 2021. "Identity Propaganda: Racial Narratives and Disinformation." *New Media and Society* 25 (2): 14614448211029293.

Refiti, Albert. 2010. "Whiteness, Smoothing and the Origin of Samoan Architecture." *Interstices: A Journal of Architecture and Related Arts* 10. https://openrepository.aut.ac.nz/server/api/core/bitstreams/68b8f4e4-d424-4fd0-91fe-a2ed21563bbd/content.

Reo, Nicholas James, and Kyle Powys Whyte. 2012. "Hunting and Morality as Elements of Traditional Ecological Knowledge." *Human Ecology* 40 (1): 15–27.

Resnicow, Ken, Robin Soler, Ronald L. Braithwaite, Jasjit S. Ahluwalia, and Jacqueline Butler. 2000. "Cultural Sensitivity in Substance Use Prevention." *Journal of Community Psychology* 28 (3): 271–290.

Reyes, Nicole Alia Salis. 2018. "A Space for Survivance: Locating Kānaka Maoli through the Resonance and Dissonance of Critical Race Theory." *Race Ethnicity and Education* 21 (6): 739–756.

Reyes-García, Victoria, Adrien Tofighi-Niaki, Beau J. Austin, Petra Benyei, Finn Danielsen, Álvaro Fernández-Llamazares, Aditi Sharma, Ramin Soleymani-Fard, and Maria Tengö. 2022. "Data Sovereignty in Community-Based Environmental Monitoring: Toward Equitable Environmental Data Governance." *BioScience* 72 (8): 714–717.

Reyes-García, Victoria, Álvaro Fernández-Llamazares, Pamela McElwee, Zsolt Molnár, Kinga Öllerer, Sarah J. Wilson, and Eduardo S. Brondizio. 2019. "The Contributions of Indigenous Peoples and Local Communities to Ecological Restoration." *Restoration Ecology* 27 (1): 3–8.

Ricart, Aurora M., Dorte Krause-Jensen, Kasper Hancke, Nichole N. Price, Pere Masqué, and Carlos M. Duarte. 2022. "Sinking Seaweed in the Deep Ocean for Carbon Neutrality Is ahead of Science and beyond the Ethics." *Environmental Research Letters* 17 (8): 081003.

Ricciardi, A., and J. Cohen. 2007. "The Invasiveness of an Introduced Species Does Not Predict Its Impact." *Biological Invasions* 9:309–315.

Rights of Nature and Future Generations Bill. 2019. https://www.parliament.wa.gov.au/Parliament/Bills.nsf/A83E23DAE4373236482584AB002386A7/$File/Bill151-1.pdf.

Rigney, Lester-Irabinna. 1997. "Internationalism of an Aboriginal or Torres Strait Islander Anti-Colonial Cultural Critique of Research Methodologies: A Guide to Indigenist Research Methodology and Its Principles." *Research and Development in Higher Education: Advancing International Perspectives* 20:629–636.

Risam, Roopika. 2018. "Decolonizing the Digital Humanities in Theory and Practice." In *The Routledge Companion to Media Studies and Digital Humanities*, edited by Jentery Sayers, 78–86. New York: Routledge.

Ritschl, D. 2001. "Can Ethical Maxims Be Derived from Theological Concepts of Human Dignity?" In *The Concept of Human Dignity in Human Rights Discourse*, edited by D. Kretzmer and E. Klein, 37–59. New York: Kluwer Law International.

Rodney, Walter. 2018 [1972]. *How Europe Underdeveloped Africa*. Repr. New York: Verso Books.

Rodríguez Aguilera, Meztli Yoalli. 2022. "Grieving Geographies, Mourning Waters: Life, Death, and Environmental Gendered Racialized Struggles in Mexico." *Feminist Anthropology* 3 (1): 28–43.

Rodríguez, Dylan. 2012. "Racial/Colonial Genocide and the 'Neoliberal Academy': In Excess of a Problematic." *American Quarterly* 64 (4): 809–813.

Rose, Jeff, Aleksandra Pitt, Rose Verbos, and Lark Weller. 2022. "Incorporating Movements for Racial Justice into Planning and Management of US National Parks." *Journal of Park and Recreation Administration* 40 (1).

"Rules of Warfare—Francisco De Vitoria (1483–1546)." 2008. *The Wonderful World of Reno Ohio* (blog). October 14. sandhillumc.wordpress.com/2008/10/14/rules-of-warfare%E2%80%94francisco-de-vitoria-1483-%E2%80%93-1546/.

Russell, B. 1948. *Human Knowledge: Its Scope and Limits*. New York: Simon and Schuster.

Russell, J. C., and T. Blackburn. 2017. "The Rise of Invasive Species Denialism." *Trends in Ecology and Evolution* 32 (1): 3–6.

Saad, Layla F. 2020. *Me and White Supremacy*. Naperville, IL: Sourcebooks.

Said, Edward. 2014 [1978]. *Orientalism: 25th Anniversary Edition*. Repr. New York: Random House.

Salas Jr., Victor M. 2011. "Francisco de Vitoria on the Ius Gentium and the American Indios." *Ave Maria Law Review* 10:331.

Salmón, Enrique. 2000. "Kincentric Ecology: Indigenous Perceptions of the Human–Nature Relationship." *Ecological Applications* 10 (5): 1327–1332.

Salmón, Enrique. 2017. "Resilience and Rebellious Memory Loops: Further Musings of an American Indian Ethnoecologist." *American Indian Culture and Research Journal* 41 (3): 127–132.

Sandin, S. A., J. E. Smith, E. E. DeMartini, E. A. Dinsdale, S. D. Donner, A. M. Friedlander, T. Konotchick, et al. 2008. "Baselines and Degradation of Coral Reefs in the Northern Line Islands." *PLOS One* 3 (2): p.e1548.

Sandoval, Cueponcaxochitl D. Moreno, Rosalva Mojica Lagunas, Lydia T. Montelongo, and Marisol Juárez Díaz. 2016. "Ancestral Knowledge Systems: A Conceptual Framework for Decolonizing Research in Social Science." *AlterNative: An International Journal of Indigenous Peoples* 12 (1): 18–31.

Sarkki, Simo, Rob Tinch, Jari Niemelä, Ulrich Heink, Kerry Waylen, Johannes Timaeus, Juliette Young, Allan Watt, Carsten Neßhöver, and Sybille van den Hove. 2015. "Adding 'Iterativity' to the Credibility, Relevance, Legitimacy: A Novel Scheme to Highlight Dynamic Aspects of Science-Policy Interfaces." *Environmental Science and Policy* 54:505–512. https://doi.org/10.1016/j.envsci.2015.02.016.

Saulters, O., E. Sheets, and M. Junker. 2021. "Indigenous Brownfields: Visioning, Listening, and Co-Creating the Future." Presentation, Tribal Lands and Environment Forum, Northern Arizona University. August 17. https://

mediaspace.nau.edu/media/Indigenous+BrownfieldsA+Visioning%2C+Listening %2C+and+Co-Creating+the+Future/1_4emi2ti9.

Schachter, Oscar. 1983. "Human Dignity as a Normative Concept." *American Journal of International Law* 77 (4): 848–854.

Schillmoller, Anne, and Alessandro Pelizzon. 2013. "Mapping the Terrain of Earth Jurisprudence: Landscape, Thresholds and Horizons." *Environmental and Earth Law Journal* 3:1.

Schneider, Tsim D., and Katherine Hayes. 2020. "Epistemic Colonialism: Is It Possible to Decolonize Archaeology?" *American Indian Quarterly* 44 (2): 127–148.

Schultz, P. Wesley. 2000. "New Environmental Theories: Empathizing with Nature: The Effects of Perspective Taking on Concern for Environmental Issues." *Journal of Social Issues* 56 (3): 391–406.

Schultz, P. Wesley. 2001. "The Structure of Environmental Concern: Concern for Self, Other People, and the Biosphere." *Journal of Environmental Psychology* 21 (4): 327–339.

Schwartz, Shalom H. 2007. "Universalism Values and the Inclusiveness of Our Moral Universe." *Journal of Cross-Cultural Psychology* 38 (6): 711–728.

Scott, Joe. 2022. "Traditional Ecological Inquiry Program (TEIP)." Long Tom Watershed Council. January 12. https://www.longtom.org/community/teip/.

Settles, Isis H., NiCole T. Buchanan, and Kristie Dotson. 2019. "Scrutinized but Not Recognized: (In)visibility and Hypervisibility Experiences of Faculty of Color." *Journal of Vocational Behavior* 113:62–74.

Shaffril, Hayrol Azril Mohamed, Nobaya Ahmad, Samsul Farid Samsuddin, Asnarulkhadi Abu Samah, and Mas Ernawati Hamdan. 2020. "Systematic Literature Review on Adaptation towards Climate Change Impacts among Indigenous People in the Asia Pacific Regions." *Journal of Cleaner Production* 258:120595.

Sharma, Nitasha Tamar. 2021. *Hawai'i Is My Haven: Race and Indigeneity in the Black Pacific.* Durham, NC: Duke University Press.

Shaw, Alex, Anam Barakzai, and Boaz Keysar. 2019. "When and Why People Evaluate Negative Reciprocity as More Fair Than Positive Reciprocity." *Cognitive Science* 43 (8): e12773.

Sheehan, Linda. 2013. "Realizing Nature's Rule of Law through Rights of Waterways." In *Rule of Law for Nature: New Dimensions and Ideas in Environmental Law*, edited by Christina Voight, 222–240. Cambridge, UK: Cambridge University Press.

Sherwood, Y. P. 2021. "Indigenous Womxn and Environment Justice: She & the Basket Folded Us In." *Footnotes Magazine* 49 (3). https://www.asanet.org/footnotes-article/indigenous-womxn-and-environment-justice-she-basket-folded-us/.

Shils, Edward. 1958. "Ideology and Civility: On the Politics of the Intellectual." *Sewanee Review* 66 (3): 450–480.

Shultziner, Doron. 2004. "Human Dignity—Functions and Meanings." *Global Jurist Topics* 3 (3).

Silva, Noenoe K. 2004. *Aloha Betrayed: Native Hawaiian Resistance to American Colonialism.* Durham, NC: Duke University Press.

Simati, Benita Kumar. 2011. "The Potential of Vā: An Investigation of How 'Ie Tōga Activate the Spatial Relationships of the Vā, for a Samoan Diaspora Community." PhD diss., Auckland University of Technology.

Simpson, Audra. 2014. *Mohawk Interruptus: Political Life across the Borders of Settler States.* Durham, NC: Duke University Press.

Simpson, Leanne Betasamosake. 2014. "Land as Pedagogy: Nishnaabeg Intelligence and Rebellious Transformation." *Decolonization: Indigeneity, Education and Society* 3 (3).

Simpson, Leanne R. 1999. "The Construction of Traditional Ecological Knowledge, Issues, Implications and Insights." Winnipeg: University of Manitoba. https://mspace.lib.umanitoba.ca/handle/1993/2210.

Sinclair, Raven. 2003. "Indigenous Research in Social Work: The Challenge of Operationalizing Worldview." *Native Social Work Journal* 5:117–139. https://zone.biblio.laurentian.ca/handle/10219/407.

Sirgy, M. Joseph. 1986. "A Quality-of-Life Theory Derived from Maslow's Developmental Perspective: 'Quality' Is Related to Progressive Satisfaction of a Hierarchy of Needs, Lower Order and Higher." *American Journal of Economics and Sociology* 45 (3): 329–342.

Smith, Diane E. 2016. "Governing Data and Data for Governance: The Everyday Practice of Indigenous Sovereignty." In *Indigenous Data Sovereignty: Toward an Agenda*, edited by Tahu Kukutai and John Taylor, 117–138. Canberra: Australian National University Press.

Smith, Linda Tuhiwai. 1996. "Kaupapa Maori Health Research." In *Hui Whakapiripiri: A Hui to Discuss Strategic Directions for Maori Health Research*, 14–30. Wellington: Te Ropu Rangahau Hauora a Eru Pomare.

Smith, Linda Tuhiwai. 2012. *Decolonial Methodologies: Research and Indigenous Peoples.* London: Bloomsbury.

Smith, Linda Tuhiwai. 2021 [1999]. *Decolonizing Methodologies: Research and Indigenous Peoples,* 3rd ed. London: Bloomsbury.

Smith, Mitch, and Julie Bosman. 2022. "Congress Told Colleges to Return Native Remains. What's Taking So Long?" *New York Times*, September 15. https://www.nytimes.com/2022/09/15/us/native-american-remains-university-of-north-dakota.html.

Snively, Gloria, and Lorna Wanosts Williams. 2018. *Knowing Home: Braiding Indigenous Science with Western Science*. Book 2. University of Victoria Libraries, ePublishing Services.

Sonnenblume, Kollibri terre. 2016. "A Century of Theft from Indians by the National Park Service." *Economist*, March 29. https://theecologist.org/2016/mar/29/century-theft-indians-national-park-service.

Soranno, Patricia A., Kendra S. Cheruvelil, Kevin C. Elliott, and Georgina M. Montgomery. 2015. "It's Good to Share: Why Environmental Scientists' Ethics Are Out of Date." *BioScience* 65 (1): 69–73.

Sosa, John R. 1985. "The Maya Sky, the Maya World: A Symbolic Analysis of Maya Cosmology." PhD diss., State University of New York at Albany. https://www.

proquest.com/openview/7aae2770c2432bfc023c32757b93a346/1?pq-origsite=gs
cholar&cbl=18750&diss=y.

Spade, Dean. 2020. *Mutual Aid: Building Solidarity during This Crisis (and the Next)*. New York: Verso Books.

Spence, Mark David. 1999. *Dispossessing the Wilderness: Indian Removal and the Making of the National Parks*. Oxford: Oxford University Press.

Spencer, Michael S., Taurmini Fentress, Ammara Touch, and Jessica Hernandez. 2020. "Environmental Justice, Indigenous Knowledge Systems, and Native Hawaiians and Other Pacific Islanders." *Human Biology* 92 (1): 45–57.

Spokane Tribe of Indians. nd. "The History of the Spokane Tribe of Indians." https://spokanetribe.com/history/.

SSIR (School Status and Improvement Report). 2018. School Year 2017–18. Accountability Section, Assessment and Accountability Branch, Office of Strategy, Innovation and Performance. Hawaii State Department of Education.

Stannard, David E. 1989. *Before the Horror: The Population of Hawaiʻi on the Eve of Western Contact*. Honolulu: University of Hawaiʻi Press.

Starck, Christian. 2002. "The Religious and Philosophical Background of Human Dignity and Its Place in Modern Constitutions." In *The Concept of Human Dignity in Human Rights Discourse*, edited by David Kretzmer and Eckart Klein, 179–193. Leiden: Brill Nijhoff.

Statman, Daniel. 2002. "Humiliation, Dignity and Self-Respect." In *The Concept of Human Dignity in Human Rights Discourse*, edited by David Kretzmer and Eckart Klein, 209–229. Leiden: Brill Nijhoff.

Steeves, Paulette Faith. 2015. *Decolonizing Indigenous Histories, Pleistocene Archaeology Sites of the Western Hemisphere*. PhD diss., State University of New York at Binghamton.

Steeves, Paulette F. C. 2021. *The Indigenous Paleolithic of the Western Hemisphere*. Lincoln: University of Nebraska Press.

Stern, Theodore. 1998. "Columbia River Trade Network." *Handbook of North American Indians* 12:641–652.

Stevens, Stan, ed. 2014. *Indigenous Peoples, National Parks, and Protected Areas: A New Paradigm Linking Conservation, Culture, and Rights*. Tucson: University of Arizona Press.

Stevenson, Marc G. 1998. "Traditional Knowledge in Environmental Management? From Commodity to Process." Working Paper 1998-14. Sustainable Forest Management Network. https://era.library.ualberta.ca/items/26253b73-96ed-42bb-a003-82ed9045d574/download/815ac251-99df-495d-8c54-f72136db4314.

Stevenson, Marc G. 1999. "What Are We Managing? Traditional Systems of Management and Knowledge in Cooperative and Joint Management." Conference notes, 1999 Sustainable Forest Management Network conference, Edmonton, Canada, February 14–17. https://www.osti.gov/etdeweb/biblio/334423.

Stone, C. D. 1996. *Should Trees Have Standing? and Other Essays on Law, Morals and the Environment*, 25th anniv. ed. New York: Oceana Publications.

Struthers, Roxanne. 2001. "Conducting Sacred Research: An Indigenous Experience." *Wicazo Sa Review* 16 (1): 125–133.

Stuart, J., and S. Stephens. 2006. "North Coast Bioregion Fire in California's Ecosystems." In *Fire in California's Ecosystems*, edited by Neil G. Sugihara, 147–169. Berkeley: University of California Press. https://nature.berkeley.edu/stephenslab/wp-content/uploads/2015/04/Stuart-Stephens-North-Bioregion-AFE-9-06.pdf.

Sua'ali'i-Sauni, Tamasailau, Maualaivao Albert Wendt, Vitolia Mo'a, Naomi Fuamatu, Upolu Luma Va'ai, Reina Whaitiri, and Stephen L. Filipo. 2014. *Whispers and Vanities: Samoan Indigenous Knowledge and Religion*. Wellington, Aotearoa: Huia Publishers.

Subramaniam, Banu, and Sigrid Schmitz. 2016. "Why We Need Critical Interdisciplinarity: A Dialogue on Feminist Science Technology Studies, Postcolonial Issues, and Ecodiversity." *FZG—Freiburger Zeitschrift für Geschlechterstudien* 22 (2): 13–14.

Suh, E. M. 2000. "Self, the Hyphen between Culture and Subjective Well-Being." In *Culture and Subjective Well-Being*, edited by E. Diener and E. M. Suh, 13–36. Cambridge, MA: MIT Press.

Sultana, Farhana. 2022a. "Critical Climate Justice." *Geographical Journal* 188 (1): 118–124.

Sultana, Farhana. 2022b. "The Unbearable Heaviness of Climate Coloniality." *Political Geography* 99:102638.

Supreme Court of Colombia. 2018. "Luis Armando Tolosa Villabona, Magistrado Ponente, STC4360-2018 Radicacion No. 11001-22-03-000-2018-00319-01, Bogota, D.C." April 5. http://www.cortesuprema.gov.co/corte/wp-content/uploads/2018/04/STC4360-2018-2018-00319-011.pdf.

Suquamish Tribe. 2015. "Chief Seattle's 1854 Oration"—ver. 1. Suquamish Tribe. https://suquamish.nsn.us/home/about-us/chief-seattle-speech/.

Tachine, A., and Z. Nicolazzo, eds. 2023. *Weaving an Otherwise: In-Relations Methodological Practice*. Abingdon, UK: Taylor & Francis.

Táíwò, Olúfẹ́mi, and Beba Cibralic. 2020. "The Case for Climate Reparations." *Foreign Policy* 10.

Tatum, Beverly Daniel. 2017 [1997]. *Why Are All the Black Kids Sitting Together in the Cafeteria? And Other Conversations about Race*. London: Hachette UK.

Te Awa Tupua (Whanganui River Claims Settlement), Act 2017. 2017. Te Awa Tupua, New Zealand. March 20. http://www.legislation.govt.nz/act/public/2017/0007/latest/whole.html.

Teneva, Lida T., Eva Schemmel, and John N. Kittinger. 2018. "State of the Plate: Assessing Present and Future Contribution of Fisheries and Aquaculture to Hawai'i's Food Security." *Marine Policy* 94:28–38.

Teuton, Christopher B., America Meredith, Hastings Shade, Sammy Still, Sequoyah Guess, and Woody Hansen. 2012. *Cherokee Stories of the Turtle Island Liars' Club*. Chapel Hill: University of North Carolina Press. doi:10.5149/9780807837498_teuton.

Thambinathan, Vivetha, and Elizabeth Anne Kinsella. 2021. "Decolonizing Methodologies in Qualitative Research: Creating Spaces for Transformative Praxis." *International Journal of Qualitative Methods* 20:16094069211014766.

The Mauna Kea Syllabus Project. 2021. *The Mauna Kea Syllabus*. https://www. maunakeasyllabus.com/.

Thoegersen, Jennifer. 2015. "Examination of Federal Data Management Plan Guidelines." *Journal of Escience Librarianship* 4 (1). doi:10.7191/jeslib.2015.1072.

Thwaites, Reuben Gold, ed. 2001 [1905]. *Original Journals of the Lewis and Clark Expedition: Vol. 4*. Digital Scanning. https://books.google.com/books?hl=en&lr=&id =RG34CgAAQBAJ&oi=fnd&pg=PR7&dq=Thwaites,+Reuben+Gold,+ed.+2001 +%5B1905%5D.+Original+Journals+of+the+Lewis+and+Clark+Expedition:+Vol .+4+.+Digital+Scanning+&ots=RMo75KPYzv&sig=P 7YR_rRdCZYYn3lQ-7K2iikzkTA#v=onepage&q&f=false.

Tierney, Brian. 1992. *JH Burns. Lordship, Kingship, and Empire: The Idea of Monarchy, 1400–1525*. The Carlyle Lectures, 1988. New York: Clarendon Press of Oxford University Press.

Tom, Erica, Melinda M. Adams, and Ron W. Goode. 2023. "Solastalgia to Soliphilia: Cultural Fire, Climate Change, and Indigenous Healing." *Journal of Ecopsychology*. https://doi.org/10.1089/eco.2022.0085.

Tompkins, Peter, and Christopher Bird. 2002. *The Secret Life of Plants*. New York: Harper/Perennial.

Topkok, Charles Sean Asiqluq, and Beth Leonard. 2015. *Iñupiat Ilitqusiat: Inner Views of Our Iñupiaq Values*. Fairbanks: University of Alaska.

Towes, Christian, and Kendra Germany-Wall. 2022. "Born through a Donation 175 Years Ago, the Choctaw-Irish Bond Remains Strong Today." Choctaw Nation of Oklahoma. https://www.choctawnation.com/biskinik/ born-through-a-donation-175-years-ago-the-choctaw-irish-bond-remains- strong-today/.

Trask, Haunani-Kay. 1999. *From a Native Daughter: Colonialism and Sovereignty in Hawaii* Rev. ed. Honolulu: University of Hawai'i Press.

Triandis, Harry C. 2000. "Cultural Syndromes and Subjective Well-Being." In *Culture and Subjective Well-Being*, edited by E. Diener and E. M. Suh, 13–36. Cambridge, MA: MIT Press.

Trigger, D. 2004. "Anthropology in Native Title Court Cases: 'Mere Pleasing, Expert Opinion, or Hearsay.'" In *Crossing Boundaries: Cultural, Legal, Historical and Practice Issues in Native Title*, edited by Sandy Toussaint, 24–33. Carlton, AUS: Melbourne University Publishing.

Trigger, David, Jane Mulcock, Andrea Gaynor, and Yann Toussaint. 2008. "Ecological Restoration, Cultural Preferences and the Negotiation of 'Nativeness' in Australia." *Geoforum* 39 (3): 1273–1283.

Trondheim, Gitte. 2010. "Kinship in Greenland—Emotions of Relatedness." *Acta Borealia* 27 (2): 208–220.

Trosper, Ronald L., and John A. Parrotta. 2012. "Introduction: The Growing Importance of Traditional Forest-Related Knowledge." In *Traditional Forest-Related Knowledge*, edited by John A. Parrotta and Ronald L. Trosper, 1–36. Dordrecht: Springer.

Tsosie, Krystal S., and Katrina G. Claw. 2020. "Indigenizing Science and Reasserting Indigeneity in Research." *Human Biology* 91 (3): 137–140.

Tsosie, Krystal S., Joseph M. Yracheta, Jessica A. Kolopenuk, and Janis Geary. 2021. "We Have 'Gifted' Enough: Indigenous Genomic Data Sovereignty in Precision Medicine." *American Journal of Bioethics* 21 (4): 72–75.

Tsosie, Rebecca. 2019. "Tribal Data Governance and Informational Privacy: Constructing 'Indigenous Data Sovereignty.'" *Montana Law Review* 80 (2).

Tuagalu, I'ougafa, 2008. "Heuristics of the Vā." *AlterNative: An International Journal of Indigenous Peoples* 4 (1): 107–126. https://doi.org/10.1177/117718010800400110.

Tuck, Eve. 2009. "Suspending Damage: A Letter to Communities." *Harvard Educational Review* 79 (3): 409–428.

Tuck, Eve, and C. Ree. 2013. "Exemplar Chapter 33: A Glossary of Haunting." https://static1.squarespace.com/static/557744ffe4b013bae3b7af63/t/557f2d6ce4b029eb4288a2f8/1434398060958/Tuck+%26+Ree%2C+A+Glossary+of+Haunting.pdf.

Tuck, Eve, and K. Wayne Yang. 2012. "Decolonization Is Not a Metaphor." *Decolonization: Indigeneity, Education and Society* 1 (1): 1–40.

Turner, Dale. 2020. "On the Politics of Indigenous Translation." In *The Routledge Handbook of Critical Indigenous Studies*, edited by Brendan Hokowhitu, Aileen Moreton-Robinson, Linda Tuhiwai-Smith, Chris Andersen, and Steve Larkin, 175–185. London: Routledge.

Turner, Kieron. 2022. "Disrupting Coloniality through Palestine Solidarity: Decolonizing or Decolonial Praxis?" *Interfere* 3:6–34.

Turnhout, Esther, Tamara Metze, Carina Wyborn, Nicole Klenk, and Elena Louder. 2020. "The Politics of Co-Production: Participation, Power, and Transformation." *Current Opinion in Environmental Sustainability* 42 (2018): 15–21.

Tynan, Lauren. 2021. "What Is Relationality? Indigenous Knowledges, Practices and Responsibilities with Kin." *Cultural Geographies* 28 (4): 597–610.

UN General Assembly. 1948a. International Bill of Human Rights. Adopted December 10. A/RES/217(III)A-E.

UN General Assembly. 1948b. Universal Declaration of Human Rights. Adopted December 10. UNGA Res 217 A(III) (UDHR) art 5.

UN General Assembly. 1966a. International Covenant on Civil and Political Rights. Adopted December 16, 1966, entered into force 23 March 23, 1976. 999 UNTS 171 (ICCPR) art 7.

UN General Assembly. 1966b. International Covenant on Economic, Social and Cultural Rights. December 16, 1966. 993 U.N.T.S. 3; S. Exec. Doc. D, 95-2 (1978); S. Treaty Doc. No. 95-19; 6 I.L.M. 360.

UN General Assembly. 2002. "Resolution Adopted by the General Assembly on 20 December 2018." https://www.un.org/pga/73/wp-content/uploads/sites/53/2019/04/A.RES_.73.235.pdf.

UN General Assembly. 2007. "United Nations Declaration on the Rights of Indigenous Peoples." September 13. https://www.un.org/development/desa/indigenouspeoples/wp-content/uploads/sites/19/2018/11/UNDRIP_E_web.pdf.

United Nations. 2012a. "Permanent Forum on Indigenous Issues." Economic and Social Council. Supplement No. 23. https://www.un.org/development/desa/indigenouspeoples/unpfii-sessions-2/unpfii-eleventh-session.html.

United Nations. 2012b. "Impact of the 'Doctrine of Discovery' on Indigenous Peoples." June 1. https://www.un.org/en/development/desa/newsletter/desanews/dialogue/2012/06/3801.html.

United Nations. 2015. *Transforming Our World: The 2030 Agenda for Sustainable Development*. New York: United Nations, Department of Economic and Social Affairs.

UN Human Rights Council. 2018. "Free, Prior and Informed Consent: A Human-Rights Based Approach." U.N. Doc A/HRC/39/62, 2. https://sdgs.un.org/2030agenda.

US DOI (Department of Interior). 2009. "Tribal Consultation Policy." Secretary of the Interior. https://www.doi.gov/sites/doi.gov/files/migrated/tribes/upload/SO-3317-Tribal-Consultation-Policy.pdf.

US DOI (Department of the Interior). 2022. "Interior Department Strengthens Tribal Consultation Policies and Procedures." Press release, February 1. https://www.doi.gov/pressreleases/interior-department-strengthens-tribal-consultation-policies-and-procedures.

US DOI NPS (Department of the Interior National Park Service). 1988. "Management Policies." http://npshistory.com/publications/management/mgt-policies-1988.pdf.

US EPA (Environmental Protection Agency). 2017. Memorandum from Office of Land and Emergency Management (OLEM). Considering Traditional Ecological Knowledge (TEK) during the Cleanup Process. https://www.epa.gov/sites/default/files/2020-10/documents/considering_traditional_ecological_knowledge_tek_during_the_cleanup_process_updated_link.pdf.

US EPA (Environmental Protection Agency). nd. "Water Quality Standards Tools for Tribes." Accessed May 7, 2023. https://www.epa.gov/wqs-tech/water-quality-standards-tools-tribes.

US GAO (Government Accountability Office). 2005. "Indian Tribes: EPA Should Reduce the Review Time for Tribal Requests to Manage Environmental Programs." October 31. GAO-06-95. Washington, DC: GAO. https://www.govinfo.gov/content/pkg/GAOREPORTS-GAO-06-95/html/GAOREPORTS-GAO-06-95.htm.

Uzawa, Kanako. 2020. "Crafting Our Future Together: Urban Diasporic Indigeneity from an Ainu Perspective in Japan." PhD diss., Arctic University of Norway.

Valenzuela-Vermehren, Luis. 2013. "Vitoria, Humanism, and the School of Salamanca in Early Sixteenth-Century Spain: A Heuristic Overview." *Logos: A Journal of Catholic Thought and Culture* 16 (2): 99–125.

Van Doren, Charles. 1992. *A History of Knowledge: Past, Present, and Future*. New York: Ballantine Books.

Varcoe, Colleen, and Holly A. McKenzie. 2022. "Decolonizing Research." In *Women's Health in Canada: Challenges of Intersectionality*, 2nd ed., edited by Marina Morrow, Olena Hankivsky, and Colleen Varcoe. Toronto: University of Toronto Press.

Vaughn, Kēhaulani. 2019. "Sovereign Embodiment: Native Hawaiians and Expressions of Diasporic Kuleana." *Hūlili Journal* 11 (1): 227–245.

Vaughan, Mehana Blaich. 2018. *Kaiaulu: Gathering Tides*. Corvallis: Oregon State University Press.

Vaughan, Mehana Blaich, and Margaret R. Caldwell. 2015. "Hana Pa'a: Challenges and Lessons for Early Phases of Co-Management." *Marine Policy* 62 (December): 51–62. https://doi.org/10.1016/j.marpol.2015.07.005.

Veenhoven, R. 2000. "Freedom and Happiness: A Comparative Study in Forty-Four Nations in the Early 1990s." In *Culture and Subjective Well-Being*, edited by E. Diener and E. M. Suh, 257–288. Cambridge, MA: MIT Press.

Vinyeta, Kirsten, Kyle Whyte, and Kathy Lynn. 2016. "Climate Change through an Intersectional Lens: Gendered Vulnerability and Resilience in Indigenous Communities in the United States." https://papers.ssrn.com/sol3/papers. cfm?abstract_id=2770089.

Vizenor, Gerald, ed. 2008. *Survivance: Narratives of Native Presence*. Lincoln: University of Nebraska Press.

Vold, Vivi. 2020. "Illumination of Opportunities and Challenges at the Crossroads between Research on Greenland and Greenlandic Society—Reflection and Analysis of the Visual Material *From Where We View the World*." FilmFreeway. Ilisimatusarfik, University of Greenland. https://filmfreeway.com/ Fromwhereweviewtheworld.

Von Bismarck, Helen. 2012. "Defining Decolonization." *British Scholar Society* 27.

Wagamese, Richard. 2016. *Embers: One Ojibway's Meditations*. Vancouver, CAN: D & M Publishers.

Wahkinney, Jared. 2019. "Comanche Food Attitudes." PhD diss., Oklahoma University. https://hdl.handle.net/11244/321136.

Walia, Harsha. 2021. *Border and Rule: Global Migration, Capitalism, and the Rise of Racist Nationalism*. Chicago: Haymarket Books.

Wall, Tamara U., Alison M. Meadow, and Alexandra Horganic. 2017. "Developing Evaluation Indicators to Improve the Process of Coproducing Usable Climate Science." *Weather, Climate, and Society* 9 (1): 95–107.

Walter, Maggie, and Chris Andersen. 2016. *Indigenous Statistics: A Quantitative Research Methodology*. London: Routledge.

Walter, Maggie, Raymond Lovett, Bobby Maher, Bhiamie Williamson, Jacob Prehn, Gawaian Bodkin-Andrews, and Vanessa Lee. 2021. "Indigenous Data Sovereignty in the Era of Big Data and Open Data." *Australian Journal of Social Issues* 56 (2): 143–156.

Walter, Maggie, and Stephanie Russo Carroll. 2021. "Indigenous Data Sovereignty, Governance and the Link to Indigenous Policy." In *Indigenous Data Sovereignty and Policy*, edited by Maggie Walter, Tahu Kukutai, Stephanie Russo Carroll, and Desi Rodriguez-Lonebear. New York: Routledge.

Warne, Donald, and Linda Bane Frizzell. 2014. "American Indian Health Policy: Historical Trends and Contemporary Issues." *American Journal of Public Health* 104 (S3): S263–S267.

Watermeyer, Tsering Dolkar, and Miu Chung Yan. 2022. "Indigenization without 'Indigeneity': Problematizing the Discourse of Indigenization of Social Work in China." *British Journal of Social Work* 52 (3): 1511–1528.

Watts, V. 2013. "Indigenous Place-Thought and Agency amongst Humans and Non Humans (First Woman and Sky Woman Go on a European World Tour!)." *Decolonization: Indigeneity, Education and Society* 2 (1).

Weston, Burns H. 2008. "Human Rights and Nation-Building in Cross-Cultural Settings." *Maine Law Review* 60:317.

Whaley, Gray H. 2006. "'Trophies' for God: Native Mortality, Racial Ideology, and the Methodist Mission of Lower Oregon, 1834–1844." *Oregon Historical Quarterly* 107 (1): 6–35.

Wheaton, Henry. 1863. *Elements of International Law*. Vol. 1. Boston: Little, Brown.

Whittemore, Mary Elizabeth. 2011. "The Problem of Enforcing Nature's Rights under Ecuador's Constitution: Why the 2008 Environmental Amendments Have No Bite." *Pacific Rim Law and Policy Journal* 20:659.

Whyte, Kyle Powys. 2013. "On the Role of Traditional Ecological Knowledge as a Collaborative Concept: A Philosophical Study." *Ecological Processes* 2 (1): 1–12.

Whyte, Kyle. 2018. "Settler Colonialism, Ecology, and Environmental Injustice." *Environment and Society* 9 (1): 125–144.

Whyte, Kyle Powys, Joseph P. Brewer, and Jay T. Johnson. 2016. "Weaving Indigenous Science, Protocols and Sustainability Science." *Sustainability Science* 11:25–32.

Wilcove, D. S., D. Rothstein, J. Dubow, A. Phillips, and E. Losos. 1998. "Quantifying Threats to Imperiled Species in the United States." *BioScience* 48:607–615.

Wildcat, Daniel R. 2010. *Red Alert!: Saving the Planet with Indigenous Knowledge*. Arvada, CO: Fulcrum Publishing.

Wildcat, Daniel R. 2013. "Introduction: Climate Change and Indigenous Peoples of the USA." In *Climate Change and Indigenous Peoples in the United States: Impacts, Experiences and Actions*, edited by Julie Koppel Maldonado, Benedict Colombi, and Rajul Pandya, 1–7. Cham: Springer International.

Wilder, Craig Steven. 2013. *Ebony and Ivy: Race, Slavery, and the Troubled History of America's Universities*. New York: Bloomsbury.

Wilderson III, Frank B. 2020. *Afropessimism*. New York: Liveright Publishing.

Wilkerson, Isabel. 2020. *Caste: The Origins of Our Discontents*. New York: Random House.

Wilkinson, Mark D., Michel Dumontier, IJsbrand Jan Aalbersberg, Gabrielle Appleton, Myles Axton, Arie Baak, Niklas Blomberg, et al. 2016. "The FAIR Guiding Principles for Scientific Data Management and Stewardship." *Scientific Data* 3 (1).

Wilkinson, Richard. 2004. "Why Is Violence More Common Where Inequality Is Greater?" *Annals of the New York Academy of Sciences* 1036 (1): 1–12.

Wilkinson, Richard G., Ichiro Kawachi, and Bruce P. Kennedy. 1998. "Mortality, the Social Environment, Crime and Violence." *Sociology of Health and Illness* 20 (5): 578–597.

Williams, Michael. 2000. "Dark Ages and Dark Areas: Global Deforestation in the Deep Past." *Journal of Historical Geography* 26 (1): 28–46.

Williams Jr., Robert A. 1992. *The American Indian in Western Legal Thought: The Discourses of Conquest*. Oxford: Oxford University Press.

Williamson, Bhiamie, Sam Provost, and Cassandra Price. 2022. "Operationalising Indigenous Data Sovereignty in Environmental Research and Governance." *Environment and Planning F:* 26349825221125496.

Wilson, Gemma. 2020. "Indigenous Fire Practitioner: 'Let Us Drive for a Change.'" *SBS News*, February 4. https://www.sbs.com.au/news/insight/article/indigenous-fire-practitioner-let-us-drive-for-a-change/u1yft4mp1.

Wilson, Nicole J. 2014. "The Politics of Adaptation: Subsistence Livelihoods and Vulnerability to Climate Change in the Koyukon Athabascan Village of Ruby, Alaska." *Human Ecology* 42:87–101.

Wilson, Shawn. 2001. "What Is an Indigenous Research Methodology?" *Canadian Journal of Native Education* 25 (2).

Wilson, Shawn. 2008. *Research Is Ceremony: Indigenous Research Methods.* Nova Scotia: Fernwood.

Wilson, Waziyatawin Angela. 2004. "Introduction: Indigenous Knowledge Recovery Is Indigenous Empowerment." *American Indian Quarterly* 28 (3/4): 359–372.

Wilson-Hokowhitu, Nālani. 2019. *The Past Before Us: Moʻokūʻauhau as Methodology.* Honolulu: University of Hawaiʻi Press.

Winter, Kawika B., Kamanamaikalani Beamer, Mehana Blaich Vaughan, Alan M. Friedlander, Mike H. Kido, A. Nāmaka Whitehead, Malia K. H. Akutagawa, Natalie Kurashima, Matthew Paul Lucas, and Ben Nyberg. 2018. "The Moku System: Managing Biocultural Resources for Abundance within Social-Ecological Regions in Hawaiʻi." *Sustainability* 10 (10): 3554.

Winter, Kawika, Noa Lincoln, Fikret Berkes, Rosanna ʻAlegado, Natalie Kurashima, Kiana Frank, Puaʻala Pascua, et al. 2020. "Ecomimicry in Indigenous Resource Management: Optimizing Ecosystem Services to Achieve Resource Abundance, with Examples from Hawaiʻi." *Ecology and Society* 25 (2).

Wolfe, Patrick. 2006. "Settler Colonialism and the Elimination of the Native." *Journal of Genocide Research* 8 (4): 387–409.

Wright, Erin Kahunawaikaʻala. 2003. "Education for the Nation: Forging Indigenous Hawaiian Identity in Higher Education." PhD diss., University of California, Los Angeles.

Wulf, Andrea. 2015. *The Invention of Nature: The Adventures of Alexander von Humboldt, the Lost Hero of Science.* London: Hachette UK.

Wyban, Carol Araki. 2020. *Tide and Current: Fishponds of Hawaiʻi.* 2nd ed. Honolulu: University of Hawaiʻi Press. https://doi.org/10.2307/j.ctvz0h8mc

Wynecoop, Monique D., Penelope Morgan, Eva K. Strand, and Fernando Sanchez Trigueros. 2019. "Getting Back to Fire Sumés: Exploring a Multi-Disciplinary Approach to Incorporating Traditional Knowledge into Fuels Treatments." *Fire Ecology* 15 (1): 1–18.

Xego, Zipho, and Emeka E. Obioha. 2021. "Knowledge of Current Conservation Methods and Infusion of Indigenous Knowledge Systems among Local Communities in Dwesa Cwebe Protected Area, South Africa." *Indilinga African Journal of Indigenous Knowledge Systems* 20 (2): 263–281. https://hdl.handle.net/10520/ejc-linga_v20_n2_a9.

Yalom, I. D. 1980. *Existential Psychotherapy.* New York: Basic Books.

Yamane, Cherry YEW, and Susana Helm. 2022. "Indigenous Culture-as-Health: A Systematized Literature Review." *Journal of Prevention* 43: 167–190.

Yarra River Protection (Wilip-Gin Birrarung Murron) Act. 2017. No. 49.https://content.legislation.vic.gov.au/sites/default/files/2020-04/17-49aa005%20authorised.pdf.

Young, Michaela. 2016. "Then and Now: Reappraising Freedom of the Seas in Modern Law of the Sea." *Ocean Development and International Law* 47 (2): 165–185.

Younging, Gregory. 2018. *Elements of Indigenous Style: A Guide for Writing by and about Indigenous Peoples*. Edmonton: Brush Education.

Yuen, Jonathan. 2021. "Pathogens Which Threaten Food Security: Phytophthora infestans, the Potato Late Blight Pathogen." *Food Security* 13 (2): 247–253.

Zenk, Henry B. 1976. "Contributions to Tualatin Ethnography: Subsistence and Ethnobiology." MA thesis, Portland State University. https://pdxscholar.library.pdx.edu/open_access_etds/2279/.

Zhao, Ping, Yue Tian, Yongkui Li, Guofa Xu, Subo Tian, and Zichen Huang. 2020. "Potato (Solanum tuberosum L.) Tuber-Root Modeling Method Based on Physical Properties." *PLOS One* 15 (9): e0239093.

Zidny, Robby, Jesper Sjöström, and Ingo Eilks. 2020. "A Multi-Perspective Reflection on How Indigenous Knowledge and Related Ideas Can Improve Science Education for Sustainability." *Science and Education* 29 (1): 145–185.

Zvobgo, Luckson, Peter Johnston, Portia Adade Williams, Christopher H. Trisos, Nicholas P. Simpson, and Global Adaptation Mapping Initiative Team. 2022. "The Role of Indigenous Knowledge and Local Knowledge in Water Sector Adaptation to Climate Change in Africa: A Structured Assessment." *Sustainability Science* 17 (5): 2077–2092.

四ツ倉典滋 [Yotsukura, Norishige]. 2021. 北海道大学北方生物圏フィールド科学センター 忍路臨海実験所. [Field Science Center for Northern Biosphere, Hokkaido University Oshoro Marine Station]. 日本水産学会誌 [*The Japanese Society of Fisheries Science Journal*] 87 (1): 55.

石原真衣 [Ishihara, Mai]. 2018. 沈黙を問う:「サイレント・アイヌ」というもうひとつの先住民問題 [Questioning Silence: The "Silent Ainu," Another Indigenous Problem. 北方人文研究 [*Northern Humanities Studies*] 11:3-21.

石原真衣 [Ishihara, Mai]. 2020. 〈沈黙〉の自伝的民族誌―サイレント・アイヌの痛みと救済の物語 [*Autoethnography of "Silence": The Story of the Pain of Silent Ainu and Their Care*]. 北海道大学出版会 [Hokkaido University Press].